Troubled Times

Readings in Social Problems

Robert H. Lauer

and

Jeanette C. Lauer

U.S. International University

Roxbury Publishing Company

Los Angeles, California

Library of Congress Cataloging-in-Publication Data

Troubled times: readings in social problems / [edited] by Robert H. Lauer and
Jeanette C. Lauer
  p. cm.
  Includes bibliographical references and index.
  ISBN 1-891487-19-1
  1. Social problems—United States. 2. United States—Social conditions—1980- 3.
United States—Economic conditions—1981- I. Lauer, Robert H. II. Lauer, Jeanette
C.
HN59.2.T732000
306′.0973—dc21   98-44608
                                                                          CIP

Publisher and Editor: Claude Teweles
Copy Editor: Elizabeth Vaughn
Production Editor: Dawn VanDercreek
Production Assistants: Remy Goldsmith and Renée Burkhammer
Typography: Synergistic Data Systems
Cover Design: Marnie Deacon Kenney
Cover Photo: Photograph by Richard Gardner, © 1977. Used by permission of The Com-
mercial Appeal.

Printed on acid-free paper in the United States of America. This paper meets the standards
for recycling of the Environmental Protection Agency.

ISBN: 1-891487-19-1

Roxbury Publishing Company
P.O. Box 491044
Los Angeles, California 90049-9044
Tel: (310) 473-3312 • Fax: (310) 473-4490
Email: roxbury@crl.com

To those who are our haven in a troubled world:
Jon, Kathy, Julie, Jeffrey, Kate, Jeff, Krista, Benjamin,
David, and John Robert

Contents

Part I: Troubled Institutions: Problems in the System

Part II: Troubled Groups: Problems of Inequality

Part III: Troubled Behavior: Problems of Deviance

Preface

Why are there poor people in the United States? There are always those who give a simplistic answer: people are poor because they are unwilling to work—"If you are poor, it is your own fault. And if it is your own fault, we don't have a social problem. Rather, you have a personal problem."

In other words, many Americans turn social problems into purely individual difficulties. They exhibit two tendencies that inhibit a sociological understanding. First, they tend to analyze problems in simplistic terms, so that the solution takes the form of "If people would only . . . , the problem would no longer exist." Second, they tend to judge that problems have individual causes and solutions, and in so doing fail to recognize the crucially important social factors involved.

This book addresses these tendencies by stressing the interplay of macro- (large-scale or social-structural) factors and micro- (small-scale or social-psychological) factors involved in all social problems. For each problem discussed, both macro- and microfactors are identified in one or more of the selections and in our introduction to them.

Because many problems are exacerbated for women and members of minority racial or ethnic groups, the selections highlight issues of gender and race or ethnicity. In each part, one of the selections focuses specifically on gender, race or ethnicity, or both. Other selections provide insights on gender and race or ethnicity as part of a broader discussion.

The book is organized by the general type of problem, from systemic problems to problems of deviance. Each of the three parts begins with a brief introduction which explains the nature of that type of problem. Within each part, we examine a number of specific problems, using three or more selected readings to probe its various facets.

Because we believe that the study of social problems should be informative, stimulating, and relevant, we have included some pedagogical aids. Focus questions precede each selection to help you identify major points. Critical evaluation questions at the end of each selection are designed to help you examine the issue from other points of view, to think about implications of the discussion, and to consider whether the author's case is a convincing one. We believe that no matter how much you may initially agree or disagree with an author's position, you should always try to evaluate it objectively and think about how people with a different perspective would respond. In other words, the critical evaluation questions remind you not to mindlessly accept a reading.

Finally, at the end of each section is a project for personal application and class discussion. These projects personalize each problem in some way. We believe that if each student in the class does the project, the results can be used for a stimulating and informative class discussion.

We are grateful to the reviewers whose thoughtful comments have helped shape this book: Deborah A. Abowitz (Philadelphia College); James A. Glynn (Bakersfield Junior College); Valerie Jenness (University of California, Irvine); Thomas Kando (California State University, Sacramento); Peter Kivisto (Augustana College); John Linn (Gustavus Adolphus College); Scott Sernau (Indiana University, South Bend); Peter J. Stein (William Paterson University); Kathleen Tiemann (University of North Dakota); Mark A. Winton (University of Central Florida); Morrison Wong (Texas Christian University). ✦

About the Contributors

George M. Anders is a senior special writer for *The Wall Street Journal.*

Barry Bluestone is a professor of political economy at the University of Massachusetts, Boston.

Judith A. Chafel is an associate professor in the Department of Curriculum and Instruction at Indiana University, Bloomington.

Robert C. Davidson teaches in the Department of Family and Community Medicine and the Center for Health Services Research at the University of California, Davis.

Jerelyn Eddings writes for *U.S. News & World Report.*

Marvin D. Free, Jr. is an assistant professor of sociology at the University of Wisconsin, Whitewater.

David Gordon is Dorothy H. Hirshon Professor of Economics and director of the Center for Economic Policy Analysis at the New School for Social Research.

Lawrence A. Greenfeld is a statistician at the Bureau of Justice Statistics, U.S. Department of Justice.

John Harte is a professor of energy and resources at the University of California, Berkeley.

J. David Hawkins teaches social work at the University of Washington, Seattle.

Susan Headden writes for *U.S. News & World Report.*

Madeline E. Heilman is a professor of psychology and coordinator of the industrial and organizational psychology program at New York University.

Martha Honey is a freelance journalist and research fellow at the Institute for Policy Studies, Washington, DC.

Sarah Ingersoll is special assistant to the administrator at the Office of Juvenile Justice and Delinquency Prevention, U.S. Department of Justice.

Demie Kurz teaches at the University of Pennsylvania in the Women's Studies Program.

Donni LeBoeuf is senior program manager at the Office of Juvenile Justice and Delinquency Prevention, U.S. Department of Justice.

Ernest L. Lewis is the associate dean for student affairs and teaches in the Department of Urology at the University of California, Davis.

Timothy Maher is an associate professor of sociology at the University of Indianapolis.

Lynn Olson is a contributor to *Education Week.*

Todd Oppenheimer writes for *The Atlantic Monthly.*

Dale F. Pearson is a professor of social work at Brigham Young University.

H. Wesley Perkins is a professor of sociology at Hobart and William Smith Colleges, Geneva, New York.

Anthony M. Platt is a member of the editorial board of *Social Justice* and a professor of social work at California State University, Sacramento.

Samantha Quan is an economist in the Bureau of Labor Statistics.

Stephen Rose is senior research analyst in the Education Testing Service, Washington, DC.

Charles M. Sennott is on the staff of *The Boston Globe.*

Earl Shorris is a contributing editor of *Harper's Magazine.*

Joseph S. C. Simplicio is chair of the Education Department of Caldwell College, New Jersey.

Jane Sprague Zones is a medical sociologist at the University of California, San Francisco, and a long-time women's health advocate.

Louis Uchitelle writes for *The New York Times.*

Virginia Valian is a professor of psychology and linguistics at Hunter College and the City University of New York Graduate Center in New York City.

Susan Walzer teaches at the State University of New York, at Albany.

Henry Wechsler is director of the College Alcohol Study at the Harvard School of Public Health.

Catherine J. Weinberger teaches in the Department of Economics at the University of California.

Cathy Spatz Widom teaches at the State University of New York, at Albany.

NOTE: Biographical information has been provided where available. A few of the authors do not appear on the above list. ✦

Introduction

Millions of American women are the victims of violence at the hands of husbands or acquaintances every year. Is this a social problem? Along with the majority of Americans, you would probably answer yes. Among the Yanomamo Indians of South America, husbands typically beat, disfigure, and occasionally kill their wives (Chagnon 1977). Is that a social problem? You would probably answer yes, but the Yanomamos—both men and women—do not generally regard the violent treatment of wives as a problem. So what exactly do we mean by the phrase "social problem?"

What Is a Social Problem?

The phrase "social problem" first appeared in the 19th century among French and German writers (Schwartz 1997). It made its first appearance in English in the work of the philosopher John Stuart Mill, in about the middle of the 19th century. In all of these writings, "the social problem" referred to the unequal distribution of wealth and, in particular, to the struggle between labor and capitalist factory owners. In other words, the idea of a social problem began as a sense of something wrong in society—of suffering and deprivation growing out of a situation of injustice. The current usage reflects that same basic idea, but adds to it. In essence, a social problem is some condition or pattern of behavior in society that people define as incompatible with their desired quality of life (Lauer 1998).

That is why wife beating is a social problem in the United States but not among the Yanomamo Indians. Of course, to say that something isn't a social problem is not to say that we approve of or accept the situation or behavior. There may be, from the perspective of an outsider or a future generation, many things wrong in a society that the people themselves do not regard as social problems. Wife rape was not considered a social problem in this country until the late 1970s. Prior to a change of the law in Oregon in 1977, the legal code in all states exempted husbands from rape statutes. Poverty was not considered a social problem in this country until the 1960s. Prior to that time, most assumed that even if poor people did exist, the economy was gradually eliminating poverty.

Clearly, wives were raped before 1977 and people lived in poverty before the 1960s. But until something is recognized as detrimental and unacceptable, we do not treat it as a social problem. And if something is not defined as a social problem, little or nothing will be done to change the situation.

What Are Your Chances of Being Affected by a Social Problem?

To put it bluntly, your chances of being affected by a social problem are 100 percent. In fact, you are likely to be affected by more than one, and in all probability you already have been. For example, you have already experienced a social problem if you answer yes to any of the following questions:

- Have you or has anyone in your family abused alcohol or any other drug?

- Have you been a victim of any crime? Have you had something stolen? Have you been assaulted? Have you ever feared for your safety or well-being because of the threat of crime? Have you shared in the suffering of someone close to you who was victimized?

- Have you spent part or all of your life in poverty?

- Do you ever experience mistreatment of any kind because of your gender, your race, or your ethnic background?

- Have you or your parents ever been unemployed (which means that you wanted to work but were unable to get a job) or underemployed (which means that you worked in a job for which you were overqualified or underpaid, or that you worked part time when you wanted to work full time)?

- Has anyone in your family lost a job because of corporate downsizing?

- Have you attended a school that failed to give you a high-quality education?

- Did you grow up in a family where there was violence, a family disrupted by divorce, or a single-parent home?

- Has anyone in your family suffered from inadequate medical care?

- Has someone in your family died or been disabled in war?

- Have you or has anyone in your family become ill from pollution or contaminated food?

We could extend the list. In addition to the above, you could be affected by some problems of which you are unaware—for instance, by the abuse of governmental power. You might think that such abuse does not affect you directly, but what if the money Congress appropriates to unnecessary, pork-barrel projects means that less federal money goes to schools, hospitals, or urban projects? The quality of your education, health care, or area of residence could be lower than it should be.

What about the abuse of corporate power? Abuses such as price fixing affect the cost of the products you buy. Misleading advertising may induce you to purchase products that do not fulfill what they promised. Corporate benefits from the government may deprive you of benefits in the same way that pork-barrel projects do.

You are likely, then, to be affected both directly and indirectly by a number of social problems. Sometimes the effects may be relatively mild: for example, you may believe a misleading advertisement and spend a modest amount of money on a product that fails to do what you expected. Sometimes the effects may be severe, as those who are traumatized by such things as violence, divorce, addiction, unemployment, and poverty can testify.

Obviously, this is not the most encouraging discussion for you. But it is important because it is hoped you will become a part of those Americans who contribute in some way to the amelioration of social problems. We believe that you are more likely to work to remedy social problems when you recognize that these problems are pervasive, that they affect all of us, and that all of us must work together to minimize the trauma they cause.

According to some observers, the majority of Americans in the 1990s showed little or no ability to sympathize with their fellow citizens who were suffering severely from social problems (Mills 1997). Selfishness and callousness combined to make them indifferent to such things as poverty and homelessness.

We are not convinced that Americans today exhibit the "triumph of meanness." To be sure, some people are selfish and calloused. But many people get so wrapped up in the demands of living in a fast-paced world that they never see the suffering masses. Others do not respond to the suffering because they do not understand the extent to which people are victimized by numerous factors, at least some of which are beyond their control.

To reflect upon how you are now, and will continue to be in future, caught up in various social problems can sensitize you to the fact that everyone around you also has to deal with those problems. Studying the problems can inform you about the many factors that contribute to them, and to be sensitive and informed is to be prepared to contribute to their resolution.

How Can Social Problems Be Explained?

If you agree that something is a social problem, you will probably want to do something about it—or at least want *someone* to do something about it. Some of the issues that arise in trying to attack social problems will be discussed in Part I. Before anyone can do anything, however, one needs to understand the problem in question: what caused it and what tends to perpetuate it? How does it affect people? Whose responsibility is it to deal with it? These are complex questions. With regard to what causes and perpetuates a particular problem, the answer is, "many things." Many elements contribute to a social problem, both macrofactors, such as the uneven distribution of power and wealth, the economy, and social norms and roles, and microfactors, such as attitudes, concepts of self, and social interaction. (Lauer 1998). The kinds of macrofactors and microfactors may be illustrated by the problem of unemployment. For example, a black woman loses her management position because of corporate downsizing. After six months of looking, she is still unable to secure another position. What are some of the possible factors that help explain her situation?

One macrofactor may be the economy: a downturn can lead to cutbacks in the work force and a higher level of unemployment. Another macrofactor is government: at one time, affirmative action programs would have helped the woman, but with such programs currently under governmental and judicial attack she has lost a powerful tool. Still another macrofactor may be a social norm that prevails in some businesses—"we hire only those who are like us and who will therefore fit in easily." Since those who are "like us" are white males, the woman (white or black) has no chance.

Among the microfactors are attitudes of prejudice. The woman may run into covert prejudice against both African Americans and women. Such attitudes reinforce the norm to hire only those "like us." Interaction with other businessmen may justify the attitudes and the norm; perhaps the men are all members of the same club and privately acknowledge, mutually support, and joke about their shared feelings. Finally, after numerous failures, the woman's self-concept may suffer. She may begin to doubt herself, a fact picked up in interviews that makes it even less likely that she will secure a position.

Thus, race, gender, social institutions, norms, attitudes, interaction patterns, and self-concept are all involved in understanding the woman's situation. Similar scenarios could be created for other kinds of social problems. That is why we noted earlier that people may be caught up in numerous factors, at least some of which are beyond their control. And that is why simplistic analyses fail adequately to explain problems.

What is a simplistic analysis? In contrast to identifying the various macro- and microfactors involved in any problem, a simplistic analysis tends to focus on one factor. Sometimes it is a valid one, but it is only one. And sometimes that factor may be of questionable validity.

Thus, it is simplistic to argue that the high rate of poverty among African Americans is due to their lack of motivation. Using national data over a 10-year period, James R. Kluegel (1990) found that whites tend to accept such an explanation. The percentage who believe it has declined, but large numbers still accept it. It is naive, of course, to argue that no African Americans lack motivation, just as it is naive to argue that all white Americans possess it. There may be some individuals, both black and white, who are poor because they lack motivation. But all the evidence indicates that there are so few such individuals that motivation is not a valid factor in explaining poverty (Lauer 1998).

Similarly, it is simplistic to argue that any one factor, such as single-parent families, is the major cause of most or all the nation's social problems. For instance, as Arlene Skolnick (1997) points out, the emphasis on "family values" in the 1990s led some observers to identify single-parent families as the source of most of our ills. As David Popenoe (1996) has discussed in detail, single-parent homes are indeed related to many problems people have. But to say that the single-parent home is a factor in some problems is quite different from saying that it is the major factor in most problems. After all, the majority of those who are addicted, who commit crime, who suffer mental distress, or who have a troubled work history do not come from single-parent homes. Clearly, other factors are at work.

Understanding and explaining social problems, then, requires you to examine them carefully and identify the full range of elements involved. Whatever the problem is, you can be sure that many factors—at both the macrolevel and the microlevel—are involved.

What Can Be Done About Social Problems?

Once something is defined as a social problem, conflict typically results because not everyone agrees with the definition. And those who agree that a problem exists do not agree on what to do about it. Some Americans resist antipoverty programs. They see poverty, as noted earlier, not as a social problem but as a problem of individuals who lack the necessary motivation. Among those who agree that crime is a social problem, some advocate a get-tough policy on criminals, while others argue that such get-tough measures as imprisonment, longer prison terms, and the death penalty are not only counterproductive but unworthy of a civilized society. Among those who agree that we have a serious race problem, some urge continuing governmental intervention such as affirmative action programs, while others insist that such programs are no longer needed and perpetuate rather than resolve the problem.

Why the differences? At least three things can be said. First, those who hold to simplistic explanations of social problems are likely to offer simplistic solutions. For example, some Americans believe that improving education will solve most of our social problems (Applebome 1997). To be sure, education is part of the answer to some problems. Education has helped to counter various myths, such as the innate inferiority of African Americans, the inability of women to function appropriately in the business world, the notion that women who are raped "asked for it and really wanted it," and the idea that the earth is an unlimited supply of resources that can be freely exploited rather than a vulnerable system that needs careful management.

Second, some people have a knee-jerk reaction to any social problem based on their general perspective, whether radical, liberal, or conservative. Rather than looking at the data and trying to see the problem in all of its dimensions, they proceed on the basis of assumptions that are rooted in their political philosophy. For example, we believe that one of today's most serious social problems is the condition of the family, particularly the high rates of family violence and disruption by divorce. In discussions of the problem, Marxists' knee-jerk reaction is to argue that the real problem is not the family but the capitalist society. Family life, they insist, cannot be salvaged because it, like everything else, is corrupted by capitalism. Similarly, liberals' knee-jerk reaction is to assert that too much is made of divorce, and that single-parent families are as legitimate and as conducive to people's well-being as the nuclear family, while conservatives' knee-jerk reaction is to agree that the family is in serious need of repair and to argue that only the defeat of liberal philosophy and the return to traditional values will achieve that goal.

Third, differences exist because, although some people see a proposed effort to deal with a social problem as socially beneficial, others see their own interests threatened. Virtually every piece of legislation designed to facilitate social progress was strongly attacked at the time it was introduced by those acting in behalf of their self-interest.

Of course, no one identifies his or her opposition to a particular proposal as self-interest. Rather, the opposition is framed in terms of the proposal's potential threat to general social well-being. Men fought women's right to vote on the grounds that women were too emotional and would dilute the rationality of the political process. Management fought labor's right to collective bargaining on the grounds that it was un-American, a socialist plot, and a threat to the economic system. State politicians fought federal child-labor laws on the grounds that they undermined necessary states' rights and that, in any case, moral persuasion rather than legislation should be used. Physicians fought Medicare and Medicaid on the grounds that they are socialized medicine and that the nation cannot afford the costs of such a system. Business interests fought environmental protection laws on the grounds that they take away jobs from people and represent one more intrusion into American life by big government.

Because of simplistic understandings, political philosophies, and self-interest, efforts to deal with social problems will always be plagued by conflicting positions. The point is, the fact that such conflicting positions exist does not mean that you cannot make a rational judgment about how to deal with a particular problem. Rather, they mean that people draw their conclusions for a variety of reasons, only one of which is a reliance upon evidence.

We shall return briefly to the matter of solving social problems in the epilogue. Here we want to emphasize the point that in spite of the difficulties and complexities, progress can be, and has been, made. Women can vote and choose a professional career. African Americans can live in places other than racial ghettoes and work in high-status jobs side by side with whites. The poor can obtain some medical care. Workers are protected from many job hazards and from arbitrary firing. Such statements could not have been made during much of the nation's history.

We make them here not to suggest that problems are no longer severe, but to illustrate that progress can be made. And progress will be faster to the extent that people understand the many factors involved in social problems and minimize the tendency to let their own biases (political philosophies and self-interest) affect their judgments about how to attack those problems.

References

Applebome, Peter. 1997. "School as America's Cure-all." *New York Times*, January 12.

Chagnon, Napoleon A. 1977. *Yanomamo*, second ed. New York: Holt, Rinehart and Winston.

Kluegel, James R. 1990. "Trends in Whites' Explanations of the Black-White Gap in Socioeconomic Status, 1977-1989." *American Sociological Review* 55: 512-225.

Lauer, Robert H. 1998. *Social Problems and the Quality of Life*, seventh ed. New York: McGraw-Hill.

Mills, Nicolaus. 1997. "Challenging Our Culture of Spite and Cruelty." *Chronicle of Higher Education* 44 (September 19): B13.

Popenoe, David. 1996. *Life Without Father*. New York: Free Press.

Schwartz, Hillel. 1997. "On the Origin of the Phrase 'Social Problems.'" *Social Problems* 44: 276-296.

Skolnick, Arlene. 1997. "Family Values: The Sequel." *The American Prospect*, May-June, p. 86. ✦

PART I

Troubled Institutions: Problems in the System

The Government and Power

M any social scientists believe that power is the name of the game. Power in this context is the ability to control the behavior of others in order to reach personal goals. The distribution of power means how much power can be exercised by various groups, organizations, and institutions.

Social scientists do not agree on who has the most power in American society. Some, such as C. Wright Mills, argue that power is concentrated in a relatively small number of political, economic, and military leaders. There is also a middle level of power in the form of interest groups that lobby Congress. Nevertheless, these scholars contend that the great majority of citizens are relatively powerless and are controlled by the power elite.

In contrast, other social scientists argue that power is distributed fairly equally among interest groups. These interest groups—such as the American Medical Association, the National Rifle Association, and the National Association of Manufacturers—act on their own or in coalition with other groups to sway public opinion and bring about political action that reflects their interests.

Whatever their beliefs about the distribution of power, observers agree that the government is a major wielder of power and that social problems involve the exercise of power. However, power may be a part of a problem or it may help ameliorate a problem—depending upon how it is exercised. This first section looks at a number of ways that government and the exercise of power are a part of the nation's social problems.

References

Mills, C. Wright. 1956. *The Power Elite*. New York: Oxford University Press. ✦

1

The $150 Billion 'Welfare' Recipients: U.S. Corporations

Charles M. Sennott

Government has enormous power because it controls resources such as personnel and money, and has the authority to require obedience to laws. Corporations also have enormous power from resources such as money, jobs, skills, and the capacity to influence elections. Politicians may yield to corporate power to preserve their own positions, giving corporations considerable advantages to the detriment of citizens. Indeed, many sociologists criticize those politicians who readily hand out benefits to corporations but argue against government programs aimed at giving benefits to needy individuals.

Charles Sennott's chapter on corporate welfare shows how the exercise of power at the macrolevel of government increases corporate profits through programs like subsidies, giveaways, and tax breaks. At the same time, and because of that corporate welfare, at the microlevel of individual aspirations and needs, many suffer.

Focus Questions

1. In what sense are corporations "welfare" recipients?

2. Why does corporate welfare persist?

3. What does the author mean by "culture of dependence"?

It comes down to priorities. And to understand the choices made every day by the federal government on who should benefit from taxpayers' money, consider these stark examples:

- Walt Disney Corp, whose profits in 1995 exceeded $1 billion, received $300,000 in federal assistance last year to perfect fireworks displays. But Joseph and Phyllis Fagone of East Boston, who are in their mid-80s and struggling on a fixed income, were among 1,000 state residents whose federally funded fuel assistance ran out before Christmas.

- Kopin Corp, a Massachusetts technology company, has received $30 million in federal subsidies the last four years and tens of millions more in savings through the lease of a state-owned laboratory. Despite this huge public investment, the company plans to send more and more of its new manufacturing jobs overseas.

Meanwhile, it looks like Derek Davis, 17, of Roxbury will be among the thousands of Boston youths who won't get summer jobs due to limited federal and state funding. He was hoping to save money for college.

Every year, an estimated $150 billion—in the form of direct federal subsidies and tax breaks that specifically benefit businesses—is funneled to American companies. Critics call it "corporate welfare."

The $150 billion for corporate subsidies and tax benefits eclipses the annual budget deficit of $130 billion. It's more than the $145 billion paid out annually for the core programs of the social welfare state: Aid to Families with Dependent Children (AFDC), student aid, housing, food and nutrition, and all direct public assistance (excluding Social Security and medical care).

Now, a growing number of voices from both ends of the political spectrum question whether it is fair to provide such help to businesses while cutting back on aid to poor people—questions which at a minimum seek to frame corporate assistance as the missing piece of the national debate on welfare reform.

Stirrings on the corporate welfare issue have been set in motion by an unlikely coalition of politicians, policy makers and think tanks, ranging from Labor Secretary Robert

Reich to Republican presidential candidate Pat Buchanan; from liberal Democrat Sen. Edward Kennedy to conservative Republican Sen. John McCain; and from the libertarian Cato Institute to the Progressive Policy Institute.

They feel that if the White House and Congress were sincere about achieving a balanced budget, they could begin by cutting billions of dollars in direct subsidies to giant multinational companies. The subsidies range from $1.4 billion annually in price supports for large sugar farming interests; to nearly $2 million to help McDonald's market Chicken McNuggets in the Third World; to $20,000 for golf balls that defense manufacturer Lockheed Martin billed the federal government as an "entertainment" expense.

"Americans have been asked to tighten their belts across the board, from families who receive food stamps to our men and women in uniform," said McCain of Arizona, who has challenged fellow Republicans on the issue. "We are morally obliged to ensure that the corporate sector shares in the sacrifice. The public cannot understand why we are shelling out billions of dollars to powerful corporate interests when we simply cannot afford such largesse."

Robert Shapiro, an analyst for the Progressive Policy Institute, a think tank of the centrist Democratic Leadership Conference, said, "The hypocrisy on corporate welfare is glaring. We are in an era in which the Congress was able to find nearly a trillion dollars in cuts over seven years, the bulk of it from social services to the poor. But less than 2 percent of those cuts came from subsidies to industry."

"I don't blame the businesses for trying to get whatever they can. But I do blame the government for being willing to sacrifice the tax dollars of average people to satisfy these well-heeled and well-organized special pleaders," adds Shapiro, who has researched federal subsidies. "We have encrusted the economy with layer upon layer of these subsidies to the point where it is having a profound impact on the economy and the allocation of limited resources."

Said Gloria Larsen, who until recently was Gov. William F. Weld's secretary of economic affairs and served as deputy director of the Federal Trade Commission under President Bush: "The personal responsibility argument is so readily tied to social welfare. Now it is time that it is tied to corporate welfare."

Talk, but Little Action

Despite such sentiments to cut back, corporate assistance continues. President Clinton's administration . . . has used the bully pulpit against these expenditures, but done relatively little to actually prevent them. In some instances, Clinton has even sought to increase subsidies. The Republican-controlled Congress has been equally recalcitrant about any proposed changes to tax provisions that steer billions of dollars to big business. And in Massachusetts, Weld has endorsed an active policy of subsidizing business through trade missions, support services, tax breaks and state offices that guide businesses, big and small, on how to tap federal money.

Corporate welfare goes virtually unmentioned in political campaigns, where candidates like Clinton and Bob Dole square off on how to reform social welfare. Neither has proposed "two years and out" for corporations receiving federal assistance. And only recently has there been any policy debate on "personal responsibility" of corporations to the communities where they profit and receive public money.

Corporate welfare persists largely because of parochial politics. State by state, politicians are applauded for bringing home corporate pork with little regard for its drain on the national economy.

"Corporate welfare is a fashionable phrase inside the Beltway," says Sheila Krumholz, research director for the Washington-based Center for Responsive Politics, which tracks campaign finance issues. "But when it comes to biting the hand that feeds them, politician after politician is walking away from their rhetoric. They cave in to each individual subsidy, every one of which . . . can be defended and rationalized."

A Boston Globe examination of the issue has found:

- A host of questionable federal give-aways, such as the $200 million a year Market Promotion Program which over the last two years gave Massachusetts-based Ocean Spray some $700,000 and California-based Gallo about $4 million to market "Cranapple" juice and wine all over the world. Hundreds of thousands of dollars more were given to Concord-based Welch's and a Lynn-based company that makes marshmallow fluff.

- While many federal programs have the stated purpose of creating jobs, some subsidized companies are downsizing. AT & T, General Electric, Raytheon and Digital—among many large companies receiving federal assistance—have laid off about 100,000 workers among them. And defense contractor Lockheed Martin is expected to receive $1 billion to help defray the cost of its $10 billion merger, including more than $16 million in pay and performance bonuses for top executives while nearly 50,000 of the conglomerate's employees have been laid off in the last five years.

- Government subsidies to high-tech industries have resulted in tens of thousands of jobs going overseas. Federal officials and corporate chiefs boast about the promise of high-paying jobs created by "partnerships" with government. But they say little or nothing about the fact that many of the jobs created end up in Ireland, Malaysia, Singapore or Thailand because of low labor costs and taxes. The roughly $100 million a year Sematech consortium helped Digital Equipment Corp. and other semiconductor companies, but Digital still has shifted part of its workforce and capital to Ireland and Singapore.

- There is little hard data and even less oversight of many federal programs, especially in the technology and science industries, to assess whether they are accomplishing their stated goals of creating jobs and stimulating the economy. In the Advanced Technology Program, for example, Massachusetts companies participated in $90 million worth of projects, but a state-funded study found that only 150 jobs were directly created as a result of the projects.

A rush by the federal government and states to accommodate business with favorable tax rates has created a historic shift in America's tax burden. After World War II, the nation's tax bill was roughly split between corporations and individuals. But after years of changes in the federal tax code and international economy, the corporate share of taxes has declined to a fourth the amount individuals pay, according to the US Office of Management and Budget. A parallel trend has occurred at the state level. In Massachusetts, corporations pay $900 million, or 8 percent, of the $13 billion in state tax revenue annually.

Many business leaders defend the tax breaks and subsidies they receive as necessary to create a "level playing field" in the global marketplace. Industries in most of Europe and Asia, they note, are heavily subsidized by their governments. Proponents of government partnerships argue that not just big business, but thousands of small startup companies rely on federal dollars to research and develop products with potential for great public benefit, products that would otherwise go unfunded. It is an issue of great import to Massachusetts, which by many accounts is the most dependent of 50 states on federal research dollars. The hundreds of millions of dollars that pour into the state every year are the lifeblood of the commonwealth's universities, hospitals and high tech firms.

Culture of Dependency

Defenders of corporate subsidies and tax benefits also point to technological breakthroughs, such as the Internet, created through federal research and development programs and largely paid for by the US Defense Department. Others point out that because of agribusiness subsidies, Americans pay less for food than citizens of most other industrialized countries.

Joel Johnson, vice president of the Aerospace Industries Association and a top lobbyist for a business sector which every year receives billions of dollars in subsidies and tax breaks, defends the flow of public money to profitable companies. "There are business leaders and political leaders who recognize that the only way the government—whether it is the Defense Department or the Energy Department—can afford the new technology is if it works with business," he says. "But that is a partnership, not welfare."

Still, critics insist that if social welfare has created a "culture of dependency," so too has corporate America grown reliant on federal help. Many benefits seem to remain entrenched in legislation for decades, even though their purpose has become anachronistic. Many agriculture subsidies, for example, were adopted as post-Depression safeguards against famine.

Putting a precise dollar figure on corporate welfare depends on how it is defined. The Cato Institute considers corporate welfare to be the 125 Cabinet-level programs that provide direct subsidies to individual industries. Cato's estimate, generally regarded as conservative, is that such subsidies total $75 billion in 1996.

Ralph Nader's Center for the Study of Responsive Law offers a more expansive definition that includes federal tax breaks, many of which are designed to funnel money to specific industries. The center estimates total corporate aid at $167 billion annually, a figure most experts consider high.

The big money in corporate welfare comes in the subsidies to agribusiness, the oil industry and energy plants. Comparatively, Massachusetts companies are smaller players, but the commonwealth is considered the leading recipient per capita of federal research and development money, specifically subsidies to the defense, technology, science and medical industries.

Historically, the movement of technology from federal laboratory to the marketplace was commercial kismet. It was often a byproduct of defense research, but the government played a passive role. Market forces and competitive corporations took the federal research and turned it into everything from television to Tang.

But there has been a profound change in the seven years since the end of the Cold War. Now, Washington wants to play an active role in bringing government research into the marketplace. This has spawned an array of programs, including Small Business Innovative Research, the Advanced Technology Program and the Technology Reinvestment Program—all aimed at creating partnerships with business. In total, these partnerships with government provide an estimated $6 billion a year to industry giants in what critics have dubbed "techno-pork."

Some programs, such as Cooperative Research and Development Grants, go largely unregulated, with little expert evaluation of the validity of the proposed work and great criticism of the process used to select commercial partners. Although the Office of Science and Technology keeps track of the number of projects, critics point out there is almost no accounting of the return on this investment, or whether it is in the public interest.

The Department of Energy's own advisory board reported in February 1995 that Cooperative Research and Development Grants, while valuable, leave federal laboratories "vulnerable to charges that the selection process is flawed and that the competitive playing field is unfairly tilted toward the labs' chosen partners."

In other words, the government ends up picking winners and losers in the marketplace. Tom Glynn, president of Maine-based Lighthouse Software is angry that the federal government has given about $40 million to help Icon Industrial Controls Corp. of Louisiana develop a product that Lighthouse already manufactures.

Says Glynn, whose company makes software to control robots in the machine tool industry, a growing international market: "I'm furious as a businessman, and I'm furious as a taxpayer that the federal government is funding my competition."

An Incentive to Leave

Corporate dependence on federal dollars may be distorting the free-market system. Many critics, including conservative economists and free-market chief executives, believe some tax-code loopholes and many subsidies have created damaging incentives for companies to send jobs and capital overseas. They have kept management focused on maintaining federal funding rather than increasing market share.

Says Stephen Moore, who has written a series of reports on corporate welfare for the Cato Institute: "The point is, we have very efficient capital markets in this country. The government has never been good at picking winners and losers. The Commerce Department and Congress are influenced by lobbying more than the market. That makes for a corruption of the market. And this in the long run is bad for the national economy."

Moore says he knows the growing attack on corporate welfare has struck a raw nerve within American business. Since he wrote a much-discussed and controversial report on the issue last year in response to a challenge by Secretary Reich, he says, "IBM and the big guys want to have lunch with us a lot lately.

They are dying to tell us how important these programs are."

"But what people need to know is who gets hurt. And that is the small business owners, who don't have lobbyists in Washington and trade associations bringing them billions of federal dollars. And they certainly aren't in Washington taking us out to lunch."

Critical Evaluation

1. How might a corporate executive respond to this chapter?

2. Has the author been fair in presenting both the pros and cons of corporate welfare? Why or why not?

3. Do you think that the author's sources of information are reliable? Why or why not?

Charles Sennott, "The $150 Billion 'Welfare' Recipients: U.S. Corporations." In *The Boston Globe*, 7 July 1996. Copyright © 1996 by *The Boston Globe*. Reprinted by permission. ✦

2

The FBI and Covert Repression

Kevin Gotham

What do people expect from government? Ideally, the government should protect the citizenry and serve the interests of all citizens equally. But because the federal government has such enormous power, it can act covertly against citizens who are opposed to current political policies and practices. People who are doing nothing illegal, who are merely protesting an existing situation or asserting their rights, can find themselves repressed rather than protected by the government.

In this selection, Kevin Gotham shows how the FBI engaged in covert surveillance and repressive activities against Americans engaged in the civil rights and anti-Vietnam War movements. In theory, the American government is set up to protect the right of citizens to protest. In practice, government officials may take covert action to suppress protest. Although such protest may be officially defined as threatening to the nation, at least in some cases the threat is actually to the political beliefs of those in power.

At the structural level, then, all the resources of the federal government may be brought to bear against protest groups. This repression is legitimated and perpetuated by the attitudes of those Americans who accept the government's definition of what and who are threats to the society.

Focus Questions

1. What is the "fundamental paradox" of the U.S. government?

2. How do government officials justify covert surveillance?

3. In what ways did the FBI attempt to suppress the civil-rights and anti-Vietnam War movements?

Introduction

In recent years the covert intelligence operations of the Federal Bureau of Investigation (FBI) have become an important topic of investigation (Donner, 1990; Churchill and Vander Wall, 1990; Keller, 1989; O'Reilly, 1988). Scholarly research and Congressional investigations have uncovered a wealth of data on FBI covert operations against legal dissident groups who have challenged state policy (e.g., Robbins, 1992; Theoharis, 1989; Theoharis and Cox, 1988; Blackstock, 1988; Thomas, 1981; U.S. House, 1976; U.S. Senate, 1976a, 1976b, 1976c). What these data reveal is a history of significant political repression, which, for the most part, remain hidden from both the American people and the media, and denied by mainstream political discourse (Glick, 1989). Although the sociological literature recognizes the covert nature of the American state, questions concerning the contradictory relationship between covert repression and democratic legitimacy have yet to be examined. This paper seeks to address the operational and structural contradictions of organized state power and democratic legitimacy by examining the FBI's counterintelligence programs (COINTELPROs) against the civil rights and anti-Vietnam war movements. These historical case studies illustrate state responses to dissident movements including the rhetorical construction of domestic security threats through the stigma of "subversion." I argue that while covert repression has been an institutionalized response to dissent, its actual implementation is mediated by political, individual, and organizational factors that are historically contingent.

A basic assumption of this paper is that the American state system is shot through with contradictions (Poulantzas, 1978; Offe, 1984). One tension exists between the domestic security interests of the state and the constitutional rights of the citizenry. On the one hand, the state must neutralize dissident threats to its security interests in order to survive; on the other hand, it must maintain the appearance as an unbiased referee of competing societal interests to legitimate its power. I argue that using covert techniques of repression against dissident groups and activity is one way the American state attempts, yet never fully succeeds, to reconcile the contradictions between state power and democratic legitimacy. Covert techniques include the use of confidential informants, agents provocateur, disinformation, electronic surveillance, and a host of other surreptitious techniques designed to conceal the identity of the sponsoring agency and to disrupt and neutralize adversarial organizations and political activity (Barak, 1991; Churchill and Vander Wall, 1990; Marx, 1974). Covert repression gives the American state the anonymous capacity to influence events and thwart dissident efforts to challenge state policy while at the same time denying the targeted victims the direct opportunity to legally challenge the actions taken against them (Donner, 1980; Marx, 1988). The victims of covert repression may never suspect that their misfortunes and failures are the intended result of governmental coercion since covert techniques are difficult to trace and confirm.

In what follows I explore the covert nature of FBI domestic security operations. First, I lay out the theoretical orientation of the paper, focusing on the structural and operational contradictions of organized state power and democratic legitimacy. Second, I present an historical overview of FBI domestic security operations; and, third, I present two historical case studies to illustrate the actual ways covert repression was implemented. I find that despite formal procedures and strict organizational routines, the selection of groups for repression was arbitrary and inconsistent, and depended on field office discretion. Findings indicate that covert repression is not directly shaped by a unified state that is a reflection of the agents of the capitalist class or a power elite. The implementation of covert repression reflects the individual biases and prerogatives of agents who respond to a myriad of complex factors at a given historical moment.

Theoretical Orientation

The range of options available to domestic security agencies to contain dissident threats is shaped, in part, by the state itself (Keller,

1989:7). Unlike the agencies in totalitarian and military states, the range of political control options available to the FBI is severely limited due to the decentralized structure of state power. Under democratic systems of government the coercive power of the state is frustrated, theoretically, by a constitutional system of administrative checks and balances among the different branches of the federal government. The arbitrary use of violence by the executive branch, for example, could not be easily undertaken due to the constitutional restraints within the U.S. justice system. Violent and overt tactics of repression such as the absence of due process, indefinite imprisonment, torture, and mass assassinations, that are readily employed by military states, are usually not a feature of liberal democracies. Although abhorrent exceptions have occurred during eras of international unrest and public disorder (e.g., the Palmer Raids of 1919–1920, the mass internment of Japanese-Americans in 1942, and the public outlawing of the Communist Party U.S.A. in 1954), violent state actions such as the 1989 Tiananmen Square massacre in Communist China, and the 1992 anti-government executions in Iran have no equivalent in liberal democracies. Overt repression and naked force would likely undermine the state's democratic legitimacy.

In the U.S., there exists a fundamental paradox between the constitutional rights of individuals and the domestic security interests of the state. Max Weber recognized that a central feature of modern states was their "monopoly of the *legitimate* use of physical force within a given territory" (Weber, 1972a:78). The state's monopolistic claim to use physical force must be seen as legitimate by the citizenry if that state is to survive. In democratic societies, state power is considered legitimate to the extent to which it appears to represent the consent of the governed. The state draws its legitimacy from the protection of the constitutional liberties of freedom of expression and organized dissent that are a crucial means of indicating consent (Clark and Dear, 1986:164). However, as Weber recognized, since the state's "absolute end" is to preserve the "external and internal distribution of power" it is "absolutely essential . . . to appeal to the naked violence of coercive means in the face of outsiders as well as in the face of internal enemies" (Weber, 1972b:334). Therefore, when confronted with ideological threats to its economic and political interests the domestic security concerns of the state will take precedence over the constitutional rights of its citizenry. But if the democratic state imposes any restraints on the constitutional rights of its citizenry then its *raison d'être* of the consent of the governed may be undermined. Should political elites violate the procedures of constitutional democracy and the rule of law in a substantial way then legal redress and informal protests may occur and result in a crisis of legitimacy (Habermas, 1976). Hence the American state faces contradictory tasks: On the one hand, it must neutralize dissident threats to its security interests to survive; on the other hand, it must respect and protect the constitutional rights of the citizenry to legitimate its power.

The need to maintain the legitimacy of constitutional democracy while simultaneously neutralizing dissident threats makes the use of covert methods of repression compelling. Acting covertly allows the state to clandestinely influence events and thwart threatening political movements while maintaining democratic appearances. As the chief federal agency discharged with domestic security functions in the United States, it has been the FBI's traditional responsibility to investigate and neutralize dissident threats to the state as defined by the agency itself (Keller, 1989:15). Since the advent of World War II, the FBI's clandestine activities have been insulated from public scrutiny, interest group pressures, the judicial procedures of the law and courts, and democratic accountability (Barak, 1991; Donner, 1990: Halperin et al., 1976). The insular nature of FBI internal operations has enabled the agency to conceal its repressive actions in such a way as to deny the targeted groups the direct opportunity to legally challenge the actions taken against them. The logic of this modus operandi is that the ability to conceal instances of political repression from the citizenry will prevent any damage to the regime's legitimacy, since what is not publicly known cannot have public consequences. . . .

I argue that the labeling of oppositional political groups and activity as "subversive" and the use of covert repression are ways the American state attempts to meet the challenges of dissident movements while at the same time maintaining democratic appearances. This does not mean that the rhetorical construction of domestic security threats and implementation of covert repression reflects the conscious intent of a unified power elite or a class conscious ruling class. The selection of targets for repression can be arbitrary and inconsistent, and depend "as much upon opportunity, personal bias, and individual discretion as upon formal or tacit directives shaped by state power" (Thomas, 1981:52-3). This suggests that the implementation of covert repression is not directly shaped by a unified state but is mediated by individual and organizational factors that are historically contingent.

Domestic Security for the American State

The domestic security apparatus of any modern state is the product of its historical development. The emergence of the United States as a world power at the beginning of the century, the impact of two world wars and the Cold War, and the increasing centralization and growth of state authority and control have contributed to the development of the FBI as a permanent agency of the federal bureaucracy (Halperin et al., 1976). The first substantial domestic security responsibilities of the federal government were established during World War I with Congressional passage of the Espionage Act of 1917, the Immigration Act of 1918, and the Sedition Act of 1918 (U.S. Senate, 1976b:378-9). In the years preceding World War II, President Franklin Delano Roosevelt established the FBI's modern day domestic security structure by directing the agency to take charge of investigative work in matters relating to "espionage, sabotage, subversive activities, and violations of neutrality laws" (U.S. Senate, 1976a:25-27, 1976b:392-396).

Wartime exigencies provided the impetus for the establishment of the FBI's domestic security structure while at the same time creating an inherent contradiction for the state: that in order to ensure domestic stability, it was necessary for the Executive, with the tacit consent of Congress, to suppress certain constitutionally protected forms of political activity in order to prevent foreign espionage, subversion, and sabotage to the U.S. war effort. By authorizing the agency to investigate "subversive activities," ideological considerations and "potential" for subversion and lawbreaking were given priority over actual violations of the law (Thomas, 1981:49-50; Halperin et al., 1976). During the 1940s, the scope of the agency's "subversive activities" investigations included targeting individuals showing "sympathy for Communist objectives and policies," "suspected" Communist Party members, and genuine domestic groups such as the American Civil Liberties Union (ACLU), the National Alliance for the Advancement of Colored People (NAACP), and the John Birch Society (U.S. Senate, 1976b:31-2, 48-49; Theoharis, 1989; Theoharis and Cox, 1988:174).

The FBI's domestic security functions were expanded and institutionalized during the Cold War. Executive authority to investigate "subversive activity" was reaffirmed by President Truman on July 24, 1950, and by President Eisenhower on December 5, 1953 (U.S. Senate, 1976a:25-26, 45-46; 1976b:393-396). By the late 1950s, the FBI was extending its investigative efforts to cover the "entire spectrum of the social and labor movement in the country" as part of its COMINFIL (Communist Infiltration) and COINTELPRO programs (U.S. Senate, 1976a:45, 1976b:449). Under the COMINFIL program, the FBI disseminated political information to the President and Attorney General about domestic organizations seeking to influence public policy with the intention of determining if "subversive campaigns" were involved (U.S. Senate, 1976a:46-9, 1976b:448-52). Beginning in 1956 and continuing to the early 1970s, the foundation of the FBI's domestic security operations was a series of top-secret "COINTELPROs," specifically designed to "expose, disrupt, misdirect, discredit, or otherwise neutralize" dissident individuals and political organizations. The COINTELPROs were centrally directed and nationally targeted programs designed to formalize the implementation of covert repression which, prior to 1956, had been undertaken on an ad hoc, informal, and localized basis (U.S. Senate, 1976a:66, 1976b:19-23; Theoharis, 1978:136-151; Powers, 1987:339-343). The formal nature of COINTELPRO necessitated that local field offices and headquarters communicate extensively over specific disruptive operations and methods. Hundreds of thousands of FBI memoranda were recorded detailing the bureaucratic operation of COINTELPRO, the specific functions and objectives of the program, and the results of individual COINTELPRO operations. A huge volume of bureaucratic paper was generated that paradoxically led to the program being publicly exposed during the 1970s through Freedom of Information Act (FOIA) suits and congressional investigations (U.S. Senate, 1976b:3-77, 1976c:372-397; U.S. House, 1976).

Revelations in the mid 1970s of FBI illegalities associated with COINTELPRO led to the establishment of more stringent guidelines on FBI domestic security investigations by Attorney General Levi (Eliff, 1979). Levi's guidelines were modified in 1981 by President Reagan's Executive Order No. 12333 of 4 December 1981, and by Attorney General William French Smith's directive of 7 March 1983 that broadened the FBI's investigative discretion from "subversive activities" to "terrorism" while permitting the agency to resume intrusive and disruptive operations (Churchill and Vander Wall, 1990:330; Theoharis, 1989:102-110; Glick, 1989:31).

In sum, the FBI's covert actions against legal dissident activities and organizations does not simply represent aberrant acts or excesses which were limited in time and confined to a few overzealous officials. Covert repression has been an institutionalized feature of the American state for most of this century and reflects the continued policies of liberal as well as conservative administrations. If the FBI's domestic security authority to investigate "subversive activities" provides a justification for targeting legal dissident activities, it also reflects the tension between the security interests of the state and the rules of constitutional democracy. In order to meet the challenges of dissident movements while at the same time retaining the niceties of civil liberties, it becomes necessary to construct an ideological label such as "subversive activities" or "terrorism" to "delegitimate dissident ideas and activities . . . even though those ideas and activities are lawful" (Grace and Leys, 1989:89). Domestic security operations require not only an apparatus but a target for covert repression. Once a target has been rhetorically constructed it becomes necessary to act covertly in order to circumvent the constitutional restraints within the U.S. justice system. I now turn to two historical case studies, the civil rights movement and the anti-Vietnam war movement, in order to examine how covert repression was actually implemented, and to illustrate how the state attempts to delegitimate legal dissident activities in an effort to legitimate state action against them.

The Civil Rights Movement

The events associated with the rise of the civil rights movement and the widespread urban riots of the 1960s appear to have generated considerable conflict and confusion within the FBI. For example, the extent of communist influence in the civil rights movement was a source of disagreement and dissension between Director J. Edgar Hoover and his officials in the FBI's Domestic Intelligence Division (DID) during the early 1960s. Hoover's orders in the summer of 1963 were that FBI field offices were to be "extremely alert to data indicating interest, plans, or actual involvement of the [Communist] Party in the current Negro movement."[1] However, four days before the March on Washington on August 26, 1963, the DID sent a sixty-eight page report to Director Hoover contending that there had been an "obvious failure" on the part of Communists to infiltrate groups such as the NAACP and the Southern Christian Leadership Conference (SCLC) and that communist influence on the civil rights movement had been "infinitesimal."[2] Hoover refused to accept the DID's conclusions and castigated the division:

"This memo reminds me vividly of those I received when Castro took over Cuba. You contended then that Castro and his cohorts were not Communists and not influenced by Communists. Time alone proved you wrong" (U.S. Senate, 1976b:1057). Hoover's admonishment prompted the DID to reverse its previous conclusion implying to Hoover that "we did not put the proper interpretation upon the facts which we gave to the Director." Hoover concurred with the DID's recommendation for "increased coverage of communist influence on the Negro," and on October 3 disseminated a memorandum to FBI field offices emphasizing that "imaginative and aggressive tactics be utilized" for purposes of "neutralizing the [Communist] Party's activities in the Negro field" (U.S. Senate, 1976b:110-111).

Within a year, Hoover was reporting before the House Appropriations subcommittee that outbreaks of urban rioting around the country were linked to communist efforts to "generate racial tensions . . . and control . . . the Negro population" (O'Reilly, 1989:154). Over the next three years, Hoover continually disseminated memoranda to the White House, Justice Department, and members of Congress indicating few ties between the Communist party and the civil rights movement e.g., civil rights disturbances were "not communist inspired but communist encouraged"—but emphasizing that the "CPUSA [Communist Party U.S.A.] views every noncommunist organization as a target for infiltration" (O'Reilly, 1989:136, 234). These FBI reports as well as more rioting in Watts in August 1965, followed by rioting in over 250 cities over the next three years encouraged the White House and Justice Department to believe that there was a communist conspiracy at the heart of the riots (O'Reilly, 1988; U.S. Senate, 1976a:240-2).

By the summer of 1967 the White House was ordering the agency to supply the "correct information" indicating that all the riots were "well-planned" and "in very many cases" directed by "the same people" (O'Reilly, 1989:245; Davis, 1992:97-103; Donner, 1990:77-9; Powers, 1987:422-7). Attorney General Ramsey Clark directed the agency "to use the maximum available resources, investigative and intelligence, to collect and report all the facts bearing upon the question as to whether there has been or is a scheme or conspiracy by any group of whatever size, effectiveness or affirmation, to plan, promote, or engage in riot activity."[3] On August 28, FBI Headquarters responded by directing twenty-three field offices to institute a counterintelligence program (COINTELPRO) to "expose, disrupt, misdirect, discredit, or otherwise neutralize black nationalist hate groups."[4] In March 1968, Hoover expanded this COINTELPRO to all forty-seven field offices directing field agents to submit a summary of black nationalist movement in their territory and a "progress letter summarizing counterintelligence operations proposed . . . , operations effected, and tangible results." Field offices were directed to "prevent the coalition of black nationalist groups"; "prevent the rise of a 'messiah'" who could unify black nationalist groups; prevent groups and leaders from gaining "respectability"; and "prevent the long-range growth of black nationalist organizations."[5]

The nebulousness of the "black nationalist hate-groups" label was demonstrated by the lack of consensus in the agency as to which groups constituted a legitimate threat. Under this program targeting included, according to one COINTELPRO supervisor, "a great number of organizations that you might not today characterize as black nationalist but which were primarily black."[6] Thus, on paper, this COINTELPRO targeted a range of organizations from the black power advocates such as the Black Panther Party (BPP) and the Student Non-Violent Coordinating Committee (SNCC), to peaceful organizations such as the Southern Christian Leadership Conference (SCLC) and the Congress of Racial Equality (CORE), as well as every Black Student Union and other black student groups.[7] However, the Omaha field office reported no "organized Black Nationalist Movement" in the area, and both the Kansas City and Milwaukee field offices reported little or no black nationalist groups other than the Nation of Islam. Field offices in Pittsburgh, Newark, New York, Detroit, and Cleveland identified few groups to target except for non-violent peaceful groups such as

CORE and SCLC, who did not pose a danger and therefore required little counterintelligence attention (O'Reilly, 1989:277-8).

Not all field offices agreed with the aims or philosophy of this COINTELPRO and there is evidence of considerable resistance to the program at the New York and San Francisco field offices, among others (Davis, 1992:106). The New York field office, the most active field office in the nation, was admonished for not providing a sufficient quantity of counterintelligence proposals (O'Reilly, 1989:290). In May 1969, the Special Agent in charge of the San Francisco field office was severely reprimanded for his protests against using counterintelligence actions against the local chapter of the Black Panther Party (BPP). Hoover informed him that he had "obviously missed the point" and that his outlook was "not in line with Bureau objectives."[8] While such a reprimand may have been rare, it indicates that organizational conflict and dissension within the agency was not uncommon. As one of the requirements of this COINTELPRO, field offices were required to develop a certain number of "ghetto informants" to provide information regarding the "racial situation" and "racial activities" (U.S. Senate, 1976a:75-6; 1976b:293, 494; 1976c:17). If a particular area did not include any black nationalist groups or any ghetto areas, the field agent had to "so specify by memorandum"—"so that he will not be charged with failure to perform." Because FBI agents in charge of field offices had to recruit a large number of additional racial informants, many invented ghetto informants on paper or reclassified criminal informants as ghetto informants (O'Reilly, 1989:268-9). FBI Headquarters also established a quota system that required field offices to report a sufficient number of counterintelligence results or face reprimand or reassignment. This prompted some field offices to engage in deception, subterfuge, and outright lying to meet the extraordinary demands and stringent requirements of Headquarters (Davis, 1992:101-123; O'Reilly, 1989:276-85).

In sum, FBI documents indicate considerable conflict and confusion between field offices and headquarters over which civil rights groups constituted a legitimate threat. Field offices responded to Headquarters' demands for information on the communist influence in the civil rights movement by targeting non-communist and non-violent organizations as well as inflating counterintelligence results and reclassifying criminal informants as ghetto informants. This would suggest that despite strict organizational routines and lines of authority, targeting was ad hoc, and depended on the individual discretion and biases of field agents at a given field office more than the conscious intent of high level political elites.

The Anti-Vietnam War Movement

The decision to launch a COINTELPRO against the anti-Vietnam war movement was in response to what the FBI believed to be communist efforts to dominate and control anti-war protest and dissent. Although Hoover could never give conclusive proof, his barrage of FBI reports to the White House and Justice Department insinuated that communist penetration of the anti-war movement was pervasive and intense. In April 1965 Hoover was reporting to President Johnson that the anti-war group Students for a Democratic Society (SDS) was "largely infiltrated by communists and [has] woven into the civil rights situation which we know has large communist influence."[9] In January 1966 Hoover warned that the Communist Party had an "ever increasing role in generating opposition to the United States' position in Vietnam" (Powers, 1987:429). In his annual presentation before the House Appropriations subcommittee in 1968, Hoover claimed that the Communist Party was attempting to unite the civil rights and anti-war movements "to create one massive movement which they hope will ultimately change our government's policies." Hoover also maintained that student groups of the New Left have been "infiltrated by Communist Party members" who have "seized upon every opportunity to foment discord among the youth in this country."[10]

Escalating anti-war protest and campus demonstration combined with the inability to discredit the anti-war movement by link-

ing it to communist subversion provided the impetus to launch COINTELPRO-New Left in May 1968 (Davis, 1993:133; Powers, 1987:430). As with the Black Nationalist CO-INTELPRO, the New Left COINTELPRO had no clearly defined target and there was never any firm definition as to what constituted "New Left." Field offices were instructed that the New Left was a "subversive force"—the supervisor of this COINTELPRO characterized it as "more or less an attitude"—dedicated to destroying "our traditional values."[11] Other FBI documents indicate that although the New Left had "no definable ideology," it did have "strong Marxist, existentialist, nihilistic, and anarchist overtones."[12] By September 1968 FBI Headquarters was instructing field offices that the "New Left" did not refer to "a definite organization," but to a "loosely-bound, freewheeling, college-oriented movement."[13]

The scattered and unstructured character of the anti-war movement limited the effectiveness of some covert operations such as anonymous mailings, stigmatizing protest leaders as FBI informants (e.g., the "snitch jacket" technique), and dissemination of disinformation that had worked well against specific organizations.[14] According to one COINTELPRO document, the "disruption of the New Left . . . poses problems which have not been previously present" due to the anti-war movement's decentralized, open, and diffuse character.[15] The inability to find a concrete target, except for the SDS, resulted in continuous reclassification of categories for monitoring dissident individuals: from the Rabble Rouser Index in August 1967, to the Agitator Index, to the Key Activist Index in January 1968 (U.S. Senate, 1976b:511-18). These reclassifications as well as the problems with informants assaulting local police and looting riot torn areas, and an inability to recruit under-21 college-age informants (FBI guidelines required informants to be 21 years old) to infiltrate campus anti-war organizations hindered the effectiveness of this program and contributed to its haphazard coordination (Davis, 1993:17, 155).

Despite the enthusiasm in FBI Headquarters, it appears that some field agents remained indifferent to this counterintelligence program. Several field offices were reprimanded for their lack of effort in seeking specific data depicting the "depraved nature and moral looseness of the New Left" and "using this information to the best advantage."[16] Other field offices were taken to task for not submitting enough counterintelligence proposals or for their lack of "imagination" and enthusiasm in proposing specific counterintelligence proposals (Davis, 1993:130-53). On July 23, 1968, Hoover disseminated a stinging memorandum to all field offices indicating that he was "appalled by the reaction of some of our field offices" for their lack of vigor in pursuing the New Left. Hoover castigated his field offices for their failure to recognize the "subversive" character of the New Left: "I have reminded you time and again that the militancy of the New Left is escalating daily. Unless you recognize this and move in a more positive manner to identify subversive elements . . . this type of activity can be expected to mount in intensity. . . . This must not be allowed to happen and I am going to hold each Special Agent in charge responsible to insure that the Bureau's responsibilities in this area are completely met and fulfilled."[17]

Hoover's admonishment is indicative of the frustrations and tensions experienced by the agency in an attempt to contain the escalating campus protests and anti-war demonstrations during an era of unparalleled domestic strife and unrest. The popularity of the anti-war movement handicapped the effectiveness of this program and resulted in inconsistent targeting and conflict between Headquarters and field offices. The failure of field offices to adequately neutralize anti-war opposition was interpreted by Headquarters as a "failure to perform." Individual field offices responded in a variety of ways by targeting not only anti-war demonstrations and organizations but also university professors and administrators, and students demonstrating against anything (U.S. Senate, 1976a: 173; 1976b:23-7, 29-33; Blackstock, 1988). This would suggest that despite the centralization of decision making and coordination of operations, the actual implementation of covert repression was erratic and inconsistent and depended on field office discretion and bias.

Discussion and Conclusion

The historical analysis presented in this paper is based on the view that covert repression reflects a myriad of tensions and contradictions within the American state system and the FBI itself. The FBI's counterintelligence campaigns arose in response to the challenges of the civil rights and anti-Vietnam war movements. White House and Justice Department officials directed the agency to investigate incidents of possible subversion in these movements and then left it up to the agency to determine which political activities were subversive and how those activities should be investigated (U.S. Senate, 1976a: 157-9). The FBI in turn monitored both civil rights and anti-war groups on the premise that legitimate dissident activity was subject to communist influence. As civil rights and anti-war demonstrations mushroomed into consolidated national movements the agency responded by implementing covert programs of political repression. The COINTELPROs were nationally targeted formal programs specifically designed to circumvent the constitutional restraints of the U.S. justice system thereby denying targeted groups and individuals the capacity to directly challenge the legality of the coercive actions taken against them. Acting covertly against legal dissident groups and activity was politically advantageous as a means of denying the legal significance of political activity and pacifying peoples' political agency as "citizens." Any attempt to prosecute domestic dissidents within the legal system would have legitimated a defendant's politics and confirmed his/her status as an American citizen, entitled to the legal protections of the U.S. Constitution (Donner, 1980:21). COINTELPRO enabled the agency to bypass the constitutional restrictions that otherwise would have been invoked if overt repression was employed.

This historical analysis has demonstrated that the premise of FBI repression was that dissident groups or individuals needed to be neutralized not because what they were doing was illegal, but because they might be influenced by "communists." The FBI invariably took a broad view of its mandate to investigate subversion by targeting not merely alleged instances of subversive activity, but "potential" subversives (e.g., Martin Luther King Jr.), and "subversive" beliefs and attitudes—which were viewed as a condition for engaging in subversive activities (U.S. Senate, 1976b:79-184). The label of subversion was invoked to stigmatize civil rights and anti-war protest as communist inspired in order to delegitimate legal efforts to challenge state policy. While FBI documents indicate that there was considerable conflict and indecisiveness between Headquarters and field offices over which groups and activities should be targeted for repression, there was never any doubt that oppositional forms of political behavior should be monitored and controlled. The broad and all-inclusive nature of the concept of subversion was not a liability or handicap to state surveillance but the requisite for targeting legal dissident activities and political opposition. . . .

Researchers examining the revelations of covert repression have tended to focus on the "paranoid" and "egomaniacal" leadership style of J. Edgar Hoover as explanations of FBI improprieties (Summers, 1993; Gentry, 1991; Wise, 1976). Although Hoover's perceptions, values, and vision influenced the FBI, it is also true that the FBI's modus operandi reflected the attitudes, beliefs, and perceptions of superordinate officials, no matter how autonomous the agency may have been under Hoover's rule. Both President Johnson and Attorney General Ramsey Clark actively sought and relied upon FBI intelligence on communist activity and directed the agency to expand its investigative efforts to uncover communist efforts to infiltrate domestic organizations (Powers, 1987:422-34; O'Reilly, 1989:264-5; U.S. Senate, 1976a:78-80, 250-2, 266-88). Former Assistant Attorney General Fred Vinson testified before Congress in 1975 that in 1967, the Justice Department averaged "fifty letters a week from Congress" insisting that "people like [Stokely] Carmichael be jailed" (U.S. Senate, 1976a:280). Therefore, FBI repression against civil rights and anti-war groups should not be seen as the

handicraft of one leader, but rather reflected the view within the federal government on the necessity of suppressing forms of political opposition during the 1960s and early 1970s.

Criticisms of individuals also tend to divert attention away from the institutional factors that determine the persistent reliance upon covert repression. In assessing the covert nature of FBI domestic security operations, much research has suggested that covert intelligence operations and activities reflect the internal structure and organizational routines of agencies themselves rather than logics of state power. Manning (1980) contends that the unique modes of information acquisition and processing peculiar to police work facilitate covert intelligence operations. Thomas (1981:51) suggests that the "secrecy of surveillance may be as much a reflection of organizational requisites as of any intent or need of those controlling state power." The historical analysis presented in this paper is based on the view that the covert nature of FBI domestic security operations, while a reflection of the organizational routines of the agency, is also shaped and conditioned by the constitutional set of laws and administrative checks and balances. The constitutional freedoms of thought, speech, and association legitimate the existing political system but they can also conflict with the security interests of the state. Covert repression serves to mitigate this conflict by secretly thwarting dissident mobilizations and activity while at the same time formally retaining the constitutional freedoms that protect political dissent. This does not mean that the reliance on covert repression always reflects the conscious intent of state officials to suppress mass insurgents by manipulating or circumventing constitutional rules. Covert repression is not directly shaped by a unified state but embodies contradictory features. These include target inconsistency, field office discretion, and conflict between field offices and Headquarters despite formal organizational polices and routines.

As the twentieth century draws to a close, recent developments in telecommunications, electronic surveillance, and covert intelligence operations are enhancing the information-gathering powers of the state and redefining meanings of individual freedom and constitutional democracy (Leo, 1992; Marx, 1988). Technological developments that are creating new possibilities for people to communicate in private are conflicting with the security requirements of the state and leading to invasions of privacy (Marx and Corbett, 1991; Marx, 1990). A prime example is the current debates, lawsuits, and attempts by the federal government to regulate computer software programs that can secretly access electronic forms of communication (Lyon, 1993). What these debates and controversies indicate is that as technology creates the means to communicate and associate in private, state security concerns are leading to attacks on freedoms that are legally protected in non-electronic forums. The paradox of contemporary surveillance technologies is that while they amplify the repressive capacity of the state, they can also protect liberty, privacy, and security, and may generate new forms of political opposition and struggle. This suggests that despite their manifest repressive power, the surveillance powers of the state can create new understandings of state power, individual freedom, and constitutional democracy.

Notes

1. Airtel from Director, FBI to SAC, Albany 6/27/63. U.S. Senate, 1976c: 64- 3, 697.

2. Memorandum from F.J. Baumgartner to William C. Sullivan, 8/22/63, quoted in U.S. Senate, 1976b:480; see also O'Reilly, 1989:128-9.

3. Memorandum from the office of the Attorney General, to Director, FBI, 9/14/67. U.S. Senate, 1976a:171-2, 1976c:528-30.

4. Director, FBI to SAC, Albany, 8/25/67. U.S. Senate, 1976c:383-5.

5. Airtel from Director, FBI to SAC Albany, 3/4/68. Memorandum from W.C. Sulivan to G.C. Moore, 2/29/68. U.S. Senate, 1976c:386-92. Churchill and Vander Wall, 1990:107-11.

6. Black Nationalist Supervisor, 10/17/75, quoted in U.S. Senate, 1976b:4.

7. Airtel from Director, FBI to SAC, Albany, 11/4/70. U.S. Senate, 1976c:698-9.

8. Airtel from Director, FBI to SAC, San Francisco, 5/27/69.

9. Hoover memorandum, 4/28/65, quoted in U.S. Senate, 1976a:251.

10. *New York Times* 19 May, 1968, "Hoover Finds Period in New Left Action" p.1.

11. Memorandum from W.C. Sullivan to C.D. Brennan, 5/9/68. U.S. Senate, 1976c:393-4. Memorandum from Director, FBI to SAC, Newark, 5/27/68. Churchill and Vander Wall, 1990:181-2.

12. SAC Letter No. 68-21, 4/2/68, quoted in U.S. Senate,1976b:507.

13. Airtel from Director, FBI to SAC, Albany, 9/28/68. U.S. 82 Senate, 1976c:669-71.

14. Memorandum from Director, FBI to SAC, Chicago, 5/19/69; and 5/21/69. Churchill and Vander Wall, 1990:210-1. Memorandum from Director, FBI to SAC, Albany, no date. U.S. Senate, 1976c:395-7; See also Churchill and Vander Wall, 1990:183-4; Donner, 1980:232; Powers, 1987:432.

15. Memorandum from Director, FBI to SAC, Philadelphia, 5/29/69.

16. Airtel from Director, FBI to SAC, Albany, 10/9/68. U.S. Senate, 1976c:612- 3.

17. FBI Memorandum, Headquarters to Field Office, 7/23/68.

References

Barak, Gregg. 1991. "Toward a Criminality of State Criminality." Pp. 3-18 in Gregg Barak (ed.), *Crimes by the Capitalist State*. State University of New York Press.

Bierne, Piers, and James Messerschmidt. 1991. *Criminology*. New York: Harcourt Brace Jovanovich.

Blackstock, Nelson (ed.). 1988. *COINTELPRO: The FBI's Secret War on Political Freedom*. New York: Monad Press.

Churchill, Ward, and Jim Vander Wall. 1990. *The COINTELPRO Papers: Documents from the FBI's Secret Wars against Domestic Dissent*. Boston: South End Press.

Clark, Gordon L., and Michael Dear. 1984. *State Apparatus: Structures of Language and Legitimacy*. Boston: Allen and Unurn, Inc.

Davis, James Kirkpatrick. 1992. *Spying on America: The FBI's Domestic Counterintelligence Program*. New York: Praeger.

Donner, Frank. 1991. *Protectors of Privilege: Red Squads and Police Repression in Urban America*. Berkeley: University of California Press.

——. 1980. *Age of Surveillance: The Aims and Methods of America's Political Intelligence Community*. New York: Vintage Books.

Eliff, John T. 1979. *Reform of FBI Domestic Intelligence Operations*. Princeton: Princeton University Press.

Gelbspan, Ross. 1991. *Break-ins, Death Threats, and the FBI: The Covert War Against the Central American Movement*. Boston: South End Press.

Gentry, Curt. 1991. *J. Edgar Hoover: The Man and the Secrets*. New York: W. W. Norton and Company.

Glick, Brian. 1989. *War at Home: Covert Action Against U.S. Activists and What We Can Do About It*. Boston: South End Press.

Grace, Elizabeth, and Colin Leys. 1989. "The Concept of Subversion and Its Implications." Pp. 62-85 in C.E.S. Franks (ed.), *Dissent and the State*. Toronto: Oxford University Press.

Habermas, Jurgen. 1976. *The Legitimation Crisis*. Translated by Thomas McCarthy. Boston: Beacon Press.

Halperin, Morton H., Jerry J. Berman, Robert L. Borosage, and Christine M. Marwick. 1976. *The Lawless State: Crimes of the U.S. Intelligence Agencies*. New York: Penguin.

Keller, William W. 1989. *The Liberals and J. Edgar Hoover: The Rise and Fall of a Domestic Intelligence State*. Princeton: Princeton University Press.

Leo, R. A. 1992. "From Coercion to Deception: The Changing Nature of Police Interrogation in America." *Crime, Law, and Social Change*. 18(1-2):35-60.

Lyon, David. 1993. *Rise of the Surveillance Society: Computers and Social Control in Context*. Cambridge: Polity Press.

Manning, Peter K. 1980. *The Narc's Game: Organizational and Informational Limits on Drug Law Enforcement*. Cambridge: MIT Press.

Marx, Gary. 1990. "Privacy and Technology." World and I. 3(Sept.):523-41.

——. 1988. *Undercover: Police Surveillance in America*. Berkeley: University of California Press.

——. 1974. "Thoughts on a Neglected Category of Social Movement Participant: The Agent Provocateur and the Informant." *American Journal of Sociology*. 80(2): 402-442.

Marx, Gary, and Ronald Corbett. 1991. "Critique: No Soul in the New Machine: Technofallacies in the Electronic Monitoring Movement." *Justice Quarterly*. 8(3):399-414.

Offe, Claus. 1984. *Contradictions of the Welfare State*. London: Hutchison.

O'Reilly, Kenneth. 1989. *Racial Matters: The FBI's Secret File on Black America, 1960-1972*. New York: Free Press.

——. 1988. "The FBI and the Politics of the Riots, 1964-1968." *Journal of American History*. 75(1): 91-114.

Poulantzas, Nicos. 1978. *State, Power, Socialism*. London: New Left Books.

Powers, Richard Gid. 1987. *Secrecy and Power: The Life of J. Edgar Hoover*. New York: Free Press.

Robbins, Natalie. 1992. *Alien Ink: the FBI's War on Freedom of Expression*. New York: William Morrow and Company, Ink.

Summers, Anthony. 1993. *Official and Confidential: The Secret Life of J. Edgar Hoover*. New York: G. P. Putnam's Sons.

Theoharis, Athan G., and John Stuart Cox. 1988. *The Boss: J. Edgar Hoover and the Great American Inquisition*. Philadelphia: Temple University Press.

Theoharis, Athan. 1989. "The FBI and Dissent in the United States." Pp. 86-110 in C. E. S. Franks (ed.), *Dissent and the State*. Toronto: Oxford University Press.

——. 1978. *Spying on Americans: Political Surveillance from Hoover to the Huston Plan*. Philadelphia: Temple University Press.

Thomas, Jim. 1981. "Class, State, and Political Surveillance: Liberal Democracy and Structural Contradictions." *Insurgent Sociologist*. 11-12(Summer-Fall):47-59.

United States House, Select Committee on Intelligence. 1989. *The FBI Investigation of CISPES: Hearings before the Permanent Select Committee on Intelligence*. House of Representatives, 100th Congress, 2nd session. Washington: U.S. Government Printing Office.

United States House. House Select Committee to Study Government Operations with Respect to Intelligence Activities. 1976. *Hearings. Part 3. U.S. Intelligence Agencies and Activities Domestic Intelligence Programs*. 94th Congress, 1st Session. Washington, DC: U.S. Government Printing Office.

United States Senate. Select Committee on Intelligence. 1988. *Senate Select Committee on Intelligence Inquiry into the FBI Investigation of the Committee on Solidarity with the People of El Salvador (CISPES)*. Hearings. 100th Congress, 2nd Session. Washington, DC: U.S. Government Printing Office.

United States Senate. Senate Select Committee to Study Governmental Operations with Respect to Intelligence Activities. 1976a. *Final Report. Book II. Intelligence Activities and the Rights of Americans*. 94th Congress, 2nd Session. Washington, DC: U.S. Government Printing Office.

——. 1976b *Final Report. Book III. Supplementary Detailed Staff Reports of Intelligence Activities and the Rights of Americans.* 94th Congress, 2nd Session. Washington, DC: U.S. Government Printing Office.

——. 1976c. *Hearings, Vol. 6. Federal Bureau of Investigation.* 94th Congress, 1st Session. Washington, DC: U.S. Government Printing Office.

Weber, Max. 1972a. "Politics as Vocation." Pp. 77-128 in H. H. Gerth and C. Wright Mills (eds.) *From Max Weber: Essays in Sociology.* New York: Oxford University Press.

——. 1972b. "Religious Rejections of the World and Their Directions." Pp. 323-59 in H. H. Gerth and C. Wright Mills (eds.) *From Max Weber: Essays in Sociology.* New York: Oxford University Press.

Wise, David. 1976. *The American Police State: The Government Against the People.* New York: Random House Books.

Critical Evaluation

1. The author notes that the FBI met resistance even from within. Does this mean that their efforts at covert repression are not a matter for concern? Why or why not?

2. Under what, if any, circumstances would you support government efforts at covert repression?

3. How would a political conservative respond to this chapter? How would a political liberal respond?

Kevin Gotham, "The FBI and Covert Repression." In *The Journal of Political and Military Sociology* 22:2, pp. 203-222. Copyright © 1994 by *The Journal of Political and Military Sociology.* Reprinted by permission. ✦

3

Can Local Governments Solve All Our Problems?

Rob Gurwitt

There is a trend to shift responsibility for dealing with various problems from the federal to the local level—to state and city governments. Many liberals and conservatives support the idea that the federal government should turn over the responsibility for dealing with problems—ranging from gun control to educational reforms—to local governments (Berke 1997). At first, the trend may seem to be a victory for those who have long championed states' rights over federal rights. But some local officials complain that the federal government simply wants to rid itself of responsibility for problems rather than increase the influence of local governments.

Apart from motivation, the question remains: Can local governments solve the problems? It is doubtful. For one thing, structural change hampers cities. For example, many cities suffered severe loss of revenue when residents and businesses moved to the suburbs. This structural change is unlikely to be reversed, at least in the near future. And it is reinforced by an important social psychological factor—negative attitudes about city living. A national survey found that fewer than one in ten Americans say they prefer to live in a large city (Fisher 1997). The reasons include expense, the fast pace of living, crime, poverty, and other social problems.

Rob Gurwitt's analysis provides another reason why cities may have difficulties dealing with social problems. He points out that the dispersal of power in many cities can virtually paralyze government. Such a dispersal may be supported at the microlevel of people's attitudes, but it leaves a city severely handicapped in its efforts to bring about needed change.

References

Berke, Richard L. 1997. "Social Issues Shift to the States." *New York Times*, October 19.

Fisher, Christy. 1997. "What We Love and Hate About Cities." *American Demographics*, October.

Focus Questions

1. Why does the author assert that "nobody runs Kansas City?"

2. What are the "disquieting trends" the author sees in "depressed central cities?"

3. What are the pros and cons of fragmented power in cities?

In the end, Larry Brown had little choice but to resign as city manager of Kansas City, Missouri. By late June, when he finally agreed to give up his office atop the city's oddly graceful, Depression-era skyscraper of a city hall, Brown was a man beset, openly mistrusted by the council and sniped at by employees. His imminent departure was a universal assumption within local political circles.

There are those in Kansas City who, in hindsight, trace Brown's downfall to his 1994 arrest for drunken driving, which they contend cost him the respect of city staff. Others point to his decisions last year to give his top aides large pay raises and to send them to California's Napa Valley for taxpayer-supported training sessions—steps that turned into public-relations nightmares. By April, when a city council majority lambasted his proposed budget and yanked funding from his efforts to transform city government, it was just a matter of time.

But the truth is that the seeds of Brown's departure were sown at the beginning, at the very moment he was hired. Never short on ambition, Brown wanted nothing less than to assert the authority of the city manager to run Kansas City government as he saw fit. Instead, encountering more and more resistance the harder he tried, Brown learned a painful and expensive lesson: Nobody runs Kansas City. And a complex array of political forces is organized to keep it that way.

Power rests everywhere within the community—in the corporate boardrooms, with neighborhood developers and community organizations, within city agencies, on appointed boards, with the city council, in the hands of the mayor and in the office of the city manager. Building consensus on any issue is a time-consuming, frustrating process, and it is made harder by a structure that deliberately impedes the clear-eyed exertion of political will. Yet, as Brown discovered, so many people have a vested interest in the status quo that—for a city manager, at least—trying to change this state of affairs may be impossible.

This is a schizophrenic moment in the political history of America's big cities. For many of them, even some that were once branded ungovernable, the 1990s have brought a restoration of managerial competence, symbolized by New York's attack on crime, Cleveland's downtown revival, Chicago's school reform crusade and Philadelphia's return from the brink of bankruptcy.

All of the surging cities of this decade have had leaders with the ability to articulate and then enforce their priorities. These may be, as in New York, Chicago and Philadelphia, strong mayors in both the structural and political sense. Or they may be, as in Phoenix, a dynamic and widely admired city manager working with an elected council. But, in every case, there is a palpable sense that someone is in charge, setting an agenda about what is needed to make them attractive places to live and work.

Meanwhile, however, another set of cities, symbolized by Kansas City, Cincinnati, Miami and Dallas, among others, is stuck at the opposite end of the scale—mired in bickering, divided responsibility and long-standing political confusion. Nobody is in charge in these places. And it seems to take forever for anything to get done.

For the most part, these cities never fell quite as far as the Philadelphias and Clevelands of America. As a result, they have not been forced to look as hard at remaking local government. But, in the end, they will have

no alternative. In the coming years, the struggle for urban viability will be hard enough, even under the best of circumstances. The fragmented cities will be at a profound disadvantage.

And they may finally be realizing it. In Kansas City, in the wake of Brown's resignation, popular but constitutionally weak Mayor Emanuel Cleaver has begun talking about the need to give more authority to his successors. In Cincinnati, there have been nine attempts during the past decade to give the mayor more control, and another—with the quiet backing of the current mayor, Roxane Qualls, and the city's business leadership—is in the works. Dallas, shocked by a decade of political incivility following generations of close-knit cooperation, is openly debating where it went wrong, and what sort of governmental structure it might need to set things right. The forces backing change in all of these cities seem to agree that, although there may be no one formula for success in urban government, there is a recipe for failure, and it is the absence of leadership.

At first glance, it might seem odd to include Kansas City anywhere near the top of the list of troubled American cities. The regional economy is doing just fine, with unemployment in the metropolitan area below 4 percent. The city itself has seen new employers—Gateway 2000 and Harley-Davidson among them—set up plants in town. According to U.S. Census Bureau estimates, Kansas City actually has grown in population since 1990—although pretty much all of that growth has been in the long-annexed rural and suburb-like reaches north of the Missouri River.

Mayor Cleaver has embarked on a revitalization effort that includes creating a jazz hall of fame and a Negro Leagues baseball museum. Several of the city's leading businessmen are hoping to launch a huge hotel and entertainment complex on a dormant parcel of downtown land. And a committee that draws from both sides of the Missouri-Kansas state line is overseeing the resurrection of Kansas City's famous beaux arts Union Station as a hands-on science center.

Still, beneath the glowing press releases, there is trouble. Kansas City faces the same disquieting trends as other depressed central cities. "Projections show an increase in the number of jobs in the core, but as a share of the region's jobs, Kansas City's will either not increase or will decline," says David Warm, of the Mid-America regional council. "Most of the jobs, wealth and people are locating at the edges of the region. So there is the same clear and continuing pattern of decline in the center, disinvestment in the inner-tier suburbs and rapid growth on the edges that you see elsewhere." In the competition with its suburbs, in other words, Kansas City is, at the moment, losing.

On the day he announced Larry Brown's resignation, Emanuel Cleaver made it clear that there is another competition that weighs on him as well. Pressed by reporters about what he thought of a governmental structure that, in essence, makes him merely the most prominent member of the city council, Cleaver could not hold back his frustration. "Kansas City is now a big-league city," he said, "and when the mayor of the city sits around with the president and CEO of a major corporation trying to get them to relocate here, the mayor is at a disadvantage, because other mayors can cut the deal at the table. We are at a disadvantage in many instances when we are out competing."

The fact is, running Kansas City is mostly a matter of indirection. Mayors and city managers have to deal not only with a set of department heads who historically have had great room to pursue their own priorities, but also with circumstances that couldn't be better designed to water down their authority. The police are funded by the city but controlled by a state board. Libraries are under a separate board. Economic development, which is much of what Cleaver has been about in recent years, is under the control of the Economic Development Corp., which has become a sort of independent deal-maker for the city. The schools have been answerable to a federal court for 20 years, foster care services are in court hands as well, and the housing authority is in receivership. No one who wants to get things done in Kansas City, in other words, can do it directly.

As you might expect, many Kansas Citians have grown to like this state of affairs—it leaves each player within city government, along with those who try to affect it, with a fair degree of autonomy. It also means, though, that when their agendas differ, the city looks rudderless. "When communities have well-organized voices or a broad community ethic that's widely shared," says the head of one organization in Kansas City, "when there's a strong leader with clear ideas and directions, when there are well-organized plans and a well-organized and directed civic leadership that pursues those plans, that's when you get a healthy politics of ideas. Kansas City is not there at the moment. The city is up for grabs."

In the year or so leading up to Brown's forced resignation, there were at least three distinct sets of priorities being laid out in city hall. Cleaver's had to do with bringing in new economic development, redeveloping Kansas City's historically black neighborhoods and tackling the issue of race relations head-on. The city council was focusing on how to pay for the city's infrastructure needs and shoring up basic services to residents. With all this going on, Brown was maneuvering to redesign the entire process by which Kansas City government worked. In retrospect, there was no way he could have succeeded.

In his defense, Brown was doing pretty much what the council had said it wanted when it hired him, back in 1993. Its members had asked for someone to bring Kansas City government in line with the movement toward cost containment and quality service that other cities had been pursuing. "We wanted someone to take charge and run the city wisely and economically and efficiently," says George Blackwood, the council's mayor pro tem. "We said, 'We're out of control. Get good people, get the job done, let's create a lean, mean fighting machine.'"

Brown's response was a process he called "transformation." Part of his goal was to introduce the notions of customer service and efficient, responsive bureaucracy that have taken hold elsewhere. But he also set out to break down the barriers that, over the decades, had grown up among departments that had become accustomed to being treated as sovereign entities. Most important, Brown wanted to reestablish the city manager's authority over the day-to-day running of the organization. Over the years, not only had department heads grown accustomed to following their own lead but city council members also had grown accustomed to making requests directly of department heads and even mid-level managers. The result was a city organization in which the right and left hands often didn't keep track of each other.

Brown made every effort to deal with this problem. As it turned out, though, few of his efforts sat well with others in city hall. Although some departments and lower-level managers responded to the service-oriented freedom Brown offered them—the city's fire department being, perhaps, the leading example—others resisted; they found sympathetic ears on a council that already saw Brown cutting off its direct pipeline to city departments.

The council was especially vulnerable on this point because there was no real leadership pushing it to embrace the principles that "transformation" was supposed to instill; indeed, there was no particular leadership pushing it in any direction at all. A set of scandals during the past few years—four council members have been indicted on corruption charges—has created an ominous level of mistrust, turning the council into a set of 12 independent players who may come together around specific priorities.

Given those circumstances, council members' political legitimacy has rested, in large part, on their day-to-day involvement in city government; it was Brown's difficulty grasping the importance they placed on this that, more than anything else, undermined him. The budget he submitted to the city council this spring is a good example: It was essentially all text, a budget designed to get the council to think about policy without worrying about particular line-items. As a matter of theory, this should be all a council needs from a city manager in order to pass judgment on the general direction city government is headed. But as Cleaver points out, "Politics 101 is, Don't call the politicians stupid. His statement, as I interpreted it, was, 'You guys set policy, I'll worry about the rest.' Well, in 1997, politicians don't fade into the woodwork. That ain't going to happen any-

more." When it became clear that Brown had no intention of setting aside his priorities in favor of the council's and the mayor's—that, indeed, there was no way to reconcile them—he left.

There are those in Cincinnati, too, who have become increasingly impatient with a political process that treats issues crucial to the city as though they were mice let loose among a swarm of cats. "I think that the city of Cincinnati is an essentially scandal-free, well-managed city with a work force of good, dedicated people," says Nick Vehr, a recently retired Republican councilman. "But . . . things get mired down in endless political debate and a kind of bureaucratic morass that pounds them to a pulp before they can be implemented."

Cincinnati, too, is a council-manager city. Unlike Kansas City, however, its mayor isn't even elected separately. Instead, he or she is simply the council member who gets the most votes in the general election. Because no one actually runs for mayor, and because the mayor is no more powerful than any other member of the city council, there is very little political accountability in Cincinnati. The result, says Zane Miller, a political scientist at the University of Cincinnati, is an "absence of coherent leadership."

"The city bounces from problem to problem," agrees John Fox, editor of City Beat, Cincinnati's local alternative weekly newspaper. "The bottom line is city government becomes a reactionary body rather than a proactive body that says, 'Here's our vision for where we're going in the next 10 years.'"

This is not necessarily for lack of trying. For two years, in fact, administrative staff worked with the council to develop a strategic planning process that was to produce a clear set of priorities on which the city manager could focus. In a series of sessions with the council, however, city hall's vision of the future became muddier, not clearer. Rather than establish a handful of priorities with a few "action steps" attached to each, council members decided they had dozens of priorities. The "strategic plan" sank under its own weight.

Visiting Cincinnati, one does not get a sense of a city at loose ends. Its long-neglected riverfront is about to become a new focus for city life as two sports stadiums—one for the football Bengals, the other for the baseball Reds—are built there. Main Street, which was pretty much derelict 10 years ago, now has become a restaurant- and bar-filled entertainment zone at night. Parts of the neighborhood known as Over-the-Rhine, which was essentially a ghetto sitting on downtown's heels, are rapidly being gentrified. A new department store is going up on a prime downtown parking lot that many had despaired would never be replaced. "If you look ahead 10 years," says Al Tuchfarber, director of the Institute for Policy Research at the University of Cincinnati, "you're going to see a very revitalized downtown and riverfront."

Yet, the good things that are taking place in Cincinnati are taking place more in spite of city government than because of it. The revitalization of Over-the-Rhine might have materialized years ago had the city not set up barriers to redevelopment there. The new department store on Fountain Square West took a decade to materialize because the council spent most of that decade squabbling over just how the land ought to be used.

Perhaps the most troubling example of the city's problems, though, is the stadium deal. Given a deadline by the Bengals to come up with a plan that would keep the team in town, the city—after much hair-tearing—essentially punted. The financing deal was finally put together by surrounding Hamilton County, which, with three county board members, can move much more quickly. In exchange, the county will own the stadiums. "It wasn't until we shifted authority to the county," Nick Vehr says, "that the sports franchises seriously began negotiating to stay in this town. . . . I think there's a general perception in this community that the ability to manage the future no longer resides, as it did in the past, in city hall."

There are, to be sure, plenty of people in both Kansas City and Cincinnati who believe that their cities are better off precisely because power is so fragmented. "The successful person negotiates coalitions and puts them together on a given issue," says one former Kansas City government staffer, "and that's not a bad thing. With coalition-building, there's

some kind of consensus reached. Maybe it takes longer and demands more skill, but maybe the stuff that results is more durable."

It can also, of course, be argued that forceful leadership is hardly a panacea for American cities. If it were, neither Detroit under Coleman Young nor Washington, DC, under Marion Barry would have fallen into the disrepair both cities now struggle against.

But for a much larger number of cities these days, it is fractured leadership—not abused personal power—that constitutes the main political problem. In Miami, for instance, the fiscal insolvency and corrupt practices of its former city manager and finance director flourished in no small part because each major player in city government was content to go his own way—the manager pursued his own political goals, each city commissioner was wrapped up in his own pursuits, the finance director was given a free hand, and the business community and many onlookers were convinced that the city itself did not matter. There was, simply put, no one in charge who cared about Miami as a whole.

Dallas, meanwhile, has been an exhibit of fragmentation for the entire decade of the 1990s. Once, it was a prime example of the opposite: a place where decisive mayors and city managers worked quietly and efficiently with a single-minded business establishment to set clear community priorities. Thirty years ago, when Mayor Erik Jonsson felt he needed a blueprint for long-term urban planning, he simply rounded up 80 civic leaders, spirited them off to a country club for a weekend and returned with a short list of major goals for the 1970s—most of which were implemented.

But that Dallas power structure eventually succumbed to its own weaknesses. It was so tightly controlled, so exclusive and so overwhelmingly affluent, male and white that it bred longstanding resentments among the groups in town that felt left out of its processes. When the establishment expired, it set in motion a long period of chaos during which the newly enfranchised elements jostled for power without paying much attention to the interests of the community as a whole.

In 1991, under court pressure, Dallas switched from a council whose members were elected at-large to a district-by-district system. Ever since then, the council's deliberations have been one long bout of factionalism—ethnic, ideological and geographic. Presided over by a mayor with little formal power, the council has drifted from one crisis to another.

Recently, some of the tumult on the council has quieted down amid Mayor Ron Kirk's efforts to build a consensus around long-term plans for the city. At the same time, however, the school board threatens to explode under the pressure of racial feuding—for the most part between African-Americans and Hispanics—and much of the rest of the city's political leadership is finding it difficult to avoid being dragged into that battle.

It may be too much to say that all fragmented cities are alike these days, but all of them seem to be a little like Dallas, Cincinnati and Kansas City: so enmeshed in rivalries and personal politics that they are having trouble living up to their potential—or even seeing clearly just what that potential might be. If they are to remain competitive when it comes to attracting businesses, rebuilding the public schools and drawing middle-class residents back to their neighborhoods, they somehow need to rely upon leaders who can help them coalesce around coherent visions of where they're going. Such people clearly exist in all of these cities; the only question is whether they will be allowed to emerge.

"Leaders shackled by unreasonable restrictions are forced to engage in compromises and deal-making that slows forward movement and inhibits development of wide-ranging vision," the editor of the Kansas City Star's editorial page wrote not long ago, in a commentary that just as easily could have been applied to Cincinnati and any number of other places casting about for direction these days. "The way Kansas City's government now works," Rich Hood wrote, "there are so many safeguards built in to prevent dramatic leadership (or risky gambles that might not pay off) that we too frequently witness government by paralysis."

Critical Evaluation

1. The author argues for more centralized power in cities. What are some possible pitfalls of such centralization?

2. If city governments become effective in taking action, will they then be able to address their social problems? Why or why not?

3. How else might a city be run so as to avoid both the inaction of fragmented power and the abuse of personal power?

Rob Gurwitt, "Nobody in Charge." In *Governing Magazine* September 1997. Copyright © 1997 by *Governing Magazine*. Reprinted by permission. ✦

Project for Personal Application and Class Discussion: The Government and Power

Make a cost-benefit analysis of government in terms of your own life. In a cost-benefit analysis, you list all the costs (in terms of such things as dollars, emotional costs, time consumed, effort required, etc.) of something and compare those costs with the benefits (again, in terms of dollars, emotional gains, time saved, effort saved, etc.) You may or may not be able to assign an exact dollar amount or value to the various items. In some situations, you may have simply to consider the two lists and decide whether the benefits outweigh the costs or vice versa for you.

Keeping in mind the various levels of government (federal, state, and local) and the materials in this section, list as many benefits as you can that you receive from government (do not forget such indirect benefits as federal aid to education). Also make a list of what government costs you.

Which is greater, your costs or your benefits? How do you think your lists might change when you are 30 years older? How do you think your lists would compare to those of someone of another race or the other gender?

As noted in the introduction to this section, government is a major wielder of power. How much power do you think you have over your life? How much power do you have to influence government? How would you exercise that power? What could you do to gain more power? ✦

The Economy and Work

Economic well-being and meaningful work are central to people's overall well-being. When people lose their jobs, or when they work at jobs that are highly stressful, they are likely to suffer various emotional and physical ills. As unemployment goes up, for example, so do the rates of suicide, admission to mental hospitals, alcohol abuse, and heart attacks (Lauer 1998).

The availability of work—and the kind of work that is available—depends on the economy. Early in the nation's history, most people worked in agriculture. Today, its highly technological, capitalist economy offers more than 30,000 different occupations, including many that are highly stimulating and meaningful. However, many of these occupations are also highly stressful. For example, routine work can be both physically and emotionally stressful. Certain work conditions, such as factories with heavy machinery or toxic materials, can pose health hazards. Work situations, such as an overbearing boss, may deprive workers of job satisfaction.

In sum, both the lack of work and working under stressful conditions are detrimental to human well-being. This section looks at a number of problems in the U.S. economy and at practices in businesses and corporations that affect people's ability to find meaningful work and secure an adequate income.

Reference

Lauer, Robert H. 1998. *Social Problems and the Quality of Life*. 7th ed. New York: McGrawHill. ✦

4

Overworked and Underemployed

Barry Bluestone
Stephen Rose

The American economy, as dramatized by the stock market, has been in a boom period. Does that translate into increasing financial well-being for American workers and their families? Not necessarily. Barry Bluestone and Stephen Rose's analysis indicates that many Americans, particularly those with less education, are both overworked and underemployed—underemployed being working for wages that are too low, working part-time when full-time work is desired, or working at a job below one's skill level.

Bluestone and Rose's analysis focuses on structural factors that contribute to the problem—the job and income instability of the present economy. Of course, the government is another structural factor that enters the picture, because the government can either allow employers to continue exploiting workers or pass legislation that protects workers. The structural problems generate attitudes of insecurity that tend to perpetuate the situation. Their analysis also illustrates another challenge to understanding social problems—how to find the data that can give us the information we need properly to assess a problem.

Focus Questions

1. Why are Americans overworked?
2. Which workers are overworked and underemployed?
3. What is the relationship between overwork and underemployment?

At least since the 1980s people have said that they work "too hard"—that they are spending too much time on the job, with too little left for family, chores, or leisure. In 1991 this frustration became conventional wisdom thanks to Juliet Schor's best-seller, *The Overworked American*, which demonstrated that Americans worked an average of 163 more hours in 1990 than they had in 1970—or the equivalent of nearly an extra month of full-time work per year. According to Schor, men were working two and a half more weeks per year; women an average of seven and a half more weeks. These were startling statistics, reversing more than a century of gradual reduction in working time as society became richer and more productive. If Americans were working this much longer, then they were not only overworked by traditional U.S. standards, they were setting new world records.

But critics challenged Schor's data and pointed to a logical flaw in her argument. Today, more people work part-time because they can't find full-time work; more are temping or working as short-term independent contractors. Job insecurity is rampant, and other statistics show that the number of weekly hours on the typical job has actually shrunk steadily since World War II. It seemed implausible that Americans were simultaneously "overworked" and "underemployed," thus prompting the question: Were Schor and all the harried Americans who cheered her book's appearance wrong?

Not necessarily. It's possible, for instance, that we are mixing apples and oranges. The number of contingent jobs and average weekly hours refers to "jobs," not people. If individuals are moonlighting more—working multiple jobs in any given week—then the average workweek reported by employers can still shrink while the average workweek reported by workers can actually expand. It is also possible that one sector of the workforce is "overworked" while another portion is "underemployed."

But the real story turns out to be even more intriguing and complicated. Based on a new analysis of the data, we have found that Americans are indeed working longer than they once did, if not quite as much as Schor would have us believe. But, more importantly, we have also found that many Americans are both overworked and underemployed. Because of growing job instability, workers face a "feast and famine" cycle: They work as much as they can when work is available to compensate for short workweeks, temporary layoffs, or permanent job loss that may follow. What's more, while American families as a whole are putting in more time, that work isn't producing significant increases in living standards. For the typical two-breadwinner household, having both parents work longer hours may not mean an extra trip to Disney World or nicer clothes for school; more likely, it means keeping up car payments or just covering the costs of food and housing.

Multitasked

At one extreme are workers like Bill Cecil, a 50-year-old United Auto Worker member recently portrayed in the *Wall Street Journal.* Averaging four hours a day in overtime and volunteering to work seven days a week for most of the year, Cecil clocks an average of 84 hours a week at a Chrysler plant in Trenton, Michigan, where he works as a skilled millwright. In the past two years, Cecil's extraordinary work effort has paid off. He has averaged more than $110,000 a year in gross pay. Sacrificing, by his own admission, "freedom and time with family," he works as much overtime as the company will let him in order to help send his four kids to college, fill his lunch pail with lobster salad rather than luncheon meat, and underwrite his golf habit, which he indulges whenever a vacation or a layoff permits. While Bill Cecil's case is exceptional, 70 percent of the skilled-trades workers at his engine production facility are working at least some extra hours most weeks.

Increasing overtime is becoming more commonplace throughout the manufacturing industry. For the first four out of five post-World War II business cycles, average weekly hours of work for production and nonsupervisory workers in manufacturing remained roughly constant, varying only slightly between 40.1 and 40.4 hours. However, during the current business cycle, from 1989 to 1996, the average workweek has jumped to 41 hours—with average overtime reaching a post-World War II peak of 4.7 hours per week in 1994.

A *Fortune* magazine poll of Fortune 500 CEOs in 1990 found a similar tendency toward more work among executives. Sixty-two percent of CEOs reported their executives were working longer hours than they had ten years before. They reported that nearly nine out of ten of their high-level executives normally put in more than 50 hours a week while three-fifths of middle managers did the same.

Moonlighting is also on the rise. In 1979, 4.9 percent of U.S. workers reported working more than one job during the same workweek. By 1995, the percentage was up to 6.4 percent. Virtually all of this increase has occurred among women, who now represent nearly half of all multiple job holders. According to a recent survey sponsored by the *Washington Post,* the Kaiser Family Foundation, and Harvard University, two out of five families report they have sent an additional family member into the paid labor force or had an existing working member take on an additional job—simply because the family needed extra money.

Working more makes sense from both the employers' and the employees' perspectives. Manufacturing firms like Chrysler do not hesitate to schedule large amounts of overtime when product demand outstrips supply, even if it means paying time and a half, double time, or triple time during holidays, because it is still less expensive than covering the high fixed costs of recruitment, training, and possibly the underwriting of future severance pay associated with hiring new workers. For salaried white-collar employees who are exempt from hours regulations, the arithmetic is even simpler—the extra hours often cost the company nothing at all.

Fortune 500 CEOs and their executives say they need to put in overtime just to keep up with global competition and compensate for internal restructuring or middle-level management downsizing. But why would blue-collar workers so willingly give up leisure or family time? Schor has identified one factor, which she calls "capitalism's squirrel cage"— an "insidious cycle of work and spend" where people work long hours to support a material lifestyle always a bit beyond their reach. But that suggests the increased work hours are buying a rising standard of affluence, which is somewhat misleading. Indeed, a more compelling reason for extra work is the slowdown in wage growth during the past two decades. Between 1947 and 1973, real hourly wages for production and nonsupervisory employees rose by 79 percent. Since 1973 hourly wages have actually declined by more than 13 percent. For many workers, working longer hours is the only way to compensate for lower hourly wages.

Of course when pollsters ask people, "Would you like to work less?", most say "yes." But when pollsters include a caveat—that fewer working hours would mean less take-home pay—the answer changes sharply. Over the last 20 years, surveys with this appropriately worded question have been answered with great consistency: Approximately 60 percent say they prefer their current work schedule and pay. Of those who express a desire to change their working time, more people, by about three to one, express the desire to work longer rather than shorter hours.

Union negotiators in the U.S. know this, which is why they so rarely make reducing work time a priority in collective bargaining. In fact, many workers complain bitterly whenever management prerogative or union contract restrict overtime hours. In a "real experiment" on this issue, New York's state government in 1984 began allowing their workers to take voluntary reductions in work schedules without affecting their career statuses. The plan was flexible and permitted workers to move on and off "V-time." Since its inception, however, the program has never enrolled more than 2 percent of the workforce.

This expressed desire for more hours is consistent with the trend toward more contingent work. At the same time that many workers are looking to expand their number of working hours, the economy has shifted steadily from manufacturing to sectors like retail trade and services, where part-time work is more common. One estimate for 1995 places the total number of contingent workers (part-time, temporary, and contract workers) at close to 35 million—28 percent of the civilian labor force. Of these, 18 percent of the workforce or 23 million workers were part-time, working 35 hours or less per week. Smaller in absolute numbers, but growing much faster, is the temporary workforce, which between 1982 and 1995 more than tripled to 1.4 million workers. Manpower, Inc. now boasts it is the largest employer in America, submitting more W-2 forms to the Internal Revenue Service each year than any other firm. The number of contract and self-employed workers is also growing rapidly, indeed explosively. The U. S. General Accounting Office has reported that the number of individuals who are self-employed or working under personal contract was growing at more than 13 percent a year in the late 1980s. By 1988, 9.5 million Americans worked for themselves either full-time or as a supplement to regular or part-time employment.

A large proportion of the contingent workforce has chosen voluntarily to work part-time, as temporaries, or as independent contractors. Still, involuntary part-time employment is growing much faster than the voluntary variety. In 1973, 19 percent of total part-time employment was accounted for by individuals who wanted full-time jobs but could not find them. By 1993, this proportion was up to 29 percent. The incidence of involuntary part-time work is especially high among men. In 1985, one in four part-time women reported their part-time status was involuntary; nearly half of all part-time men did so.

For the labor force as a whole, these numbers begin to add up. Since 1994, the Bureau of Labor Statistics (BLS) has been compiling a new set of alternative measures of unemployment and underemployment—what the Labor Department calls "labor resource underutilization." In addition to the official unemployment rate, the BLS adds three types of "underutilized" workers: (1) those who have stopped looking for work only because they have become discouraged by their apparent job prospects; (2) those who are "marginally attached" to the civilian labor force; and (3) those who are working part-time only because they cannot find full-time jobs. The "marginally attached" include those who want and are available for a job and have recently searched for work, but have left the official labor force because of such constraints as child care or transportation problems.

The official unemployment rate in 1995 was 5.6 percent with an average of 7.4 million failing to find work each month. Adding discouraged workers to the total brings the "underemployment" rate up to 5.9 percent. Adding the "marginally attached" ups the rate to 6.8 percent. Finally, adding in the involuntarily part-time brings the rate to 10.1 percent. In what was a good year for the economy and employment growth, 1995, the total number of unemployed and underemployed workers reached nearly 13.5 million—one in ten of the total labor force.

All of these trends contribute to the decline in the average workweek reported by employers since at least World War II . . . from 1947 to 1958 the average workweek was nearly 40 hours, the "full-time" standard for much of this century. In the most recent business cycle, the average workweek fell below 35 hours, the cutoff normally used to define a "part-time" job. Ironically, in what is supposed to be an "overworked" nation, the typical job is now part-time! Again, we should ask, "overworked," "underemployed," or perhaps both?

Whose Numbers Should We Believe?

Whether we believe that Americans are overworked or underemployed depends, in part, on whether we believe the work time data. Many economists question Juliet Schor's findings and it's not hard to understand why: The idea that Americans are, on average, spending the equivalent of an extra month a year in paid work seems almost unbelievable.

But is it? According to one recent study, Schor's basic finding holds up, but her estimates of overwork appear somewhat exaggerated. Using data from the Current Population Survey, Larry Mishel and Jared Bernstein of the Economic Policy Institute have re-estimated annual work hours for various years. Their research confirms the general proposition of increased annual working

hours, but for a comparable period (1973 to 1992) their estimate is only three-fifths as large as Schor's. They calculate that in 1973, the average workweek (for both employed and self-employed workers toiling in the public as well as the private sector) was 38.4 hours. The average work year was 43.2 weeks, yielding an annual estimate of 1,659 hours of work. By 1992, the average workweek had climbed by 0.6 hours while the average work year had increased to 45.2 weeks. Hence, annual average hours had risen to 1,759, an increase of 100 hours or 6 percent—but 63 hours less than Schor's estimate.

Yet even these more reasonable figures raise questions.

Note that the steady decline in the average workweek reported by employers . . . suggests that for average hours per job to decline while average hours per worker increases, there would have to be enormous increases in moonlighting. This seems implausible, because even with the recent increase in moonlighting, only 8 million workers out of a workforce of more than 125 million report holding more than one job.

The problem may be with the very survey data upon which Schor, Mishel, and Bernstein all rely. The estimates of hours worked come from the March Current Population Survey (CPS) for each year, which the U.S. Census Bureau and the Department of Labor compile annually. Among several dozen questions about labor market activity, the CPS asks respondents to report "hours worked last week" and "usual weekly hours of work last year." Individuals have only a few seconds to answer these questions. In making what may be a wild guess, particularly for those people whose hours vary substantially from week to week, the individuals frequently guess high. And the more harried and rushed they feel, the higher they guess. Could you account for the actual number of hours you spent working last week?

A more accurate measure of hours worked comes from special studies that target the work time issue by asking respondents to keep a 24-hour time diary of everything they do over a one- to two-day period. Such time diary surveys were first carried out by the University of Michigan Survey Research Center in 1965 and 1975, and then again by the University of Maryland in 1985. The accuracy of work time estimates derived from this survey approach is presumably superior to CPS measures for two reasons. First, the exercise's sole purpose is studying the use of time; second, respondents do not have to plum their memories for what they did a week ago or try to calculate instantly how many weeks they worked all of last year.

Sure enough, a comparison of CPS-estimated hours of work and diary entries suggests that people overestimate how much they work—and that the overestimates get bigger the more hours they put in. According to John Robinson of the University of Maryland and Ann Bostrom of Georgia Tech University, who studied the two sets of surveys, among those estimating 20 to 44 weekly hours, the CPS-type estimates were only slightly higher than the diary entries. But among workers claiming to "usually" work more than 55 hours per week, the gap was 10 hours or more per week. Robinson and Bostrom concluded that "the diary data suggest that only rare individuals put in more than a 55- to 60-hour workweek, with those estimating 60 or more hours on the job averaging closer to 53-hour weeks." Moreover, using the diary studies for 1965, 1975, and 1985, Robinson and Bostrom found a systematic increase in the size of the estimate gap over time. The gap rose from just one hour in 1965 to four hours in 1975 to six hours in 1985, which is more than enough to account for the alleged "overwork" that Schor and Mishel and Bernstein claim to have found.

When Robinson and Bostrom analyzed diaries for 1965, 1975, and 1985 more carefully, they found only small changes in hours worked among those who normally work 20 hours or more per week. Between 1965 and 1985, men's average hours declined by 0.7 hours per week from 47.1 to 46.4 hours, while working women's hours increased by the same amount (0.7) from 39.9 to 40.6 hours. If these numbers are believed then the source of increased hours worked that Schor observed must be new entrants to the labor force—again, many of them women—and part-timers who have increased their part-time hours. Of course, whether this should be

counted as "overwork" or not is a matter of deeply divided opinion.

'Schoring' Up the Findings

What can we make of such sharply different findings? To answer this question, we decided to pursue still another approach, using yet another type of survey instrument. So far, all of the research on working hours has relied on data snapshots at different points in time using either the CPS or diary information. An alternative approach is to use longitudinal data—in other words, information about the same people gathered year after year—to track working hours. Using this information, we can follow the work time pattern of, say, a particular age group over several years . . . or follow the same workers over time. Here we do both in order to provide completely new estimates of work time. We use the Panel Study of Income Dynamics (PSID), a data set of families that the University of Michigan Survey Research Center has been following since 1968. The long-running nature of the PSID permits a comparison of working time during two ten-year periods—the 1970s (1969–1979) and the 1980s (1979–1989). (These periods had similar growth rates in real output per person and in job creation, and each encompassed two complete business cycles. Hence, the comparison is a reasonable one to make.) We also combine the two decades of data to follow a particular age group (in this case, prime age workers with job experience) in order to derive typical trends in annual work hours for men and women, whites and blacks, and for segments of the population with differing amounts of schooling.

While the PSID does not provide the full detail nor perhaps the precision of hours estimates culled from the diary method, its data on hours worked is superior to that of the CPS. First, PSID asks respondents to detail their work experience by recalling how many days they were on vacation, on sick leave, on strike, or on leave due to other family members' illness. It then asks respondents to answer questions about regular hours of work per week and weeks worked on his or her main job. Then it poses the same questions concerning up to three other jobs respondents held during the year. Finally, all of this information is combined to yield an estimate of annual hours. Obviously, this approach suffers from recall problems, much as the CPS does, but the detail on each job presumably permits a better estimate.

The first part of our analysis is based on computing the average hours of work in each year from 1967 through 1989 for prime age workers (ages 25–54). . . . There is clear evidence of variation related to the business cycle. Average hours dip sharply in 1970–71, in 1975, and then again during the steep 1981–82 recession. But overwhelming the business cycle is a U-shaped trend in hours of work. Average hours appear to decline through the early 1980s and then begin a sharp recovery throughout the decade. If we compare 1979 and 1989, the last two business cycle peaks, there does indeed appear to be an increase of 79 hours per year for the average worker. But over a longer period, this increase marks not so much a startling increase as a return to levels that prevailed in the late 1960s.

To obtain a more accurate estimate of the trend in hours, we ran a statistical exercise to control for the business cycle. Having done this, we find a small, but statistically significant, overall upward trend in annual hours for prime age workers as a group. The trend amounts to only 3.3 hours per year. Hence, over a 20-year period, we find a 66-hour increase in annual work—the equivalent of 1.5 weeks of full-time work per year. This is well below Schor's estimate of 163 hours and a third below that what Mishel and Bernstein found. But, importantly, the trend is decidedly upward, in contrast to the essentially flat line Robinson and Bostrom found for the 1965–1985 period using the diary method.

Among men, working hours declined slightly, after we control for the business cycle. But for women, hours increased significantly. Indeed, our estimate of 18.8 additional hours per year translates into a 20-year total somewhat greater than even Schor's estimate. We also find significant differences in the hours trajectories by race. Reflecting trends well documented elsewhere, our estimate of a decline of 7.7 hours per year for black men translates into an average work year in the late 1980s more than 150 hours shorter than in the late 1960s. In 1989, we estimate that black men averaged only 1,950 hours per year compared with just under 2,300 hours for white men. Higher unemployment rates are responsible for part of this difference. Shorter workweeks explain the remainder. This suggests that the continuing earnings gap between white and black men is only partly accounted for by differences in wage rates—the traditional measure of labor market "success." A large amount of the gap is also due to differences in hours worked. Wage rates matter, but what is really killing black men in the labor market is their inability to find full-time, full-year jobs as readily as their white counterparts.

The racial gap in hours worked among women shows an intriguing time pattern. On an annual basis, there appears to have been virtually no gap in work hours in 1967. The gap then widened significantly, so that by the mid-1970s black women were working almost 200 hours more per year than white women. White women caught up again, and by 1989 white and black women were working virtually the same amount. To close the gap, white women's cycle-adjusted hours had to rise substantially faster than that of black women. This is precisely what happened. Over 20 years, white women's annual hours increased by the equivalent of 10.3 weeks of full-time work, nearly double the 5.4 weeks for black women.

As a general rule, then, there has been a slight reduction in men's work hours and a large increase in women's hours. Given these trends, we can ask what has happened to family work effort as America has undergone the transition from the prototypical "Ozzie and Harriet" division of labor of the 1950s to the dual-career family of the 1980s and 1990s.

To investigate the trend in family effort, we have estimated the combined hours of work for "prime age" families in which both husband and wife are working. . . . There is a clear and nearly unbroken trend toward much greater work effort, interrupted only modestly by the recessions of 1971, 1974–75, and 1980–1982. By 1988, prime age working couples were putting in an average of 3,450 hours per year in combined employment, up from 2,850 two decades before. . . .

Adjusting for business cycle effects, we calculate that for all husband-wife working couples, family work effort increased by more than 32 hours per year for each year of the 1970s and 1980s. Hence, in the span of just two decades, working husband-wife couples increased their annual market work input by a cycle-adjusted 684 hours or 4 months of full-time work. The typical dual-earner couple at the end of the 1980s was spending an additional day and a half on the job every week. If individuals are not more overworked than before, families certainly are.

Increases in family work effort differ significantly depending on race and education. The increase in working hours among white working couples was 60 percent larger than the increase for black couples—a reflection of both the sharp decline in black men's hours and the large increase in white female work effort. More-educated working couples also increased their work effort more than those with less schooling. Those in which the husbands had at least undergraduate college degrees increased their combined work effort by nearly 730 hours compared to an increase of only 490 hours for couples headed by high school dropouts. The "overeducated" are the ones most "overworked."

Has this enormous increase in work effort paid off in terms of increased family earnings? . . . For prime age working couples as a group, combined real earnings rose by 18.5 percent between 1973 and 1988. (This represents an increase from $43,851 to $51,955 in 1989 dollars.) Most of this modest increase, however, did not come from improved wages, but from increased work effort. The 18.5 percent increase in real earnings was purchased with a 16.3 percent increase in hours worked. Over the entire 15-year period, the combined average husband-wife hourly wage increased by only 1.8 percent—the equivalent of a real hourly wage increase of less than 30 cents over the entire period, or 2 cents each year!

As such, Schor's "squirrel cage" does not appear to be far off the mark. American mythology holds that long hours will pay off in a steadily increasing standard of living; in other words, sacrificing time with family can

pay for a dishwasher or microwave and, down the road, a more expensive college for one's children. Yet from a purely material perspective, all the extra hours from the "average" working family have yielded only a very modest improvement in the amount of goods and services they can buy.

But even this story is too sanguine for most families. When we break down the hours and earnings data by education group the tale gets even more depressing. Most Americans are not working harder so they can afford a fancier minivan; they're just trying to make payments on their old car or cover the rent. When you remove from the equation families headed by a worker with at least a college degree, it turns out that the enormous increase in work effort over the past 20 years has allowed families to maintain their old standard of living—but almost nothing more. For families headed by high school dropouts, the situation is the most dismal. Between 1973 and 1988, such families increased their annual work effort by nearly 12 percent yet ended up with 8 percent less annual income. For families headed by high school graduates or some college, work effort was up by 16 to 17.4 percent, producing less than a 4 percent increase in total earnings. These families are trapped in an *Alice in Wonderland* world, running faster and faster just to stay in the same place. For all of these families, the "family" hourly wage has fallen precipitously, by as much as 17 percent in the case of the high school dropout.

Of course, more work still pays off for one group: families headed by a college graduate. These families increased their work effort by about the same percentage as those headed by high school graduates or those with some college, yet their material consumption standard increased by nearly a full third between 1973 and 1988. Unfortunately, such well-educated families comprise less than a third of all American dual income families.

Feasting Before the Famine

To this point, we have been concerned with trends in hours worked and earnings for particular demographic groups. We now shift our attention to an equally important issue.

What can we say about the year-to-year variation in work hours for individual workers? This is of obvious importance given the debate over the apparent growth in job insecurity. If a worker is insecure about his job, then it is possible he may voluntarily work as much overtime as he can in order to cushion the blow of depressed income from future joblessness. Or, for that matter, he may work extra hours because he has to pay off credit card debts that accumulated in the last bout of underemployment. . . .

To measure inter-year variation in work hours for these prime age workers, we have developed a special measure we call "Hi-Lo." This statistic measures the proportion of individuals in a group who, during a decade, experience at least one year in which they work more than 2,400 hours and at least one year of 1,750 hours or less. The "Hi" value is equivalent to an average workweek of approximately 46 hours or more. The "Lo" value is equivalent to less than 35 hours per week. These cutoffs correspond to common definitions of "overtime" work and "part-time" work.

According to our analysis, among all prime age males, nearly three out of ten workers (28 percent) had at least one year of substantial "overtime" and at least one year of significant "underemployment" during the 1980s. Compared to the 1970s, the proportion of such individuals experiencing such hours variation was up by nearly 8 percent.

For black men, the incidence of Hi-Lo variation is substantially higher than among white men, with 37 percent of black men experiencing this variety of "feast and famine" employment history. Those who have completed a high school diploma or college degree appear to experience less hours variation than those who drop out of high school or do not complete college.

But by the far the strongest indicators of the feast-or-famine syndrome emerge when we break the Hi-Lo numbers down according to earnings levels and the number of job changes. Among men in the lowest 20 percent of the earnings ladder, four out of ten experience Hi-Lo hours variation—more than double those in the top 20 percent. Those who have low earnings even when they are working full-time are the most likely to experience a feast-and-famine work life. Not surprisingly, those who change employers more often face the highest rates of Hi-Lo activity. More than half of prime age men who change employers at least four times in a decade face years of "overtime" and years of "underemployment." For women, the "overworked-underemployed" phenomenon expanded as well between the 1970s and 1980s. In the earlier decade, only 12 percent experienced such Hi-Lo work histories. In the 1980s, nearly 21 percent of women spent their lives on the work time roller coaster.

High school dropouts have seen a substantial rise in Hi-Lo activity between the two decades. But so have college graduates and the top-quintile earners. One might conjecture from these findings that those with the fewest skills and those in the ranks of middle managers have been particular victims of downsizing. Future research with the PSID should be able to provide more evidence to test this hypothesis.

Taken together, the results for men and women suggest that increased job instability has led to increased hours variability for men and increased hours and variability of work for women. While the data presented here cannot prove that male job instability causes men to work more overtime when it is available and at the same time increases women's workforce participation, the results are fully consistent with such a thesis. In short, we can conjecture that "underemployment" of men may be leading to "overwork" for families. Because Dad's work prospects are more uncertain than ever, Mom is working harder than ever before.

In the end, then, it turns out that both Schor and her critics were partially right. There is compelling evidence of both overwork and underemployment not only across the workforce, but for individual workers (particularly men) who may face bouts of full-time work interspersed with years in which part-time hours are the rule. In both the 1970s and the 1980s, more than one-quarter of men experienced a decade in which they worked at least one year of "overwork" (more than 46 hours per week) and at least one year of "underemployment" (less than 35 hours per week). How much of this is voluntary cannot be judged, but the finding is consistent with other research that shows growth in job instability and income insecurity. Adding to this evidence is our finding that those workers who change jobs more than four times in a decade are more than three times as likely to face bouts of "overwork" and "underemployment" as those who have at most one job change during the same period.

The reason for this overwork, ironically, turns out to be underemployment. Men are working overtime to compensate for expected job loss in the future. Women have expanded their work effort to cover for what otherwise would be a sharp reduction in family living standards.

What does this foreshadow for family and community? Americans will not find a better balance between work and leisure, between earning a living and spending time with loved ones, between wage earning and "civic engagement," until the economy provides long-term employment security and rising wages. If past is prologue, the last 25 years of U.S. labor market history should not make us sanguine about the possibilities.

There is serious political talk, now and then, about legislating shorter weeks. But no matter how much we may complain about being overworked and no matter how much we worry about latchkey kids, few American workers will support political action unless it is tied to a much broader set of policies aimed at improving material living standards along with more leisure.

Critical Evaluation

1. The authors stress the effects of the economy and the practices of employers. What, if anything, do workers contribute to the problem of overwork and underemployment?

2. What kind of workers are most likely to be affected by the problem discussed by the authors?

3. As the authors note, it is possible for people to believe they are overworked when data do not support the belief. Which is more important—what people believe about overwork and underemployment or what objective data show?

5

Race and Gender Wage Gaps

Catherine J. Weinberger

When people start a career or a new job, they usually expect a salary based on such things as their education, training, and experience. But the workplace is not yet blind to gender or race. In fact, some observers believe that the plight of certain groups has grown worse. Ernest Spaights and Ann Whitaker, for example, argue that although many black women have made occupational and economic gains, black women as a whole are worse off in some respects than they were in 1970. Even those women who have made gains may face stress in the workplace from racist attitudes and wage discrimination.

In this selection, Catherine Weinberger looks at both race and gender in her analysis of wage gaps among college graduates. She notes various factors at both the macrolevel and the microlevel that help account for the wage differentials. When all the structural factors that would reasonably make a difference in wages—such as type of occupation and amount and quality of education—are accounted for, there is still a gap (not included here is Weinberger's statistical analysis). We are left with the conclusion that prejudicial attitudes explain a part of the gap.

Reference

Spaights, Ernest and Ann Whitaker. 1995. "Black Women in the Workforce." *Journal of Black Studies* 25: 283-296.

Focus Questions

1. What factors enter into race and gender wage gaps?

2. Is discrimination still a factor in wages earned?

3. What groups suffer the greatest wage loss because of discrimination?

Introduction

Women and black men have lower average hourly earnings than white men with the same number of years of education (Corcoran and Duncan 1979; Blau and Ferber 1987a). Part of these "wage gaps" may be due to labor market discrimination, whereas part may be due to differences in productivity between the typical members of different demographic groups. For example, it is often suggested that the racial wage gap reflects a tendency for black students to receive a lower quality of education than white students with the same number of years in school (Nechyba 1990; Juhn, Murphy, and Pierce 1991). Similarly, it has been suggested that women lack the mathematical ability to pursue college degrees in more remunerative technical fields (Paglin and Rufolo 1990) and that women choose to pursue degrees in fields where the associated careers are compatible with their anticipated family responsibilities (Polachek 1978, 1981; Blakemore and Low 1984). In all these examples, adding appropriate controls to the wage equation for the type and quality of education attained should reduce or eliminate the estimated wage gap.

One approach is to control for the occupation of employment. If we believe that labor markets allocate individuals to the jobs for which they are best suited, then occupation is a good proxy for an individual's productivity and preferences. Adding controls for occupation significantly reduces estimated race and gender wage gaps (Blinder 1973; Trieman and Hartman 1981; Blau and Ferber 1987b; Ferber and Green 1991). The more narrowly occupation is defined, the smaller is the estimated gender wage gap (Gunderson 1989; Groshen 1991). This observation is interpreted by some as evidence that the gender wage gap results from gender differences in productivity or preferences.

The limitation of this method is that occupation is a labor market outcome. Occupational assignments may themselves be affected by labor market discrimination (Brown, Moon, and Zoloth 1980; Blau 1984; Bielby and Baron 1984; Ferber and Green 1991; Gill 1994). If so, then occupation measures neither an employee's productivity nor preferences, and differences in occupation cannot be used to "explain" differences in wages.

An alternative approach is to control carefully for the skills and preferences that an individual takes into the labor market. For example, estimates of the wage differential between white male and white female recent college graduates are reduced by about one-half when controls for four to eight broad college major categories are included in the wage equation (Polachek 1978; Daymont and Andrisani 1984; Eide and Grogger 1992; Rumberger and Thomas 1993; Eide 1994). Given that increasingly detailed designations of an individual's occupation lead to diminishing estimates of the gender wage differential, an interesting question is whether increasingly detailed measures of the type and quality of education will reduce estimated wage gaps between white men and other groups of young recent college graduates.

While many economic studies focus on differences in outcomes between white men and white women or between black men and white men, this study examines wage outcomes for men and women who identified themselves as white, black, Hispanic, or Asian. This broader focus can reveal relationships in the data that would otherwise not be recognized. For example, Hispanic children face disadvantages in quality of education similar to those faced by black children (Oakes 1990; NCES 1994). Yet, unlike black men, U.S. born Mexican-American men do not earn much less than white men with the same number of years of education (Trejo 1995). Or, for example, controls for occupation lead to larger estimates of the wage disadvantage faced by Asian-American men (Duleep and Sanders 1992).

This study uses a unique sample of recent college graduates. The *1985 Survey of Recent College Graduates* reports the earnings, exact college major, college grade point average, and educational institution attended for over 8000 young college graduates. The sample includes several hundred graduates who identified themselves as black, Asian, or Hispanic.

Each individual in the sample completed a four-year bachelor's degree in an academic field one to two years before the 1985 survey date. These young graduates have very low levels of previous work experience and are homogeneous with respect to the number of years of education completed. College major, college grades, and the college attended represent both exceptionally detailed measures of the type and quality of education attained and an indication of the ability of each graduate to work productively at the broad range of tasks involved in completing college coursework. In addition, college major provides an indication of each graduate's occupational preferences. This sample therefore provides a unique opportunity to observe whether race and gender wage differentials remain after controlling very carefully for the education, productive ability, and preferences an individual takes into the labor market.

The limitation of this analysis is that it examines the wage differential in only a small sector of the economy. This analysis does not even begin to explore whether earlier discrimination affected the educational attainments of these college graduates or of their less educated age-mates. In particular, black and Hispanic young people are much less likely than white young people to become college graduates and enter this sample (Berryman 1983). This analysis has nothing to say about whether individuals with more or less education face comparable wage differentials or what will happen to these wage differentials as the cohort ages. However, this data set provides a unique opportunity to learn whether wage differentials can be found even in the markets for these highly and equally educated young men and women.

The Data

This study is based on the *1985 Survey of Recent College Graduates*. The survey was conducted by the U.S. Department of Education, National Center for Education Statistics. In 1985, 13,200 recent college graduates were sampled from a random sample of 404 institutions in the United States. Each of the graduates surveyed had earned a bachelor's or master's degree from a sampled institution between July 1983 and June 1984. The probability that an institution was sampled and the number of students sampled from an institution were generally proportional to the usual number of bachelor's and master's degrees granted. Institutions with high minority enrollments and individuals with certain college majors were oversampled. The effective response rate was 78 percent of students sampled (NCES 1988). Of the 10311 respondents, the 964 master's degree recipients and the 1217 bachelor's degree recipients over age 30 were not used in the analysis, leaving 8130 bachelor's degree graduates no more than 30 years old.

The analysis was further restricted to the 5952 bachelor's degree graduates no more than 30 years old who, in April 1985, were not enrolled in school full time, were either employed full time or involuntarily employed part time, earned more than $1 an hour, and had data present for earnings, work experience, college major, and college grades. Only 1 percent of this sample was lost due to missing data or extremely low wages.

This group of 5952 respondents has less educated parents, more pregraduation work experience, and lower college grades than the 2178 bachelor's degree graduates no more than 30 years old who were omitted from the analysis. The majority of those who were omitted were enrolled in school, so the observed differences between those in and out of the sample reflect the ability of graduates from wealthier families to delay working until after completing a lengthy education and the higher propensity of academically talented students to continue their education. Graduates with liberal arts degrees in the humanities, sciences, or social sciences are also less likely to go directly into the labor market than graduates with professional degrees in business, computer science, education, engineering, or nursing and are underrepresented in this sample. . . .

The data set is very well suited to determine the average wages of graduates with a given college major. Surveyed individuals were asked to identify their college major from a list of over 300 major fields and subspecialties, of which 246 are represented in this sample. The level of detail includes, for example, 32 types of biology major, 19 types of business major, 55 types of education major, and 25 types of engineering major. Collapsed major categories are used in some of the analysis, and these categories are business, communications, computer science, economics, education, engineering, humanities, mathematics, nursing, science, social sciences (other than economics), and "other."

Research about which colleges open the doors to higher paying jobs is at a very early stage. There is statistical evidence that graduates of the most selective private colleges earn higher wages than graduates of other colleges (Brewer, Eide, and Ehrenberg 1996), but knowledge about the relative returns to attending the majority of colleges is speculative. Existing rankings of "college quality" are based on various characteristics of schools that may or may not lead to higher wage jobs. In addition, these rankings are not complete orderings. . . .

College grade point average is self-reported. Self-reported grades are generally accurate, with no gender difference in the tendency to inflate self-reported grades (Freeberg 1988; Maxwell and Lopus 1994). Therefore, we do not expect the estimated wage gaps to be affected by misreported grades. College grade point average was recorded from a categorical variable . . . to a continuous variable. All ranges were recorded to the midpoint of the range.

The graduates are grouped demographically by gender and into the following five subgroups: non-Hispanic white (N=5025), non-Hispanic black (N=403), Asian or Pacific Islander (N=157), Hispanic (N=349), and American Indian or Native Alaskan (N=18). . . .

Employment data were gathered for the week of April 29, 1985. Respondents had the option of reporting wages or earnings on an hourly, daily, weekly, monthly, or annual basis. Hourly earnings are computed from whatever wage or income figures were reported and from reported hours worked per week. Those reporting their occupation as "teacher" and their salary on an annual basis were assumed to earn that salary in only ten months.

Two separate variables reflecting work experience are included in the analysis. The first is actual full-time work experience prior to receiving the bachelor's degree, excluding summer or other temporary jobs. This question was specifically asked of the graduates in the survey. The second is postdegree experience, defined as time elapsed since college graduation, which varies from ten to twenty-two months in this sample. This "potential experience" variable is a common proxy for work experience.

A final labor market variable included in the analysis is hours worked per week. . . .

White Women

For white women, differences in broadly defined college major explain nearly half the estimated wage disadvantage relative to white men. Adding further controls for narrow college major, geography, or institution attended has absolutely no additional affect on the estimated 9 percent white female wage disadvantage. This means that within a broad college major category, women do not choose less remunerative majors on average. It also means that, on average, white women and white men attend colleges whose graduates are similarly valued.

Black Men

For black men, controls for college major and institution attended have no effect on the 9 percent estimated wage disadvantage relative to white men. This means that black male college graduates, on average, choose equally remunerative college majors as white men. In addition, black male college graduates attend colleges whose graduates are as highly valued in the labor market as the colleges attended by white men. Because these black male and white male college graduates come from families with similar levels of education, it is not surprising that their educational attainments are similar in type and quality.

Black Women

Unlike black men, black women attend colleges whose graduates are less valued by the labor market, on average, than those attended by white men. This difference may reflect the fact that the black women in this sample came from less affluent families. Like white women, black women have less remunerative college majors than white men. However, black women have somewhat less

remunerative college majors than white men within as well as between broad college major categories. Altogether, controls for college major and the educational institution attended explain two-fifths of the black female wage disadvantage relative to white men, reducing the estimated wage disadvantage from 25 percent to 16 percent. This remaining wage gap is still the largest of any demographic group.

Hispanic Men

Hispanic male college graduates earn somewhat more than white men until controls for college attended are included. After controlling for type and quality of college education received, the Hispanic male recent college graduates in this sample face no wage disadvantage relative to white men.

Hispanic Women

Like Hispanic men who complete college, Hispanic women attend colleges whose graduates are highly valued by the labor market. Controls for college major reduce the estimated wage disadvantage faced by Hispanic women from 11 percent to zero. However, further controls reveal that there is a 6 percent gap relative to white men who attended the same college. The 6 percent estimated wage disadvantage faced by Hispanic women has a large standard error. Therefore, we can conclude only that Hispanic women probably face some wage disadvantage and that it is no larger than that faced by other women.

Asian Men and Women

For Asian men and women, controlling for college major and institution attended reveals a hidden wage disadvantage. Asian men and women tend to choose more remunerative college majors, to live in higher-wage geographic regions, and to graduate from colleges with better-paid graduates than other men and women. All these factors contribute to relatively high average wages. However, Asian men and women actually face the same 10 to 15 percent wage disadvantage as white women, black women, and black men relative to white male graduates of the same institution and college major . . .

Summary and Conclusions

The question of whether race and gender differentials in pay among individuals with the same number of years of education are due to labor market discrimination or to unobserved differences in career preferences and the type and quality of education attained is difficult to answer. The focus of this paper is a large survey of recent college graduates. This data set contains extremely detailed information about the productive characteristics and career preferences that an individual takes into the labor market. The available controls include narrowly defined college major, college grades, and the exact educational institution attended by each graduate. This paper examines the effects on estimated wage differentials of including increasingly detailed controls for the type and quality of education attained.

This analysis shows clearly that among recent college graduates, white women, black men, black women, Asian men, and Asian women all face the same 10 to 15 percent wage disadvantage relative to white men with the same type and quality of college education. If labor market discrimination is defined as a mechanism that causes individuals with the same productive characteristics but different ascriptive characteristics to be valued differently by the labor market, then this is very strong evidence that discrimination operates in the market for recent college graduates.

References

Bielby, William, and James Baron. 1984. "A Woman's Place Is with Other Women: Sex Segregation within Organizations." In *Sex Segregation in the Work-place*, edited by Barbara Reskin, pp. 27-55. Washington, DC: National Academy Press.

Berryman, Sue. 1983. *Who Will Do Science? Trends and Their Causes in Minority and Female Representation Among Holders of Advanced Degrees in Science and Mathematics. A Special Report.* New York: The Rockefeller Foundation.

Blakemore, Arthur E., and Stuart A. Low. 1984. "Sex Differences in Occupational Selection: The Case of College Majors." *Review of Economics and Statistics* 66 (February): 157-63.

Blau, Francine. 1984. "Occupational Segregation and Labor Market Discrimination." In *Sex Segregation in the Workplace*, edited by Barbara Reskin, pp. 117-143. Washington, DC: National Academy Press.

Blau, Francine, and Marianne Ferber. 1987a. "Discrimination: Empirical Evidence from the United States." *American Economic Review* 77 (May): 316-20.

———. 1987b. "Occupations and Earnings of Women Workers." In *Working Women: Past, Present, and Future*, edited by Karen S. Koziara, Michael Maskow, and Lucretia D. Tanner. Washington, DC: Bureau of National Affairs.

———. 1991. "Career Plans and Expectations of Young Women and Men: The Earnings Gap and Labor Force Participation." *Journal of Human Resources* 26 (Fall): 58 1.

Blinder, Alan S. 1973. "Wage Discrimination: Reduced Form and Structural Estimates." *Journal of Human Resources* 8 (Fall): 436-55.

Brewer, Dominic, Eric Eidec, and Ronald G. Ehrenberg. 1996. "Does it Pay to Attend and Elite Private College? Cross-Cohort Evidence of the Effects of College Quality on Earnings." Unpublished paper.

Brown, Randall S., Marylyn Moon, and Barbara S. Zoloth. 1980. "Incorporating Occupational Attainment in Studies of Male-Female Earnings Differentials." Journal of human Resources 15 (Winter):3-28.

Corcoran, Mary, and Greg J. Duncan. 1979. "Work History, Labor Force Attachment, and Earnings Differences between the Races and Sexes." *Journal of Human Resources* 14: 1-20.

Constantine, Jill. 1995. "The Effect of Attending Historically Black Colleges and Universities on the Future Wages of Black Students." *Industrial and Labor Relations* 48: 53 1-46.

Daymont, Thomas, and Paul Andrisani. 1984. "Job Preferences, College Major and the Gender Gap in Earnings." Journal of Human Resources 19: 408-28.

Duleep, Harriett, and Seth Sanders. 1992. "Discrimination at the Top: American-Born Asian and White Men." *Industrial Relations* 31 (Fall): 416-32.

Eide, Eric, and Jeff Grogger. 1992. "Omitted-Ability Bias, Major-Specific Wage Premia, and Changes in the Returns to College Education." Unpublished Paper, University of California, Santa Barbara.

Eide, Eric. 1994. "College Major and Changes in the Gender Wage Gap." *Contemporary Economic Policy* 12 (April): 55-64.

Ferber, Marianne, and Carole Green. 1991. "Occupational Segregation and the Earnings Gap." In

Essays on the Economics of Discrimination, edited by Emily P. Hoffman. Kalamazoo, MI: W.E. Upjohn Institute.

Freeberg, Norman. 1988. "Analysis of the Revised Student- Descriptive Questionnaire. Phase 1: Accuracy of Student-Reported Information, College Board Report 88-5." College Entrance Examination Board, New York (ERIC: ED304460).

Fuller, Rex, and Richard Schoenberger. 1991. "The Gender Salary Gap: Do Academic Achievement, Internship Experience, and College Major Make a Difference?" *Social Science Quarterly* 72 (December): 715-26.

Gill, Andrew M. 1994. "Incorporating the Causes of Occupational Differences in Studies of Racial Wage Differentials." *Journal of Human Resources* 29 (Winter): 20-4 1.

Grogger, Jeff, and Eric Eide. 1995. "Changes in College Skills and the Rise in the College Wage Premium." *Journal of Human Resources* 30 (Spring): 280-310.

Groshen, Erica L. 1991. "The Structure of the Female/Male Wage Differential." *Journal of Human Resources* 26 (Summer): 457-72.

Gunderson, Morley. 1989. "Male-Female Wage Differentials and Policy Responses." *Journal of Economic Literature* 27 (March): 46-72.

Juhn, Chinhui, Kevin Murphy, and Brooks Pierce. 1991. "Accounting for the Slowdown in Black-White Wage Convergence." *In Workers and Their Wages: Changing Patterns in the U.S.* edited by Marvin Kosters. Washington, DC: American Enterprise Institute Press.

Koch, James V. 1972. "Student Choice of Undergraduate Major Field of Study and Private Internal Rates of Return." Industrial and Labor Relations Review 26 (October):680-5.

Oakes, Jeannie. 1990. Multiplying Inequalities: The Effects of Race, Social Class, and Tracking on Opportunities to Learn Mathematics and Science. Santa Monica, CA: Rand Corporation (ERIC ED329615).

Maxwell, Nan L., and Jane S. Lopus. 1994. "The Lake Wobegon Effect in Student Self-Reported Data." *American Economic Review* 84 (May): 201-5.

National Center for Education Statistics (NCES). 1988. *Employment Outcomes of Recent Master's and Bachelor's Degree Recipients*, CS 88-25 1. Washington, DC: U.S. Department of Education.

National Center for Education Statistics (NCES). 1994. *The Conditions of Education 1994.* Washington, DC: U.S. Department of Education.

Nechyba, Thomas J. 1990. "The Southern Wage Gap, Human Capital, and the Quality of Education." *Southern Economic Journal* 57 (October): 308-22.

Paglin, Morton, and Anthony M. Rufolo. 1990. "Heterogeneous Human Capital, Occupational Choice, and Male-Female Earnings Differences." *Journal of Labor Economics* 8: 123-44.

Polachek, Solomon. 1978. "Sex Differences in College Major." *Industrial and Labor Relations Review* 31 (July): 498-508.

Rumberger, Russeel W., and Scott Thomas. 1993. "The Economic Returns to College Major, Quality, and Performance: A Multilevel Analysis of Recent Graduates." *Economics of Education Review* 12 (March): 1-19.

Trieman, Donald, and Heidi Hartmann, editors. 1981. *Women, Work, and Wages: Equal Pay for Work of Equal Value*. Washington, DC: National Academy Press.

Trejo, Stephen. 1995. "Why Do Mexican Americans Earn Low Wages?" Unpublished Paper, University of California, Santa Barbara.

Weinberger, Catherine J. 1997a. "Mathematics Test Scores, Gender, and Undergraduate Participation in Engineering, Mathematics, and Science." Unpublished Paper, University of California, Santa Barbara.

Weinberger, Catherine J. 1997b. "What's the Difference? Characteristics of Mathematically Talented Men and Women Who Do Not Pursue College Degrees in Engineering, Mathematics or Science." Unpublished Paper, University of California, Santa Barbara.

Wood, Robert G., Mary E. Corcoran, and Paul N. Courant, 1993. "Pay Differentials Among the Highly Paid: The Male-Female Earnings Gap in Lawyers' Salaries." *Journal of Labor Economics* 11 (3): 417-41.

Critical Evaluation

1. What other factors might enter into the race and gender wages gaps reported by the author?

2. How might an employer respond to the author's findings?

3. What action is needed in order to close the gap in wages that results from discrimination?

Catherine J. Weinberger, "Race and Gender Wage Gaps in the Market for Recent College Graduates." In *Industrial Relations* 37:1, pp. 67-84. Copyright © 1998 by Blackwell Publishers. Reprinted by permission. ✦

6

When Workers Become Victims

Many Americans have been hurt by the current trend of corporate "downsizing." This practice causes severe problems of low morale and distrust of management (Koretz 1997). Nevertheless, driven by the desire for maximum profits, companies continue to downsize, and millions of American workers have lost their jobs as a result. Ironically, as Luis Uchitelle points out, many of these workers return as "rentals" (contract workers), often to the very companies that laid them off. The workers also suffer consequences of downsizing at the microlevel—including lower self-concepts, anger, and bitterness.

Not all employees are equally likely to be victims of downsizing. David Gordon argues that corporations are still "fat" at the managerial level. In fact, he asserts that the major source of American economic problems is "the way most U.S. corporations maintain bloated bureaucracies and mistreat their workers" (Gordon 1996: 3). Gordon's data show that workers have experienced a "wage squeeze" since 1979 and that minorities and lower-level workers suffered the most, while those at the top did well during the downsizing years.

References

Gordon, David M. 1996. *Fat and Mean: The Corporate Squeeze of Working Americans and the Myth of Managerial 'Downsizing.'* New York: The Free Press.

Koretz, Gene. 1997. "The Downside of Downsizing." *Business Week*, April 28, p. 26.

A.

More Downsized Workers Are Returning as Rentals

Louis Uchitelle

Focus Questions

1. What is a "rental," or contract worker?

2. What are the effects on workers of being downsized and returning as contract workers?

3. How are relationships with co-workers affected by being a contract worker?

The call came while Linda Corbett was in her yard gardening. A supervisor at Pacific Bell, a man she knew, told her that his staff was overwhelmed with work. He wanted to know whether Ms. Corbett would consider returning to the company from which, just six months earlier, she had been "severed involuntarily," as she still puts it bitterly.

Ms. Corbett, who is 42, resisted at first. She had reacted to her ouster by plunging into suburban life. She became active in the Chamber of Commerce, took courses in how to start a small business, gave parties with her husband and tended her vegetables and flowers. But she finally gave in, returning last May to a sales job at the company that had employed her since high school.

Instead of going back as an employee, however, she returned as a contract worker, on the payroll of one of the temporary-help agencies that have sprung up around Pacific Bell, like pilot fish around a whale, renting workers to the giant even as it sheds employees.

That contract workers are widely used is well known. What is just coming to light is that as many as one-fifth of them, probably more than a million, are people like Ms. Corbett who have returned to their old companies, many after having been pushed off payrolls or lured off with lucrative buyouts. New surveys are beginning to document the trend, which appears to be another move toward a system in which companies and employees feel less obligated to each other.

"Many companies don't want to lose experienced people and they don't want to keep them on expensive career tracks," said Alan Krueger, a Princeton labor economist. "So they have come up with contract-worker status for ex-employees. And that is an important step that companies are taking toward rewriting the implicit contract that bound them to their workers."

As they grow in number, these former employees returning on contract become a subculture in the workplace. They are people with an employee's mindset spliced centaur-like to an outsider's role as a rented worker. That was clear in interviews with more than a dozen of them.

Not having careers to advance, some praise the liberation from enervating office politics, and from the stress of competing for raises and promotions. They talk of a greater flexibility to work only when they please. But their altered status cuts at their self-esteem. They are sometimes shunned by co-workers. They are often less effective than they had been. Many find themselves no longer going the extra mile to get a job done or acquire a new skill.

Some come to realize, as Ms. Corbett has, that what they have returned to are set tasks, rather than work that draws on their ingenuity and ambition. And company benefits like health insurance and pensions become only a memory for many. Corporations view these workers as skilled reserves who can jump back in without losing time learning the routine. But productivity suffers when they find themselves less motivated in their new role.

The Labor Department recently produced the first major statistical evidence of people cycling back to their old employers as contract workers. Its report found that among five million contingent workers, 17 percent of a representative sample surveyed in 1995 said they had had a "previous different relationship" with the companies that now, in effect, rent them. Seven million people who describe themselves as self-employed were not represented in the survey, and some may also be back at their old companies on contract.

Similarly, the American Management Association, in a survey of 720 companies that recently shed workers, found that 30 percent had brought back downsized employees, on contract or as rehired employees.

Temporary-help agencies offer additional evidence. Shelley Wallace, the president of the Wallace Law Registry, which rents lawyers to corporations that have made cuts in their legal departments, estimates that 10 percent of the lawyers rented out by her agency and others go to their former employers.

And William Ostler, the president of Training Delivery Service, the temporary-help agency supplying the largest number of contract workers to Pacific Bell, says former employees make up 80 percent of the 900 to 1,000 people that his agency supplies to the phone company on an average day.

Pacific Bell says it is using 4,200 temporary and contract workers in addition to 44,000 regular employees (down from 54,600 in 1991). Other companies also engage in the practice. The list includes Xerox, Hoffman-LaRoche, Delta Air Lines, Digital Equipment and Chevron, as well as smaller places like Bronson Methodist Hospital in Kalamazoo, Mich.

Seldom, however, will the companies or their workers discuss what they do in any detail. Pacific Bell is an exception. A class action brought by 1,600 former employees, a suit charging that Pacific Bell violated a job-guarantee agreement, has illuminated the process at that company. Some of those listed as plaintiffs, including Ms. Corbett, were willing, now that their names are public, to talk about their experiences.

The High Cost of Independence

Linda Corbett speaks like a person whose spouse has thrown her out, unexpectedly, and has now invited her back—on very different terms. She is bitter, and she finds the experience hard to put behind her.

"Restore my seniority, my vacation time and my pension," she said of the possibility that she return to a permanent job at the company, "and I'll consider it." On the other hand, the invitation back to the company that once rejected her has made her feel better about herself. "I feel I have value. Otherwise, they would simply drop my contract."

Ms. Corbett came back to a sales job in the phone company's Third Street office downtown, a job she had held until 1992. The insult of having been forced out has been somewhat offset by the welcome she received from former colleagues who quickly shifted work to her.

The $40 an hour she earns on the payroll of a temporary-help agency is $10 an hour more than her base salary as an employee, she calculates. That makes her feel even better. And exercising the new control she says she has over her life, she took four weeks off to tour Asia with her husband.

But Ms. Corbett has also been confronted by the fact that her old sales job, at a Pacific Bell office north of here, was not eliminated, as she was told it would be, but refilled, by an acquaintance. For this Ms. Corbett comes down hard, not on her replacement but on the company. She was, she reasons, the victim of "a numbers game" in which low-level managers were given downsizing quotas, regardless of workload.

Michael Rodriguez, Pacific Bell's vice president for human resources, conceded "there were jobs that we hoped would go away when those in them did, but some of the work did not go away as quickly as we would have liked."

Shelley McGuinness, who is 44, has had a rougher return to Pacific Bell. Like Ms. Corbett, she was in marketing, selling voice and data services. Like Ms. Corbett's job, hers was declared "surplus" last fall, and like Ms. Corbett, she was given the choice of a $70,000 buyout or 60 days to find another job within Pacific Bell. Failing in the latter, she took the former.

A temporary-help agency recruited her and in July Ms. McGuinness found herself back in the Third Street building, at $20 an hour—two-thirds of her old pay—doing part of her old job, but on another floor. One floor below, her former colleagues carry on, without a new hire in her old seat. But candidates are interviewing for the post. That rattled Ms. McGuinness, who had been told, she says, that the job would be eliminated as part of a reorganization.

Some of her ex-office mates are rattled, too. They limit their contacts with her to small talk, eyes often averted. "You think you are getting over this," Ms. McGuinness said, "and then you bump into someone in the elevator and you feel defensive and hurt, and all the old feelings come back. They don't talk to me much. It is as if they think they might catch what I have, if they really talked to me."

She fingers a paper ID badge that she pastes to her sweater, with a redmarker "C" on it, for contract worker. "Some days it feels like a scarlet letter," she said, "and other days it makes me feel like I am an independent contract worker, and I can go home at night and not worry about this place."

Former colleagues try to rationalize what happened. "Shelley was neither a shining star at her job nor at the bottom," one said. "Those who know they weren't as good feel they lucked out, and those who performed better tell themselves she should have worked harder."

Roger Colella, 51, hoped the growing use of former employees would play to his advantage. But he is not quite as sure of this as he once was.

Mr. Colella was an $80,000-a-year manager at Pacific Bell. Many companies, seeking to thin their ranks without dismissing people, have permitted employees in mid-career, or earlier, to cash in the company-financed portions of their pensions, periodically sweetening the amounts to encourage this. Pacific Bell offered the latest sweetener last March and Mr. Colella decided that he had to act, or risk losing $515,000.

Now he is working around the house, unemployed. He sees himself as a man temporarily between engagements at the company that ushered him out in September and expects him back in March, but on contract, and perhaps not as a manager. Mr. Colella says he is beginning to realize that in his second act, former subordinates will inevitably be less respectful of his authority.

Indeed, managing on contract is an oxymoron, Mr. Colella says; he would be more comfortable returning in a line job, as a peer of his former subordinates. No matter how friendly the parting, he adds: "Some level of mutual respect and authority is lost. My people might think they want me back, but if I returned they would view me as temporary, and say, 'This guy is only here for a short time; we'll do as we wish.'"

Some of Mr. Colella's former subordinates express the hope that his old job will still be open in March, when Mr. Colella, with his calming ways, will be eligible to return on contract. "We are living in a void until then," one said.

The experiences of Ms. Corbett, Ms. McGuinness and Mr. Colella, multiplied many times, are forcing change on the American workplace and on the economy. Productivity is particularly at issue. Ms. Corbett, for example, says that in theory she works on a par with another woman in her new position. But in practice, they are not equals. Excluded from training, Ms. Corbett says she is no longer acquiring technical knowledge to market new products, so the workload falls increasingly on her partner, who parcels out to Ms. Corbett only the tasks she can handle.

Uncertain of the future, she no longer goes out of her way to cultivate people in other departments who, as a favor, might speed up her customers' orders for circuits and equipment, as they once did. For Jeffrey Pfeffer, a management expert at the Stanford Business School, stories like that demonstrate a setback for the nation's economic effectiveness. "Companies don't think about the relationship between job tenure and productivity," he said.

The phenomenon of former employees' cycling back to their companies as contract workers is still relatively small, but if it spreads, says Mr. Krueger, the Princeton labor economist, we come "that much closer to a world in which employment is no longer the primary source of pensions and health care, and we may have to choose other arrangements."

Ms. McGuinness offers herself as vivid example of the issue. Her $42,000 pension settlement is not a match for what she would have received had she remained at Pacific Bell until retirement, another 15 years. And the company's health insurance, for which she paid only $50 a month for full family coverage, expired six months after her job did.

Within those six months, her husband was found to have cancer (in remission now). He managed to shift to a group policy at the carpeting business he owns, but at a cost to himself of more than $300 a month. Ms. McGuinness bought a separate policy for herself and her son, at $129 a month. The family's out-of-pocket health insurance, in sum, rose nearly ninefold, and Ms. Corbett found herself without the five weeks of paid vacation she had accumulated.

"I'll never get that back," she said. "My biggest heartache is what happened to my benefits."

Critical Evaluation

1. The author begins with a woman's experience, suggesting that her reaction is typical for contract workers. Is it?

2. Are the author's sources of information adequate for the conclusions he makes?

3. Does the author identify all the adverse consequences of contract work? What other consequences are there?

Louis Uchitelle, "More Downsized Workers Are Returing as Rentals." In *The New York Times* December 8, 1996. Copyright © 1996 by *The New York Times* Company. Reprinted by permission. ✦

B.
Fat and Mean: The Corporate Squeeze of Working Americans

David M. Gordon

Focus Questions

1. What is meant by the "wage squeeze?"

2. How have those in top corporate positions fared in recent times?

3. How are gender, race, and education related to the wage squeeze?

Andrew Flenoy, a twenty-one-year-old living in Kansas City, did better in 1994 than many, holding down a steady job paying a cut above the minimum wage. In fact, he had even enjoyed some recent promotions, rising at a food catering firm from dishwasher to catering manager. Through that sequence of promotions, however, his earnings had increased from $5.50 an hour to only $6.50 an hour—the equivalent of only about $12,000 a year working full-time year-round. Whatever satisfaction he had enjoyed from his promotions had quickly paled. "Now he is tired of the burgundy and black uniform he must wear," a reporter concluded, "and of the sense that he works every day from 6 a.m. to 2 p.m. just to earn enough money so that he can come back and work some more the next day." "My resolution for 1994," Flenoy remarked, "is that if nothing comes along, I'll relocate and start from scratch somewhere else."

Flenoy attended only a semester of community college after high school and suffered the additional employment disadvantage of being African American. Many are inclined to assume, indeed, that the wage squeeze has mostly afflicted the young, the unskilled, and the disadvantaged.

Although some have suffered more than others, however, a much wider band of the working population has been caught in the vise. For most Americans, the wage squeeze has been a profoundly democratizing trend.

Indeed, the data on the breadth of the wage squeeze seem finally to have persuaded skeptics not normally known for their empathy with workers. Recently confronted with some of these data, for example, Marvin Kosters, a well-known conservative economist at the American Enterprise Institute who had earlier challenged reports about trends toward growing inequality, admitted surprise at the variety of subgroups affected by wage erosion. "It's really quite amazing," he acknowledged. The data would scarcely seem "amazing," of course, to those who've been directly feeling the pinch.

In order to assess the breadth of the wage squeeze, we need to turn to data from household surveys, which unlike the establishment surveys afford considerable detail on workers' personal characteristics. We can look at trends in real hourly earnings between 1979 and 1993 for a variety of different groups in the private nonfarm workforce, since it is trends in the private sector with which I am most concerned. . . . Looking at this universe, we find that real hourly earnings for all private nonfarm employees, including those at the top, remained essentially flat from 1979 to 1993—barely rising from $11.62 to $11.80 (in 1993 prices). (Government workers did somewhat better.)

But we know that those at the top did fairly well. The more telling comparison looks at real wage trajectories for the bottom four-fifths of the real wage distribution and for the top fifth. As anticipated from the data for production workers reviewed in the previous section, it was the bottom 80 percent that experienced actual real wage decline, with the 1993 level dropping by 3.4 percent below the 1979 figure. For the top 20 percent times were not so harsh; they enjoyed a healthy rate of increase, with their real hourly earnings rising by 1993 to almost three times those for the bottom four-fifths.

We can also compare workers by race and ethnic origin. Looking at workers in the bottom 80 percent of the overall wage distribution, it is true, not surprisingly, that African Americans and Hispanics fared less well than whites. But even among whites in the bottom 80 percent, real hourly earnings dropped by nearly 3 percent. (Of course, a much larger percentage of African Americans and Hispanics were situated in the bottom four-fifths of the wage distribution than of whites.) Not just the disadvantaged but the advantaged racial group joined the wake.

Looking at wage trends by gender, we find a major difference in the impact of the wage squeeze. While male workers in the bottom 80 percent of the distribution experienced devastating declines in their real hourly earnings—facing a decline of close to 10 percent—women workers in the bottom 80 percent enjoyed modest real wage growth, with a total increase over the full period of 2.8 percent. Despite these gains, however, women's wages still lagged substantially behind men's. In 1993, the median female hourly wage had reached barely more than three-quarters of the median male wage, at 78 percent. Women were gaining on men, to be sure, but their gains occurred primarily because real male wages were plummeting, not because real female earnings were themselves growing rapidly. Indeed, almost three-quarters of the decline in the wage gap between men and women from 1979 and 1993 can be attributed to the decline in male earnings—a trend which undoubtedly contributed to the widespread frustration which many males have apparently been feeling and venting.

A final comparison looks at the experience of workers with different levels of education. It was the bulk of workers on the bottom, those with less than a college degree, who experienced actual wage decline. Only those with a college degree or better were able to gain some measure of protection against the

Table 1

The Wage Squeeze Across the Work Force
Real Hourly Earnings, Nonfarm Private Sector ($1993)

	1979	1993	% Change
All workers	$11.62	11.80	1.5%
Bottom 80 percent	8.93	8.59	−3.4
Top 20 percent	22.41	24.66	10.04
White workers, bottom 80 percent	9.03	8.77	−2.9
Black workers, bottom 80 percent	8.28	7.98	−3.6
Hispanic workers, bottom 80 percent	8.53	7.86	−7.9
Male workers, bottom 80 percent	9.94	9.05	−9.0
Female workers, bottom 80 percent	7.94	8.16	2.8
High school dropout	10.31	8.19	−20.6
High school graduate	11.11	10.05	−9.5
Some college education	13.12	11.03	−15.9
College graduate	16.01	16.57	3.5
Postgraduate	19.84	21.59	8.8

Sources and Notes: Based on author's own tabulations from data samples extracted from Current Population Survey.

Source: Reprinted with the permission of The Free Press, a Division of Simon & Schuster from *Fat and Mean: The Corporate Squeeze of Working Americans and the Myth of Managerial "Downsizing"*, by David M. Gordon. Copyright © 1996 by David M. Gordon.

unfriendly winds. And the most recent trends have been harsh even for a large number in that group. From 1989 to 1993, for example, even male workers with just a college degree, but no postgraduate education, were hit with declining real earnings.

Table 1 pulls together these separate tabulations for different groups of workers. The wage squeeze has caught a huge proportion of U.S. workers in its grip.

Critical Evaluation

1. Using Gordon's figures, the loss for the bottom 80 percent of full-time workers would be $13.60 a week. Is that a significant amount?

2. What are some possible explanations for the figures Gordon gives in Table 1?

David M. Gordon. 1996. *Fat and Mean: The Corporate Squeeze of Working Americans and the Myth of Managerial 'Downsizing'*. Copyright © 1996 by David M. Gordon. Reprinted by permission of The Free Press, a Division of Simon & Schuster. ✦

Project for Personal Application and Class Discussion: The Economy and Work

Think ahead to the time when you will have completed your education and begun a career. Answer as fully and realistically as you can the following questions:

1. What do you expect your starting salary to be?

2. What is the minimum annual salary you would accept?

3. What do you expect your employer to give you in the way of fringe benefits?

4. What, in addition to your salary, do you expect to gain from the work you do?

5. Do you anticipate that your work will make the best use of your skills and interests?

6. What do you expect to give to your employer?

Discuss your answers with someone who works or has worked in the type of career you have chosen. Are your answers realistic in terms of this person's experience? How do you think you would handle the situation if your expectations were violated by some of the factors discussed in this section—underemployment, race or gender discrimination, or downsizing? ✦

Education

Most Americans value education and view it as an essential ingredient for a high-quality life. Education is the gateway to better jobs and higher income levels. But like government and the economy, education can become a part of, as well as a solution to, social problems. Education, for example, has helped to combat the myth of racial inferiority, the idea that women who are raped were in some sense "asking for it," and the notion that we can treat the earth as an endless source of resources rather than as a vulnerable home that needs care.

But education also poses problems. Both the content of education (e.g., for a good part of the nation's history, African Americans—except for the issue of slavery—were virtually ignored in children's schoolbooks) and access to education (women, the poor, and minorities have not had the same access to educational opportunities as white males) have been troublesome issues. This section examines some of the prominent problems and controversies that surround education today. ✦

7

Quality Counts, but Do We Have It?

Education Week

For education to improve individual and social well-being, it must be high in quality. In 1983 the National Commission on Excellence in Education issued a report criticizing education at all levels as a "rising tide of mediocrity." Has education improved since then? Education Week evaluated and graded the nation's schools from B to C– in five important areas. The journal also identified the ways in which minorities obtain an education of lesser quality than that of whites.

Numerous factors contribute to the deficiencies noted. At the macrolevel, inadequate and inequitable government support for education, inadequately trained teachers, and insufficient parent and community involvement help explain the problems. These factors are supported at the microlevel by such things as parental indifference and teachers' low expectations for poor and minority students.

Focus Questions

1. Why is education important?

2. What are the categories used to evaluate education?

3. How does grading vary by category and by state?

4. How does education for the poor and minorities differ from that of others?

Part 1: The State of the States: Executive Summary

Public education systems in the 50 states are riddled with excellence but rife with mediocrity. Despite 15 years of earnest efforts to improve public schools and raise student achievement, states haven't made much progress.

As the new millennium approaches, there is growing concern that if public education doesn't soon improve, one of two outcomes is almost inevitable:

- Our democratic system and our economic strength, both of which depend on an educated citizenry, will steadily erode; or,

- Alternative forms of education will emerge to replace public schools as we have known them.

This will not happen next year or perhaps even in the next 10 years. But in time, if our education systems remain mediocre, we will see one of those two results. Either would be a sad loss for America.

The nation's governors realize this. . . . [T]hey met at the National Education Summit to reaffirm their commitment to school reform. They invited the voters to hold them accountable and called for "an external, independent, nongovernmental effort to measure and report each state's annual progress."

We agree that Americans should hold their representatives —and themselves—accountable for the quality of their public schools. . . . *Education Week's* editors spent the better part of the past year studying the condition of public education in the states. We reviewed thousands of pages of data from a variety of government and private sources, surveyed policy makers and business leaders in every state, and polled educators.

We then compiled statistics on more than 75 specific indicators and graded states on their policies and performance in four major categories—academic standards, quality of teaching, school climate, and funding. We also ranked the states on their students' scores on the National Assessment of Educational Progress.

We relied on research and experience in choosing the most useful indicators to evaluate public education in the states. Our goal was to focus on policies that really matter, that research tells us are most likely to result in better schools and more learning.

In addition, staff writers have summarized the progress and problems in each state. They searched 15 years of *Education Week's* archives, pored over numerous state reports, and interviewed hundreds of experts. Their summaries . . . make up the bulk of this report.

In a nutshell, here is what we found:

1. Standards and Assessments

What do we expect students to know and be able to do and how do we judge their performance? That question goes straight to the purpose and nature of public schooling. It is being discussed in every state, and it is one that every parent and taxpayer should be involved in.

High standards for student performance lay the foundation for the significant changes that must follow. And the work in this area appears to be paying off. This is where the states earned their highest overall grade—a solid B. Encouraging as that is, we must note that the B, at this point, is more for effort than results. In most states, the standards haven't found their way into classrooms. Teachers, by and large, are not prepared to teach to them. We don't know how rigorous they are. The tests aren't yet in place to measure student progress. And few states are ready to hold either schools or students accountable for meeting the new standards.

- **Overall grade for the states: B.**
- 22 states earn A's.
- 13 get B's
- 2 states net F's, mainly because they have decided not to develop statewide standards and assessments.

2. Quality of Teaching

How are teachers prepared and supported? The system can only be as good as its teachers. Research shows that a good teacher in every classroom is the most effective way of improving student performance. Great strides have been made at the policy level to turn teaching into a real profession with higher standards for training and more rigorous licensing requirements. At the national level, the crucial pieces of a system are falling into place, but there is much work to be done. On average, four out of 10 secondary teachers do not have a degree in the subject they teach. Too many unlicensed teachers are in classrooms. Not enough prospective teachers receive the high-quality education they need. On-the-job education for teachers is still more of a goal than a reality.

- **Overall Grade for the states: C.**
- 8 states get B's.
- 3 get D's.
- The rest receive C's.

3. School Climate

How should a school be organized and run to be effective? We know a lot about what makes good schools. They should be small enough for teachers to know their students and work effectively with their colleagues. They should have a clear, shared sense of mission and be focused on student learning. They should capitalize on what we now know about how children learn. And they should be safe and orderly. That is the goal. The reality is that nearly half of our elementary teachers have classes of 25 or more pupils; more than half of high school English teachers teach 80 or more students a day. There is not enough parent and community involvement.

Strong traditions of local control dilute the effectiveness of state policy in changing the way schools are organized and operated. And ultimately, it is in the school and the classroom where we win or lose. In school climate, states get their lowest scores.

- **Overall, the states earn a C–.**
- No states get A's.
- 4 states receive B's.
- 19 get D's, and the rest get C's.

4. Resources

Are states allocating enough money to do the job? Most states are spending more money for education than they did 10 years ago, and the increases generally have out-paced inflation. But too few of the additional dollars have reached classrooms. Most of the increased funding has been spent on the approximately 12% of students in special education, on trying to keep up with enrollment growth, and on rising salaries for an aging teaching force.

- **Overall, states get a C+ on whether they spend enough.**
- 5 states get A's, and 20 get B's.
- 17 states get C's, and 7 states get D's.
- 1 state gets an F.

Do States Make Sure That Everyone Gets a Fair Share? After more than three decades of lawsuits and legislative haggling, the system has become somewhat more equitable. But progress notwithstanding, intolerable disparities persist between rich schools and poor schools within states and across states, and the extent of that inequity is not revealed in the letter grades. The fact is that the quality of a child's education depends greatly on skin color, family income, and where he or she lives. The problem is most severe in inner cities and poor rural areas.

- **Overall, the states get a low B– on equity.**
- 5 states get A's.
- 6 states get D's.
- The rest earn B's and C's.

Do States Spend Their Money on the Right Things? How money is spent is as important as how much is spent. States do not concentrate enough funding in the classroom—on teaching and learning. Technology has great potential to increase productivity in a labor-intensive endeavor. Schools have made remarkable gains in acquiring computer equipment, but there is little evidence that it is being effectively used to help all children. Finally, states have failed to make sure that school buildings are sound and safe. Districts have deferred maintenance to the point where millions of children attend schools that need to be replaced or substantially repaired.

- **States get a C– in the allocation of dollars.**

- 6 states get B's.
- 28 states get C's.
- 16 states either barely passed or failed.

5. Student Achievement.

This is the bottom line. The question of student achievement can't be answered as fully and accurately as it should be because the states don't collect the necessary information to permit comparisons—data such as course-taking, dropout rates, and attendance rates. The only comparable measures of student performance are the NAEP scores, and they are discouraging.

- Maine has the best score in the nation on the 1994 NAEP 4th grade reading test, and 59% of its 4th graders could not read at a proficient level.
- Iowa led the nation on the 1992 NAEP math exam, and 69% of its 8th graders were below the proficient level.
- 85% of Louisiana's 4th graders read below the proficient level.
- 94% of Mississippi's 8th graders score below proficient in math.

The public education systems in the 50 states have been a century or more in the making. They cannot be transformed quickly, but they can be significantly improved. In every state, there are examples of successful, effective schools. Their success does not permit us to tolerate mediocrity any longer or anywhere.

Part 2:
Race and Demography
by Lynn Olson

Quality Counts focuses on what states can do to raise the achievement of all students. Stress the word "all." Raising standards, improving teaching, and creating better schools are only the first steps. States also must ensure that all children have access to a demanding curriculum, high-quality instruction, and nourishing classrooms.

[Recently] a revealing report from the Education Trust underlined just how far states have to go to fulfill their obligation to all students. The Washington-based nonprofit organization directs its efforts toward closing the performance gap between children from poor and minority families and their more advantaged peers.

It found that after decades of progress, the achievement gap between white and minority students is widening again. Between 1970 and 1988, minority students made striking gains in academic performance, while the achievement of white students remained flat.

During that time, the difference in performance between white and African-American students on the National Assessment of Educational Progress—which tests a representative sample of students nationwide—narrowed by about one-half. The gap between white and Hispanic students closed by one-third.

But beginning in 1988, this progress stopped. And in some subjects at some grades the gap began to yawn once more. Today, African-American, Hispanic, and American Indian students still perform well below other students in all subjects at all grade levels tested. In some cases, the gap has widened because the scores of minority students have declined; in other cases, the performance of white students has improved, while the performance of minority students has remained relatively stable.

"The fact that progress in minority achievement has stopped at a time when minorities comprise a growing portion of the student population should sound a wake-up call to the whole country," the Education Trust says in its report, *Education Watch: The 1996 Education Trust State and National Data Book.* "For while virtually all minority students master basic skills by age 17, disproportionately few master the higher-level skills they need to assume productive roles in society."

Researchers attribute the dramatic gains of the 1970s and early 1980s, in part, to changes in family characteristics and demographics. In particular, more black parents were better educated, had fewer children, and were less likely to live in poverty by the late 1970s. And all of these characteristics are strongly correlated with higher test scores.

But David Grissmer, a senior research scientist at the RAND Corp., argues that changing family characteristics alone cannot explain the large gains made by minority students. He calculates that changes in families accounted for only about a third of the total gain.

"Teachers and schools with large numbers of minority students may have been responsible for the most significant gains in test scores over the past 20 years," he suggests.

Massive desegregation of the schools, federal programs focused on boosting the basic reading and mathematics skills of disadvantaged students, and increased public spending on education all may have contributed to the academic progress of minority children.

The problem now, says the Education Trust report, is one of will. Experiences from real schools show that poor and minority students can excel if they are taught at high levels. "But most schools don't teach all students at the same high level," the report says. "In fact, we have constructed an educational system so full of inequities that it actually exacerbates the challenges of race and poverty, rather than ameliorates them. Simply put, we take students who have less to begin with and give them less in school, too."

The Education Trust report documents the following disparities:

- Poor and minority students are less likely to be in classes with teachers who at least minored in their fields. In the 1990–91 school year, for example, only 42% of math classes in high schools with majority-minority enrollments were taught by teachers who were math majors. By comparison, in high schools with few minority students—less than 15% of enrollment—69% of math classes were taught by math majors. More than two-thirds of African-American and Hispanic students attend predominantly minority schools.

- In schools where more than 30% of the students are poor, 59% of teachers report that they lack sufficient books and other reading resources. By contrast, only 16% of teachers in more affluent schools report such shortages.

- Poor and minority students are more likely to be taught a low-level curriculum with low standards for performance. Only one in four students from low-income families is placed in a college-preparatory sequence of courses. In contrast, poor and minority students are overrepresented in less challenging general and vocational education programs.

- Roughly 55 out of every 100 white and Asian students complete Algebra 2 and geometry. Only 35% of African-American and American Indian seniors take this math. Although one in four white seniors takes physics, only one in six black seniors and one in seven Hispanic seniors completes this course.

Some states provide disadvantaged students with better teachers and a more challenging curriculum than others do, the report says. For example:

- In Tennessee, 23% of public K–12 students were black in 1992, and 24% of students in Advanced Placement mathematics and science courses were black. By contrast, in Virginia, 26% of public K–12 students were black, but only 7% of students in AP math and science courses were black.

- In New York state in 1992, 20% of public K–12 students were African-Americans, and 20% of students in gifted-and-talented programs were black. In Mississippi, 51% of public K–12 students were black, but African-Americans made up only 7% of those in gifted-and-talented programs.

Poor and minority students also achieve significantly more in some states than in others. Mr. Grissmer calls these "value added" states because their students perform better on national assessments than their family and demographic characteristics would predict.

Take the case of Texas and California. Both states have a similar percentage of poor and black students. And Texas has a higher percentage of Hispanic students. Yet on the National Assessment of Educational Progress, poor and minority students in Texas perform

significantly better than similar students in California.

For example, in Texas, 44% of 4th graders in disadvantaged urban schools performed at the "basic" level or above on the 1992 NAEP math assessment, compared with only 27% in California. Hispanic 4th graders also fared significantly better in Texas than in California. On the 1994 NAEP reading assessment, about one-third of the students tested in both states were Hispanic. But in Texas, 41% read at the "basic" level or above; in California, only 22% did so.

Mr. Grissmer speculates that one reason for the difference may be the investment Texas has made in reducing class sizes in the early grades. About 90% of Texas' elementary teachers now have fewer than 25 children. Until this year, that was true for only 7% of California's elementary teachers.

The point is that while states cannot control the demographic or family characteristics of their students, some states do a much better job providing a decent education to all of their students than others do. When it comes to education, quality counts—for all children. And states should be held accountable for how well all students perform.

Critical Evaluation

1. Are all of the indicators equally important? Could students learn well in a school that received a C or lower grade on some of the indicators?

2. The report focuses on school factors. What other factors are important in whether students learn?

3. What could be done in the schools and elsewhere to improve the education of poor and minority students?

Adapted from "Examining Race and Demography," by Lynn Olsen, and "The State of the States" by the Editors of *Education Week*. In *Quality Counts: A Report Card on the Condition of Public Education in the 50 States*, a supplement to *Education Week* 16, January 22, 1997, pp. 1, 10–11. Copyright © 1997 by *Education Week*. Reprinted by permission. ✦

8

The Fearful, the Truant, and the Suspended/ Expelled

Sarah Ingersoll
Donni LeBoeuf

For millions of American students, school is a threatening or repugnant place. Many fear for their safety. As always, the bully is a menace. Even greater fear is caused by the presence of gangs and large numbers of students who bring weapons to school. Unfortunately, fear is a psychological state that inhibits learning.

Because students are afraid or find school disagreeable for other reasons, truancy is also a problem. Some students will not adjust to or abide by the rules and are therefore suspended or expelled. Clearly, such students cannot acquire a high-quality education. Sarah Ingersoll and Donni LeBoeuf provide details on the three issues of fear, truancy, and suspension or expulsion. The authors also note that these obstacles to education are more likely to hamper minorities and that they contribute to other social problems. The authors also explore possible solutions.

Focus Questions

1. What creates a fearful atmosphere in schools?

2. Why are students truant?

3. What are the main reasons for suspending or expelling students?

4. What can be done to deal with the problems of fear, truancy, and suspension or expulsion?

In many schools, crime and fear of crime are interfering with the education process. Students are concerned about crime in their neighborhoods and schools—with one in five African American and Hispanic teens indicating that crime or the threat of crime has caused him or her to stay home from school or cut class. The increase in disruptive and violent behaviors and weapons possession in schools has been accompanied by a proportionate increase in suspensions and expulsions.

The costs of these problems, both for children and for society, are prohibitively high. Children who are not educated will more than likely lack adequate skills to secure employment and become self-sufficient adults. In 1993 approximately 63 percent of high school dropouts were unemployed. When they are employed, high school dropouts are often on the low end of the pay scale without employee benefits or job security. Over their lifetimes, high school dropouts will earn significantly less than high school graduates and less than half of what college graduates are likely to make in their lifetimes. Similarly, dropouts experience more unemployment during their work careers and are more likely to end up on welfare. Many dropouts struggle to maintain a minimum standard of living, often requiring welfare system support. Indeed, individuals who do not receive a basic education must overcome tremendous barriers to achieve financial success in life or even meet their basic needs.

In addition to harming their chances of future success, children who are not attending school regularly or who drop out can pose significant problems for school administrators, police officers, juvenile court judges, probation officers, and the public. Many youth who are habitually truant and experience school failure are the same youth who bring weapons to school, bully or threaten their classmates, or regularly disrupt the school's learning environment. When they are not in school, truants and dropouts may be engaging in delinquent behavior. Research has demonstrated that youth who are not in school and not in the labor force are at high risk of delinquency and crime. In Milwaukee, for example, prior to the introduction of the

Truancy Abatement/Burglary Suppression Program (TABS), truants were responsible for a significant number of daytime violent crimes. With the inception of TABS, significant reductions occurred in the area of violent crime. In 1993–94, during scheduled school days, homicides were down 43 percent, sexual assaults were down 24 percent, aggravated assaults were down 24 percent, and robberies were down 16 percent. In 1994–95 daytime crime declined even further in all areas except homicide.

Society pays a high price for children's school failure. An estimated 34 percent of [prison] inmates in 1991 and 29 percent in 1986 had completed high school. In 1993, 17 percent of youth under age 18 entering adult prisons had not completed grade school (eighth grade or less). One-fourth had completed 10th grade, and 2 percent had completed high school or had a general equivalency diploma. Each year's class of dropouts costs the Nation more than $240 billion in lost earnings and foregone taxes over their lifetimes. Billions more will be spent on crime control (including law enforcement and prison programs), welfare, healthcare, and other social services. The staggering economic and social costs of providing for the increasing population of youth who are at risk of leaving or who have left the education mainstream are an intolerable drain on the resources of Federal, State, and local governments and the private sector.

Fearful Students

Problem Summary

Many students are genuinely afraid to attend school. In 1991 approximately 56 percent of juvenile victimization happened in school or on school property; 72 percent of personal thefts from juvenile victims occurred in school; and 23 percent of violent juvenile victimization occurred in school or on school property.

In a 1993 U.S. Department of Health and Human Services study, one in seven male students in grades 9 through 12 reported having carried a gun within the past 30 days. Another 1993 poll found this to be consistent across grades. Of 2,508 students surveyed

from 96 elementary, middle, and senior high schools nationwide, 15 percent reported they had carried a handgun on their person within the previous 30 days, 4 percent said that they had taken a handgun to school during the previous year, and 22 percent said that they felt safer having a handgun on their person if they were going to be in a physical confrontation. According to a report by the Center to Prevent Handgun Violence, in the 4 years between 1986 and 1990, there were 71 handgun-related deaths and 201 woundings at schools across the Nation.

Many students bring weapons to school because of the proliferation of gangs, drug activity, and other students carrying weapons. The upward trend of juvenile violence and victimization can create a climate of fear that pervades the school setting. Parents fear for their children's safety going to and from school, and children are often apprehensive at school from fear of bullying or threats of violence. In 1993 more than half of a nationally representative sample of 6th through 12th grade students were aware of incidents of bullying with 42 percent having witnessed bullying.

In a 1995 survey of 2,023 students in grades 7 through 12, almost half stated that they had changed their behavior as a result of crime or the threat of crime. For example, to protect themselves, one in eight has carried weapons, and one in nine has stayed home from school or cut class. Students in at-risk neighborhoods were four times as likely to have carried weapons, stayed home from school, or cut class to protect themselves. A 1993 survey by *USA Weekend*, based on mail-in responses of 65,193 students in grades 6 to 12, reported that 37 percent of students did not feel safe in school and 50 percent knew someone who switched schools to feel safer. Of those responding to the survey, 43 percent avoided school restrooms, 20 percent avoided school hallways, and 45 percent avoided school grounds in general.

Promising Approaches

Various types of partnerships between school officials and law enforcement officers have addressed the problem of youth who are afraid to leave their homes or go to school because of violence, bullying, or gang activities.

Improving the School Atmosphere. Some approaches focus on improvement in the school atmosphere by:

- Formulating school security plans and establishing school safety teams that involve students.
- Providing crime prevention training for students.
- Forging partnerships with community agencies that enhance school resources and activities.
- Increasing communication among teachers, students, and law enforcement officials.
- Organizing parent-student patrols and safe corridors.
- Legislating drug- and gun-free school zones.
- Sponsoring campuswide cleanups.
- Fostering parent involvement.
- Offering teachers school safety training.
- Creating schoolwide violence prevention curriculums.
- Establishing peer mediation and conflict resolution programs.

Responding to Perpetrators of Violence. Other programs respond to the perpetrators of violence and fear through curriculums that engage bullies, gang members, and violent students in learning anger management, conflict resolution, resistance to peer pressure, and appreciation of diversity. A number of communities have implemented victim/offender programs that require juvenile offenders to make restitution to victims for damage or losses incurred, or to perform community services. Others have established crisis intervention teams that help students cope with troubling violent incidents in and around school.

Many jurisdictions also focus on fear related to gang violence. They employ strategies that include teams of community volunteers, school officials, and youth-service providers. Working together, they conduct special outreach programs to juvenile gang members designed to reduce gang threats, recruitment, and revenge; remove gang graffiti in and near the school campus; control campus access; provide afterschool programs; and establish comprehensive dress codes or uniform policies that eliminate gang signs and colors from the school environment.

Targeting Weapons. These program strategies include antiweapon campaigns that increase student engagement with school officials, anonymous hotlines for reporting weapons and other criminal activity, school resource officers, locker searches, and clear school policies and discipline codes. The majority of weapon reduction programs involve curriculums that emphasize the prevention of weapon misuse, the risks involved with the possession of a firearm, and the need for learning conflict resolution and anger management skills. Programs often use videotapes showing the tragic results of gun violence and may also include firearm safety instruction, public information campaigns, counseling programs, partnerships with hospital emergency rooms, and crisis intervention hotlines.

Truants

Problem Summary

Across the Nation many children as young as elementary school age are staying away from school for a variety of reasons. Some are slow learners, some lack personal and educational goals because of an absence of academic challenge, some fear violence, and some have parents who are guilty of "educational neglect." With daily absentee rates as high as 30 percent in some cities, it is not surprising that truancy is listed among the major problems facing schools. The statistics speak volumes:

- In New York City, the Nation's largest school system, about 150,000 of its 1 million public school students are absent on a typical day.
- The Los Angeles Unified School District, the Nation's second largest district, reports that an average of 62,000

students (10 percent of its enrollment) are out of school each day.

- In Detroit, 40 public school attendance officers investigated 66,440 chronic absenteeism complaints during the 1994–95 school year.

The impact of truancy extends beyond the loss of educational opportunity. Many police departments report that daytime crime rates are rising, in part because some students who are not in school are busy committing crimes such as burglaries, vandalizing cars, shoplifting, and scrawling graffiti on signs and office buildings. When police in Van Nuys, California, conducted a 3-week-long school truancy sweep, shoplifting arrests fell 60 percent. Police in St. Paul, Minnesota, reported that crimes such as purse snatching dropped almost 50 percent after police began picking up truants and taking them to a new school attendance center.

Truancy has become such a significant problem that some cities are now passing ordinances allowing police to issue a citation to either the parent or the truant, which can result in a $500 fine or 30 days in jail for the parent and suspension of the youth's license to drive. In addition to fining parents, courts can order them to attend parenting classes and hold them in contempt of court. In some cases the court may take a child away from a parent and make the child a ward of the court.

Promising Approaches

Team Approaches. Schools are joining with district attorneys' offices and law enforcement, social services, and community agencies in their attempts to address truancy. This team approach focuses on both the parents and child. It determines what issues (educational, health, economic, psychological, behavioral) are contributing to the child's truancy. The team addresses the identified needs and gives a clear message on school attendance to the parents and the child. If these efforts do not result in regular school attendance, the team refers the case to the district attorney's office for a hearing. Reports indicate that in many instances this approach is working. In cases where truancy

persists, the district attorney's office will refer the student, the parents, or both to court. Court dispositions may include counseling on communication, conflict resolution education, parenting skills, and community service or a fine.

Truancy Centers. Centers dedicated to truancy reduction are being established across the country as a tool that school, law enforcement agencies, and community organizations can use to address their truancy problems. Boys and Girls Clubs and other youth-serving organizations are making their facilities available to schools to support truancy center programs. Jurisdictions are giving police officers authority to stop and question youth who are in the community during school hours. Police take those youth who do not have a legitimate excuse for being absent from school to a truancy center, where professionals assess the family situation to determine what family-based or other services may be needed and whether followup may be required. The center contacts the school and either releases the child to a parent or guardian or transfers the child to an alternative facility pending release. In order to return to school, the student must be accompanied by his or her parent or guardian.

Community Assessment Centers. Sometimes referred to as juvenile assessment centers, the community assessment center concept is being adopted by jurisdictions to comprehensively address the needs of at-risk and delinquent youth. Assessment centers combine the efforts of law enforcement with social service and mental health agencies to bring needed services to juveniles who commit first-time, minor, or status offenses, including truancy. Based on an assessment provided by a multidisciplinary team housed at the assessment center, services are provided in a timely and comprehensive manner. This comprehensive and immediate intervention is designed to help prevent repeat offending.

Alternative Schools

Many truants benefit from the smaller classes, higher teacher-to-student ratio, and more hands-on learning found in an alternative school setting.

Suspended and Expelled Students

Problem Summary

Weapons possession, substance abuse, disruptive behavior, assaults on school staff and students, and criminal acts committed outside school are five reasons schools are removing increasing numbers of students from the educational mainstream.

- Wisconsin schools expelled about 70 percent more students in 1993–94 than in the previous school year.

- By the end of the 1993–94 school year, Colorado's public schools recorded 65,547 suspensions, some students having been suspended more than once.

- One Oregon school district expelled nearly one student per day during the first 3 months of the 1994–95 school year after enacting a zero tolerance policy on weapons.

- During the 1993–94 academic year, a record 17,046 violent incidents plagued the New York City schools. More than 4,000 teachers were assaulted, and 725 weapons were confiscated.

- According to the New York Board of Education, 150 students were caught with firearms.

Under the Improving America's Schools Act, in order to receive Title I funds from the U.S. Department of Education, a State must have a law " . . . requiring local educational agencies to expel from school for a period of not less than one year a student who is determined to have brought a weapon to school," except that the local chief administrative officer may modify the expulsion requirement on a case-by-case basis. As a result, school districts are increasingly ordering 1-year expulsions for students who bring weapons to school, spawning a large number of students ranging from elementary to high school age who must be dealt with in alternative schools, in the juvenile justice system, or on the streets. Schools and communities must face the problem of how suspended and expelled students can continue to receive an education and what kind of academic setting should be provided for them.

Promising Approaches

In-School Suspensions. Typically, disruptive students are suspended from school and placed under parental supervision for the duration of their out-of-school suspension. Students, however, often lack oversight due to parents' work schedules, repeat the same disruptive behaviors in the home and community, and miss homework assignments. Schools also lose Average Daily Attendance income. These factors created the need to alter the out-of-school suspension policy for many school districts. They concluded that disruptive students need a structured environment to help them change their behavior while staying focused on their education. In-school suspensions are one answer these school districts have chosen to address the problem of disruptive student behavior. Students with chronic discipline problems are removed from their regular classroom and placed in a highly structured environment, generally with no more than 15 students, for a specified period of time. These in-school suspension programs provide academic and counseling components, including a range of individually designed learning modules and computer tutorial programs developed to promote success in the classroom; a counseling program based on an assessment of identified needs; an interpersonal training program to develop coping and communication skills; and conflict resolution and law-related education programs. A community service component is included in many programs to help build self-esteem through helping the less fortunate while developing socially acceptable behaviors and attitudes.

Alternative Schools. Many school districts have chosen alternative schools to provide academic instruction to students expelled for such offenses as weapons possession; suspended from their regular school for a variety of reasons, including disruptive behavior; or unable to succeed in the mainstream school environment. Alternative schools come in all sizes and settings, from space in a large department store, community center, or empty office building to a portable structure. More important than location is what alternative schools offer these troubled youth. For many, an alternative school presents and reinforces the message that students are accountable for their actions. At the alternative school, they receive an assessment of their academic and social abilities and skills, are assigned to a program that allows them to succeed while challenging them to reach higher goals, and receive assistance through small group and individualized instruction and counseling sessions. In addition, students and their families may receive an assessment to determine if social services such as healthcare, parenting classes, and other program services are indicated.

To help students return to their regular schools, alternative schools develop individualized student plans. For many students, however, returning to a setting where they failed is not an attractive option. Many students want to remain in the alternative school, and some school districts permit this. Often, those who do remain in the alternative school are allowed to graduate with their mainstream school classmates. Alternative schools that succeed with this population of youth typically have the following elements:

- Strong leadership
- Lower student-to-staff ratio
- Carefully selected personnel
- Early identification of student risk factors and problem behaviors

- Intensive counseling/mentoring
- Prosocial skills training
- Strict behavior requirements
- Curriculum based on real life learning
- Emphasis on parental involvement
- Districtwide support of the programs

Many alternative schools also have a strong community service component that helps students recognize their responsibility to their community and others while gaining self-esteem for their contributions.

Critical Evaluation

1. Data on such things as threats in schools are based on surveys of students. Are their perceptions accurate? Could the threat be less than they believe? Could it be more?

2. How many of the authors' "promising approaches" to dealing with the problems are realistic or practical?

3. What are other ways to deal with the threats, truancy, and behavior that leads to suspension or expulsion?

Sarah Ingersoll and Donni LeBoeuf, "The Fearful, the Truant, and the Suspended/Expelled." U.S. Department of Justice, *Juvenile Justice Bulletin*, February 1997. ✦

9

The Computer Delusion

Todd Oppenheimer

Americans have always had a great deal of faith in money and technology. Given sufficient money and the best technology, many believe, any problem can be solved. In fact, one of the points made in the evaluation by Education Week (Chapter 7) was the need for full use of technology in addressing deficiencies. It is understandable that in the computer age, many assume that the school with the most advanced computer systems would offer the best education. But is the computer the essential answer to improved educational quality?

Todd Oppenheimer presents evidence that increasing the use of computers has mixed results. Yet, because of people's belief in the value of and need for computers combined with corporate gifts of computer systems to schools, other aspects of education continue to be pushed aside and even eliminated.

Focus Questions

1. What arguments are advanced by those who promote the use of computers in schools?

2. What are some of the negative outcomes of computer usage?

3. What is meant by a "hypertext mind?"

4. What does the author set forth as a solution to the problems he notes?

In 1922 Thomas Edison predicted that "the motion picture is destined to revolutionize our educational system and . . . in a few years it will supplant largely, if not entirely, the use of textbooks." Twenty-three years later, in 1945, William Levenson, the director of the Cleveland public schools' radio station, claimed that "the time may come when a portable radio receiver will be as common in the classroom as is the blackboard." Forty years after that the noted psychologist B. F. Skinner, referring to the first days of his "teaching machines," in the late 1950s and early 1960s, wrote, "I was soon saying that, with the help of teaching machines and programmed instruction, students could learn twice as much in the same time and with the same effort as in a standard classroom." Ten years after Skinner's recollections were published, President Bill Clinton campaigned for "a bridge to the twenty-first century . . . where computers are as much a part of the classroom as blackboards." Clinton was not alone in his enthusiasm for a program estimated to cost somewhere between $40 billion and $100 billion over the next five years. Speaker of the House Newt Gingrich, talking about computers to the Republican National Committee early this year, said, "We could do so much to make education available twenty-four hours a day, seven days a week, that people could literally have a whole different attitude toward learning."

If history really is repeating itself, the schools are in serious trouble. In *Teachers and Machines: The Classroom Use of Technology Since 1920* (1986), Larry Cuban, a professor of education at Stanford University and a former school superintendent, observed that as successive rounds of new technology failed their promoters' expectations, a pattern emerged. The cycle began with big promises backed by the technology developers' research. In the classroom, however, teachers never really embraced the new tools, and no significant academic improvement occurred. This provoked consistent responses: the problem was money, spokespeople argued, or teacher resistance, or the paralyzing school bureaucracy. Meanwhile, few people questioned the technology advocates' claims. As results continued to lag, the blame was finally laid on the machines. Soon schools were sold on the next generation of technology, and the lucrative cycle started all over again.

Today's technology evangels argue that we've learned our lesson from past mistakes. As in each previous round, they say that when our new hot technology—the computer—is compared with yesterday's, today's is better. "It can do the same things, plus," Richard Riley, the U.S. Secretary of Education, told me this spring.

How much better is it, really?

The promoters of computers in schools again offer prodigious research showing improved academic achievement after using their technology. The research has again come under occasional attack, but this time quite a number of teachers seem to be backing classroom technology. In a poll taken early last year U.S. teachers ranked computer skills and media technology as more "essential" than the study of European history, biology, chemistry, and physics; than dealing with social problems such as drugs and family breakdown; than learning practical job skills; and than reading modern American writers such as Steinbeck and Hemingway or classic ones such as Plato and Shakespeare.

In keeping with these views New Jersey cut state aid to a number of school districts this past year and then spent $10 million on classroom computers. In Union City, California, a single school district is spending $27 million to buy new gear for a mere eleven schools. The Kittridge Street Elementary School, in Los Angeles, killed its music program last year to hire a technology coordinator; in Mansfield, Massachusetts, administrators dropped proposed teaching positions in art, music, and physical education, and then spent $333,000 on computers; in one Virginia school the art room was turned into a computer laboratory. (Ironically, a half dozen preliminary studies recently suggested that music and art classes may build the physical size of a child's brain, and its powers for subjects such as language, math, science, and engineering—in one case far more than computer work did.) Meanwhile, months after a New Technology High School opened in Napa, California, where computers sit on every student's desk and all academic classes use computers, some students were complaining of headaches, sore eyes, and wrist pain.

Throughout the country, as spending on technology increases, school book purchases are stagnant. Shop classes, with their tradition of teaching children building skills with wood and metal, have been almost entirely replaced by new "technology education programs." In San Francisco only one public school still offers a full shop program—the lone vocational high school. "We get kids who don't know the difference between a screwdriver and a ball peen hammer," James Dahlman, the school's vocational-department chair, told me recently. "How are they going to make a career choice? Administrators are stuck in this mindset that all kids will go to a four-year college and become a doctor or a lawyer, and that's not true. I know some who went to college, graduated, and then had to go back to technical school to get a job." Last year the school superintendent in Great Neck, Long Island, proposed replacing elementary school shop classes with computer classes and training the shop teachers as computer coaches. Rather than being greeted with enthusiasm, the proposal provoked a backlash.

Interestingly, shop classes and field trips are two programs that the National Information Infrastructure Advisory Council, the Clinton Administration's technology task force, suggests reducing in order to shift resources into computers. But are these results what technology promoters really intend? "You need to apply common sense," Esther Dyson, president of EDventure Holdings and one of the task force's leading school advocates, told me recently. "Shop with a good teacher probably is worth more than computers with a lousy teacher. But if it's a poor program, this may provide a good excuse for cutting it. There will be a lot of trials and errors with this. And I don't know how to prevent those errors."

The issue, perhaps, is the magnitude of the errors. Alan Lesgold, a professor of psychology and the associate director of the Learning Research and Development Center at the University of Pittsburgh, calls the computer an "amplifier," because it encourages both enlightened study practices and thoughtless ones. There's a real risk, though, that the thoughtless practices will dominate, slowly dumbing down huge numbers of tomorrow's adults. As Sherry Turkle, a professor of the sociology of science at the Massachusetts Institute of Technology and a longtime observer of children's use of computers, told me, "The possibilities of using this thing poorly so out-weigh the chance of using it well, it makes people like us, who are fundamentally optimistic about computers, very reticent."

Perhaps the best way to separate fact from fantasy is to take supporters' claims about computerized learning one by one and compare them with the evidence in the academic literature and in the everyday experiences I have observed or heard about in a variety of classrooms.

Five main arguments underlie the campaign to computerize our nation's schools.

- Computers improve both teaching practices and student achievement.

- Computer literacy should be taught as early as possible; otherwise students will be left behind.

- To make tomorrow's work force competitive in an increasingly high-tech world, learning computer skills must be a priority.

- The technology programs which leverage support from the business community are badly needed today because schools are increasingly starved for funds.

- Work with computers—particularly using the Internet—brings students valuable connections with teachers, other schools and students, and a wide network of professionals around the globe. These connections spice the school day with a sense of real-world relevance, and broaden the educational community.

'The Filmstrips of the 1990s'

Clinton's vision of computerized classrooms arose partly out of the findings of the presidential task force—thirty-six leaders from industry, education, and several interest groups who have guided the Administration's push to get computers into the schools. The report of the task force, "Connecting K–12 Schools to the Information Superhighway" (produced by the consulting firm McKinsey & Co.), begins by citing numerous studies that have apparently proved that computers enhance student achievement significantly.

One "meta-analysis" (a study that reviews other studies—in this case 130 of them) reported that computers had improved performance in "a wide range of subjects, including language arts, math, social studies and science." Another found improved organization and focus in students' writing. A third cited twice the normal gains in math skills. Several schools boasted of greatly improved attendance.

Unfortunately, many of these studies are more anecdotal than conclusive. Some, including a giant, oft-cited meta-analysis of 254 studies, lack the necessary scientific controls to make solid conclusions possible. The circumstances are artificial and not easily repeated, results aren't statistically reliable, or, most frequently, the studies did not control for other influences, such as differences between teaching methods. This last factor is critical, because computerized learning inevitably forces teachers to adjust their style—only sometimes for the better. Some studies were industry-funded, and thus tended to publicize mostly positive findings. "The research is set up in a way to find benefits that aren't really there," Edward Miller, a former editor of the *Harvard Education Letter*, says. "Most knowledgeable people agree that most of the research isn't valid. It's so flawed it shouldn't even be called research. Essentially, it's just worthless." Once the faulty studies are weeded out, Miller says, the ones that remain "are inconclusive"—that is, they show no significant change in either direction. Even Esther Dyson admits the studies are undependable. "I don't think those studies amount to much either way," she says. "In this area there is little proof."

Why are solid conclusions so elusive? Look at Apple Computer's "Classrooms of Tomorrow," perhaps the most widely studied effort to teach using computer technology. In the early 1980s Apple shrewdly realized that donating computers to schools might help not only students but also company sales, as Apple's ubiquity in classrooms turned legions of families into Apple loyalists. Last year, after the San Jose *Mercury News* (published in Apple's Silicon Valley home) ran a series questioning the effectiveness of computers in schools, the paper printed an opinion-page response from Terry Crane, an Apple vice-president. "Instead of isolating students," Crane wrote, "technology actually encouraged them to collaborate more than in traditional classrooms. Students also learned to explore and represent information dynamically and creatively, communicate effectively about complex processes, become independent learners and self-starters and become more socially aware and confident."

Crane didn't mention that after a decade of effort and the donation of equipment worth more than $25 million to thirteen schools, there is scant evidence of greater student achievement. To be fair, educators on both sides of the computer debate acknowledge that today's tests of student achievement are shockingly crude. They're especially weak in measuring intangibles such as enthusiasm and self-motivation, which do seem evident in Apple's classrooms and other computer-rich schools. In any event, what is fun and what is educational may frequently be at odds. "Computers in classrooms are the filmstrips of the 1990s," Clifford Stoll, the author of *Silicon Snake Oil: Second Thoughts on the Information Highway* (1995), told *The New York Times* last year, recalling his own school days in the 1960s. "We loved them because we didn't have to think for an hour, teachers loved them because they didn't have to teach, and parents loved them because it showed their schools were high-tech. But no learning happened."

Stoll somewhat overstates the case—obviously, benefits can come from strengthening a student's motivation. Still, Apple's computers may bear less responsibility for that change than Crane suggests. In the beginning, when Apple did little more than dump computers in classrooms and homes, this produced no real results, according to Jane David, a consultant Apple hired to study its classroom initiative. Apple quickly learned that teachers needed to change their classroom approach to what is commonly called "project-oriented learning." This is an increasingly popular teaching method, in which students learn through doing and teachers act as facilitators or partners rather than as didacts. (Teachers sometimes refer to this approach, which arrived in classrooms

before computers did, as being "the guide on the side instead of the sage on the stage.") But what the students learned "had less to do with the computer and more to do with the teaching," David concluded. "If you took the computers out, there would still be good teaching there." This story is heard in school after school, including two impoverished schools—Clear View Elementary School, in southern California, and the Christopher Columbus middle school, in New Jersey—that the Clinton Administration has loudly celebrated for turning themselves around with computers. At Christopher Columbus, in fact, students' test scores rose before computers arrived, not afterward, because of relatively basic changes: longer class periods, new books, after-school programs, and greater emphasis on student projects and collaboration.

During recent visits to some San Francisco-area schools I could see what it takes for students to use computers properly, and why most don't.

On a bluff south of downtown San Francisco, in the middle of one of the city's lower-income neighborhoods, Claudia Schaffner, a tenth-grader, tapped away at a multimedia machine in a computer lab at Thurgood Marshall Academic High School, one of half a dozen special technology schools in the city. Schaffner was using a physics program to simulate the trajectory of a marble on a small roller coaster. "It helps to visualize it first, like 'A is for Apple' with kindergartners," Schaffner told me, while mousing up and down the virtual roller coaster. "I can see how the numbers go into action." This was lunch hour, and the students' excitement about what they can do in this lab was palpable. Schaffner could barely tear herself away. "I need to go eat some food," she finally said, returning within minutes to eat a rice dish at the keyboard.

Schaffner's teacher is Dennis Frezzo, an electrical engineering graduate from the University of California at Berkeley. Despite his considerable knowledge of computer programming, Frezzo tries to keep classwork focused on physical projects. For a mere $8,000, for example, several teachers put together a multifaceted robotics lab, consisting of an advanced Lego engineering kit and twenty-four old 386-generation computers. Frezzo's students used these materials to build a tiny electric car, whose motion was to be triggered by a light sensor. When the light sensor didn't work, the students figured out why. "That's a real problem—what you'd encounter in the real world," Frezzo told me. "I prefer they get stuck on small real-world problems instead of big fake problems"—like the simulated natural disasters that fill one popular educational game. "It's sort of the Zen approach to education," Frezzo said. "It's not the big problems. Isaac Newton already solved those. What come up in life are the little ones."

It's one thing to confront technology's complexity at a high school—especially one that's blessed with four different computer labs and some highly skilled teachers like Frezzo, who know enough, as he put it, "to keep computers in their place." It's quite another to grapple with a high-tech future in the lower grades, especially at everyday schools that lack special funding or technical support. As evidence, when *U.S. News & World Report* published a cover story last fall on schools that make computers work, five of the six were high schools—among them Thurgood Marshall. Although the sixth was an elementary school, the featured program involved children with disabilities —the one group that does show consistent benefits from computerized instruction.

Artificial Experience

Consider the scene at one elementary school, Sanchez, which sits on the edge of San Francisco's Latino community. For several years Sanchez, like many other schools, has made do with a roomful of basic Apple IIes. Last year, curious about what computers could do for youngsters, a local entrepreneur donated twenty costly Power Macintoshes— three for each of five classrooms, and one for each of the five lucky teachers to take home. The teachers who got the new machines were delighted. "It's the best thing we've ever done," Adela Najarro, a third-grade bilingual teacher, told me. She mentioned one boy, perhaps with a learning disability, who had

started to hate school. Once he had a computer to play with, she said, "his whole attitude changed." Najarro is now a true believer, even when it comes to children without disabilities. "Every single child," she said, "will do more work for you and do better work with a computer. Just because it's on a monitor, kids pay more attention. There's this magic to the screen."

Down the hall from Najarro's classroom her colleague Rose Marie Ortiz had a more troubled relationship with computers. On the morning I visited, Ortiz took her bilingual special-education class of second-, third-, and fourth-graders into the lab filled with the old Apple IIes. The students look forward to this weekly expedition so much that Ortiz gets exceptional behavior from them all morning. Out of date though these machines are, they do offer a range of exercises, in subjects such as science, math, reading, social studies, and problem solving. But owing to this group's learning problems and limited English skills, math drills were all that Ortiz could give them. Nonetheless, within minutes the kids were excitedly navigating their way around screens depicting floating airplanes and trucks carrying varying numbers of eggs. As the children struggled, many resorted to counting in whatever way they knew how. Some squinted at the screen, painstakingly moving their fingers from one tiny egg symbol to the next. "Tres, cuatro, cinco, seis . . . ," one little girl said loudly, trying to hear herself above her counting neighbors. Another girl kept a piece of paper handy, on which she marked a line for each egg. Several others resorted to the slow but tried and true—their fingers. Some just guessed. Once the children arrived at answers, they frantically typed them onto the screen, hoping it would advance to something fun, the way Nintendos, Game Boys, and video-arcade games do. Sometimes their answers were right, and the screen did advance; sometimes they weren't; but the children were rarely discouraged. As schoolwork goes, this was a blast.

"It's highly motivating for them," Ortiz said as she rushed from machine to machine, attending not to math questions but to computer glitches. Those she couldn't fix she simply abandoned. "I don't know how practical it is. You see," she said, pointing to a girl counting on her fingers, "these kids still need the hands-on"—meaning the opportunity to manipulate physical objects such as beans or colored blocks. The value of hands-on learning, child development experts believe, is that it deeply imprints knowledge into a young child's brain, by transmitting the lessons of experience through a variety of sensory pathways.

"Curiously enough," the educational psychologist Jane Healy wrote in *Endangered Minds: Why Children Don't Think and What We Can Do About It* (1990), "visual stimulation is probably not the main access route to nonverbal reasoning. Body movements, the ability to touch, feel, manipulate, and build sensory awareness of relationships in the physical world, are its main foundations." The problem, Healy wrote, is that "in schools, traditionally, the senses have had little status after kindergarten."

Ortiz believes that the computer-lab time, brief as it is, dilutes her students' attention to language. "These kids are all language-delayed," she said. Though only modest sums had so far been spent at her school, Ortiz and other local teachers felt that the push was on for technology over other scholastic priorities. The year before, Sanchez had let its librarian go, to be replaced by a part-timer.

When Ortiz finally got the students rounded up and out the door, the kids were still worked up. "They're never this wired after reading group," she said. "They're usually just exhausted, because I've been reading with them, making them write and talk." Back in homeroom Ortiz showed off the students' monthly hand-written writing samples. "Now, could you do that on the computer?" she asked. "No, because we'd be hung up on finding the keys." So why does Ortiz bother taking her students to the computer lab at all? "I guess I come in here for the computer literacy. If everyone else is getting it, I feel these kids should get it too."

Some computerized elementary school programs have avoided these pitfalls, but the record subject by subject is mixed at best. Take writing, where by all accounts and by my own observations the computer does en-

courage practice—changes are easier to make on a keyboard than with an eraser, and the lettering looks better. Diligent students use these conveniences to improve their writing, but the less committed frequently get seduced by electronic opportunities to make a school paper look snazzy. (The easy "cut and paste" function in today's word-processing programs, for example, is apparently encouraging many students to cobble together research materials without thinking them through.) Reading programs get particularly bad reviews. One small but carefully controlled study went so far as to claim that Reader Rabbit, a reading program now used in more than 100,000 schools, caused students to suffer a 50 percent drop in creativity. (Apparently, after forty-nine students used the program for seven months, they were no longer able to answer open-ended questions and showed a markedly diminished ability to brainstorm with fluency and originality.) What about hard sciences, which seem so well suited to computer study? Logo, the high-profile programming language refined by Seymour Papert and widely used in middle and high schools, fostered huge hopes of expanding children's cognitive skills. As students directed the computer to build things, such as geometric shapes, Papert believed, they would learn "procedural thinking," similar to the way a computer processes information. According to a number of studies, however, Logo has generally failed to deliver on its promises. Judah Schwartz, a professor of education at Harvard and a co-director of the school's Educational Technology Center, told me that a few newer applications, when used properly, can dramatically expand children's math and science thinking by giving them new tools to "make and explore conjectures." Still, Schwartz acknowledges that perhaps "ninety-nine percent" of the educational programs are "terrible, really terrible."

Even in success stories important caveats continually pop up. The best educational software is usually complex—most suited to older students and sophisticated teachers. In other cases the schools have been blessed with abundance—fancy equipment, generous financial support, or extra teachers—that is difficult if not impossible to duplicate in the average school. Even if it could be duplicated, the literature suggests, many teachers would still struggle with technology. Computers suffer frequent breakdowns; when they do work, their seductive images often distract students from the lessons at hand—which many teachers say makes it difficult to build meaningful rapport with their students.

'Hypertext Minds'

Today's parents, knowing firsthand how families were burned by television's false promises, may want some objective advice about the age at which their children should become computer literate. Although there are no real guidelines, computer boosters send continual messages that if children don't begin early, they'll be left behind. Linda Roberts [technology adviser in the Department of Education] thinks that there's no particular minimum age—and no maximum number of hours that children should spend at a terminal. Are there examples of excess? "I haven't seen it yet," Roberts told me with a laugh. In schools throughout the country administrators and teachers demonstrate the same excitement, boasting about the wondrous things that children of five or six can do on computers: drawing, typing, playing with elementary science simulations and other programs called "educational games."

The schools' enthusiasm for these activities is not universally shared by specialists in childhood development. The doubters' greatest concern is for the very young—preschool through third grade, when a child is most impressionable. Their apprehension involves two main issues.

First, they consider it important to give children a broad base—emotionally, intellectually, and in the five senses—before introducing something as technical and one-dimensional as a computer. Second, they believe that the human and physical world holds greater learning potential.

The importance of a broad base for a child may be most apparent when it's missing. In *Endangered Minds*, Jane Healy wrote of an English teacher who could readily tell which of her students' essays were conceived on a computer. "They don't link ideas," the teacher says. "They just write one thing, and then they write another one, and they don't seem to see or develop the relationships between them." The problem, Healy argued, is that the pizzazz of computerized schoolwork may hide these analytical gaps, which "won't become apparent until [the student] can't organize herself around a homework assignment or a job that requires initiative. More commonplace activities, such as figuring out how to nail two boards together, organizing a game . . . may actually form a better basis for real-world intelligence."

Others believe they have seen computer games expand children's imaginations. High-tech children "think differently from the rest of us," William D. Winn, the director of the Learning Center at the University of Washington's Human Interface Technology Laboratory, told *Business Week* in a recent cover story on the benefits of computer games. "They develop hypertext minds. They leap around. It's as though their cognitive strategies were parallel, not sequential." Healy argues the opposite. She and other psychologists think that the computer screen flattens information into narrow, sequential data. This kind of material, they believe, exercises mostly one half of the brain—the left hemisphere, where primarily sequential thinking occurs. The "right brain" meanwhile gets short shrift—yet this is the hemisphere that works on different kinds of information simultaneously. It shapes our multi-faceted impressions, and serves as the engine of creative analysis.

Opinions diverge in part because research on the brain is still so sketchy, and computers are so new, that the effect of computers on the brain remains a great mystery. "I don't think we know anything about it," Harry Chugani, a pediatric neurobiologist at Wayne State University, told me. This very ignorance makes skeptics wary. "Nobody knows how kids' internal wiring works," Clifford Stoll wrote in *Silicon Snake Oil*, "but anyone who's directed away from social interactions has a head start on turning out weird. . . . No computer can teach what a walk through a pine forest feels like. Sensation has no substitute."

This points to the conservative developmentalists' second concern: the danger that even if hours in front of the screen are limited, unabashed enthusiasm for the computer sends the wrong message: that the mediated world is more significant than the real one. "It's like TV commercials," Barbara Scales, the head teacher at the Child Study Center at the University of California at Berkeley, told me. "Kids get so hyped up, it can change their expectations about stimulation, versus what they generate themselves." In *Silicon Snake Oil*, Michael Fellows, a computer scientist at the University of Victoria, in British Columbia, was even blunter. "Most schools would probably be better off if they threw their computers into the Dumpster."

Faced with such sharply contrasting viewpoints, which are based on such uncertain ground, how is a responsible policymaker to proceed? "A prudent society controls its own infatuation with 'progress' when planning for its young," Healy argued in *Endangered Minds*.

> Unproven technologies . . . may offer lively visions, but they can also be detrimental to the development of the young plastic brain. The cerebral cortex is a wondrously well-buffered mechanism that can withstand a good bit of well-intentioned bungling. Yet there is a point at which fundamental neural substrates for reasoning may be jeopardized for children who lack proper physical, intellectual, or emotional nurturance. Childhood—and the brain—have their own imperatives. In development, missed opportunities may be difficult to recapture.

The problem is that technology leaders rarely include these or other warnings in their recommendations. When I asked Dyson why the Clinton task force proceeded with such fervor, despite the classroom computer's shortcomings, she said, "It's so clear the world is changing."

Real Job Training

In the past decade, according to the presidential task force's report, the number of jobs requiring computer skills has increased from 25 percent of all jobs in 1983 to 47 percent in 1993. By 2000, the report estimates, 60 percent of the nation's jobs will demand these skills—and pay an average of 10 to 15 percent more than jobs involving no computer work. Although projections of this sort are far from reliable, it's a safe bet that computer skills will be needed for a growing proportion of tomorrow's work force. But what priority should these skills be given among other studies?

Listen to Tom Henning, a physics teacher at Thurgood Marshall, the San Francisco technology high school. Henning has a graduate degree in engineering, and helped to found a Silicon Valley company that manufactures electronic navigation equipment. "My bias is the physical reality," Henning told me, as we sat outside a shop where he was helping students to rebuild an old motorcycle. "I'm no technophobe. I can program computers." What worries Henning is that computers at best engage only two senses, hearing and sight—and only two-dimensional sight at that. "Even if they're doing three-dimensional computer modeling, that's still a two-D replica of a three-D world. If you took a kid who grew up on Nintendo, he's not going to have the necessary skills. He needs to have done it first with Tinkertoys or clay, or carved it out of balsa wood." As David Elkind, a professor of child development at Tufts University, puts it, "A dean of the University of Iowa's school of engineering used to say the best engineers were the farm boys," because they knew how machinery really worked.

Surely many employers will disagree, and welcome the commercially applicable computer skills that today's high-tech training can bring them. What's striking is how easy it is to find other employers who share Henning's and Elkind's concerns.

Kris Meisling, a senior geological-research adviser for Mobil Oil, told me that "people who use computers a lot slowly grow rusty in their ability to think." Meisling's group creates charts and maps—some computerized, some not—to plot where to drill for oil. In large one-dimensional analyses, such as sorting volumes of seismic data, the computer saves vast amounts of time, sometimes making previously impossible tasks easy. This lures people in his field, Meisling believes, into using computers as much as possible.

But when geologists turn to computers for "interpretive" projects, he finds, they often miss information, and their oversights are further obscured by the computer's captivating automatic design functions. This is why Meisling still works regularly with a pencil and paper—tools that, ironically, he considers more interactive than the computer, because they force him to think implications through.

"You can't simultaneously get an overview and detail with a computer," he says. "It's linear. It gives you tunnel vision. What computers can do well is what can be calculated over and over. What they can't do is innovation. If you think of some new way to do or look at things and the software can't do it, you're stuck. So a lot of people think, 'Well, I guess it's a dumb idea, or it's unnecessary.'"

I have heard similar warnings from people in other businesses, including high-tech enterprises. A spokeswoman for Hewlett-Packard, the giant computer-products company, told me the company rarely hires people who are predominantly computer experts, favoring instead those who have a talent for teamwork and are flexible and innovative. Hewlett-Packard is such a believer in hands-on experience that since 1992 it has spent $2.6 million helping forty-five school districts build math and science skills the old-fashioned way—using real materials, such as dirt, seeds, water, glass vials, and magnets. Much the same perspective came from several recruiters in film and computer-game animation. In work by artists who have spent a lot of time on computers "you'll see a stiffness or a flatness, a lack of richness and depth," Karen Chelini, the director of human resources for LucasArts Entertainment, George Lucas's interactive-games maker, told me recently. "With traditional art training, you train the eye to pay attention to body movement. You learn attitude, feeling, expression. The ones who are good are those who as kids couldn't be without their sketchbook."

Many jobs obviously will demand basic computer skills if not sophisticated knowledge. But that doesn't mean that the parents or the teachers of young students need to panic. Joseph Weizenbaum, a professor emeritus of computer science at MIT, told the San Jose *Mercury News* that even at his technology-heavy institution new students can learn all the computer skills they need "in a summer." This seems to hold in the business world, too. Patrick MacLeamy, an executive vice-president of Hellmuth Obata & Kassabaum, the country's largest architecture firm, recently gave me numerous examples to illustrate that computers pose no threat to his company's creative work. Although architecture professors are divided on the value of computerized design tools, in MacLeamy's opinion they generally enhance the process. But he still considers "knowledge of the hands" to be valuable—today's architects just have to develop it in other ways. (His firm's answer is through building models.) Nonetheless, as positive as MacLeamy is about computers, he has found the company's two-week computer training to be sufficient. In fact, when he's hiring, computer skills don't enter into his list of priorities. He looks for a strong character; an ability to speak, write, and comprehend; and a rich education in the history of architecture.

Just a Glamorous Tool

It would be easy to characterize the battle over computers as merely another chapter in the world's oldest story: humanity's natural resistance to change. But that does an injustice to the forces at work in this transformation. This is not just the future versus the past, uncertainty versus nostalgia; it is about encouraging a fundamental shift in personal priorities—a minimizing of the real, physical world in favor of an unreal "virtual" world. It is about teaching youngsters that exploring what's on a two-dimensional screen is more important than playing with real objects, or sitting down to an attentive conversation with a friend, a parent, or a teacher. By extension, it means downplaying the importance of conversation, of careful listening, and of expressing oneself in person with acuity and individuality. In the process, it may also limit the development of children's imaginations.

Perhaps this is why Steven Jobs, one of the founders of Apple Computer and a man who claims to have "spearheaded giving away more computer equipment to schools than anybody else on the planet," has come to a grim conclusion: "What's wrong with education cannot be fixed with technology," he told *Wired* magazine last year. "No amount of technology will make a dent. . . . You're not going to solve the problems by putting all knowledge onto CD-ROMS. We can put a Web site in every school— none of this is bad. It's bad only if it lulls us into thinking we're doing something to solve the problem with education." Jane David, the consultant to Apple, concurs, with a commonly heard caveat. "There are real dangers," she told me, "in looking to technology to be the savior of education. But it won't survive without the technology.". . . .

The solution is not to ban computers from classrooms altogether. But it may be to ban federal spending on what is fast becoming an overheated campaign. After all, the private sector, with its constant supply of used computers and the computer industry's vigorous competition for new customers, seems well equipped to handle the situation. In fact, if schools can impose some limits—on technology donors and on themselves— rather than indulging in a consumer frenzy, most will probably find themselves with more electronic gear than they need. That could free the billions that Clinton wants to devote to technology and make it available for impoverished fundamentals: teaching solid skills in reading, thinking, listening, and talking; organizing inventive field trips and other rich hands-on experiences; and, of course, build-ing up the nation's core of knowledgeable, inspiring teachers. These notions are considerably less glamorous than computers are, but their worth is firmly proved through a long history.

Last fall, after the school administrators in Mansfield, Massachusetts, had eliminated proposed art, music, and physical education positions in favor of buying computers, Michael Bellino, an electrical engineer at Boston University's Center for Space Physics, appeared before the Massachusetts Board of Education to protest. "The purpose of the schools [is] to, as one teacher argues, 'Teach carpentry, not hammer,' " he testified. "We need to teach the whys and ways of the world. Tools come and tools go. Teaching our children tools limits their knowledge to these tools and hence limits their futures."

Critical Evaluation

1. What evidence does Oppenheimer use? Is it sufficient evidence for the conclusions he reaches?

2. If one concedes that the negative outcomes cited by Oppenheimer generally occur, do they outweigh the benefits of computer usage? Why or why not?

3. Could the effects of computer usage that the author discusses vary by the type of student? How?

Todd Oppenheimer, "The Computer Delusion." In *The Atlantic Monthly* July 1997. Copyright © 1997 by Todd Oppenheimer. Reprinted by permission. ✦

10

School Vouchers—Panacea or Pandora's Box?

Joseph S. C. Simplicio

Negative attitudes about the quality of public education (that it is too low) and the content (that it lacks values or contradicts existing values) have led to calls for a system of school vouchers. These would allow parents to send their children to private schools. Among the benefits of a voucher system, according to proponents, are higher academic performance, increased parental involvement, greater student interest in education, and better use of tax monies. In addition, they argue that competition from private schools will force public schools to improve the quality of education.

Whether a voucher system will ultimately be adopted depends upon both macrofactors (government action) and microfactors (attitudes of the public). As of this writing, advocates and opponents of a voucher system are both trying to gain public and governmental support. Joseph Simplicio points out that advocates of the system make a number of assumptions, each of which is questionable in the light of the evidence. In fact, he notes, it is possible that a voucher system would mainly benefit those who are already obtaining better education for their children.

Focus Questions

1. What is a school voucher?

2. What are the assumptions made by advocates of a voucher system?

3. How does the author respond to these assumptions?

On the surface the concept of a voucher system appears ideal. It seems to offer a unique opportunity for parents to become directly involved in their children's education at an important decision level basis. As Ogawa and Dutton (1994) point out, the process in itself appears deceptively quite simple. Parents looking at both public and private educational options simply select the school whose curricula best meet the needs of their child. With no district boundaries to worry about and with monies provided by the school district parents are freed from monetary constraints.

It all seems quite ideal. The possibilities for educational reform and student growth seem unlimited. No longer will children from small privately funded schools have an advantage over students housed in large publicly run school systems. Now that all children have the opportunity to attend either public or private institutions the playing field will be made more equal. Unfortunately, this is not necessarily true. Although there have been isolated attempts to introduce the voucher system into select school systems, as Witte (1990) has pointed out, there has been no real large scale voucher movement enacted that has involved both public and private schools. In fact, historically, such attempts have met with failure. For example, both Colorado, in 1992, and California, in 1993 defeated just such initiatives.

In addition, for the voucher system to be truly effective certain major assumptions must be validated. Paramount among these is the belief that parents will actively make informed choices concerning their children's educational options. The literature, however, does not support such a contention. In fact, studies suggest that only parents with certain characteristics will make any choices at all. One such characteristic is the tendency to be among the better educated in the district. A detailed study involving a large district in Alum Rock, California bears this out. The researchers, Bridge and Blackman (1978), discovered that despite the district's attempt to disseminate information equally, the better educated parents within the district were more informed regarding the options offered by the voucher plan and were able to obtain more detailed information through a wider array of sources. In another study conducted by Nault and Uchitelle (1982) it was again determined that parents with lower educational levels were less knowledgeable about options and alternatives offered by a local choice plan.

The findings of these two studies were consistent with data gathered from the Milwaukee Public Schools' Parental Choice Program which allowed low income families to send their children to private schools at public expense. Here the researchers discovered that those parents who chose to avail themselves of this option were the better educated in the district (Witte, 1991; Witte, Bailey & Thorn, 1992). In fact, a national survey aimed at determining how a federally funded tuition plan might affect parental choices discovered that the more affluent and better educated parents were significantly more likely to become actively involved in school choice plans (Williams, Hancher, & Hunter, 1983).

Studies have also indicated that another important shared characteristic among parents who are more likely to opt for a voucher plan is an overall dissatisfaction with the current education their children are receiving. For example, a Minnesota study which focused in on predominately Caucasian, fairly affluent, and largely Protestant parents discovered just such a significant school dissatisfaction rate among those parents who actively participated in the choice option available to them through their local school districts (Darling-Hammond & Kirby, 1985). Data gathered from a Montgomery County, Maryland survey supported this fact by showing that parents there who chose to transfer their children to other schools held high levels of dissatisfaction with the education their children were receiving (Frechtling & Frankel, 1982).

With knowledge of such data it is hard then to justify the basic premise that the majority of parents are informed enough to make crucial decisions regarding their children's education. In fact, the evidence shows quite clearly that many will choose to make no decision at all, thus dooming their children to be left behind in inferior schools (Moore & Davenport, 1988).

A second major assumption regarding the voucher system is predicated upon the belief that more parental choice will inevitably result in school systems that are more responsive to parental preferences and student needs. This will be accomplished by providing more innovative curricula and instruction. Once again though, the data do not support such an assumption. Kemerer and King (1995) noted that 85% of all private schools are religiously affiliated. Such schools are innately very conservative regarding their curricula choices and instructional methodologies. Concurring, a RAND corporation study looking at a California intradistrict public school choice program also concluded that the voucher system did not generate any truly major educational alternatives within the district (Barker, Bikson, & Kimbrough, 1981).

A third major assumption regarding a viable voucher system is the belief that school districts will mandate the necessary funds to allow parental choice. Here, though, voucher systems face quite significant opposition to any such redistribution of public funds. This challenge comes from critics who attack the very constitutionality of any such plan.

Looking to the courts for guidance in this matter reveals the judicial system's apparent ambiguity regarding the subject. Rulings have been inconsistent. In Wisconsin for example, the Supreme Court there refused to allow a public voucher plan to be expanded to include private schools. Basing their decisions on state constitutional restrictions, other courts in Massachusetts, New Hampshire, Washington, and Puerto Rico, have also dealt severe setbacks to voucher plans which would channel public funds into private institutions of learning. However, in 1994 a case brought before the Vermont Supreme Court, which was argued on the basis of federal rather than state law, resulted in a ruling by that court that a voucher system, which would require public reimbursement of up to 75% to parents of students attending private schools, did not violate the First Amendment establishment clause of the United States Constitution.

It is also quite apparent then that the legality of a voucher system pivots on several factors including the wording of its provisions, variations in the design of the program, the jurisdictional basis of the law, and judicial preferences. All of these can impact upon a court's decision. Other factors can play prominent roles as well. Plans, for example, that would funnel money directly into schools are more constitutionally vulnerable than those which establish a scholarship system distributing monies to the parents first. This premise was reinforced by a recent 1983 United State Supreme Court ruling in the case Mueller & Allen. In this case the court, by a slim 5 to 4 margin, upheld a Minnesota law that allowed parents to claim tax deductions for tuition, textbook, and transportation expenses for children in private schools. The lesson here is clear. With the absence of a clear-cut mandate from the courts, advocates of the voucher system are forced to proceed with extreme caution.

Finally, one last important assumption concerning vouchers claims that the system provides better opportunities for student interactions and more exposure to diverse cultural groups bears closer scrutiny. Critics such as Maria Montecel, executive director of the Texas-based Intercultural Development Research Association in San Antonio, disagree. She contends that minimally funded voucher systems will not provide all students with access into better schools. The result in her opinion will be the creation in essence of a two-tiered system of education.

I tend to agree. I believe that the system would simply subsidize parents who could already afford private school education. In addition, I do not believe vouchers would provide expanded opportunities for all students, including those who would not normally be able to afford such institutions, nor would they guarantee a more diverse student population. Private schools could simply adjust tuition rates upward to ensure exclusion. As a result private school parents, their children, and the schools would benefit from additional state financial support while those students whose education the funds were designed to enhance would accrue no measurable benefit. . . .

References

Baker, P., Bikson, T., & Kimbrough, J. (1981). *A study of alternatives in American education. Vol. V. Diversity in the classroom.* Santa Monica, CA: RAND.

Bridge, R., & Blackman, J. (1978). *A study of alternatives in American education. Vol. IV. Family choice in schooling.* Santa Monica, CA: RAND.

Darling-Hammond, L., & Kirby, S. (1985). *Tuition tax deductions and parent school choice: A case study of Minnesota.* Santa Monica, CA: RAND.

Frechtling, J., Frankel, S. (1982). *A survey of Montgomery County parents who transferred their children between public and private schools in 1980-81.* Rockville, MD: Montgomery County Public Schools.

Kemerer, F., & King, K. (1995). Are school vouchers constitutional? *Kappan,* 77 (4), 307-311.

Moore, D., & Davenport, S. (1988). *The new improved sorting machine.* Chicago: Designs for Change.

Nault, R., & Uchitelle, S. (1982). School choice in the public sector: A case study of parental decision making. In M.E. Manley-Casimer (Ed.), *Family choice in schooling* (pp. 85-98). Lexington, MA: Lexington Books.

Ogawa, R., & Dutton, J. (1994). Parental choice in education. *Urban Education,* 29 (3), 270-295.

Williams, M., Hancher, K., & Hunter, A. (1983). *Parents and school choice: A household survey.* Washington, DC: Office of Educational Research and Improvement.

Witte, J. (1990). *Choice in American education.* Madison: University of Wisconsin-Madison, Robert LaFollette Institute of Public Affairs.

——. (1991). *First year report: Milwaukee parental choice program.* Madison: University of Wisconsin-Madison, Robert LaFollette Institute of Public Affairs.

Witte, J., Bailey, A., & Thorn, C. (1992). *Second year report; Milwaukee parental choice program.* Madison: University of Wisconsin-Madison, Robert LaFollette Institute of Public Affairs.

Critical Evaluation

1. How would an advocate of the voucher system respond to this chapter?

2. What evidence does Simplicio offer for his assertions? Is the evidence adequate for the conclusions he draws?

3. Many arguments become an either-or proposition: e.g., either for the existing system or for a voucher system. Are there other possibilities that might satisfy both sides? What are they?

Joseph S. C. Simplicio, "School Vouchers—Pandora's Box?" In *Education* 117, Winter 1996, pp. 213-216. Copyright © 1996 by *Education.* Reprinted by permission. ✦

Project for Personal Application and Class Discussion: Education

The readings in this section have dealt with the quality of education, the climate for learning, the role of technology, and an effort to assure equal opportunity in high-quality education.

1. How would you rate the quality of the education you have received? Grade your education, from A to F, in terms of quality of teaching, school climate, and resources. Then give an overall grade for each level (elementary, junior high, high school, and college).

2. Briefly explain your grades.

3. How does your education compare with the overall assessment offered by *Education Week* in Chapter 7? Has your education been below average, average, or above average? Why? ✦

The Family

Most Americans expect the family to be, as one historian put it, a "haven in a heartless world." In other words, we expect the family to be a refuge from trouble and a source of nurture and support. Yet for many people, the family is the source of intense trauma and severe struggle. This section looks at three troublesome aspects of family life: the division of labor in the home, divorce, and domestic violence. Troubled family life also figures prominently in a number of other problems dealt with in this book. The conclusion is that those who do not have a warm, supportive family are far more likely than others to engage in various kinds of deviant behavior. ✦

11

Who's Minding the Baby?

Susan Walzer

Many social scientists have pointed out that men's and women's experiences of marriage are very different. Nowhere is this difference more vividly illustrated than in work around the home. Husbands have assumed some additional household duties in recent years, primarily in the area of child care (Spain and Bianchi 1996). Nevertheless, surveys show that women—including those who are employed full time outside the home—still perform a disproportionate share of the household work. When women define this arrangement as unfair, marital dissatisfaction and conflict are likely (Stohs 1995).

In her research on baby care, Susan Walzer shows how this inequity creates tension. She notes a strong structural factor that produces inequity—social norms that dictate who should do what around the home. People develop attitudes that support the norms and perpetuate the inequity.

References

Spain, Daphne and Suzanne M. Bianchi. 1996. *Balancing Act: Motherhood, Marriage, and Employment Among American Women*. New York: Russell Sage Foundation.

Stohs, Joanne Hoven. 1995. "Predictors of Conflict Over the Household Division of Labor Among Women Employed Full-time." *Sex Roles* 33: 257-276.

Focus Questions

1. What is "mental labor?"

2. What are the various kinds of mental labor associated with caring for a baby?

3. How does mental baby care affect the marital relationship?

The tendency for women and men to become more differentiated from each other in work and family roles upon becoming parents has been documented in longitudinal studies of transitions into parenthood (see summaries in Belsky and Kelly 1994; Cowan and Cowan 1992). New mothers are more apt than new fathers to leave or curtail their employment (Belsky and Kelly 1994). And despite couples' previous intentions (Cowan and Cowan 1992), mothers provide more direct care to babies than fathers do (Belsky and Volling 1987; Berman and Pedersen 1987; Dickie 1987; Thompson and Walker 1989). Fathers tend to act as "helpers" to mothers, who not only spend more time interacting with babies, but planning for them as well (LaRossa 1986).

This pattern of increased gender differentiation following the birth of a baby has been associated with decreases in marital satisfaction, particularly for wives (Belsky, Lang, and Huston 1986; Cowan and Cowan 1988; Harriman 1985; Ruble et al. 1988). A number of researchers have interpreted new mothers' marital dissatisfaction as connected with "violated expectations" of more shared parenting (Belsky 1985; Belsky, Lang, and Huston 1986; Ruble et al. 1988), although some researchers express surprise that wives expect so much in the first place (Ruble et al. 1988). Nevertheless, traditional divisions of household labor have been implicated in marital stress following the birth of a first baby (Belsky, Lang, and Huston 1986; Schuchts and Witkin 1989).

In this paper I focus on the more invisible, mental labor that is involved in taking care of a baby and suggest that gender imbalances in this form of baby care play a particular role in reproducing differentiation between mothers and fathers and stimulating marital tension. My use of the term "mental" labor is meant to distinguish the thinking, feeling, and interpersonal work that accompanies the care of babies from physical tasks, as has been done in recent studies of household labor (see, e.g., Hochschild 1989; DeVault 1991; Mederer 1993). I include in the general category of mental labor what has been referred to as "emotion" work, "thought" work, and "invisible" work (Hochschild 1983;

DeVault 1991); that is, I focus on aspects of baby care that involve thinking or feeling, managing thoughts or feelings, and that are not necessarily perceived as work by the person performing it (DeVault 1991).

Using qualitative data from interviews with 50 new mothers and fathers (25 couples), this paper describes three categories of mental baby care and suggests that the tendency for mothers to take responsibility for this kind of work is an underrecognized stress on marriages as well as a primary way in which mothering and fathering are reproduced as gendered experiences. While the tendency for mothers to feel ultimately responsible for babies has been identified in other studies (see, e.g., McMahon 1995), this paper describes some of the interactional and institutional contexts within which differences between maternal and paternal responsibilities are reproduced. I suggest that the way that new parents divide the work of thinking about their babies reflects an accountability to socially constructed and institutionalized differentiation between women and men. . . .

Thinking About the Baby As 'Women's Work'

Three categories of mental labor associated with taking care of a baby surfaced in my respondents' reports: worrying, processing information, and managing the division of labor (see also Ehrensaft 1987; LaRossa and LaRossa 1989).

Worrying

In this section I . . . suggest that mothers worry about babies, in part, because fathers do not . . . . The "mental" experience of being a new mother—thinking about the baby, worrying "about everything"—is one that many of the women in my sample shared (see also Ehrensaft 1987; Hays 1993):

I don't walk around like a time bomb ready to explode, I don't want you to think that. It's just that I've got this stuff in the back of my head all the time.

I worry about her getting cavities in teeth that are not even gonna be there for her

whole life. Everything is so important to me now. I worry about everything.

It's like now you have this person and you're always responsible for them, the baby. You can have a sitter and go out and have a break, but in the back of your mind, you're still responsible for that person. You're always thinking about that person.

These new mothers described thinking about their babies as something that mothers do: "Mothers worry a lot." Worrying was such an expected part of mothering that the absence of it might challenge one's definition as a good mother. One of my respondents described returning to her job and feeling on her first day back that she should be worrying about her baby. She said that she had to "remind" herself to check on how her baby was doing at the baby-sitter's "or I'd be a bad mother."

Fathers do not necessarily think about their children while they are at work or worry that this reflects on them as parents (Ehrensaft 1987). My respondents did not report feeling like "bad" fathers if they took their minds off of their babies; some even expressed stress when their babies had to have their attention:

Sitting two hours playing with him, when I first did it was like, this is a waste of my time. I said, "I have more important things to do." And I'm still thinking, "Look at the time I've spent with him. What would I have done otherwise?"

This father's concern with his perceived lack of productivity while spending time with his baby might be a response to the social construction of fathers' roles as primarily economic (see Benson 1968; Thompson and Walker 1989). Another new father in my sample described a sense of loss about time he missed with his baby when he had to travel for work, "but," he said, "it goes back to the idea of being a father. . . . I do think in a traditional sense where I'm the father, I'm the husband, it's my job to support the family."

A couple I will call Brendan and Eileen illustrate the relationship between parental worry and social constructions of motherhood and fatherhood. Brendan and Eileen both have professional/managerial careers, each reporting salaries of more than $75,000. When Eileen had to travel for work, Brendan would function as Jimmy's primary caregiver. But when she was home, Eileen wanted to do "the baby stuff." She referred to her caregiving of Jimmy as her "stake" in his life:

> This is going to be hard to say. It's really important to me that Jimmy understands I'm his mother, whatever that means, because I'm probably not a traditional mother by any stretch.

When I asked what it means to her for Jimmy to know that she's his mother, Eileen responded:

> It means that if I come home some night and he's with [his] day care [provider] and he doesn't want to leave her, it'll kill me, is what it means. So I don't know if the rest of this is trying to ensure that doesn't happen. I don't know if the rest is trying to ensure that I have that very special role with him.

For Eileen, anything that she was not doing for Jimmy had the potential to damage her "special role" with him. If she was not the most special person to him, she was inadequate as a mother— something she noted that Brendan did not feel. She connected these concerns with what she referred to as "the good mother image": all nurturing and all present and always there. She added, "Now, I'm not even going to be able to have a shot at it because I'm not a lot of those things."

Brendan said that his behavior with Jimmy was not driven by guilt and anxiety as he perceived Eileen's to be:

> I think she feels that need. She wants to be a good mother. . . .Being a father, it's not a guilt thing. It's not like I'm going to do this because I don't want to be a bad daddy.

Brendan noted that his relationship with Jimmy was based on fun while he perceived Eileen's actions to be driven by insecurity. Eileen recognized that her concerns made her less of a good mother in Brendan's eyes. "I think his issue with me as a mother is that I worry a lot. The fact is that I do, but I also think mothers worry a lot." Although Eileen worried that she couldn't match the good mother image she described herself as "absolutely" buying into, worrying itself made her feel like a good mother.

Why is worrying associated with being a mother? I suggest two general reasons, which generate two kinds of worry. The first reason is that worrying is an integral part of taking care of a baby; it evokes, for example, the scheduling of medical appointments, babyproofing, a change in the baby's diet. There appears to be a connection between taking responsibility for physical care and carrying thoughts that reinforce the care (see Coltrane 1989; Ruddick 1983). This kind of worry, which I refer to as "baby worry," is generated by the question: What does the baby need? And babies need a lot. As Luxton (1980:101) points out, women are often anxious because babies are "so totally dependent" and perceived as highly vulnerable to illness and injury.

A second reason that new mothers worry is, as I suggest above, because they are expected to, and because social norms make it difficult for mothers to know whether they are doing the right thing for their babies. I call this "mother worry," and it the question: Am I being a good mother? While it has been suggested that mothers are more identified with their children than fathers are (Ehrensaft 1987), I suggest that mothers' worrying is induced by external as well as by internal mechanisms. That is, perhaps mothers experience their children as extensions of themselves as Ehrensaft (1987) argues, but mothers are also aware that their children are perceived by others as reflecting on them. Mothers worry, in part, because they are concerned with how others evaluate them as mothers:

> I think that people don't look at you and say, "oh, there's a good mother," but they will look at people and say, "oh, there's a bad mother." Being a mother I worry about what everyone else is going to think.

The mother just quoted perceived mothers as uniquely responsible for their children's behavior, and even street violence:

> The behavior of the child reflects the mother's parenting. . . . I mean kids, you have all these things with kids shooting

people, and I blame it on . . . mothers not being around.

The association of mothers with worrying provides a source of differentiation between mothers and fathers and presents women with a paradox, often played out in interactions with their male partners. Worrying is associated with irrationality and unnecessary anxiety, and some fathers suggested that their partners worried too much about their babies:

Sometimes I say, "He's fine, he's fine," but he's not fine enough for her.

However, worrying is perceived as something that "good" mothers do. A number of fathers made an explicit connection between good mothering and their wives' mental vigilance:

She's a very good mother. She worries a lot. She's always concerned about how she's doing or she's always worried about if [child's] feelings are hurt or did she say something wrong to her.

This paradoxical message—good mothers worry; worrying too much isn't good—underlies the tendency for mothers to worry and for fathers to express ambivalence about their worrying. One mother described a division of labor in which she was stressed and got things done while her husband's job was to tell her to lighten up:

I'm the one who stresses out more. He is very laid back. He doesn't worry about things. In fact he procrastinates. And I'm the one, run run run run run. . . . But one of us has to get things done on time and the other one has to keep the other one from totally losing it and make them be more relaxed. So it kind of balances us out.

A father described the care that his wife's worrying ensures for their baby while also suggesting that some of it might be unnecessary:

She worries a lot. I'm probably too easy-going, but she makes sure he goes to the doctor, makes sure he has fluoride, makes sure he has all of his immunizations. She's hypervigilant to any time he might be acting sick. She's kind of that way herself. I

kid her about being a hypochondriac. She makes sure he gets to bed on time, makes sure he's eating enough, whereas I'm a little more lackadaisical on that.

In both of these cases, as with Brendan and Eileen, the respondents described a kind of balance between the mother and father: The mother worries, the father doesn't; his job, in fact, might be to tell her not to worry. This dynamic reinforces a gendered division of mental labor. Although there is a subtext that the mother's worrying is unnecessary and/or neurotic, she does not stop. In fact, the suggestion that the mother "relax" serves to reinforce her worrying because although she does not recognize it as work, she does recognize that worrying gets things done for the baby. If the father offered to share the worrying rather than telling the mother to stop, the outcome might be quite different.

While I would not argue that it is possible for a baby to be cared for without having some assortment of adults performing "baby worry," the "mother worry" I have described here is heightened in our society by assumptions that good parenting is done exclusively and privately by a mother (with perhaps some "help" from a father) and that veering from this model may have severe consequences for children (see Coontz 1992 for a critique of "American standards of childrearing"). Examining another area of mental labor—the work of processing "expert" information about baby care—further reveals the norms attached to the work of thinking about babies.

Processing Information: 'What to Expect'

LaRossa and LaRossa (1989) make a direct connection between the fact that wives tend to buy and read how-to books on parenting and their being "in charge" of the baby. Because mothers read the books more thoroughly, they are more informed, and both parents assume that the mother will orchestrate and implement the care: "Her purchase of the books reflects what is generally accepted: Babies are 'women's work'" (LaRossa and LaRossa 1989:144). . . .

There are a number of steps that may be involved in the mental labor of processing information about babies:

1. Deciding on the need for advice

2. Locating the advice (often from more than one source)

3. Reading/listening to the advice

4. Involving/instructing one's partner

5. Contemplating and assessing the advice

6. Planning for the implementation of the advice

What I label here as steps 1–3 are carried out by mothers usually (LaRossa and LaRossa 1989; Hays 1993). In my sample, 23 out of 25 of the mothers reported reading parenting literature while 5 of the 25 fathers did.

Step 4 occurs in a number of variations: Mothers tell fathers what to read; mothers tell fathers specifically what they have read; mothers tell fathers what to do based on their own reading. These approaches to disseminating information were apparent in my sample:

He would say, "Well you're the mother, so what's the answer here?" And I said, "What do you think I have that I would know just because I'm the mother?" But I would do a lot more reading.

Sarah [wife] has read quite a few and I just pretty much go with her. She hasn't really told me I'm doing anything wrong.

Every once in a while she might pull something out and show me if she found something she thinks I should read, but I usually don't have time.

Step 5—contemplation and assessment of the advice—is often complicated, since what women find in advice books is ideology as well as information. According to a content analysis performed by Hays (1993; see also Marshall 1991), underlying the advice provided by child care experts is an "ideology of intensive mothering" that, among other things, holds individual mothers primarily responsible for child-rearing and treats mothering as expert-guided, emotionally absorbing, and labor-intensive. Mothers therefore take responsibility for gathering information from sources that reinforce their primary responsibility for the care of babies. As described by one respondent below, mothers

have to confront the ideology underlying the advice in order to assess whether they can or want to implement it (Step 6).

The book relied on by a majority of the mothers in my sample was *What to Expect the First Year* (Eisenberg, Murkoff, and Hathaway 1989), a book that one of the authors writes was conceived to address new mothers' "numerous worries." Several of the women in my sample referred to it as their "bible." . . .

Following are the comments that open a consideration of when to introduce solid foods to a baby—something that a father can do whether or not the baby is being breast-fed:

The messages that today's new mother receives about when to start feeding solids are many and confusing. . . .Whom do you listen to? Does mother know best? Or doctor? Or friends? (Eisenberg, Murkoff, and Hathaway 1989:202)

This passage illustrates the mental labor that is expected to accompany the introduction of solid foods: choosing when to do it, consulting with others about the issue, making a decision about whose advice to take. It also presumes that it is the mother who is making the decision in consultation with her mother, doctor, friends, yet her male partner is not mentioned.

The one chapter addressed to fathers begins with the following question from a presumably typical father:

"I gave up a lot of my favorite foods when my wife was pregnant so I could support her efforts to eat right for our baby. But enough's enough. Now that our son's here, shouldn't I be able to eat what I like?" (Eisenberg, Murkoff, and Hathaway 1989:591)

The tone of the question suggests that the father is getting guff from someone about his diet. Implication: It may not be only babies whose diets new mothers need to worry about. Regardless of who is nagging this father, the question suggests that fathers will not be independently motivated to eat a healthy diet in the interest of their babies and themselves. . . .

As Hays (1993) points out, authors of advice books may not have created gender differentiation in parenting responsibility, but they certainly play a role in reproducing it. Mothers in my sample who already felt that they had the primary responsibility for their babies did not get any disagreement from the advice book they consulted most frequently about "what to expect":

> If your husband, for whatever reason, fails to share the load with you, try to understand why this is so and to communicate clearly where you stand. Don't expect him to change overnight, and don't let your resentment when he doesn't trigger arguments and stress. Instead explain, educate, entice; in time, he'll meet you—partway, if not all the way (Eisenberg, Murkoff, and Hathaway 1989:545).

This advice directs women to do "emotion work" (Hochschild 1983) to contain their responses to their husbands' lack of participation. Rather than experiencing stress or conflict, new mothers are directed to keep a lid on their feelings and focus on instructing and enticing their husbands into participation (and after all this, not to expect equity.)

This kind of "advice" provides reinforcement for new parents' gendered divisions of mental labor, including the tendency for mothers to have the responsibility for getting the advice in the first place. The suggestion from these experts that new mothers should not argue with or expect equity from their husbands may also be a factor in the decreases in marital satisfaction that some experience.

Managing the Division of Labor

In this section I expand the concept of "managing" that has already been applied to infant care in past studies and suggest that it is not only the baby's appointments and supplies that mothers tend to manage (Belsky and Kelly 1994), but their babies' fathers as well (see also Ehrensaft 1987). To use the language from *What to Expect the First Year*, "enticing" fathers into helping out with their babies is another invisible, mental job performed by new mothers, as one respondent said of her husband:

> Peter is very good at helping out if I say, "Peter, I'm tired, I'm sick, you've got to do this for me, you've got to do that," that's

fine, he's been more than willing to do that.

Even in situations in which fathers report that they and their partners split tasks equally, mothers often have the extra role of delegating the work, as the following fathers in my sample indicate (Coltrane 1989 and Ehrensaft 1987 also describe "manager-helper" dynamics in couples who "share" the care of children):

> I don't change her [diaper] too often—as much as I can get out of it.

> Then at night either one of us will give him a bath. She'll always give him a bath, or if she can't, she'll tell me to do it because I won't do it unless she tells me, but if she asks me to do it I'll do it.

These quotes from two fathers, who perceived that they split tasks equally with their partners, reflect a division of labor in which the mothers are the ultimate managers. Both of these fathers had described themselves as sharing tasks with their wives—when their wives told them to.

Diaper changes were a particular area in which enticing was evident:

> I mean diapering, that's hard to say. He won't volunteer, but if I say, "Honey, she needs a diaper change, could you do it?" he does it.

> It took me a little while to get him to change the nasty diapers . . . but now he changes 'em all. He's a pro.

Mothers also made decisions about when not to delegate:

> I do diapers. Joel can't handle it well. You know, he does diapers too, but not if there's poop in them.

> I'm pretty much in charge of that, which is fine because it's really not that big of a deal. And she's more, it seems like she's easier for me than she is for him when it comes to diapering 'cause I just all the time do it, you know?

The mother just quoted illustrates how habitual patterns become perceived as making sense—doing becomes a kind of knowing (Daniels 1987; DeVault 1991)—just as being the one to read the book makes the mother the expert. Another woman described how her husband sits and eats while she "knows" what is involved in feeding their baby (and him):

> I know what has to be done. I know that like when we sit down for dinner, she [child] has to have everything cut up, and then you give it to her, you know, where he sits down and he eats his dinner. Then I have to get everything on the table, get her stuff all done. By the time I'm starting to eat, he's almost finished. Then I have to clean up and I also have to get her cleaned up and I know that like she'll always have to have a bath, and if she has to have a bath and if I need him to give it to her, "Can you do it?" I have to ask . . . because he just wouldn't do it if I didn't ask him. You know, it's just assumed that he doesn't have to do it.

While on one level it appears that women are "in charge" of the division of labor, the assumption of female responsibility means that, on another level, men are in charge—because it is only with their permission and cooperation that mothers can relinquish their duties. One mother talked about feeling that she had to check with her husband before making plans that did not include their baby, while her husband did not check with her first. She described herself asking her husband, "Can I do this in 3 weeks?" Another young woman complained that her partner would leave the house while their child was taking a nap:

> It's always the father that can just say, "Okay, I'm gonna go." Well I obviously can't leave, he's ready for a nap, you know? It's nap time. Mommy seems to always have to stay. I think that fathers have more freedom.

These statements go against suggestions that mothers may not want to relinquish control to their male partners because motherhood is a source of power for women (see, e.g., Kranichfeld 1987). What is powerful, perhaps, is the desire of mothers to be perceived as good mothers, and this may be what they feel they are trading off if they are not taking responsibility for the care of their babies. While mothers may instruct their husbands to do things, the data here suggest that

husbands' responses to and compliance with orders are not compulsory (see also DeVault 1991). Fathers who considered themselves equal participants in the division of labor would use the fact that they were "willing" to do diapers as an example:

> We each will do whatever we have to do. It's not like I won't change diapers.

Mothers did not necessarily see any baby task as optional for them:

> It's kind of give and take. As far as diaper changing, I think I do more. . . . It's not one of his favorite tasks.

Women are the "bosses" in the sense that they carry the organizational plan and delegate tasks to their partners, but they manage without the privileges of paid managers. Their ultimate responsibility for baby care may, in fact, disempower them in relation to their husbands, since for many women it means a loss of economic power (see Blumberg and Coleman 1989) and greater dependence on their male partners (LaRossa and LaRossa 1989; Waldron and Routh 1981).

Mental Baby Care and Marital Changes

While having a baby may foster greater dependence by women on their husbands, Belsky and Kelly (1994) report that new mothers are often disappointed by the level of emotional support they get from their husbands. I suggest that women's disproportionate responsibility for mental baby care plays an important role in generating women's dissatisfaction. Mothers in my sample were not necessarily appreciated and were even criticized by their partners for worrying; the advice they were in charge of getting told them not to be open with their husbands about their experiences; and their sense of being ultimately responsible for their babies' care affected their access to other sources of validation and power, such as paid work and social networks.

One of the primary ways in which women's sense of responsibility for babies surfaced was in decisions they made about employment. In my sample, many women changed their paid work patterns, quitting jobs or cutting back their hours (see also Cowan and Cowan 1992). These changes had implications for the balance of power in their marriages:

> It's funny now because he is the breadwinner so there have been opportunities where he has interviewed for positions, had opportunities to relocate and get a better position and the money was better. You're just put in a position where you have to just follow. Before when we were both working we would talk it out. I'd say, "No, I want to stay here." And now you really can't.

On an institutional level, men's bigger pay checks and women's experiences of low-wage, low-prestige jobs structured some of my respondents' traditional parenting arrangements. But there were also women in my sample, such as Eileen, who made as much money as their husbands and were very satisfied with their jobs, yet felt that they had to answer for their work in ways that their husbands did not. Laura, for example, described her decision to let go of a part of her job that she enjoyed the most because she did not want to see her baby at the sitter for more hours:

> I can't do that, I can't emotionally. I probably could, we'd have to pay more money for the sitter, but I don't want him at the sitter like for 10 hours a day. To me, that's, I'm doing something that I want to do, but in the long run I'm hurting him, you know? In my mind, I think that.

Laura's husband, Stuart, had not cut back on any parts of his job and was struggling with maintaining his performance in extra-curricular activities:

> I either want to be involved and do it the right way or I almost don't want to be involved at all. Because I don't want to do a less than good job.

Laura did not mention how the hours required by Stuart's activities influenced the time spent by their child at the baby-sitter's, but she did acknowledge that her marriage was stressed by her resentment of her husband's "freedom." Even though both Laura

and Stuart were employed and made similar wages, Laura felt more directly accountable for their baby's care. She could not allow herself to stay at work, she said, because it would hurt their baby: "In my mind, I think that." What Laura resented perhaps is that her husband was free from these kinds of thoughts.

Women's disappointment with their partners may stem from their loneliness in particular with the thinking they do about their babies. One woman in my sample, who did not question her primary responsibility for baby care, was upset by her perception that her husband did not recognize what goes on inside her head (emphases added):

> It really hurts, because he doesn't know how high my intentions or whatever or goals for being a good mom are. . . . (crying) *He doesn't know what I think* and when he's at work he doesn't know when she starts screaming and throwing fits, or pulling everything out of the dishwasher when I'm trying to load it, *and I've got all this in the back of my head* that I have to do for school, and the house is a mess, and supper's not cooked and he'll be home in 30 minutes. *He doesn't know that I have to keep telling myself, "Be calm. Love your child." You know? He doesn't know. So I just get upset when sometimes I really think he would say, "Well she could be a better mom."*

Hochschild (1989) notes that when couples experience conflict about housework, it is generally not simply about who does what, but about who should be grateful to whom. This "economy of gratitude," Hochschild suggests, relates to how individuals define what should be expected of them as men and women. Applying this notion to divisions of baby care, if mental labor is defined as an idiosyncrasy of mothers rather than as work, there is nothing for a man to feel grateful for if his wife does it. If fathers are seen as doing mothers a favor when they participate in baby care, fathers will receive more appreciation from their partners than they give back, which may contribute to new mothers' disappointment in the lack of emotional support they receive from their husbands (Belsky and Kelly 1994).

Mothers' sense of responsibility may also keep them from other sources of support, which is another factor that puts stress on their marriages. Several of the mothers in my sample reported that their ability to keep up with social networks was affected by their sense of needing to get home to their babies. Women who lost contact with work or other social networks became more aware of what they did not get from their husbands:

> I need him sometimes to be my girlfriend and he's not. . . . I feel sorry for him because he wasn't ready for that. . . . You don't realize how much you need those other people until you see them less frequently.

Decreases in new mothers' marital satisfaction, I am suggesting, are related both to the lack of recognition and sharing of mental labor by their husbands and to the loss of independence and support from other people that mothers' exclusive mental responsibility generates. If men and women who become parents together shared the mental labor associated with taking care of a baby, neither one would be "free," but perhaps neither one would be unhappy. . . .

References

Belsky, Jay. 1985. "Exploring individual differences in marital change across the transition to parenthood: The role of violated expectations." *Journal of Marriage and the Family*, November:1037-1044.

Belsky, Jay, and John Kelly. 1994. *The Transition to Parenthood*. New York: Delacorte Press.

Belsky, Jay, Mary Lang, and Ted L. Huston. 1986. "Sex typing and division of labor as determinants of marital change across the transition to parenthood." *Journal of Personality and Social Psychology* 50:517-522.

Belsky, Jay, and Brenda L. Volling. 1987. "Mothering, fathering, and marital interaction in the family triad during infancy: Exploring family systems processes." In *Men's Transitions to Parenthood*, Phyllis W. Berman and Frank A. Pedersen, eds. 37-63. Hillsdale, N.J.: Lawrence Erlbaum Associates, Inc.

Benson, Leonard. 1968. *Fatherhood: A Sociological Perspective*. New York: Random House.

Berman, Phyllis W. Pedersen. 1987. "Research on men's transitions to parenthood: An integrative discussion." In *Men's Transitions to Parent-hood*, Phyllis W. Berman and Frank A. Pedersen, eds. 217-242. Hillsdale, N.J.: Lawrence Erlbaum Associates, Inc.

Blumberg, Rae Lesser, and Marion Tolbert Coleman. 1989. "A theoretical look at the gender balance of power in the American couple." *Journal of Family Issues* 10:225-250.

Coltrane, Scott. 1989. "Household labor and the routine production of gender." *Social Problems* 36:473-490.

Coontz, Stephanie. 1992. *The Way We Never Were: American Families and the Nostalgia Trap*. New York: Basic Books.

Cowan, Carolyn Pape, and Philip A. Cowan. 1988. "Who does what when partners become parents: Implications for men, women, and marriage." *Marriage and Family Review* 12:105-131.

——. 1992. *When Partners Become Parents*. New York: Basic Books.

Daniels, Arlene Kaplan. 1987. "Invisible Work." *Social Problems* 34: 403-414.

DeVault, Marjorie L. 1991. *Feeding the Family*. Chicago: University of Chicago

Dickie, Jane R. 1987. "Interrelationships within the mother-father-infant triad." In *Men's Transitions to Parenthood*, Phyllis W. Berman and Frank A. Pedersen, eds. 113-143. Hillsdale, N.J.: Lawrence Erlbaum Associates, Inc.

Ehrensaft, Diane. 1987. *Parenting Together*. New York: The Free Press.

Eisenberg, Arlene, Heidi E. Murkoff, and Sandee E. Hathaway. 1989. *What To Expect The First Year*. New York: Workman Publishing.

Harriman, Lynda Cooper. 1985. "Marital adjustment as related to personal and marital changes accompanying parenthood." *Family Relations* 34:233-239.

Hays, Sharon. 1993. "The cultural contradictions of contemporary motherhood: The social construction and paradoxical persistence of intensive child-rearing." Ph.D. dissertation, University of California, San Diego.

Hochschild, Arlie Russell. 1983. *The Managed Heart: Commercialization of Human Feeling*. Berkeley: University of California Press.

Hochschild, Arlie, with Anne Machung. 1989. *The Second Shift*. New York: Viking Press.

Kranichfeld, Marion L. 1987. "Rethinking family power." *Journal of Family Issues* 8:42-56.

Lamb, Michael E. 1978. "Influence of the child on marital quality and family interaction during the prenatal, perinatal, and infancy periods." In *Child Influences on Marital and Family Interaction*, Richard M. Lerner and Graham B. Spanier, eds. 137-164. New York: Academic Press.

LaRossa, Ralph. 1986. *Becoming a Parent.* Beverly Hills, Calif.: Sage Publications.

LaRossa, Ralph, and Maureen Mulligan LaRossa. 1989. "Baby care: Fathers vs. mothers." In *Gender in Intimate Relationships: A Microstructural Approach,* Barbara J. Risman and Pepper Schwartz, eds. 138-154. Belmont, Calif.: Wadsworth Publishing.

Luxton, Meg. 1980. *More Than a Labour of Love: Three Generations of Women's Work in the Home.* Toronto: Women's Press.

McMahon, Martha. 1995. *Engendering Motherhood: Identity and Self-Transformation in Women's Lives.* New York: The Guilford Press.

Mederer, Helen J. 1993. "Division of labor in two-earner homes: Task accomplishment versus household management as critical variables in perceptions about family work." *Journal of Marriage and the Family* 55:133-145.

Rossi, Alice S. 1985. "Gender and parenthood." In *Gender and the Life Course,* Alice S. Rossi, ed. 161-191. New York: Aldine Publishing Co.

Ruble, Diane N., Alison S. Fleming, Lisa S. Hackel, and Charles Stangor. 1988. "Changes in the marital relationship during the transition to first time motherhood: Effects of violated expectations concerning division of household labor." *Journal of Personality and Social Psychology* 55:78-87.

Ruddick, Sara. 1983. "Maternal thinking." In *Mothering: Essays in Feminist Theory,* 213-230. Savage, M.D.: Rowman and Littlefield Publishers, Inc.

Schuchts, Robert A., and Stanley L. Witkin. 1989. "Assessing marital change during the transition to parenthood." Social Casework: *The Journal of Contemporary Social Work,* February:67-75.

Thompson, Linda, and Alexis J. Walker. 1989. "Gender in families: Women and men in marriage, work, and parenthood." *Journal of Marriage and the Family* 51:845-871.

Waldron, Holly, and Donald K. Routh. 1981. "The effect of the first child on the marital relationship." *Journal of Marriage and the Family,* November:785-788.

Critical Evaluation

1. Is it more "natural" or more appropriate for a woman to engage in mental baby care than it is for a man? Why or why not?

2. What are the author's sources of data? Are they sufficient to conclude that men and women generally follow the patterns she describes?

3. What are some ways a couple might deal with inequity in mental baby care?

12

The Children of Divorce

Demie Kurz

One of the most serious problems facing the family is the high rate of disruption through divorce and separation. Many factors contribute to the rate of breakup. At the macrolevel, the factors include changed norms (divorce no longer carries a stigma), changed roles (women are not financially dependent on men), economic problems (rates are higher among those with lower incomes), and age at marriage (the younger the couple, the more likely they are to divorce). At the microlevel, certain attitudes ("If I'm not happy, I'm out of here") and interaction patterns (ongoing conflict or emerging alienation between the partners) contribute to high divorce rates.

What are the consequences of divorce? Both the partners and their children are likely to experience a variety of physical, emotional, and social problems (Lauer 1998). In this selection, Demie Kurz describes the effects of divorce on children from the perspectives of the mothers she interviewed.

Reference

Lauer, Robert H. 1998. *Social Problems and the Quality of Life,* seventh edition. New York: McGraw-Hill.

Focus Questions

1. How do the effects of divorce on children vary?

2. What do mothers describe as the positive effects of divorce?

3. What concerns do divorced mothers have for their children's well-being?

The question of how divorce affects children is critical to our understanding of the impact of divorce on families. Some believe that divorce creates many problems for children and has a generally negative impact on their well-being. They point to research showing that children from divorced families suffer higher high-school dropout rates, higher teenage marriages, and greater rates of single parenthood, which can result in low self-esteem, emotional disorders, antisocial behavior, and depression. These problems can be exacerbated by changes in their residence and school and the loss of their familiar lifestyle. Some believe that children are paying too high a price for the mistakes and flaws of their parents. A few believe that this is an important enough reason to try and curb the divorce rate and keep families together.

However, despite the fact that many researchers have studied the effect of divorce on the intellectual, social, and emotional functioning of children, many unanswered questions remain. This is because it is difficult to determine whether problems identified in children of divorce result from the divorce itself, from problems in the marriage, or from other circumstances that predated the marriage. Many studies of the impact of divorce on children assess children's adjustment at only one point in time. In these studies, researchers fail to compare the children of divorce with children in intact marriages. Such comparisons might show that problems observed in children were due to the stress and tension of the marriage, not the hardships associated with divorce. Others point out that studies fail to take into account the impact of the decline in the standard of living of the mother and children. And finally, the fact that many studies of the children of divorce are based on clinical samples calls into question their findings. Clinical samples, unlike random and representative samples, draw on selected populations from counseling or treatment programs. These samples often overrepresent the number of people with problems.

Frank Furstenberg and Andrew Cherlin stress that to avoid overestimating the problems of children of divorce, these children should be compared with children from intact families. For example, they cite data from the National Survey of Children that found that 34 percent of parents who were separated or divorced reported that their children had behavior or discipline problems at school, in contrast to 20 percent of parents from intact families. Furstenberg and Cherlin point out that while, on the one hand, these figures would seem to indicate that children of divorce have more problems than other children, on the other hand, 66 percent of all children from families of divorce did not have serious behavior problems in school. Paul D'Amato concludes that when comparing children of divorce and children of two-parent families, the average differences between children are small rather than large.[1]

Some researchers now believe that children in two-parent families where there is a lot of conflict are actually no better off—and often are worse off—than children in divorced single-parent families. These researchers find that many of the problems which children of divorce exhibit, such as behavior problems and low scores on academic tests, were in fact present while their parents were still together. They also believe that children's level of adjustment is related to the level of conflict between their parents following the divorce.[2] After examining the evidence on children's well-being after divorce, Furstenberg and Cherlin conclude that the best predictor of children's adjustment is a good relationship with the mother, and a low level of conflict between the mother and the father.

Women in this sample were asked whether they thought their divorce had any impact on their children. It is important to compare mothers' accounts of their children's behavior and reactions, and their interpretations of that behavior, with data that is based on other measures of well-being. Do mothers identify the same factors as critical to the well-being of their children as do researchers? Are most mothers positive or negative about their children's emotional development? Of course mothers have their own biases that may affect their outlook on their children. As Susan Krantz points out, mothers who are depressed and unhappy about their divorces may see only the negative impact of divorce on their children, while those who are happy

about their divorce may minimize its negative impact.[3] Nevertheless, it is very important to have the observations of mothers, who typically are the closest observers of their children's behavior.

Women were not asked fixed-choice questions about each child, but were asked to describe in their own words whether they thought the divorce had any impact on their children. A content analysis of their statements showed that a small percentage of women (8 percent) reported that the divorce was overall a positive thing for their children, and 54 percent reported the divorce had no effect on their children in the present, although some cited problems in the past. In contrast, 38 percent stated that they were concerned about some aspect of at least one child's behavior. Many of this latter group felt that the divorce had been very hard on at least one of their children.

There were no significant differences based on social class, length of time since the separation, or fathers' visitation in the mothers' reports of their children's well-being. More white women reported that their children had problems (42 percent) than black women (28 percent). Those with elementary and high-school children reported significantly more problems than those with younger children. One could speculate that this was because older children were more verbal about their discontent, or perhaps younger children were less attached to their fathers, whom they had known for less time before the divorce occurred. We really cannot draw conclusions about the effects of divorce on children of different ages, however, as it is difficult to separate the effects of age at divorce, length of time since divorce, and current age.

Mothers Report Positive Reactions

The 8 percent of mothers who reported that the divorce had a positive effect on their children saw the divorce as lifting some kind of burden from their children. Most of these women and some of their children experienced physical abuse at the hands of fathers.

She [8 years old] was thrilled that we separated, to be away from the abuse. She never wants us in the same space again. [33-year-old black secretary, married for eight years, with an 8-year-old child]

The children are happy. With all that violence they were mixed up. The oldest was worried and didn't do very well in school. But all that is better now. They are good kids. [30-year-old poverty-level Hispanic woman, married for eleven years, with four children, ages 7, 8, 11, and 13]

A 31-year-old working-class mother of two [white waitress, married for ten years] talked about how her children were much "better" and more "relaxed," especially the older one who had seen her father's drug addiction and who had seen her father being violent to her mother.

One woman described how much better her son was now because he had been severely emotionally abused by his father, who had also abused her physically. According to this mother, her ex-husband would call her son "a wimp," "a faggot," and "a baby" and would sometimes make him cry in front of his friends. She stated that both her son (14 years old) and daughter (8 years old) hated their father and never saw him. She concluded:

The divorce has made the children better people. . . . My son is a completely different kid. He has friends now and they come over to the house. Before he couldn't have friends over because my husband would embarrass him in front of his friends, or embarrass his friends. He has a lot of girls calling for him too. [36-year-old white police officer, high-school education, married for thirteen years, with one 8-year-old and one 14-year-old]

Some of these women, however, did worry that at some point in the future the divorce could cause emotional difficulties for their child or children. One woman who experienced a lot of violence in her relationship stated:

I think the divorce had more effect on the children when we were together. When he left, a great burden was lifted. While he was here, my daughter just lived in her room. My daughter has really been helped by the counseling. But my son refused to go. I think he's going to have to deal with

this at some time. Maybe it'll come up when he's 30. [37-year-old white receptionist, married for seventeen years, with two children, ages 14 and 17]

Mothers Report No Problems

Forty-six percent of the mothers reported that their children experienced no particular problems. These women gave several reasons for this. The greatest percentage of women in this group said there [we]re no problems because the marriage ended when the child or children were so young that they did not remember life before the divorce. They said things like, "He was just little, he didn't know his Dad at all"; "He left right after my son was born, my son doesn't remember him being here"; or, "She doesn't know any other way of life."

These mothers also attributed their children's lack of difficulty to the fact that their husbands were never actively involved with the children during the marriage. In some cases this was because the fathers worked a night shift and were gone evenings; in other cases, the fathers were not emotionally involved with their children. Women said things like, "He was never there. The kids didn't know him that well"; or, "He worked nights, he wasn't around when the children were here"; or, as this woman said:

They never had a father who was there like normal fathers anyway. He wasn't an easy, typical father. So it wasn't really so different after the divorce. [41-year-old white supervisor, married for twenty-two years, with three children, ages 15, 21, and 22]

Still other mothers said that because their children were seeing their father regularly, things were not that different for the children. Said a 30-year-old working-class mother of two, "In the beginning, when we first separated, I think they felt partly responsible, but now it's cooled down. They have time with their father. It's a lot like it was." [white woman with a high school education, married for seven years] Another woman's son was in high school when she left her ex-husband because of violence.

At first my son didn't like the divorce. He wanted us to stay together. I think it affected him in school. His marks came down. After a while he got out of it because he was close to his father and he maintained that relationship. [42-year-old white poverty-level nurse's aide, married for eight years, with a 19-year-old son]

Another woman said her 15-year-old son was helped by the fact that she and her ex-husband got along. She claims: "He's been great, really good. He was affected for a little bit but knowing we're friendly helped a lot" [30-year-old working-class white office worker, married for fifteen years, with one child]. One woman attributed her daughter's successful adjustment to a godfather.

My daughter wasn't affected by the divorce. She has a fantastic godfather, my girlfriend's husband. He's the only male figure in her life but he's been very important, including disciplining her. [36-year-old black working-class woman, married for thirteen years, with a 12-year-old child]

Several women mentioned that they had to deal with their children's questions about their family situation.

They don't remember living with their father so it hasn't hurt them that way. But my daughter [five-and-a-half] is starting to ask questions like "Why don't you live with Daddy?" She really wants to know that now, why she isn't like the other kids. [31-year-old working class woman, married for five years, with a 3-year-old and a 5-year-old]

Researchers report contradictory findings on the question of whether a child's well-being is related to contact with the noncustodial parent, typically the father; some believe frequent contact with the father is a factor in children's well-being, while others do not. Robert Emery concludes that there is "no clear evidence linking children's adjustment to a continuing relationship with the outside parent"; nonetheless, he believes that visitation with the noncustodial parent has considerable symbolic value for a child, which continues into adulthood. Furstenberg and Cherlin also report that a good relationship with a stepparent has a beneficial effect on children's well-being.[4]

Some women reported that their children experienced certain problems after the divorce, but were now fine. A 34-year-old woman who was married eight years said, "Initially my daughter was angry but now she feels she has the best of both worlds. She has two families, two intact sets of relationships, each with a different style" [graduate student, with one child]. Another woman said:

In the beginning the children kept saying they wanted him back. It was really hard. But now, they're just normal, adjusted kids. It doesn't bother them anymore. They go to school with so many kids who are in the same situation. [35-year-old white secretary, married for fourteen years with three children]

Some mothers reported conflicts with their children that began in the teenaged years and resulted in the children spending time at their father's home. After they returned to the mother's home some months later, these mother-child relationships improved. According to one mother, when she and her daughter had conflicts, her daughter would say, "Well I'll just go to Dad's." This woman finally sent her daughter to her father's house, which was nearby. She stayed for several months and then happily came back. This mother said she and her daughter get along much better now. Another mother reported that she and her daughter had been very close, but started having conflicts when her daughter was 14. Her daughter frequently became upset and began challenging the mother. Things escalated to the point where the daughter threw something at the mother. This woman then sent her daughter to her father's. When she came back their relationship also was much better.

Finally, some of these women said their children were fine, but that they believed the divorce had had some effect on them, although they were not sure what that is. As one woman, who was separated from her husband when her daughter was an infant, said, "I think it will affect her. It has to." Or, as another said:

They have generally reacted very well. They've had their moments of confusion, but as they get older, I feel they've handled it very well. I'm sure the divorce must have had an effect on them, although I can't say what particular effect. [47-year-old white medical secretary, married for twenty-two years with one child from her current marriage and five from her previous marriage]

A few mothers reported that their children were distancing themselves emotionally from their fathers. The implication was that the children were doing this because they were not seeing their father.

I don't think my son really thinks of him as a father. At my son's school they had them go buy Christmas presents as a way of learning about money. My son bought a present for me, my mother, and my father. And he called my father Dad. [38-year-old black middle-class woman, married for nine years, with a 6-year-old son]

One day my daughter [6 years old] said to me, "Mommy, Daddy's dead.' I said "Where did you get that idea?" She said, "He just is." I guess that's the way she deals with her anger toward him. [36-year-old black pharmacy technician, married for thirteen years, with a 12-year-old daughter]

Mothers Report Concerns About Children's Well-Being

Thirty-eight percent of the women (42 percent of the white women and 28 percent of the black women) reported concerns about the behavior of at least one of their children, with no class differences between them. Women reported that children experienced some negative effects from the divorce itself, but even more from the conflicts and problems that occurred during the marriage. Women reported three major concerns. The first was how the hard living that their children witnessed during the marriage could affect them in the future. While some of the women cited above said the divorce had been a positive thing for their children because it enabled them to escape from violence and drugs, in other cases women said that their children suffered from the effects of the domestic violence and drug use that took place during the marriage.

These women, who described their children as very angry and very hurt, worried about the long-term effects of hard-living and violence on their children. First, they mentioned the effects on their children of witnessing domestic violence.

My daughter [14-year-old] doesn't like her father. You heard her. She says she doesn't want to get married if it means getting beaten the way I was. Sometimes she scares me she's so tough. I feel like my son [17-year-old] will have to deal with all this sometime. He has a happy-go-lucky attitude like everything will be OK. But he was affected. His father beat him. [41-year-old white working-class woman, married for twenty-one years, with two children]

He's mixed up about his father. He wants us to live together. He remembers everything that happened. He saw me get cut badly when he was two. [28-year-old poverty-level black woman, married for six years, with a 5-year-old son]

Another mother said that her children, ages 11 and 13, refused to see their father because they were afraid of him. She said her ex-husband was "very rough on the children, physically and emotionally," particularly the son. The father took his daughter to court because she would not see him. The judge told the daughter she had to visit her father, but she refused. According to this woman, "My son hates his father for what he's done, but deep down inside he wants a relationship. With my daughter, when he took her to court, she really hated him and wants nothing to do with him."

Some researchers believe that children who are exposed to domestic violence experience more behavior problems, emotional difficulties, and reduced social competence than children who are not exposed to violence. While witnessing domestic violence has a strong negative impact on some children, however, it does not on others. A good relationship with the primary parent can act as a buffer against the negative effects of witnessing domestic violence.

Another mother said that her ex-husband always "came and went" during the marriage and abused alcohol.

My son [five-and-a-half years old] has suffered. He's very anxious and clingy. There were times in the past when if I left my mother's to go to the grocery store he would scream. I guess he thought I might leave him too. He saw his father leave when he was 2. [39-year-old white working-class government worker, married for seven years, with one child]

One woman reported that her 14-year-old son was very angry at his father, who was a drug addict, and that because his father stole family property to support his drug habit, her son never wanted to see him again.

All of this has been very very hard on my son [14 years old]. . . . I felt damned if I did and damned if I didn't about my son's seeing his father. I'm sorry that I listened to my mother and sister and my son had to see his father disintegrate. But also if I had forbidden my son from seeing his father then he would have been angry at me. [39-year-old white hairdresser, married for sixteen years, with 2 children, ages 1 and 14]

According to another woman, whose ex-husband was an alcoholic and used a lot of violence:

The divorce really had an effect on my older son. He's full of anger. He's insecure. He saw so much wild, crazy stuff at home. . . . He's in counseling. He'll be in counseling for a long time. There's no problem with his school work but he has behavior problems in school. His Dad let him down a few times, like not being there when he said he would. That was really hard on him. Also, he got beat up by his dad.

The younger one is just confused. He was only 2 years old when we split up. I was so preoccupied with everything that I actually didn't feed him enough. He didn't complain, so I didn't think about it. [33-year-old white middle-class woman, married for seven years, with two children, ages 5 and 7]

The following mother described her son as growing angrier, as he has been unable to get his father's attention. According to this woman, her ex-husband drank a lot and eventually ended up on drugs.

My son [15 years old] wanted his father to pay attention to him all through the marriage. But all through the marriage it was me who did that. I was the one who took him to all his sports events; it was me there with the other fathers. My husband went to bars. He was more interested in being with his drinking buddies.

His father takes him once in a while. It's not the greatest places—the mall, the flea market, watching the VCR at his place. He always talked about how he would take his son hunting and fishing. This is hunting season, isn't it?

After the divorce my son used to call his father. But he's stopped doing that. My son's starting to cool off to his father. Recently I asked him if he was going to call his father and he said, "I've had a divorce from him." Now my ex-husband is trying more to get in touch with his son. He realizes that his son is drawing away from him.

My son never had any trouble in school. He was a model student. But since the separation he's started acting out. He talked all the time in school for a while. Now I've just learned that he is starting to play hookey. I think he's just trying to get attention. But the person whose attention he wants—his father—he's not getting.

My son seems to be pulling away from my mother too. He was always close to her. I wish he would talk to a counselor. I try to get him to talk to me but it doesn't work. I know this is affecting him a lot. I just don't know what to do [sounding sad and scared]. I tell him never, ever to start drinking. [white office clerk, married for sixteen years, with one child]

In addition to the effects of domestic violence, drugs, and alcohol, women also mentioned fathers' visitation as a factor in their children's well-being. While research does not demonstrate a definitive link between children's well-being and the frequency of the fathers' visitation, some mothers believed their children were angry because they did not get to see their father enough. Said a poverty-level mother of three, "My oldest misses her father a lot. She has behavior problems in school and I think that's the reason. She doesn't feel quite whole. My son misses his dad" [32-year-old white store clerk, married for eight years with three children, ages 5, 7, and 8]. Another mother reported that her son was "angry, violent, and rebellious" because he was not seeing his father enough. During the marriage, he was close to his father, but now, according to this woman, the father was always with his new girlfriend and did not spend time with his son, who had become very bitter. One time when the son was angry, he ripped the basement door off its hinges and then ripped the stairway banister off the wall [married for nineteen years, with one child]. One woman reported that her daughter, who was 13, had become more angry recently. She believed this was because her daughter had not been able to see her father much. He was in prison and was recently transferred to a prison further away. This mother had no car. She hoped her ex-husband's sister would be able to take the children to see their father. Another mother said her children were angry because their father spent time with children in another relationship.

It has been very difficult for the children. They're nervous and angry and they're hurt and they hate sharing their father with his wife and three kids. [33-year-old white woman, married for thirteen years, with two children, ages ten and 13]

Several women reported that erratic patterns of visitation were very hard on the children.

He sees them less than once a year. I don't like it because it hurts the children but there is nothing I can do about it. The children try to stay in touch with him but he's usually not available. If he is he makes false promises. They don't really have a relationship with their father. They say they don't have a father. [33-year-old poverty-level black woman who works in a bar, married for sixteen years, with two children, ages 14 and 16]

He could see them anytime but he only comes once every five or six months. I don't pressure him into seeing them. He can be obnoxious. He kept the oldest one upset. He promised to see her, she waits all day, and he doesn't show up. So I don't pressure him because he makes promises

he doesn't keep. [52-year-old black secretary, married for eighteen years, with two children, ages 11 and 18]

In the following two cases, boys left their mothers' homes to live with their fathers and were not seeing their mothers. They were angry at their mothers, whose relationships with the fathers were also strained. In the first case, the mother said her son was very angry. She and her ex-husband, who was an alcoholic during the marriage, had a relationship that still had a lot of conflict.

We've been having terrible problems with my son. It's the hardest thing in my life. It's heartbreaking. My son has gotten kicked out of a lot of schools. Thank goodness I got him into the high school here. He's a senior but he's there by the skin of his teeth. All the counselors we've seen about his getting thrown out say he's a very angry young man. He's got his father's violent temper and my stubbornness.

My son has also been very unpleasant to my new husband. Finally one night two months ago my son hit him—my son's bigger than he is. And I said, "That's it, you're leaving." My son actually ran out of the house. He's been living with his father ever since. It's really heartbreaking [fighting tears]. I'm not sure I will ever see my son again. As I said, he's stubborn like me. [41-year-old white house cleaner, married for seventeen years, with two children, ages 17 and 20]

In another case, a mother reported that her son had been suicidal at one point and at the time of the interview had run away to his father's. His father used drugs during the marriage and still did.

Some women, whose ex-husbands left them for other women, reported that their children had particular problems. A mother of teen-aged girls thought their relationships with men would be affected by seeing their father leave.

The girls' legacy from this is that they'll have trouble trusting men. The older one, who felt betrayed, goes from boyfriend to boyfriend. The younger one was always scared of her father because he was away so much. [44-year-old white teacher, married for twenty-one years, with two children, ages 17 and 18]

Another woman worried about her son being burdened with her own sadness.

My son [6 years old] has been through a lot. One time after my husband left I just had to cry and cry. My son came over to me and said, "Mommy why are you crying?" I said, "Because Daddy hurt my feelings." My son said, "Don't cry anymore Mommy, I'll take care of you." A child shouldn't have to go through that. Of course twenty minutes later he was in the next room throwing things. [37-year-old white working-class woman, married for thirteen years, with one child]

The following mother, whose ex-husband left her for another woman, was angry and bitter at her ex-husband. She spoke of her son being protective of her. Perhaps he sensed her sadness and loss, or perhaps he was worried that she would leave him. Or perhaps because of her own anger she could only see the negative effects of the divorce.

My younger son [5 years old] doesn't want to be away from me very much. He's very protective of me, very protective. Even at the beach he wants to know if I'm OK when I've gone in the water. [34-year-old white working-class woman, seeking employment, married for eleven years, with two children, ages 5 and 9]

Finally, women expressed a variety of other concerns, particularly about their children's sense of security. Several women believed their children needed a male role model. One woman stated that her son was not sure of his manhood and craved male support. This woman worried even though the separation was fairly amicable and her daughter had developed a good relationship with her father.

My daughter [6 years old] still longs for the family to be together. The divorce has affected her. . . . In the beginning my daughter had terrible separation anxiety from me. And when she went to my ex-husband's for the weekend, at first she cried and cried. It was terrible. It's fine now. . . . A good thing is that my daughter's relationship with her father has really de-

veloped. . . . I think a negative thing though is that children like this lose their childhood very soon. You should hear her talk. They have to handle things so early. And she still would really like us to get together. [37-year-old white middle-class woman, married for six years, with one child]

This woman was dealing with feelings of guilt about leaving her marriage because of the pain it has caused her children.

I think sometimes that we adults are very irresponsible about our children and the pain we can cause them through divorce. I needed the divorce for myself but it really hurt my children. I'll never forget the look and actions of my son when we were separated. He tried everything he could to get us together. . . . He had a lot of anger. The divorce made him more insecure. It interrupts children's lives. . . . The thing I feel worst about the whole divorce is how it affected the children. [49-year-old middle-class woman, married for ten years, with two children, ages five and eight]

Notes

1. Frank Furstenberg and Andrew Cherlin, *Divided Families* (Cambridge, MA: Harvard University Press, 1991), 69. See also, Amato, "Life-Span Adjustment of Children to Their Parents' Divorce" 146.

2. See Amato, ibid., 151. See also Andrew Cherlin, Frank Furstenberg, and P.L. Chase-Lansdale, "Longitudinal Studies of Effects of Divorce on Children in Great Britain and the United States," *Science* 252 (1991): 1386-89; Jeanne H. Block, Jack Block, and Per R. Gierde, "The Personality of Children Prior to Divorce" *Child Development* 57 (1986): 827-40; Frank Furstenberg and Julien Teitler, "Reconsidering the Effects of Marital Disruption," *Journal of Family Issues* 15, no. 2 (June 1994): 173-90.

3. Susan Krantz, "The Impact of Divorce on Children," in *Feminism, Children, and the New Families*, ed. S. M. Dornbusch and M. H. Strober (New York: Guilford, 1988), 255.

4. Furstenberg and Cherlin report that child well-being is not related to contact with the father, while Judith S. Wallerstein and Joan B. Kelly, in *Surviving the Breakup: How Children Actually Cope with Divorce* (New York: Basic Books, 1980); and E. Mavis Hether-

ington, Martha Cox, and Roger Cox, in "The Aftermath of Divorce:" in *Mother-Child, Father-Child Relations,* ed. Joseph H. Stevens and Marilyn Matthews, (Washington, DC: National Association for the Education of Young Children, 1978), report that it is.

Critical Evaluation

1. To what extent can one rely on mothers' perceptions to determine the effects of divorce on children?

2. Would the children's fathers have the same perceptions as the mothers? Why or why not?

3 What could account for the differing percentages of white and black women who reported concerns about their children's behavior?

4. How could the author's data be used to mitigate the negative effects of divorce on children?

13
Violence Against Children

Perhaps the most destructive family situation is one that involves domestic violence or neglect. Although abuse and neglect occur in all social groups, they are more likely to occur among the impoverished. Thus, the economy is one structural factor that contributes to the problem. At the microlevel, patterns of interaction in families tend to perpetuate themselves. One of the best predictors of child abuse is whether the abuser suffered the same fate as a child (although it is important to point out that the majority of abused children do not become child abusers themselves). Another social psychological factor is self-esteem: child abusers are likely to have lower levels of self-esteem (Zuravin and Greif 1989).

These two selections address many questions concerning child abuse. They provide data on the amount of abuse and neglect, the consequences of abuse and neglect, and the way in which violence against children becomes a factor in other kinds of social problems.

Reference

Zuravin, Susan and Geoffrey L. Greif. 1989. "Normative and Child Maltreating AFDC Mothers." *Social Casework* 70:76-84.

A.
Answers to Frequently Asked Questions on Child Abuse and Neglect

National Child Abuse and Neglect Data System

Focus Questions

1. What is meant by the maltreatment of children?

2. How many children are victims of maltreatment each year?

3. What are the characteristics of those who abuse children?

The maltreatment of children is a national problem. Many organizations are researching child abuse and neglect in the United States to determine the scope of the problem and to determine its effects. This fact sheet synthesizes information from many sources to address 10 frequently asked questions about child maltreatment. Much of the data come from the National Child Abuse and Neglect Data System (NCANDS) and the Third National Incidence Study of Child Abuse and Neglect (NIS-3), both sponsored by the National Center on Child Abuse and Neglect (NCCAN). The NCANDS annually collects and analyzes information on child maltreatment provided by State child protective services (CPS) agencies. These CPS agencies are public social service organizations with primary responsibility for receiving and responding to reports of alleged maltreatment. The NIS periodically surveys community professionals who come into contact with children (5,600 professionals in 1993) to estimate the incidence of child maltreatment including both cases reported and not reported to CPS.

1. How Many Children Are Reported and Investigated for Abuse or Neglect Each Year?

In 1995, CPS agencies investigated an estimated 2 million reports that involved the alleged maltreatment of almost 3 million children.

2. How Many Children Are Victims of Maltreatment?

In 1995, CPS determined that over 1 million children were victims of substantiated or indicated child abuse and neglect. The term "substantiated" means that an allegation of maltreatment was confirmed according to the level of evidence required by State law or State policy. The term "indicated" is an investigation finding used by some States when there is insufficient evidence to substantiate a case under State law or policy, but there is reason to suspect that maltreatment occurred or that there is risk of future maltreatment.

Several studies suggest that more children suffer from abuse or neglect than are evident in official statistics from State CPS agencies. Based on reports received and investigated by CPS agencies in 1995, about 15 children per 1,000 younger than 18 in the general population were found to be victims of abuse or neglect. Based on surveys of community professionals, the NIS-3 estimates that 42 children per 1,000 in the population were harmed or endangered by abuse or neglect in 1993. A 1995 telephone survey of parents conducted by the Gallup Poll estimated that as many as 49 children per 1,000 in the population suffered physical abuse and 19 per 1,000 suffered sexual abuse.

3. Is the Number of Abused or Neglected Children Increasing?

As estimated by the NIS, there has been a substantial increase in the number of children harmed by abuse or neglect. Over a 7-year period, the estimated number of children who experienced harm from abuse or neglect increased 67 percent, from 931,000 children in 1986 (NIS-2) to 1,553,800 in 1993 (NIS-3). The 1993 estimate reflected an 149 percent increase over the 625,100 children estimated to have experienced harm from abuse or neglect in 1980 (NIS-1). In particular, the estimated number of seriously injured children has increased and quadrupled, from 141,700 in 1986 (NIS-2) to 565,000 in 1993 (NIS-3).

4. What Are the Most Common Types of Maltreatment?

Neglect is the most common form of child maltreatment. CPS investigations determined that 52 percent of victims in 1995 suffered neglect, 25 percent physical abuse, 13 percent sexual abuse, 5 percent emotional maltreatment, 3 percent medical neglect, and 14 percent other forms of maltreatment.

Some children suffer more than one type of maltreatment.

5. Who Are the Child Victims?

Child abuse and neglect affects children of all ages. Among children confirmed as victims by CPS agencies in 1995, more than half were 7 years old or younger, and about 26 percent were younger than 4 years old. Approximately 26 percent of victims were children ages 8 to 12; another 21 percent were youth ages 13 to 18. Case-level data from 11 States in 1995 suggest that the majority of victims of neglect and medical neglect were younger than 8 years old, while the majority of victims of other types of maltreatment were age 8 or older.

Both boys and girls experience child maltreatment. In 1995, 52 percent of victims of maltreatment were female and 47 percent were male. Some differences exist by type of maltreatment. For example, the NIS-3 found that girls were sexually abused three times more often than boys.

While children of families in all income levels suffer maltreatment, studies suggest that family income is related to incidence rates. The NIS-3 found that children from families with annual incomes below $15,000 per year were more than 25 times more likely than children from families with annual income above $30,000 to have been harmed or endangered by abuse or neglect in 1993.

6. How Many Children Die from Abuse or Neglect Each Year?

In 1995, 45 States reported that 996 children were known by CPS agencies to have died as a result of abuse or neglect. Not all child maltreatment fatalities are reported to CPS agencies.

Analysis of case-level data from 9 States in 1993 suggests that 43 percent of child fatalities were children younger than 1 year of age, and 81 percent were 3 years old or younger. Physical abuse was the maltreatment most commonly associated with the death of the child victim (33%). Another 30 percent were associated with both physical abuse and at least one other type of maltreatment.

7. Who Abuses and Neglects Children?

The majority of children in the 1993 NIS-3 were maltreated by birth parents (78%). Fewer children were maltreated by non-birth parents or parent-substitutes, such as a stepparent, foster parent, adoptive parent, separated or divorced spouse of an in-home parent, or parent's boyfriend or girlfriend (14%), or by others (9%).

Perpetrators tend to differ by type of maltreatment. Eighty-seven percent of children neglected were neglected by a female. Sixty-seven percent of abused children were abused by males.

The NIS-3 suggests that perpetrators of sexual abuse are different than perpetrators of other types of maltreatment. Slightly more than one-fourth (29%) of sexually abused children in the NIS-3 study were abused by a birth parent and one-fourth (25%) were sexually abused by a non-birth parent or parent substitute. Nearly one-half had been sexually abused by someone other than a parent or parent figure.

8. Are Victims of Child Abuse More Likely to Engage in Criminality Later in Life?

According to a 1992 study sponsored by the National Institute of Justice (NIJ), maltreatment in childhood increases the likelihood of arrest as a juvenile by 53 percent, as an adult by 38 percent, and for a violent crime by 38 percent. Being abused or neglected in childhood increases the likelihood of arrest for females by 77 percent. Physically abused children are more likely than child victims of other types of maltreatment to be arrested for a violent crime. A related 1994 NIJ study indicated that children who were sexually abused were 28 times more likely than a matching control group of non-abused children to be arrested for prostitution as an adult.

9. Is there Any Evidence Linking Alcohol or Other Drug Use to Child Maltreatment?

A 1993 study by the U. S. Department of Health and Human Services found that children in alcohol-abusing families were nearly 4 times more likely to be maltreated overall, almost 5 times more likely to be physically neglected, and 10 times more likely to be emotionally neglected than children in non-alcohol abusing families. Estimates suggest that 50 to 80 percent of all child abuse cases substantiated by CPS involve some degree of substance abuse by the childxs parents.

10. Who Reports Child Mistreatment?

In 1995, more than half of all reports alleging maltreatment came from professionals, including educators, law enforcement and justice officials, medical and mental health professionals, social service professionals, and child care providers. About 19 percent of reports came from relatives of the child or from the child. Reports from professionals are more likely to be substantiated or indicated than reports from nonprofessional sources.

Critical Evaluation

1. The figures given in this selection are based on reported cases. Do you think that there are additional cases that are not reported and remain undetected? If so, why are they not reported?

2. What is meant by "neglect"? Is it possible to measure neglect, or is it just a judgment call by a social worker?

3. What information in this report could be used to reduce the amount of child maltreatment?

National Child Abuse and Neglect Data System, "Answers to Frequently Asked Questions on Child Abuse and Neglect." In *Child Maltreatment 1995: Reports from the States to the National Child Abuse and Neglect Data System*, by the National Child Abuse and Neglect Data System. Washington, DC: Government Printing Office, 1997. ✦

B.
The Cycle of Violence Revisited

Cathy Spatz Widom

Focus Questions

1. What are some consequences of being abused as a child?

2. How likely is a maltreated child to eventually be arrested for a crime?

3. How can the cycle of violence be broken?

What happens to abused and neglected children after they grow up? Do the victims of violence and neglect later become criminals or violent offenders themselves?

A series of ongoing studies (sponsored by the National Institute of Justice, the National Institute of Alcohol Abuse and Alcoholism, and the National Institute of Mental Health) are examining the lives of 1,575 child victims identified in court cases of abuse and neglect dating from 1967 to 1971. By 1994, almost half of the victims (most of whom were then in their late twenties and early thirties) had been arrested for some type of nontraffic offense. Eighteen percent had been arrested for a violent crime—an increase of 4 percent in the 6 years since arrest records were first checked.

Another key finding was that neglected children's rates of arrest for violence were almost as high as physically abused children's. Neglect was defined by the court as an excessive failure by caregivers to provide food, clothing, shelter, and medical attention.

Although the study is not yet completed, these preliminary findings indicate a need for criminal justice and social service agencies to take a proactive, preventive stance to stop the cycle of violence. The goal is early identification of abused and neglected children and careful, sensitive handling of these cases to avoid an early criminal justice intervention that could become the first in a spiral of sanctions.

Study Methods

The study was based on documented records: a sample of 1,575 court cases of physical abuse, sexual abuse, and neglect that had occurred from 1967 to 1971 in a midwestern county. At the time the cases came to court, all of the children were under the age of 11, and the mean age was about 6. To isolate the effects of abuse and neglect from those of other variables, such as gender, race, and poverty, researchers created a control group whose members matched the sample on the basis of age, gender, race, and family social class.

Risk of Arrest

In the late eighties, researchers found that 28 percent of the sample group had been arrested—11 percent for a violent crime. Of the control group, 21 percent had been arrested—8 percent for a violent crime. They also noted that differences in arrest rates between members of the two groups began to emerge early—at the ages of 8 and 9. However, at this time, only 65 percent of the victims had passed through the peak years of violent offending—from age 20 to 25.

Six years later, almost 100 percent of the sample were 26 or older. After recompiling criminal histories, researchers found larger differences between the sample and control groups. This time, 49 percent of the overall sample group had been arrested—18 percent for a violent crime—compared with 38 percent of the control group—14 percent for a violent crime. Although rates were high for the control group (who shared such risk factors as poverty), they were significantly higher for those neglected and abused as children. . . .

An important finding was that neglect appeared to be just as damaging as physical abuse. The rate of arrest for violent crimes among those sample group members who had been neglected as children was almost as high as the rate for those who had been physically abused.

Additional Findings

During the interviews, both males and females reported having made suicide attempts. Males seemed to be at increased risk for antisocial personality disorder or psychopathy, whereas females seemed to be at increased risk for alcoholism and prostitution. Contrary to popular belief, however, no relationship was established between childhood abuse and neglect and teen pregnancy.

Critical Evaluation

1. How can you explain the fact that neglect is almost as damaging to a child as physical abuse?

2. Were the differences in arrest rates between the maltreated and the control groups large enough to conclude that maltreatment adversely affects children? Why or why not?

3. Are the author's suggestions for breaking the cycle of violence adequate? What else could be done?

Cathy Spatz Widom, "The Cycle of Violence Revisited." In *NIJ Research Preview*, February, 1996. Washington, DC: U.S. Government Printing Office. ✦

Project for Personal Application and Class Discussion:
The Family

Three family problems are addressed in the chapters in this section: equity in the division of labor, disruption by divorce, and domestic abuse. Thinking about your own experience in the family in which you grew up, along with any other families with which you were familiar, answer the following questions, assigning the number 1 to "yes" answers and 0 to "no" answers:

1. Did you hear your parents argue about household chores?

2. Do you believe your parents were dissatisfied with how much work each one did around the house?

3. Did your parents ever chastise you for not carrying your share of the load in your home?

4. Did your parents divorce?

5. Have any of your grandparents, your siblings, or other relatives with whom you have had contact divorced?

6. Were you ever afraid while growing up that your parents might divorce?

7. Do you believe your parents ever spanked you or struck you harder than necessary?

8. Did your parents ever verbally abuse you?

9. Were you or anyone you knew well physically abused as a child?

10. Did you ever see one of your parents hit the other in anger?

Your total score can range from zero to 10. The higher your score, the more you have been exposed to the three problems.

If you scored between five and 10, think about how the problems affected you, and how you still might be affected. Also think about what you can do to prevent your children (if you have or plan to have them) from experiencing similar problems.

As an interesting class exercise, let each member turn in his or her score anonymously. Let the instructor compute the average score for the class. Then discuss the possible reasons for the score and whether you think your average is close to that of all others in your age group. ◆

Health Care

W hen Americans are asked what is important to their satisfaction with life, good health is typically at or near the top of the list. And the older people grow, the more they value good health. How does one maintain good health? Many factors influence health, including genetics, lifestyle, and the availability of good health-care services. One's genetic inheritance is fixed. There is little anyone can do if, genetically, he or she has a propensity for, or likelihood of, certain diseases or disabilities.

What about the other two factors? There is much a person can do, of course, about lifestyle—including whether he or she smokes, drinks alcohol, uses illegal drugs, exercises, gets the sleep needed, and so on. But a person's choices about a health-care system are probably limited or none'istent.

This lack of control over one's health-care system is unfortunate. For, as the readings in this section show, the health-care system, which theoretically was established to provide the best medical care available, may actually be detrimental to one's well-being. ✦

14

Health Against Wealth: Problems of HMOs

George Anders

Today American health care is increasingly provided by business groups known as health maintenance organizations (HMOs). Many HMOs are, in essence, corporations out to make a profit. One consequence of the increasing corporate dominance of medicine is a growing inequality in the distribution of resources and the declining health conditions of the poor and minorities (Whiteis 1997). Corporations do not find it as profitable to operate in poor and minority communities.

Another consequence is a general decline in the quality of care. HMOs arose as a way to stem runaway costs in health care. But as George Anders contends, HMOs that are run as for-profit enterprises can seriously jeopardize the quality of health care. HMO physicians function in a structure that pressures them to consider both their own and the organization's profits. This structure affects their interaction with, and care of, their patients.

Reference

Whiteis, D.G. 1997. "Unhealthy Cities: Corporate Medicine, Community Economic Underdevelopment, and Public Health." *International Journal of Health Services* 27:227–42.

Focus Questions

1. What kind of frustrations do physicians encounter with managed care?

2. Why does managed care sometimes lead to a breakdown of trust?

3. Why is it hard to obtain a referral to a specialist in an HMO?

4. How have HMOs affected physicians' salaries and their practice of medicine?

It was a classic moment in a young doctor's education. Third-year medical student Brian Greenberg was completing back-to-back evening and night shifts at the pediatric ward of a Florida hospital. A night nurse woke him from a catnap at 2:40 A.M. and asked him to draw blood from a patient down the hall who was fighting an infection. Irritated at the interruption, Greenberg walked over to the bedside—and found a humbling sight: a 13-year-old blind boy, suffering from terminal cancer. "He had every reason in the world to be angry," Greenberg later recalled. "Much more than I did. But he wasn't angry at all. He was calm and friendly, and told me which vein would be the easiest for me to draw blood. I felt this incredible sorrow and love for him right there. I wished there was more I could do to help him. And I knew right then that I wanted to be a pediatrician."

Such dramatic personal encounters become career turning points. They can occur at any point in a medical education: in a maternity ward as a newborn safely enters the world, in a psychiatry rotation helping a mentally ill person battle schizophrenia, in an operating room as a veteran surgeon explains the intricacies of the craft. Whatever the setting, the moment marks the occasion when a young doctor suddenly knows what specialty to choose and what types of patients to help. Medical school instructors deliberately kindle that passion, telling students and doctors in training, "Do the most that you can for every single patient."

For more than a decade, Brian Greenberg has pushed himself to be the best pediatrician he can be. After graduating from medical school in 1986, he moved to California for advanced pediatric training at UCLA, concentrating on children with asthma and allergies. Today he sees nearly 150 children a week, as a pediatrician in private practice in Tarzana, a northwestern suburb of Los Angeles. He is a popular doctor, with a gentle voice and a bouncy sense of humor that makes most children regard him as an oversized playmate in corduroys. All day long he ministers to earaches, broken fingers, and asthma attacks, providing the essential primary care that has been a backbone of American medicine for more than a century. The abstract ideas of managed care seem incredibly remote in his offices, where giggles and yelps ring through the halls, where little boys and girls with stuffy noses say "Aaah," where mothers gently struggle to hold a baby still for a vaccination.

But when the children and their parents go home, Dr. Greenberg pours out a litany of frustrations with managed care. Half his patients now come via HMO contracts, something he never expected. Every day, he says, he must put up with ways that the managed-care system malfunctions, humbles him, or subverts his expertise. When he needs a blood sample drawn, managed-care plans tell him to bypass his own carefully trained nurses in favor of a cheaper site off premises—which has unfriendly technicians that leave children howling. When he wants to prescribe costly but powerful medicines, faraway HMO clerks second-guess his drug choices. And when very sick children need a specialist, managed-care rules can make it difficult or impossible to get a referral to the right one. "None of this helps me be a better doctor," the pediatrician says. "Much of it doesn't even save money in the long run. It just makes everything harder."

Dr. Greenberg's predicament points out the great paradox of managed care. It is a system that appears to work well overall from the panoramic vantage point of an HMO's head office, but that is often callous and clumsy in its dealings with individual patients. In the noisy commotion of a doctor's office, patients come in one at a time, with distinctive names, faces, and symptoms. Some of them truly need extra attention. All of them would like to believe that their doctor is committed to doing the most that he or she can to promote their well-being. Under the old medical model, that one-patient-at-a-time approach was regarded as the right way to practice. Yet managed care, with its emphasis on the aggregate, tugs doctors in a different direction. It makes physicians think like economists, causing them to pull back from individual cases and focus more on the allocation of resources across the whole patient population.

It is easy to see why managed-care companies want this sort of industrial logic brought to the primary-care doctor's office. Routine office visits are a major piece of overall medical spending, accounting for an estimated $50 billion a year, or 5 percent of total national health outlays. Not all that money is spent wisely or well; some patients in fee-for-service care get too much treatment while others get too little. Furthermore, most complex cases begin with an office visit to a person's regular doctor. As a result, managed-care companies tend to regard doctors' offices as facilities to be supervised with the same attention to cost-effectiveness that General Electric would apply to a light bulb factory or American Airlines would devote to a downtown ticket office.

Most HMOs start this efficiency campaign by assigning each member to a primary-care physician such as Dr. Greenberg, who is designated as the member's "gatekeeper." Health plans like to portray the gatekeeper as a patient's friendly personal physician, an image that is partly true. But the gatekeeper also is meant to keep a close eye on costs. Patients cannot see a specialist or have most medical tests performed without the explicit approval of either the primary-care physician or the managed-care company itself. A typical gatekeeper may handle 1,500 to 2,000 patients, with individual HMOs contributing a minimum of 100 and a maximum of the entire practice. To keep doctors efficient, HMOs every few months tally up how frequently their physicians are providing desirable, low-cost forms of care, such as immunizations, cholesterol checks, and cancer screenings. Other computer printouts keep tabs on doctors' use of costlier services such as X-rays, specialist referrals, and hospital days. Once health plans have such data at their fingertips, they can use a variety of incentives, penalties, and TQM techniques to encourage all doctors to practice in the manner that the managed-care plan has deemed "efficient."

From a patient's perspective the gatekeeper system is part of a whole family of controls built into managed care—affecting everything from a baby's birth to an elderly person's stroke or terminal illness. In theory, managed-care rules should steer patients to the right doctor at the right time. Often HMOs succeed in this. But . . . managed care's guidelines can hamper vital care. Specifically:

- When patients need heart surgery, HMOs have strong ideas about what hospitals to use. In several prominent instances HMOs have chosen to steer patients to centers that offer deep discounts, even if survival rates are far from the best available.

- When a person is diagnosed with cancer, getting an oncologist's candid advice about treatment choices is crucial. But one major HMO had its own ideas about what the cancer specialists should favor; it repeatedly lobbied doctors not to request a costly investigational treatment that the health plan didn't want to pay for.

- When an unexpected crisis strikes, HMO members must decide whether to call their managed-care plan for permission to go to the emergency room or simply dash ahead and call later. Patients who didn't ask for clearance have been stuck with medical bills as high as $26,000. Several patients who played by the rules suffered tragic delays and died.

- Mental-health spending is a favorite cost-cutting target of managed-care plans. Many have cut overall spending in half, which may leave schizophrenic and manic-depressive patients without the care that their doctors or family members believe they need.

- Millions of older Americans have found HMOs an attractive alternative to the conventional Medicare program. But a senior who suffers a stroke is likely to be discharged from the hospital while she still is having trouble moving her arms and legs, walking, or seeing clearly.

Fortunately, most Americans don't need a lot of medical care in any given year. Most people require only routine treatment, such as flu shots or ulcer medication, and for them the channels of managed care tend to work smoothly. Healthy members also are likely to appreciate HMOs' low copayments—$10 or less—and minimal paperwork. Surveys regularly show that 80 percent or more of HMO members say they are satisfied with their plans, a rating every bit as high as that of traditional insurance plans. Even in many cases of severe illness, the orderly paths sketched out by managed-care planners actually have helped patients get appropriate treatment.

Yet in a disturbing number of cases, the constraints of managed care, starting with the gatekeeper system, can lead to a breakdown of trust. Patients and their families no longer feel certain that their physician is making an all-out effort to help them. They are beginning to ask questions that never would have arisen 20 years ago: "Are you doing everything possible to treat my condition?" "What more could you be doing?" Persuading the new system to provide full medical care can become a negotiation, much like getting a plumber or car dealer to honor a service contract. Rather than the patient's friend and guardian, the doctor is simply a provider to bargain with.

In Orlando, Florida, internist Barbara Beeler felt so hemmed in by bureaucracy that she quit her staff-physician job at a Cigna HMO in the late 1980s to return to private practice. "It was all 'Spend less, do fewer tests,'" Dr. Beeler recalled. If a patient complained about blood in the urine, she found, Cigna's system required her to check with a referral coordinator and then the director of the local HMO center before getting clearance to order an intravenous pyelogram, the standard test to determine whether bleeding might be a sign of kidney cancer. Such tests cost more than $100 and usually don't find anything. But in a small percentage of cases the test indicates serious trouble. In a private-office setting, Dr. Beeler could order whatever tests she wanted right away; at the HMO it could take an extra day of paperwork to get her treatment approach approved. At Cigna, she said, "it became exceedingly difficult to feel good about what I was doing."

One of the most contentious issues for both patients and doctors involves managed-care protocol for referral to a specialist. HMOs argue, with some justification, that unmanaged care sends too many ailments directly into specialists' hands. As the health plans see it, cost-effective medicine means making greater use of a primary-care doctor rather than sending every rash to a dermatologist, every stomach ailment to a gastroenterologist. Academic researchers have found that some ailments, such as stomach disorders, often can be treated just as well by primary-care doctors and at lower cost.

As a result, managed-care plans deliberately make it hard to get specialist referrals. At the very least, plans require gatekeepers or the HMO itself to approve a visit to a specialist. Many health plans set up financial incentives for primary-care doctors; those who don't send many cases to specialists get bonuses, while frequent referrers may suffer penalties. Bonuses vary by plan, but in the course of a year, they can amount to several thousand dollars for a practice that relies heavily on HMO patients. Without such constraints, HMO executives contend, patients would be preyed upon by specialists eager to jack up their bills by using costly probes, scopes, and imaging machines as much as possible.

By tilting economic incentives in the other direction—and paying gatekeepers to withhold care—HMOs create a different set of potential problems. Those issues were spotlighted by Jerome Kassirer, editor of the *New England Journal of Medicine,* in a 1995 essay entitled "The Morality of Managed Care." He observed:

> On the one hand, doctors are expected to provide a wide range of services, recommend the best treatments and improve patients' quality of life. On the other, to keep expenses to a minimum, they must limit the use of services, increase efficiency, shorten the time spent with each patient and use specialists sparingly. Although many see this as an abstract dilemma, I believe that increasingly the struggle will be more concrete and stark: physicians will be forced to choose between the best interests of their patients and their own economic survival.

To guard against neglect of patients, HMOs periodically look for signs that their gatekeepers are not providing sufficient care. Extremely low rates of specialist referrals—less than half the norm—will set off warning bells at some plans. Numerous member complaints also may prompt action. And many HMO officials say that doctors who ignore their patients' needs ultimately will suffer financially, because manageable ailments will become much more serious and generate big medical bills that will be charged against the doctor's earnings. That safeguard only works, however, if patients stay with one plan for many years.

In any event, HMOs and their gatekeepers are hardly flawless in their efforts to deny needless referrals while allowing the essential ones to go through. A mid-1995 survey by Robert Blendon, a professor at the Harvard School of Public Health, found that 21 percent of HMO members in poor health said they hadn't been able to see a specialist when they needed to in the past year. Only 15 percent of comparable fee-for-service patients made the same complaint. Lawsuits across the United States allege that HMO gatekeepers have restricted access to specialists so tightly that medical tragedies have occurred. In an extreme case, computer programmer William Bacigalupo alleged in a 1992 lawsuit filed in New York state court for Dutchess County that he incurred temporary kidney failure at least in part because of his HMO's unwillingness to refer him to the appropriate specialist. Bacigalupo suffered from cryoglobulinemia, a blood-plasma disorder that can damage internal organs. Prior to joining Healthshield, a New York HMO, he had been seeing a rheumatologist for his condition. In his suit, Bacigalupo alleged that the HMO and his primary-care doctor had stymied his requests for referrals to a specialist, causing his condition to deteriorate. A New York State jury in May 1995 awarded the 40-year-old patient more than $1 million in damages. The HMO appealed the verdict.

Even when HMOs do allow referrals, their choice of available specialists can be problematic. Allan Schwartz, a New York cardiologist, observed, "When I used to encounter an aneurysm, I would send the patient to the best aneurysm surgeon I knew. It would be where you'd want your mother to go. Now I have to look at a list of surgeons who are in an HMO's network. I do my best to identify someone in the network who is OK. But it isn't someone of the caliber that I could get otherwise."

Aware that some doctors reluctantly join HMO networks but never fully welcome managed-care tactics, several major HMOs explicitly bar their participating doctors from making any negative comments about the health plan. Breaking this code of silence can be grounds for expulsion from the network. That provision was tested in late 1995 when David Himmelstein, a Massachusetts internist participating in U.S. Healthcare's HMOs, spoke out against the health plan on the Donahue television show. Two weeks later Dr. Himmelstein was told that U.S. Healthcare wouldn't need his services anymore. The HMO said only that it was realigning its network in Massachusetts, but Dr. Himmelstein interpreted the ouster as punishment for his comments. The Massachusetts legislature subsequently passed a law banning such HMO "gag clauses." Dr. Himmelstein eventually was reinstated into the U.S. Healthcare network.

Many physicians take a warmer view of managed care, contending that the benefits—more affordable care for the public, better data on how each doctor is performing—outweigh the flaws. The doctors who really thrive in HMO settings simply don't see limited access to tests and specialists as a major problem. "I want first crack at treating a disease," says New York internist Steven Tamarin, rather than sending everything from acne to yeast infections on to a specialist. Even more assertive is Richard Morrow, a Bronx family practitioner. Everywhere he turns he sees examples of specialists overdoing it. In his view, otolaryngologists put middle-ear tubes into far too many children who don't need them; cardiologists order batteries of tests that aren't always necessary; and back surgeons collect huge fees for operating on bulging disks that may not be the cause of patients' pain. "When you go in for all these treatments, you're just helping put those doctors' kids through school," Dr. Morrow snips.

From that point of view HMO guidelines are the best way to rein in specialists.

One of the most intense battlegrounds over managed care has been southern California. Nearly half of all workers in the area belong to HMOs, one of the highest rates of managed care in the United States. Since the early 1990s big employers have been especially aggressive in negotiating cheaper rates for health insurance. That has led HMOs to cut their payments to doctors and hospitals and to tighten the rules on what services will be paid for. Doctors have banded together into large negotiating groups in efforts to increase their clout. Health-care consultants frequently cite the southern California market as a bellwether for the rest of the country, predicting that changes occurring in the Los Angeles area will play out in similar form throughout the United States in the next three to five years.

The promise and pitfalls of the rush toward managed care come to life in the day-to-day practice of pediatrician Brian Greenberg in Tarzana. An easygoing man in his late 30s, Dr. Greenberg became an HMO gatekeeper by accident. When he finished his training at UCLA in 1991, Dr. Greenberg toyed with the idea of practicing full-time as a pediatric allergist, but decided he preferred the variety of general pediatrics. Rather than set up a solo practice, he joined a small medical group run by a veteran pediatrician, Robert Barnhard, whom he already knew and liked from his UCLA years. Dr. Greenberg agreed to share a patient population of nearly 8,000 with Dr. Barnhard and two other younger doctors, Victoria Millet and Elaine Rosen. Dr. Barnhard divided up the income from the partnership, paying Dr. Greenberg a flat salary slightly above $100,000.

Until the end of 1992 the four doctors catered only to patients with traditional fee-for-service insurance. But then parents began mentioning that changes in their health insurance might force them to look for different pediatricians. One of the biggest local employers, the Los Angeles County Unified School District, decided in late 1992 to move all its employees into HMOs. Parents began scouring for new pediatricians. The threatened exodus was especially unsettling for Dr.

Barnhard, who had been in practice for more than 25 years. In that time very few of his patients had quit, and when one did leave, he wondered whether he had disappointed them in some way. Now parents were telling Drs. Barnhard and Greenberg that everything about their practice was fine, except that the doctors weren't signed up with their HMOs.

Eager to keep their doors open to long-time patients, the doctors decided to affiliate with as many HMOs as they could. To do so, they were required to use a middleman, an independent physicians' association, or IPA, that negotiated pay rates and contracts for hundreds of doctors with managed-care leaders such as Aetna, CaliforniaCare, Cigna, and Health Net. Doctors at the local hospital sponsored one such association: Tarzana IPA. Physicians a few miles away had formed two other such groups. Drs. Greenberg, Barnhard, Millet, and Rosen promptly joined all three IPAs to be sure of keeping almost all of their patients.

The managed-care package looked soothing at first. Dr. Greenberg and his colleagues could stay in private practice and take patients with all kinds of insurance. The physicians simply needed to agree to treat HMO patients according to managed-care rules. Pay rates would change; instead of being reimbursed for each visit or test, the doctors would be paid through capitation, the system of flat monthly rates per patient. But Dr. Greenberg and his colleagues didn't foresee the enormous consequences of these changes. The physicians briefly scanned their 40-page contracts with the IPAs, then signed them.

Three years later Dr. Greenberg musters a thin smile when recalling his early optimism. HMOs now provide half his patients, and the percentage continues to climb. Managed-care companies "have taken over our practice," he says. The values that he learned in medical school no longer are universally admired—or even taken seriously. As Dr. Greenberg observes, "I think my patients like me. I believe I practice good medicine. It used to be that if you did those two things, you were in good shape. But now none of that may matter. It all comes down to contracting decisions. Which HMO do you sign up with?

Which IPA? How many patients can they send you? And will they decide to?"

Some of the most wrenching situations involve the managed-care rules for pediatric and maternal care right after a child is born. Medical experts, notably the American College of Obstetricians and Gynecologists, recommend that mothers with no complications be discharged 48 hours after a vaginal delivery and 96 hours after a cesarean. That allows time to detect any abnormal postpartum bleeding and to check that the newborn doesn't have jaundice, infections, congenital heart problems, or other complications. But the decision about when to send a mother and baby home no longer is left up to the obstetrician and the pediatrician. Power has moved over to the health plans that pay the bills, and they often put patients on a different clock. Many HMOs pay only for shorter stays: 24 hours or less after vaginal deliveries; 72 hours after cesareans.

For HMOs the monetary rewards from shorter maternity stays are immense. Whittling away one hospital day from every birth can translate each year into 5 million fewer hospital days nationwide, or roughly $6 billion in savings. But such financial gains may carry hidden costs. Pediatric journals carry accounts of life-threatening infections and congenital heart problems in newborns that were spotted only in the second day of a maternity stay. Rapid medical treatment or surgery can save such children; delays may prove fatal. Such cases are rare. As Dr. Greenberg puts it, "The overwhelming majority of babies are fine, no matter what you do." Even so, the notion of losing even one rescuable newborn appalls him.

So, like many physicians, Dr. Greenberg now feels pressured to practice two-tier medicine. Patients with generous insurance can remain in the hospital for the full maternity stay recommended by medical panels. Patients with skimpier HMO coverage must settle for the shorter stay unless the family wants to pay for extra care themselves or Dr. Greenberg can outwit the managed-care guidelines. He has a few favorite ruses that can win his patients a few extra hours in the hospital, such as the sudden "meeting" that prevents him from signing discharge papers right away. By and large, though, he has ended up doing what managed-care companies want—and he is not proud of it. "I don't want to live in a world where insurance companies have decided to sacrifice a few patients to save a buck," he says.

On this life-and-death issue, doctors and patients have mobilized fast against HMOs' cost-saving guidelines. In the 1995–96 legislative cycle, more than a dozen states passed laws requiring insurance companies to pay for 48-hour maternity stays. A similar bill was introduced in the U.S. Congress and won support from President Clinton. HMOs generally opposed such bills as unnecessary meddling in medical issues. Health plans contended that some publicized deaths of quickly discharged newborns didn't constitute a trend, noting that a study of 30,000 deliveries at Kaiser Permanente showed no connection between short stays and higher complication or mortality rates for newborns. But HMOs' statistics couldn't allay public concern about the well-being of mothers and babies sent home barely one day after birth. Besides, other researchers found evidence that short-stay babies might be at greater risk, particularly for conditions such as jaundice. . . .

Managed-care rules can create more mischief in a baby's first year of life, typically the pediatrician's busiest time. Infants receive a battery of immunizations against mumps, diphtheria, and a half-dozen other diseases. They are supposed to have a well-baby checkup every two or three months. Inevitably, most infants also see the doctor at least once or twice for fevers and other ailments. Those repeated brief visits allow pediatricians to do a great deal of preventive care, something that HMOs play up in their marketing brochures. But when it comes to paying the pediatrician, managed-care pay scales vary tremendously. Some companies pay as much as $600 for a year's worth of infant care; others' rates may be less than $50 for the same work. Such pay scales leave doctors seething; they also raise the risk that physicians will skimp on care.

Curiously, the managed-care system starts with enough money that it could pay its front-line soldiers—the primary-care doctors—

quite well. But each premium dollar travels a long path, from a corporate employer through an HMO and other intermediaries, before reaching physicians. At each stage middlemen who never see patients skim off their share. By the time Dr. Greenberg presses a stethoscope to a baby's chest or asks a mother if her child is eating properly, only a sliver of the original premium dollar is left. . .

Some of the skimpiest paychecks in 1994 and early 1995 came from Southern California IPA, known as SCIPA. At that time, the IPA paid Dr. Greenberg $108 a year for children between ages two and 18. For children under two, he got $266.40 a year. But that apparent pay boost for infants was deceptive. The pediatrician himself had to pay for vaccines, which cost $222 in an infant's first year. The money left over, $44, was meant to cover managed care's contributions to doctors' incomes, overhead, and supplies. It barely matched what parents might pay for a single oil change and tune-up at the local gas station.

"How can you do decent care on $44 a year?" Dr. Greenberg asked. When he chose pediatrics, he knew he was going into one of the lowest-paying areas of medicine. His yearly income is far higher than that of most Americans, but barely half what his medical-school classmates who went into radiology, pathology, or other specialties can command. And his income is largely at the mercy of plans such as SCIPA, which links doctors with most of southern California's dominant HMOs: Cigna, Aetna, FHP, PruCare, and nearly a dozen more. SCIPA in late 1995 boosted its pay rates considerably after being acquired by a larger IPA, Huntington Provider Group. But for several years the managed-care plan valued Dr. Greenberg's work at less than 50 percent of what he charged fee-for-service patients. Inevitably, he speeded up his rate of seeing patients, to about six an hour, trying to cover expenses by shuttling more patients through the office in a day.

Such pay gripes are part of a fundamental worry among some physicians: that HMOs regard the fine points of doctoring with disdain if they think about them at all. Managed-care companies can track several dozen aspects of a doctor's practice, including such essentials as a pediatrician's immunization rate for all children assigned to that doctor. Over the past decade, many HMOs have nudged doctors to do better in most of those categories, often surpassing the rates of preventive-care measures in fee-for-service medicine. Physicians applaud those gains. But they contend that their best work is in subtle, impossible-to-quantify areas that won't ever show up on HMO spreadsheets.

At least a half-dozen times a day, for example, Dr. Greenberg carries out a 10-minute well-baby visit. Such a session may seem like merely a friendly chat with the baby's mother or father, but it is packed with rapid, careful probes for potential problems. Are the infant's feet and hands cold? Maybe there is a circulation problem. How does the heart sound? Maybe there is a congenital problem that can be caught early. Is the baby rolling over? Starting to crawl? Making different sounds? This is where development problems can be spotted early and treated if necessary. How is the child sleeping? Eating? Such questions check that the parents are caring for the child correctly. If there are problems, they can be discussed before the child's well-being suffers. "I think that's important," Dr. Greenberg says. "But all the HMO wants to know is: did I do the immunizations on time?"

Managed care is at its best in the treatment of routine illnesses. The capitation system ensures that doctors get their flat monthly payment even if they provide only a few minutes of phone advice for a nervous parent. A meaningful part of primary care consists of brief oral advice: the equivalent of "Put ice on it" or "Take two aspirin and call me in the morning." For basically healthy children, Dr. Greenberg finds, the capitation system lets him treat simple ailments simply, without feeling any financial incentive to insist on an office visit.

HMOs also try to make sure that doctors follow managed-care formularies—and don't prescribe costly drugs when cheaper alternatives will do. Among antibiotics, for example, generic amoxicillin is a favorite, costing $10 or less for a multiweek prescription. Stronger new antibiotics that can cost $50 or more are off-limits unless a doctor can make an overpowering case for using them. Nationwide cost savings from following formularies may total $1 billion a year or more, money that can go toward other types of care or lower insurance premiums.

Yet almost every doctor can cite cases where overly strict HMO formularies led to mean-spirited or wrong decisions. Dr. Greenberg, for example, sees a fair number of children under age six who have minor eye infections. He can prescribe several different antibiotics that are generally effective. His top choice, Polytrim, can be administered painlessly. But on several occasions HMOs vetoed that prescription and told him to switch to a cheaper substitute, sodium Sulamyd, which must be applied four times a day and can sometimes sting a child's eyes. Boxed in, he had no choice but to rewrite the prescription or tell parents to pay for the better drug out of their own pockets. "To me it matters a lot whether a four-year-old is in pain. . . but to the HMO it's just money, they don't see the child and they don't care." [Dr. Greenberg says.]

This bargain-hunting approach faces its toughest test in managed-care coverage of the seriously ill. It is a health insurance truism that the sickest 3 percent of policyholders account for 40 percent of all medical spending. Those are the cases that an HMO most avidly wants to avoid—or at least "manage." Managed-care executives like to portray themselves as watchful shepherds of sick members, lining up the best possible care while occasionally saving a few nickels. But primary-care physicians such as Dr. Greenberg see a different picture.

Tensions start when Dr. Greenberg wants to refer an ailing child to a specialist, which happens several times a day. Dr. Greenberg's general skills let him treat 90 percent or more of the children who walk in his door, but when a young boy's bladder disorder doesn't respond to the first two programs of treatment, or a teenager's mood swings alarm a parent it is time to call in an expert. Under traditional indemnity insurance, such referrals are a snap. Pediatricians simply tell parents whom to see next and let the insurer pick up his bill. Parents can even hunt for a specialist on their own if they disagree with their pediatrician's suggestions. But in managed care Dr. Greenberg must fill out a referral form, send it over to his IPA, and wait for approval. Patients may wait a week or two— sometimes more— before they see the specialist, unless a dire emergency exists. And the choice of specialists is a far cry from the medical all-star team to which Dr. Greenberg can steer his fee-for-service patients.

On a bookshelf next to Dr. Greenberg's examination rooms are two thin folders listing all the specialists to whom he can send his managed-care patients. The 32-page SCIPA list is in a blue folder; the 28-page TIPA list is in red. As the last patients leave his office one evening, Dr. Greenberg flips through the list and marvels at his lack of choices. In the TIPA folder there are only two dermatologists, neither of whom specializes in children. The list of general surgeons has shrunk to two. Originally there were five, but three pulled out because they were not getting paid on time. Only two oncologists are listed, and one of them isn't really available. Next to the cancer specialist's name, Dr. Greenberg's office manager, Vernalie Dermajian, has written "No new patients!"

That skimpy roster of experts vexes Dr. Greenberg. "I don't expect to be able to use the best in the world every time," he says. "But I do expect conscientious care." Some doctors on the approved lists were chosen, he suspects, mostly because they agreed to discount their fees 45 percent or more, accept outside review of how often they order tests, and otherwise play by managed care's rules. Top specialists won't agree to such terms, Dr. Greenberg notes. His most trusted dermatologist, in fact, briefly was part of the TIPA network, but dropped out when the managed-care plan tried to cut her fees further.

Sometimes Dr. Greenberg and his colleagues can persuade a managed-care plan to bend its rules and allow a patient to see a nonnetwork specialist. Such a request, however, almost always is a struggle. One such case involved a young girl with eosinophilic leukemia, a rare blood cancer. After five weeks of haggling with IPAs and HMOs, one of Dr. Greenberg's colleagues, Dr. Millet, won the right for the girl to be treated by a top pediatric oncologist at Children's Hospital in Los Angeles. During that time, though, the girl's treatment was delayed because the managed-care companies tried to steer her to an in-network adult oncologist who had limited experience treating the child's condition. By eventually getting the girl to the appropriate specialist, Dr. Millet believed she put her on the road to remission and perhaps outright cure. But she remained troubled by the lost five weeks and the narrowly avoided outcome of sending a very sick child to the wrong expert.

When specialists agree to work under managed-care rules, they surrender their long-standing freedom to bill insurers for whatever tests and equipment they think are needed. Dr. Greenberg, for example, continues to practice part-time as an allergist, treating children with asthma. He would like health insurance to cover whatever he prescribes, but his HMO patients sometimes run into nasty surprises. In one case he prescribed six inhalers, a three-month supply, for a boy. The parents' HMO approved only five. To a managed-care company that cut represents a 17 percent saving. To Dr. Greenberg such cutbacks squeeze out a margin of safety and make it more likely that the child will run out of medicine before his refill date. If that happens, the boy could succumb to an uncontrolled asthma attack—a scary outcome for him and a potential trigger for a $1,000 emergency-room visit that would wipe out the HMO's earlier cost savings. . .

In the worst predicament of all are children with major chronic diseases struggling to fit into the capitated, gatekeeper system of managed care. Such children may need a raft of specialist referrals every month, and never-ending tests and office visits. Those needs don't square well with a system that pays doctors a flat monthly rate for each patient. Dr. Greenberg, for example, gets $8 to $12 a month for children older than two, without any extra cash for patients who need the most care. Easy and hard cases are supposed to average out. But his monthly capitation checks don't begin to cover the costs of seeing a child with muscular dystrophy, Down's syndrome, or juvenile rheumatoid arthritis.

As a result some doctors with HMO contracts are quietly closing their doors to high-risk patients. The standard excuse among such physicians: "I don't know if I'm skilled enough to take care of such a child. Try someone else." The dodging of high-risk patients has long been an unpleasant aspect of the health insurance industry. Now, as HMOs push the financial responsibility for patients onto doctors' shoulders, some physicians are starting to behave like insurance companies themselves—redlining the patients that could annihilate their capitation budgets. "I think it's unethical," says Dr. Greenberg, who takes in some of these economically orphaned children. "But if you get only $96 a year to take care of these children, they will be a financial drag on your practice. I know I'm going to see them every month, and every visit will mean five referrals."

At 6 p.m. one autumn day, Drs. Greenberg and Barnhard sit at their small desks in the back room of their Tarzana office suite and debate a tantalizing question. What would happen if they shed all their HMO contracts and went back to a pure fee-for-service practice? Both doctors can cite what they believe are deep flaws with managed care and its gatekeeper system: underpayment for important preventive treatment, undue meddling in the doctors' choice of labs and pharmaceuticals, and limited access to good specialists who can help the sickest children. Yet after a few minutes of discussion, the two doctors realize that the idea of breaking away from managed care is only a pipe dream.

"Overnight, we'd lose 15 percent to 40 percent of our revenue," Dr. Greenberg says. "Maybe patients would switch insurance so they could keep seeing us. But a large percentage would just drop us and go to another doctor. Either we've never established a relationship with them, or they just don't want to pay more."

Dr. Barnhard is even blunter. "We could say 'We don't like managed care, and we'd like to go back to what was.' But the truth is, the old practice doesn't exist anymore."

Critical Evaluation

1. How might an HMO executive respond to Anders?

2. Could HMOs be set up in a way to avoid the kind of problems the author discusses? How?

3. Do patients benefit from HMOs? If so, in what ways?

4. The problem of adequate health care continues to be nettlesome in the United States. Do any other nations have a system that is more effective and that would be practical for us?

15

Minority Health

Dale F. Pearson

A *person's health and the kind of health care he or she receives may differ depending on whether the person is male or female, white or a member of a racial minority. As a report from the U.S. Department of Health and Human Services (1991: iii) put it: "The health status of minority and other disadvantaged populations in this country continues to fall far short of the levels that access to health services has made possible for most Americans." The report noted that minorities suffer a greater number of both physical and mental problems than do those of the white majority.*

Various factors at the macro- and microlevels help account for the health differentials. A greater proportion of minorities live in poverty and the deprivations of poverty adversely affect both physical and mental health regardless of race. The poor may also develop skeptical or negative attitudes about health care, or they may weigh the costs of a visit to the doctor with other pressing needs and decide against medical care unless the need is dire.

In this selection, Dale Pearson discusses the health problems of one group of minority persons—African American men. These health problems are related, among other things, not only to the structural factor of higher rates of poverty but also to the social psychological factor of pervasive prejudice.

Reference

U.S. Department of Health and Human Services. 1991. *Health Status of Minorities and Low-Income Groups*. Washington, DC: U.S. Government Printing Office.

Focus Questions

1. How do African American men's mortality rates compare with those of whites?

2. What are some of the major health issues faced by African American men?

3. What can be done to improve the mortality statistics and health of African American men?

The Black male in today's society continues to be at risk on a variety of important sociocultural and health issues, which impact negatively on his life, and on the lives of his family, friends, and the community. Recent studies have portrayed the Black man as rapidly becoming an endangered species (Parham 1987; Gibbs, 1984; Leavy, 1983). It is clear from popular and scientific literature that the Black male is experiencing enormous pressure in many areas. These stresses are unique to the Black man, and have implications for Black youth as well as for older Black men who struggle with concerns about survival in a White-dominated society. This chapter addresses the external and internal factors faced by a majority of Black men and gives recommendations to educators and service providers on how to better provide for the apparent needs of Black males, with suggestions as to how Blacks may take greater initiative for survival.

Life Expectancy

As recorded for 1988, the life expectancy for an American Black male was 64.9 years compared to 72.3 years for a White male; in other words, a difference of 7.4 fewer years of life for a Black man compared to a White man (U.S. Department of Health and Human Services 1990). Although these statistics are global and reflect averages, many Black men do not achieve even these years of life expectancy.

Homicide is the leading cause of death among young Black men. In 1988, the Black homicide rate (59 per 100,000) was more than 7 times the homicide rate for White youth (8 per 100,000 population) (U.S. Department of Health and Human Services 1990). Poussaint (1983) reported that "Black homicide rates are 7 to 8 times those of Whites . . . and contribute significantly to the shortened life span of the Black male"(p. 162).

Homicide statistics, reported by race and sex for the United States for 1987, indicate that Black males accounted for a total of 7,518 victims. In 1988, Black adults between the ages 25 and 44 had the highest death rate(367 per 100,000 population), or 2.5 times the rate for White adults (149 per 100,000) (U.S. Department of Health and Human Services 1990). From these figures it is apparent that Black self-hatred, as well as the frustration that activates rage and incites a perpetrator to commit homicide on another Black male, may account for the justification and legitimacy of this violent attack.

A recent study, which highlighted mortality rates in New York City's Central Harlem health district, revealed that 90% of the inhabitants were Black and 41% lived below the poverty line. This group's age-adjusted rate of mortality from all causes was the highest in New York City, more than double that of U.S. Whites and 50% higher than that of U.S. Blacks, both male and female. During a 20-year period, 1960–1980, the death rate from homicides rose from 25.3 to 90.8 per 100,000 population. Central Harlem has a high mortality rate for persons under age 65. "A large proportion . . . directly due to violence and substance abuse . . . cirrhosis, homicide, accidents, drug dependency, and alcohol use were considered the most important underlying causes of death in 35% of all deaths among people under 65" (McCord & Freeman, 1990 p. 175).

Health Issues

The United States in 1986 spent $458 billion on health care for all residents (Health Care Financing Administration 1987). Hospital care accounted for 39% or $180 billion of the total. In that same year, Blacks below age 65 were 1.6 times more likely than Whites to have no adequate health coverage (Harper 1990). Medicaid, which originally aimed at providing medical services to low-income families, has become the "largest third-party financier of long-term care in the United States. Total Medicaid benefits (including both federal and state shares) came to $44 billion in 1986, of which $16 billion was for nursing home care" (Harper 1990, p. 241).

Throughout the years, Blacks have experienced more difficulty than Whites in benefiting from the health care system and have expressed greater displeasure with those services. During 1983, Blacks spent an average of 8.2 days in hospitals, compared to Whites' average of 6.5 days per episode (Harper 1990, p. 242). Many Blacks find it difficult to gain access to the health care system for a variety of reasons. Russo (1982) mentioned that although poor Black people have Medicare and Medicaid available to them, they are less likely than Whites and people with higher incomes to have regular health care maintenance.

Cancer

In general, Black men are at greater risk for developing cancer than are White men; data through 1985 reported that the average annual age-adjusted incidence for black males was 450 per 100,000 compared to 375 per 100,000 population for White males (U.S. Department of Health and Human Services 1990). Lung cancer for Black males continues to lead as the most lethal form of cancer, accounting for a 44% greater incidence than in White males. Black men smoke more cigarettes than are smoked by any other age-sex group, with the result that the mortality rate for Black men is at least 18% higher than for White men (Johnson 1983). Other cancers in Black males are also high compared to White males. Prostate cancer, as reported for 1977, had 110 incidences per 100,000 population, whereas White men reported 65 incidences per 100,000. The incidence of esophageal cancer is 4 times higher for Black males than for White males (U.S. Department of Health and Human Services 1986a).

Most researchers tend to agree that the majority of cancers are directly related to environmental exposures. "Substances or conditions known to be related to the risk of cancer are tobacco, alcohol, high fat diet, asbestos, drugs, suppression of immune capacity, and ionizing radiation" (Jarris & Parron 1982, p. 137). Even under conditions of equal employment, social/epidemiologic research, where available, has identified that minorities experience higher exposure to certain pathogenic agents (Jarris & Parron 1982, p. 137). Many Black men have been employed in the lowest paid and often least desirable jobs, which, being hazardous to general health, are literally "killing them" (Michaels 1982, p. 147). It has also been reported that among workers in steel mills, Blacks often have higher rates of death from cancer than Whites. Black men working in the coke ovens experience the greatest source of carcinogenic exposure of all men in the steel industry (U.S. Department of Health and Human Services 1986b). There are a disproportionate number of Blacks working in the mixing and compounding areas of rubber production plants, and these "workers have elevated rates of stomach, lung, blood, bladder, and lymphatic cancer" (Michaels 1982, p. 44).

Sickle-Cell Anemia

Blacks are one of the major groups at risk for sickle-cell anemia. The trait for this hereditary disease is estimated to affect 1 out of every 10 to 12 Blacks, or 8% to 10% of the entire Black population in America (Williams 1977). This disease transmits the abnormal hemoglobin in the blood as the major factor in the perpetuation of one of the major debilitating conditions affecting Blacks today. Although it is usually diagnosed in childhood, it is not uncommon for a person to reach adulthood before clear symptoms occur. The clinical crisis may include "attacks of bone and joint pain or abdominal pain . . . fever lasting hours or days . . . headaches, paralysis, and convulsion" (Harper 1990, p. 245). Clinical manifestations can vary greatly, and prognosis is varied; children may die from cerebral hemorrhage, whereas adults may live relatively long lives. Early diagnosis and treatment appear to be important in the course of this disease.

In a recent report Vichinsky et al. (1990) reviewed the uses of transfusion therapy on Black patients with sickle-cell anemia. Historically, because of a variety of complications with this disease, red-cell blood transfusions have been the treatment of choice (Patten, Patel, Sotto, and Gayle 1989; Piomelli, 1985; Schmalzer, Chien, and Brown 1982). "The majority of patients with sickle cell anemia have received a red-cell transfusion by the time they reach adulthood"

(Samaik, Schomack, and Lusher 1986; Orlina, Unger, and Koshy 1978).

However, alloimmunization, an abnormal reaction to the transfusion process, can make it difficult for some patients successfully to receive compatible donor blood. Vichinsky et al. (1990) compared 107 Black patients with sickle-cell anemia who received transfusions with 51 Black patients who received no transfusions and 19 non-Black patients who received transfusions of red-cell blood for other forms of chronic anemia. This research attempted to determine whether the racial background of the blood-donor population contributed to the high rate of alloimmunization. Giblett (1961) earlier reported that the rate of alloimmunization was higher when Black recipients were administered red-cell blood from White donors. Generally patients with sickle-cell anemia receive blood from White donors because this blood is more readily available (Ambruso, Githens, and Alcom 1987; Patten et al. 1989). In Galveston, Texas, for example, 98% of donors are White, and in Washington, DC, 88% are White (Luban 1989; Mallory, Malamut, and Ginther 1989). Blacks account for a "disproportionately small part of the donor population" (Vichinsky et al. 1990, p. 1620). In this present study, 30% of Black patients with sickle-cell anemia had an alloimmunization response; 11% had delayed transfusion responses. Results indicate that "antigen mismatching between largely white donors and Black recipients accounted for this high incidence of alloimmunization" (Vichinsky et al. 1990 p. 1621). Black persons must be aggressively enlisted as donors to offset this problem of transfusions in Blacks.

Tuberculosis

The prevalence of tuberculosis among Blacks is known to be about twice that among Whites (Stead and To 1987; Stead, To, Harrison, and Abraham 1987; Stead, Lofgren, Warren, and Thomas 1985). Moreover, the rates for tuberculosis are considerably higher among the disadvantaged. In 1981, non-Whites experienced over 3 times the rate (37.6) of all races combined (Stewart 1972, p. 9). There are indications that susceptibility to tuberculosis may be inherited. There are some physiological conditions such as malnutrition, fatigue, and diabetes that render persons less resistant to disease and thus prime candidates for tuberculosis (Burton, Smith, and Nichols 1980, p. 277). Malnutrition, overcrowding, and poor sanitation contribute to the reception and spread of many infectious diseases, including tuberculosis (Ventura, Taffel, and Spratley 1975).

Stead et al. (1990) studied the prevalence of tuberculosis among Blacks confined to 165 racially integrated nursing homes in Arkansas and found, based on a database analysis of more than 53,000 residents, that Blacks were infected more readily by mycobacterium tuberculosis than Whites. Three groups of nursing homes were studied and the percentage of residents infected with tuberculosis tended to be "larger in homes with a higher proportion of Blacks," both male and female (Stead, Senner, Reddick, and Lofgren 1990, p. 423). Stead et al. (1990) also studied two levels of exposure to mycobacterium tuberculosis among men in two Arkansas prisons. The analysis of the data supports a finding of greater tuberculosis infectability among Black men. The data in these studies confirm the well-known and accepted fact that the prevalence of tuberculosis infection among Blacks, particularly Black males, is about twice that of Whites. The data further suggest strong heritable differences between individuals and groups as regards the human body's innate defense system. Some groups have defenses that function before infection develops, "as distinct from the immune system that develops afterward . . . the role of differences in infectability is significant" (Stead et al. 1990, p. 426).

Hypertension

An estimated 60 million people in the United States have some form of elevated blood pressure, which increases their chances for illness and premature death. Hypertension, when left untreated, is the largest single contributor to stroke, heart disease, and kidney failure. During 1980, an estimated 25.1 million patients saw outpatient physicians for hypertensive disease. In 1980,

Black males had one and one third the prevalence rate of White males (Harlan et al. 1983). It has been suggested that today Blacks, both male and female, are at one third greater risk of high blood pressure than are all Whites (Raloff 1990).

There are several risk factors associated with cerebrovascular disease in Blacks, including high blood pressure and diabetes, which contribute to a greater risk of developing a stroke than is true for Whites. Black death rates run 80% higher than death rates for Whites, and the disadvantaged have higher rates of several risk factors associated with stroke and hypertension (National Center for Health Statistics 1983, p. 32).

The study by Harburg et al. (1973) found that Blacks were most affected by the relationship between anger and blood pressure. Dimsdale (1986) examined the relationship of suppressed anger and systolic blood pressure and found this relationship statistically significant for White men (< .04) but only demonstrated as a trend in Black men and thus not statistically significant (p. 432). Results of both studies reveal inconclusive data regarding the relationship between anger and blood pressure in Black men.

The sodium/potassium ratio, Na/K, "was observed to be related to blood pressure in Black but not white persons" (Harlan et al. 1983, p. 24). To reduce hypertension, Blacks would need to reduce their sodium/potassium ratio (U.S. Department of Health and Human Services 1986c, p. 113)

A question still needs to be answered. Are Black men at greater risk for hypertension than are White men? From 1980 data, it appears that the incidence of the disease has decreased for all Blacks but that the risk is still high among Black males in the United States.

Drinking Patterns

Arteriosclerosis, commonly called hardening of the arteries, is one of the 10 leading causes of death, and in 1980 accounted for 6.4 deaths per 100,000 population for Blacks, as compared to 5.6 deaths for Whites (U.S. Department of Health and Human Services 1986d).

Throughout the years, sociocultural studies have provided conflicting data on drinking patterns among Black males. Some studies have suggested that drinking and drunkenness are pervasive among Blacks (Hannerz 1970). Often studies have suggested that Blacks are at much greater risk for alcoholism and other alcohol-related problems than Whites (Garagliano, Lilienfeld, and Medeloff 1979; Herd 1985; National Institute on Alcohol Abuse and Alcoholism 1980). Harper (1976) reports the following:

> Alcoholism is one of the most serious mental health issues facing the black community. Three times as many blacks die from alcoholism as whites. . . . Alcohol abuse is associated with over 50% of the deaths from accidents. . . . Alcohol is both a depressive drug and one that releases inhibitions. . . . It is closely linked to violent behaviors . . . rape, child abuse, and spouse battering. (p. 35)

A 1984 national survey found more similarities than differences in drinking patterns among Black and White men. Notable differences suggested that young Black men are less likely to be frequent heavy drinkers than are White men in the 18–29 age group, but Black men in the 30–39 age group show increases in frequent drinking. In the 40–49 age group, both Black and White men show declines in frequent high maximum drinking patterns, as well as increases in abstention and/or infrequent drinking. Comparing income between Black and White men suggests that the heaviest drinking groups among Black men are those with modest incomes, and that Black men with the highest incomes of $30,000 per year or more are drinking considerably less than White men at similar income levels (Herd 1990). Results suggest that young Black men (aged 30–39) with modest incomes are at greatest risk for the heaviest drinking patterns.

Depression

Because Black men often have more negative life experiences than White men (Gary 1985a) as a result of unemployment, lower earnings, and higher death rates, one would expect Black men to experience a higher rate of depression than White men. But in reality the picture is quite different and many studies

> have reported a low incidence of depression among blacks partly as a result of bias on the part of white researchers. . . . Reports show . . . blacks are more likely to be diagnosed as schizophrenic (Bell and Mehta 1981; Cannon and Locke 1977; Collins, Rickman, and Mathura 1980). It has also been widely believed by some investigators that depression is low in blacks because for many decades the suicide rate for blacks was reported to be only one half the rate of whites. (Ruiz, 1990, p. 45)

A depression study was developed with a nonrandom sample of 142 Black male adults, who potentially would reflect a variety of lifestyles. These men, whose median age was 33 years, were young and poor, and when living in large households had considerable conflict with women. The findings suggested that younger Black males under the age of 30 are more likely to have depressive symptoms than older Blacks. Married men had higher depressive scores than men who had previously been married. Men who were never married had the very highest mean depressive scores. Other causes for high depression scores among Black males included unemployment and conflict with women; men residing in extended families tended to have higher depression scores than Black men living in nuclear families. The data from Gary & Berry's (1985) study suggested that those Black men who were "young, poor, unemployed, lived in larger household units and had considerable conflict with women had the highest depression scores" (p. 126).

Acquired Immune Deficiency Syndrome (AIDS)

Currently in the United States, the most urgent public health problem and a major cause of increased deaths among minorities is AIDS, or Acquired Immune Deficiency Syndrome. Some medical experts predict that during the next 5 years, between 1 and 4 million people will die of AIDS (Walsh 1987, p. 9A). The number of AIDS cases has risen exponentially since 1981. Approximately

50,000 to 125,000 people in the United States show signs of infection. Currently, more than 361,000 AIDS cases have been reported in the United States (Utah Department of Health 1994).

AIDS continues to be contagious, incurable, and fatal. The body, under the conditions of the disease, loses its innate ability to ward off infections and illnesses, among them opportunistic infections such as parasitic pneumonia, a cancer called Kaposi's sarcoma, and meningitis. The majority of AIDS victims are White; Blacks, who make up 12% of the total U.S. population, account for 24% of all AIDS cases. Almost two thirds of Black and Hispanic adults who have contracted AIDS reside in the states of New York, New Jersey, and Florida (Harper 1990, p. 246).

Susan Blake of the American Red Cross (Harper 1990), who reviewed all public opinion polls and attitudes about AIDS concerning White and non-White perceptions of this critical problem published since 1983, found that:

1. Minorities are more likely to have misconceptions about some alleged modes of transmission than Whites. In 1987, for instance, 12% of Whites thought casual contact could result in AIDS, compared to 25% of minorities. These misconceptions need to be corrected.

2. Many more minorities reported feeling vulnerable and/or concerned about AIDS. Some 32% of minorities polled in 1987 (versus 15% of Whites) indicated concerns about AIDS. These fears are based on reality but need to be channeled into constructive action.

3. A positive difference is a reportedly higher level of interest among minorities in reading or watching programs about AIDS. In 1987 some 64% of minorities, compared with 42% of Whites, said they would read an entire article or watch a program about AIDS.

4. More Blacks than Whites report that they have changed their sexual behavior because of AIDS. When asked in a 1986 poll whether they had altered their sexual behavior to protect themselves against AIDS, only 4% of Whites, compared to 25% of minorities, said yes. This change in behavior appears to have been in reference to limiting the number of sexual partners (pp. 246-247).

Although the AIDS epidemic presents some unique challenges to American society, one important variable in coping with this issue is not just education but psychoeducation (Fullilove, Fullilove, and Morales 1988).

> Psychoeducation is based on the assumption that individuals (and members of groups) can be taught to change their behavior, particularly if they are shown how. Specifically, psychoeducation interventions: (1) present technical information about disease, (2) help participants practice communication skills, (3) teach behavior management techniques, and (4) demonstrate how to accept the consequences of disease. (p. 144)

It is important that Whites, Blacks, and other non-Whites be given sufficient information to address both their fear of AIDS and, in the case of those at risk of infection, their personal responsibility to change their behavior. Those people who are unable to change—and they include adolescents experimenting with drugs and sex, adult drug abusers using needles, and others who are alone and isolated from family and friends—will be the ones whom a variety of therapists and counselors will encounter in treatment. This situation demands early intervention.

Recommendations for Health Care Providers

In view of the critical need for appropriate intervention in focusing on the major health concerns, the following steps could be helpful:

1. Help the health care providers fully appreciate the unique characteristics of the Black man as a part of today's society.

2. Encourage awareness of the cultural and social forces that affect Blacks in America.

3. Understand the Black extended family kinship system and how it provides a network of mutual aid and social support to the family and neighbors.

4. Assess the social and emotional concerns of Black males as they relate to health care challenges.

5. Understand the Black man and his family's strengths and resources in coping with the demands and expectations of daily living.

6. Teach Blacks concerning the health care system, keeping in mind respect for differences.

7. Provide necessary health and social services as well as other human services as needed to help Black clients attain a better social, emotional, and physical adjustment.

8. Assist Black men and their families with the personal and environmental needs that affect them, predispose them to health stresses, and limit their ability fully to make use of health resources and services.

Values of Comprehensive Assessment

Logan, Freeman, and McRoy, (1990) have suggested a strong model for assessment, presented here in its entirety:

A sound assessment is of utmost importance as the basis for effective helping. It provides the treatment team with relevant psychological, social and cultural data needed for effective interprofessional intervention. When the black client with an acute or chronic illness and disability is assessed, the practitioner should consider the following factors:

1. The client's current and past life experiences

2. The client's beliefs, behavior, and family interaction, particularly those related to health

3. The impact of the illness on the family's overall functioning

4. The cultural background, including religious and spiritual perspective, of the client

5. The client's financial situation

The Client's Life Experiences

An effective care plan must be geared to the client's present situation—the here and now, with knowledge of the past and the anticipated future—from a physical, emotional, and mental health point of view. However, it is impossible to understand the client's current needs without an assessment of the total situation. This requires knowledge not only of the individual's past life experiences but also of the client's physical condition and history of illness, the client's developmental stage in life, and the client's style of coping, which in Blacks may be culturally determined. Essentially, the health care worker should have knowledge about the client's fears, anxieties, frustrations, life goals, and aspirations, as well as the client's actions and reactions to the illness. With Black clients who have had negative experiences with the health care delivery system, it is important that the health care worker's strategies of intervention focus on the client's perception of current needs, the illness, avoidance of seeking treatment, and the meaning of the illness, as well as on the response to care, treatment, and management.

Beliefs, Behavior, and Family Interaction

The manner in which families respond to acute and chronic illness reflects their style of coping. The patterned behavior results from long-standing attitudes and beliefs about health, illness, and dying. Very often, old wives' tales, folk medicine, and superstitions have a greater influence on the client's recovery than professional medical care (Kleinman, Eisenberg, and Good 1978; Sheham 1973).

Helping professionals must understand the impact of chronic and acute illness on the family unit as well as on the individual. With respect to the individual, the concern is whether he or she feels secure, loved, and cared for. But it is also important to understand the family's coping and problem-solving techniques. For example, in coping with illness does the family, like many Black families, engage in role reversals and consider home care the treatment of choice?

The Family's Religious and Cultural Perspective

Family functioning is also influenced by its ways of being in the world, its feelings about wholeness, connectedness, and openness to the concept of a universal consciousness or supreme being. A family's cultural experience influences not only its view of the role assumed by a sick family member but also its perception of dying and death—for example, is this a leave-taking tantamount to going home, escaping from a world of pain, sorrow, and discrimination, or is it an anxiety-producing, fearful ordeal? Black culture is greatly influenced by religious heritage and spirituality, but it is important to understand the diversity within this context; meaning and practices will vary from client to client.

Financial Issues

The financial situation of the client will affect and reflect the type of medical, health, and social care, the place of care, and follow-up care. Practitioners must have adequate knowledge of a client's financial situation to understand the family's level of survival, the ongoing continuity of care, and the quality and quantity of that care. This will help the practitioner intervene appropriately in making referrals for services.

According to Germain (1984), assessment is dynamic and everchanging. It not only considers how personal, environmental, and cultural factors interact with illness but is also concerned with stress level and available coping resources. Equally important, however, is the use of assessment to point up the need for intervention at the interpersonal as well as community level, specifically, the type of interventions that require advocacy, outreach, and organizing (Germain 1984, pp. 251-253).

References

Ambruso, D. R., Githens, J. H., and Alcorn, R. (1987). Experience with donors matched for minor blood group antigens, in patients with sickle cell anemia who are receiving chronic transfusion therapy. *Transfusion* 27, 94-98.

Bell, C., and Mehta, H. (1981). Misdiagnosis of Black patients with manic depressive illness: Second in a series. *Journal of the National Medical Association* 73(2), 101-107.

Billingsley, A. (1968). *Black Families in White America*. Englewood Cliffs, NJ: Prentice-Hall.

Burton, L. E., Smith, H. H., and Nichols, A. W. (1980). *Public Health and Community Medicine*. Baltimore, MD: Williams and Wilkins.

Cannon, M. S., and Locke, B. Z. (1977). Being Black is detrimental to one's mental health: Myth or reality? *Phylon* 38(4), 408-428.

Collins, J. L., Rickman, L. E., and Mathura, C. B. (1980). Frequency of schizophrenia and depression in a Black inpatient population. *Journal of the National Medical Association* 72(9), 851-856.

Dimsdale, J. E. (1986). Suppressed anger and blood pressure: The effects of race, sex, and social class, obesity, and age. *Psychosomatic Medicine* 48, 430-436.

Fullilove, M., Fullilove, R. III, and Morales, E. (1989). Psychoeducation: A tool for AIDS prevention in minority communities. *Journal of Teaching in Social Work* 2, 143-160.

Garagliano, C. E., Lilienfeld, A. M., and Medeloff, A. I. (1979). Incidence rates of liver cirrhosis and related diseases in Baltimore and selected areas of the United States. *Journal of Chronic Diseases* 32, 543-553.

Gary, L. E. (ed.). (1981). *Black Men*. Beverly Hills, CA: Sage.

Gary, L. E., and Berry, G. L. (1985). Depressive symptomatology among Black men. *Journal of Multicultural Counseling and Development* 13, 121-129.

Germain, C. B. (1984). *Social Workpractice in Health Care: An Ecological Perspective*. New York: Free Press.

Gibbs, J. T. (1984). Black adolescents and youth: An endangered species. *American Journal of Orthopsychiatry* 54, 6-21.

Giblett, E. R. (1961), A critique of the theoretical hazard of inter- vs. intra-racial transfusion. *Transfusion* 1, 233-238.

Hannerz, U. (1970). What ghetto males are like: Another look. In N. C. Whitten, Jr., and J. R. Szwed (eds.), *Afro-American Anthropology: Contemporary Perspectives* 313-327. New York: Free Press.

Harburg, E, Erfurt, J., Hauenstein, L, Chape, C., Schull, W., and Schork, M. (1973). Socioecological stress, suppressed hostility, skin color and Black-White male blood pressure: Detroit. *Psychosomatic Medicine* 35, 276-296.

Harlan, W. R., Hull, A. L., Schmouder, R. P., Thompson, F. E., Lacking, F. E., and Landis, J.R. (1983). Dietary intake and cardiovascular risk factors, part 1. Blood pressure correlates:United States, 1971-75. *Vital and Health Statistics*, Series U, No. 226, 83-1676.

Harper, B.C.O. (1990). Blacks and the healthcare delivery system: Challenges and prospects. In S.M.L. Logan, E. P. Freeman, and R. G. McRoy (eds.), *Social Workpractice With Black Families*, 239-256. New York: Longman.

Harper, F. (ed.). (1976). *Alcohol Abuse and Black America*. Alexandria, VA: Douglas.

Herd, D. (1985). The socio-cultural correlates of drinking patterns in Black and White Americans: Results from a national survey. Unpublished doctoral dissertation, University of California at San Francisco.

———. (1989). The epidemiology of drinking patterns and alcohol-related problems among U.S. Blacks. In D. L. Speigier, D. A. Tate, S. S. Aitken, and C. M. Christian (eds.), *Alcohol Use Among U.S. Ethnic Minorities* (NIAAA Research Monograph No. 18, DHSS Pub. No. ADM 89-1435), 3-5. Washington, DC: U.S. Government Printing Office.

———. (1990). Subgroup differences in drinking patterns among Black and White men: Results from a national survey. *Journal of Studies on Alcohol*, 51, 221-232.

Jarris, R. F., and Patron, D. L. (1982). Cancer and social disadvantage. In D. L. Parron, F. Solomon, and C. D. Jenkins (eds.), *Behavior Health Risks, and Social Disadvantage: Interim Report No. 6*. Washington, DC: Institute of Medicine.

Johnson, J. (1983, March). Why Black men have the highest cancer rate. *Ebony*, 69-72.

Kleinman, A., Eisenberg, L., and Good, B. (1978). Culture, illness, and care. *Annals of Internal Medicine* 88, 251-288.

Leavy, W. (I 983, August). Is the Black male an endangered species? *Ebony*, 41-42, 46.

Logan, S.M.L., Freeman, E. M., and McRoy, R. G. (1990). *Social Work Practice With Black Families*. New York: Longman.

Luban, N.L.C. (1989). Variability in rates of alloinimunization in different groups of children with sickle cell disease: Effect of ethnic background. *American Journal of Pediatric Hematology Oncology* 11, 314-319.

Mallory, D., Malamut, D., Ginther, A. (1989). Rare blood for patients with sickle cell anemia: Sickle cell disease. *Annals of New York Academy of Science* 565, 432-433.

McCord, C., and Freeman H. P. (1990). Excess mortality in Harlem. *New England Journal of Medicine*, 322, 173-177.

Michaels, D. (1982). Minority workers and occupational cancer: The hidden costs of job discrimination. In D. L. Parton, F. Solomon, and C. D. Jenkins (eds.), *Behavior, Health Risks, and Social Disadvantage*. Washington, DC: Institute of Medicine.

National Center for Health Statistics. (1983). [Article title unavailable]. Washington, DC: U.S. Government Printing Office.

National Health Expenditures (1987, Summer). *Health Care Financing Administration* 8(4), 1986-2000.

National Institute on Alcohol Abuse and Alcoholism. (1980). *National Alcoholism Program Information System, NAPIS Statistical Report on NIAAA Funded Treatment Programs for Calendar Year 1980*. Rockville, MD: National Institute on Alcohol Abuse and Alcoholism.

Orlina, A.R., Unger P.J., and Koshy, M. (1978) Post-transfusion allioimmunization in patients with sickle cell disease. *American Journal of Hematology* 5, 101-106.

Parham, T. A. (1987). Black men, an endangered species: Who's really pulling the trigger? *Journal of Counseling and Development* 66, 24-27.

Patten, E., Patel, S., Sotto, B., and Gayle, R. (1989). Transfusion management of patients with sickle cell disease: Sickle cell disease. *Annals of New York Academy of Science* 565, 446-448.

Piomelli, S. (1985). Chronic transfusions in patients with sickle cell disease: Indications and problems. *American Journal of Hematology Oncology* 7(51-55).

Poussaint, A. F. (1983). Black on Black homicide: A psychological-political perspective. *Victimology* 8(3-4), 161-169.

Raloff, J. (1990). Lead heightens hypertension risk in Blacks. *Science News* 137(26), 1.

Ruiz, D. S. (ed.). (1990). *Handbook of Mental Health and Mental Disorder Among Black Americans*. New York: Greenwood.

Russo, R. M. (1982, July). Poverty: A major deterrent to America's good health. *Urban Health*, 45-48.

Samaik, S., Schomack, J. L., and Lusher, J. M. (1986). The incidence of development of irregular red cell antibodies in patients with sickle cell anemia. *Transfusion* 26, 249-252.

Schmalzer, E., Chien, S., and Brown, S. (1982). Transfusion therapy in sickle cell disease. *American Journal of Pediatric Hematology Oncology* 4, 395-406.

Sheham, M. (1973). *Blacks and American Medical care*. Minneapolis: University of Minnesota Press.

Stead, W. W., Lofgren, J. P., Warren, E., and Thomas, C. (1985). Tuberculosis as an endemic and nosocomial infection among the elderly in nursing homes. *New England Journal of Medicine* 312, 1483-1487.

Stead, W. W., Senner, J. W., Reddick, W. T., and Lofgren, J. P. (1990). Racial differences in susceptibility to infection by mycobacterium tuberculosis. *New England Journal of Medicine* 322, 422-427.

Stead, W. W., and To, T. (1987). Significance of the tuberculin skin test in elderly persons. *Annals of Internal Medicine* 107, 837-842.

Stead, W. W., To, T., Harrison, R. W., and Abraham, J. H. III. (1987). Benefit-risk considerations in preventive treatment for tuberculosis in elderly persons. *Annals of Internal Medicine* 107, 843-845.

Stewart, G. T. (ed.). (1972). *Trends in Epidemiology: Application to Health Service*. Springville, IL: Charles C. Thomas.

Turner, S. M., and Jones, R. T. (eds.). (1982). *Behavior Modification in Black populations: Psychosocial Issues and Empirical Findings*. New York: Plenum.

U.S. Department of Health and Human Services. (1986a). *Black and Minority Health: Cancer* 3. Washington, DC: U.S. Government Printing Office.

U.S. Department of Health and Human Services. (1986b). *Black and Minority Health: Cardiovascular and Cerebrovascular Disease* 4, pt. 1. Washington, DC: U.S. Government Printing Office.

U.S. Department of Health and Human Services. (1986c). *Black and Minority Health: Cardiovascular and Cerebrovascular Disease* 4, pt. 2. Washington, DC: U.S. Government Printing Office.

U.S. Department of Health and Human Services. (1986d). *Black and Minority Health: Chemical Dependency and Diabetes* 7. Washington, DC: U.S. Government Printing Office.

U.S. Department of Health and Human Services. (1990). *Health Status of Minorities and Low-income Groups*. Washington, DC: U.S. Government Printing Office.

Utah Department of Health. (1994, May 27). *Total AIDS Cases, Utah and United States*. Utah: Bureau of HIV/AIDS.

Ventura, S. J., Taffel, S. M., and Spratley, E. (1975). Selected vital and health statistics in poverty and non-poverty areas of 19 large cities, United States, 1969-7 1. *Vital and Health Statistics* (Series 21, No. 26, DHEW Pub. No. HRA 76-1904) 1-63. Washington, DC: U.S. Government Printing Office.

Vichinsky, E. P., Earles, A., Johnson, R. A., Hoag, M. S., William, A., and Lubin, B. (1990). Alloimmunization in sickle cell anemia and transfusion of racially unmatched blood. *New England Journal of Medicine* 322, 1617-1621.

Walsh, W. B. (1987, September 11). [Article title unavailable]. *St. Louis Dispatch*, 9A.

Williams, R. A. (ed.). (1977). *Textbook of Black-related diseases*. New York: McGraw-Hill.

Critical Evaluation

1. The author states that it is "apparent" that self-hatred and frustration account for high homicide rates among African American. Is this conclusion justified from the evidence presented? What other explanations might be given?

2. How many of the health problems discussed would be reduced if African American poverty rates were brought down to the same level as white rates?

3. Which of the author's recommendations for health-care providers are most needed? Are some unnecessary?

Dale F. Pearson, "The Black Man." In *Journal of Black Studies* 25, pp. 81–98. Copyright © 1994 by Sage Publications, Inc. Reprinted by permission. ✦

16

Teens and Tobacco: Facts, Not Fiction

Centers for Disease Control

The single most preventable cause of illness is the use of tobacco. We have long known about the harm of smoking. Yet nearly 4 million adolescents smoke cigarettes, and more than 3,000 become regular smokers each day (Centers for Disease Control 1998). As a result, more than 5 million young people now under the age of 18 will die prematurely from a smoking-related disease.

So why do people continue to take up smoking? One important social psychological factor is interaction patterns—young people are far more likely to start smoking if their friends also smoke. How do group norms favoring smoking develop? An important structural factor is effective advertising. The following report from the Centers for Disease Control furnishes important data about factors involved in teens starting to smoke as well as some of the consequences of tobacco use.

Reference

Centers for Disease Control. 1998. "Teens and Tobacco: Facts Not Fiction." *Fact Sheet.* CDC Website.

Focus Questions

1. How prevalent is cigarette smoking among adolescents?

2. What are the health consequences of smoking?

3. In what sense is teen smoking an "early warning sign?"

Every day in the United States, more than 3,000 young people become regular smokers—that's more than 1 million new smokers a year.

- After years of remaining steady, teen smoking rates have increased each year since 1992. In 1996, 22.2% of high school seniors smoked daily—up from 17.2% in 1992. Between 1991 and 1996, past-month smoking increased from 14.3% to 21.0% among eighth graders and from 20.8% to 30.4% among tenth graders.

- More than 5 million young people under the age of 18 who are currently alive will die prematurely from a smoking-related disease.

- In adults, cigarette smoking causes heart disease and stroke. Studies have shown that early signs of the blood vessel damage present in these diseases can be found in adolescents who smoke.

- Starting smoking at an early age greatly increases the risk of lung cancer. A person's risk for most other smoking-related cancers also rises with the length of time that a person smokes.

- Teenage smokers suffer from shortness of breath almost three times as often as teens who don't smoke and produce phlegm more than twice as often as teens who don't smoke.

- Smokeless tobacco use among youth is a continuing problem. Data from recent school-based surveys indicate that about one in every five male students in 9th through 12th grades uses smokeless tobacco.

- Smokeless tobacco can cause gum disease and cancer of the mouth, pharynx, and esophagus. It may also increase the risk of heart disease and stroke.

- In 1991, teenage cigarette smokers consumed an average of 28.3 million cigarettes per day (516 million packs per year). During this same period, an estimated 225 million packs of cigarettes were sold illegally to young people under the age of 18. The tobacco industry generated approximately $190 million in profit from the illegal sale of cigarettes to minors in 1991.

- In 1995, approximately 57% of students in grades 9–12 who currently smoked usually bought their cigarettes from a retail store, from a vending machine, or through another person who purchased cigarettes for them.

- Several studies have found nicotine to be addictive in ways similar to those of heroin, cocaine, and alcohol. Among young smokers, the transition from experimentation to dependence occurs just as frequently as it does among users of cocaine and heroin.

- Among adolescents aged 10–18, about three-fourths of daily cigarette smokers and daily smokeless tobacco users report that they continue to use tobacco because it is really hard for them to quit. About 93% of daily cigarette smokers and daily smokeless tobacco users who previously tried to quit report at least one symptom of nicotine withdrawal. Young people who try to quit smoking suffer the same withdrawal symptoms as adults who try to quit.

- Cigarette products are among the most heavily advertised and promoted products in the United States. In 1994, tobacco companies spent an estimated $5 billion—or more than $13 million a day—to advertise and promote cigarettes.

- In 1991, about 82% of smokers who had ever smoked daily began smoking before age 18, and by that age, 53% had become daily smokers.

- A national survey found that about 86% of adolescent smokers who bought their own cigarettes preferred Marlboro, Camel, or Newport cigarettes—the most heavily advertised brands. In contrast, only 35% of adults chose these brands.

- Teen smoking is often an early warning sign of future problems. Teens who smoke are three times as likely as non-smokers to use alcohol, eight times as likely to use marijuana, and 22 times as likely to use cocaine. Smoking is also associated with numerous other high risk behaviors, including fighting and having unprotected sex.

Reference

Schoenborn, Charlotte A. 1986. "Health Habits of U.S. Adults." *Public Health Reports* 101:571–580

Critical Evaluation

1. Is advertising a factor in causing teens to start smoking or only a factor in which brand they choose? Why?

2. How would a cigarette manufacturer respond to this chapter?

3. The chapter doesn't mention family life. What role do parents play in teen smoking?

Centers for Disease Control, "Teens and Tobacco: Facts, Not Fiction." Centers for Disease Control Website, 1997. ✦

Project for Personal Application and Class Discussion: Health Care

There are a number of things you can do, or refrain from doing, that affect your health. In a study of residents of Alameda County, California, seven habits were associated with better physical health and lower mortality: regular exercise, not smoking, moderate drinking of alcohol, sleeping seven to eight hours a night, maintaining proper weight, avoiding snacks, and eating breakfast regularly (Schoenborn 1986). Maintaining your proper weight and avoiding snacks involves keeping your intake of fat low (25 percent or less of total calories is recommended).

Put a check in the columns below for yourself, your friends, and your family (parents, siblings, and spouse) for each of the health habits you observe (for friends and family, check if the majority observe the habit):

	myself	friends	family
1. Exercise regularly			
2. Do not smoke			
3. Drink in moderation			
4. Sleep 7 to 8 hours			
5. Eat breakfast regularly			
6. Keep fat intake low			

How many checks do you have? How do you compare with your friends and family? The point of checking friends and family is that it is much easier to maintain good health habits if your friends and family also observe them.

If you have not checked any of the columns, what can you do to begin the habit? To what extent will your friends and family be supportive or helpful?

Nationally, the consumption of fat per person has increased since 1970, and less than half of Americans exercise regularly. How does your class rate in observing the habits? ✦

The Environment

If anything can end the world, in T. S. Eliot's words, with a whimper rather than a bang, it will be a problem in the environment. Experts in the study of war and nuclear weapons talk about a worldwide holocaust. Experts in the study of environmental problems, however, talk about a depleted and toxic earth that will no longer be able to sustain human population.

One of the ironies of environmental problems is that the very things that enhance our quality of life—the knowledge and products of our scientific and industrial civilization—are at the heart of the threat of a depleted and toxic earth. For example, the use of the automobile confronts us with a dilemma (Bronner 1997). On the one hand, the automobile has a tremendous impact on the American economy and lifestyle, and Americans cherish the mobility the automobile gives them. On the other hand, the more than half billion automobiles on the world's roads are a major factor in such problems as air pollution, which, in turn, contributes to a variety of health problems.

Similar dilemmas surround other environmental issues. The pesticides that increase agricultural production pose a serious health hazard. The industrial processes that offer us a wealth of desirable goods are a central factor in global warming. This section will examine the problems of pesticides and global warming. It will also look at an issue that shows clearly that even environmental problems are more intense for minorities— the location of toxic waste sites.

Reference

Bronner, Michael Eric. 1997. "The Mother of Battles: Confronting the Implications of Automobile Dependence in the United States." *Population and Environment* 18:489–507. ✦

17

Pesticides: Nowhere To Hide

Martha Honey

Increased productivity is a miracle of modern agriculture—a necessary miracle because of the planet's greatly increased population. At the same time, the use of pesticides to boost productivity is a major hazard to human health and life. But are pesticides necessary? Martha Honey explores the question and discusses some of the microlevel consequences of using pesticides. She also identifies structural factors—the power of the farm lobby and the determination to protect corporate profits—that maintain the use of pesticides. Not all experts agree with her conclusions or with the quotes from activists that she cites. Such differences among experts lead to contradictory attitudes about environmental problems and greater difficulties in dealing with them appropriately and effectively.

Focus Questions

1. What is meant by the "circle of poison?"

2. How do pesticides affect people's health?

3. Why is there conflict over the use of pesticides?

4. What are people doing to counter the effects of pesticides?

Walk into almost any supermarket these days, any month of the year, and feast your eyes: towering pyramids of grapefruit, baskets of unblemished tomatoes and cucumbers, heaping bins of avocados and kiwifruit, stacks of ripened strawberries. Nowadays, the health-conscious U.S. consumer, transcending the inconveniences of the season, is serviced 12 months of the year by fruit and vegetable growers the world over. But if you're concerned that the produce section at your local market has come to resemble a wax museum, you have good reason. The abundance and variety of fresh, picture-perfect produce is brought to you and your family at a price—and not just at the cash register.

More than 30 years have passed since Rachel Carson called world attention to the health and environmental hazards of DDT and other pesticides in her landmark book, *Silent Spring*. "If we are going to live so intimately with these chemicals—eating and drinking them, taking them into the very marrow of our bones," Carson wrote, "we had better know something about their nature and their power." There is now ample proof that Carson's early warning was well founded: at least 136 active ingredients in pesticides have been found to cause cancer in humans and animals. But global pesticide use continues to escalate as farmers and food companies look for increasingly efficient methods to expand their markets. While Carson's book paved the way for the creation of the Environmental Protection Agency (EPA) in 1970, government efforts to protect the nation's food and water supply have moved at a snail's pace—of the 136 aforementioned carcinogenic chemicals, 79 are still being used on U.S. food crops. And the few, hard won legislative gains that have been made by consumer, labor, and environmental advocates are currently being torpedoed in the Republican-controlled Congress. . . .

The U.S. is one of the world's largest users of pesticides, and it's the top exporter. Sales in the U.S. total close to $8 billion. With annual overseas sales of $2.4 billion, or 44 billion pounds of chemicals, U.S. companies export more than 25 tons of pesticides *every hour*. In what has been dubbed the "circle of poison," at least one third of the pesticides exported have been banned or limited for use in this country—but they often return to consumers as residue on imported produce. While the U.S. imports only 9 percent of its vegetables, more than a quarter of the fruit sold here is imported; in winter, 40 to 60 percent of produce comes from abroad.

In the mid-1980s, the U.S. government made a major push to get many Latin American and Caribbean countries to grow new "designer" crops—strawberries, melons, and asparagus—all intended for the U.S. market and most, as they are not native to the region, heavily dependent on chemical fertilizers and pesticides. As a result, Latin America leads the Southern Hemisphere in pesticide use per acre and it supplies nearly 80 percent of U.S. fruit and vegetable imports. Not surprisingly, U.S. agricultural experts in Costa Rica, who conducted a survey of pesticide residues on strawberries in the late 1980s, refused to release their results. "But I can tell you one thing," confided one official involved in the study. "I won't eat the strawberries."

But while consumers are subject to long-term, low-level pesticide exposure from both domestic and imported produce, agricultural workers' concerns are more immediate. Each year 25 million people, primarily in the Southern Hemisphere, are poisoned through occupational exposure to pesticides; of those, 220,000 die, according to the World Health Organization (WHO). In the U.S., 300,000 farmworkers are poisoned each year.

Pesticides fall into three main categories— insecticides, herbicides, and fungicides— and they are designed to control or eliminate unwanted insects, weeds, and plant-killing fungi; each contains an "active ingredient," or the poison that kills the pest, and an "inert" carrying or spreading compound. When first developed after World War II, pesticides were hailed as miracle chemicals that would protect crops and homes, make food more plentiful and safe, and wipe out world hunger. Erika Rosenthal, Latin America Program Coordinator with the San Francisco-based Pesticides Action Network (PAN), has a late-1940s poster advertising DDT hanging in her office. The text at the bottom reads: "The great expectations held for DDT have been realized. During 1946, exhaustive scientific tests have shown that, when properly used, DDT kills a host of destructive insect pests and is a benefactor of all humanity."

But by the late 1950s, scientific evidence was already mounting that DDT was not only a potent carcinogen, but it also posed a serious threat to the environment—it is now cited as the cause of the near-extinction of the bald eagle, brown pelican, and condor. Despite its prominence in *Silent Spring*, it wasn't until 1972 that DDT was finally banned in the U.S., and it is still manufactured in Mexico, India, and Indonesia and used in some developing countries. "DDT had the dubious fame of being one of the most widespread contaminants of the ecosystem," says PAN's Rosenthal. "Dangerously high concentrations have been found in the breast milk of mothers in Central America. It's also been found in the fat of Arctic polar bears. So it's covered the globe," she says. DDT remains in the food chain as a result of soil and water contamination. As recently as 1993, a study found higher levels of DDE (which is formed when DDT breaks down) in U.S. women who had developed breast cancer than in women who had not.

Pesticides are now everywhere—in our food, drinking water, homes, yards, and air. But it's difficult to rate the worst pesticides. "It's Russian roulette. Pick your poison: acutely toxic, chronically hazardous, cancer-causing, or effect unknown," says Sandra Marquardt, pesticide consultant at Consumers Union in Washington, DC. Most often, we are exposed simultaneously to a variety of types, although the EPA sets safety levels by testing only one active ingredient at a time. And even when pesticides are banned, they are often used illegally by U.S. growers. Lax enforcement of EPA regulations by the Food and Drug Administration (FDA) makes it possible for many farmers to continue to use their pesticides of choice.

In addition to breast cancer, cancers of the reproductive system have been linked to pesticides. Infants and young children are especially vulnerable to pesticides. "Millions of children in the United States receive up to 35 percent of their entire lifetime dose of some carcinogenic pesticides by age five," reports a study by the Washington, DC-based Environmental Working Group (EWG). . . . There is growing evidence that pesticides also cause a variety of birth defects and genetic mutations. And one of the newest and most worrisome findings is that some pesticides— known as "hormone imitating" chemicals or "endocrine disrupters"—are building up in animals and humans and disrupting reproduction, immunity, and metabolism. In a recent National Wildlife Federation study, "Fertility on the Brink," University of Florida zoologist Louis Guillette writes: "We've released endocrine disrupters throughout the world that are having fundamental effects on the immune system and the reproductive system. . . . Should we be upset? I think we should be screaming in the streets."

Neither the government nor the pesticide industry has responded with much urgency to the long-term health risks faced by consumers—or the daily risks faced by farmworkers. On the evening of November 14, 1989, a few miles outside Tampa, Florida, the insecticide mevinphos was sprayed on Goodson Farms' 16 acres of cauliflower. Early the next morning, farm managers sent migrant laborers into the dewy fields to tie up the plants. Within several hours, scores were complaining of headaches, dizziness, blurred vision, slurred speech, and breathing difficulties. They began vomiting, having convulsions, and staggering out of the field; several passed out. By late afternoon an estimated 112 farmworkers were treated at the scene or at area hospitals. Thirteen were admitted to hospitals. In the following months, dozens of the workers continued to suffer symptoms, and one pregnant woman miscarried.

Florida doctors called this one of the worst cases of pesticide poisonings they had ever seen. Goodson Farms managers were fined by state authorities for sending workers into the field too soon after spraying and not giving them proper protective gear. But Goodson's fine was later reduced from $12,600 to only $7,000. And the president of Amvac Chemical Corporation, which makes mevinphos under the brand name Phosdrin, continues to praise the product: Eric Wintemute describes it as "a neat compound" and "100 percent clean" because, he says, it leaves no permanent residue on crops; its "acute toxicity" simply means it must be applied with care.

"Even if this chemical is applied as directed it can still poison the workers," remarks Michael Hancock, executive director of the Washington, DC-based Farmworker Justice Fund. He calls mevinphos "the single most harmful pesticide to farmworkers." For years, labor advocates have urged the EPA to speed up its pesticide review process and ban

chemicals like mevinphos, which is used on some 50 crops. Finally, in June 1994, the EPA made the unusual decision to issue an "emergency suspension order" that would have taken mevinphos off the market immediately.

But the day before the order was to be implemented, the EPA received a call from Amvac's lawyer, Steven Schatzow, saying the company had decided to "voluntarily" withdraw the pesticide from the U.S. market. Schatzow was no stranger to the EPA: he had been the agency's director of pesticide programs under Ronald Reagan. This was classic Washington revolving-door politics. Despite current EPA administrator Carol Browner's pledge to "break the gridlock on pesticide reform," Schatzow and the EPA struck a deal: Amvac agreed to stop producing mevinphos for use in the U.S., but the company was given until the end of 1994 to sell off its supply. And then after the Republicans' congressional sweep . . . the EPA agreed to give Amvac until the end of November 1995 "for sale, distribution, and use of existing stocks of mevinphos products."

Environmentalists are furious. "It's ridiculous. The EPA caved in," says Marquardt at Consumers Union. "It gave Amvac another year to dump this poison on the American people," adds Hancock, who sees the EPA's handling of mevinphos as a sign of the chilling effect the Republicans' Contract with America is having on the Clinton administration. "The EPA got the message not to do anything that would create headlines saying REGULATORY ACTION FORCES COMPANY OUT OF BUSINESS."

Amvac has continued to sell mevinphos overseas, in such countries as Thailand and South Africa. Under U.S. law, the 43 active ingredients in pesticides that the EPA has deemed too dangerous for use in the U.S.— along with the hundreds of pesticide ingredients that haven't been registered by the EPA—can be exported. Dr. Robert McConnell, a World Health Organization pesticides expert, says he is most worried about unregistered pesticides exported to the Southern Hemisphere because "there is virtually no data on them." And the FDA doesn't monitor imported produce any better than domestic. Although FDA border inspectors are supposed to examine a "representative sample" of produce entering the country, few fruits and vegetables are screened. "Ninety-nine percent sail through untouched," says Marquardt. "There are so few inspectors out there, and they are more concerned with testing cosmetic appearance than pesticide residues." And about one third of the shipments detected with hazardous pesticide residues reach U.S. supermarkets anyway, due to halfhearted enforcement efforts and bureaucratic delays. "It is as if we were selling bombs around the world that come back and explode in our own backyards," Congressman Sam Gejdenson (D.-Conn.) testified at 1994 hearings on pesticide exports.

Ironically, as more humans are sickened or killed by pesticides, more strains of insects, mites, weeds, and rodents are developing immunity to these chemicals. In *Silent Spring*, Carson found that 137 species of insects and mites had already become pesticide-resistant; today it is more than 500. According to Cornell University Professor David Pimentel, the amount of crops lost to insects in the U.S. "has almost doubled during the last 40 years, despite a more than tenfold increase in the amount and toxicity of synthetic insecticides used."

Nevertheless, growers, both in the U.S. and abroad, are becoming increasingly reliant on pesticides. "My greatest concern is the expanded use of pesticides—the doubling [in the U.S.] over the last 30 years—and the effect it can have on our children, our water, air, and land," says the EPA's Browner. "And it's outrageous," she adds, "that a product banned can be sold in other countries." But Browner, a longtime environmental activist, has not been able to "end the cycle of compromise" at the EPA, says Jay Feldman of the National Coalition Against the Misuse of Pesticides. She got points in early 1994 for proposing legislation that would create stricter safety standards for both domestic and imported produce, as well as stop the export of banned pesticides. But the administration's proposal never even made it out of the House agricultural committee last year, and this year it will not be reintroduced. It was "blocked by the pesticide lobby," which wields tremendous power, says Browner, particularly in the cur-

rent Republican-controlled Congress. "Now legislation is being written by the [pesticide industry] lobbyists." But labor advocates like Michael Hancock contend that the Clinton administration pressured the EPA to bow out too soon: "The agency seems to be in full retreat. They just surrender when they should stand and put up a fight over principle."

Behind the current antiregulatory fervor is the benign-sounding American Crop Protection Association, or ACPA (formerly the National Agricultural Chemical Association), the pesticide industry's main lobby. Comprised of 83 chemical companies, including such giants as DuPont, DOW, Monsanto, Velsicol, and American Cyanimid, this Washington, DC-based trade association commands enormous political clout, in part through campaign contributions to key members of the House and Senate agricultural committees. . . . ACPA member companies constitute a global pesticide supermarket, selling to virtually every country in both the Northern and Southern Hemispheres. And ACPA members have done little to ensure that workers—especially in the South—use their products safely. Scores of studies and press accounts show that workers are often given little or no training in handling the chemicals. Many cannot read labels, frequently mix pesticides with their bare hands, and carry home the poisons on their bodies and clothing. Hazardous chemicals spill or are dumped into fields, rivers, or ponds, and the poison-laced containers are reused for storing food, water, or seeds. "It's very difficult to have safe use under tropical conditions, by small farmers wearing backpacks. The packs leak and it's too hot and too expensive to wear protective clothing," says WHO's McConnell. Four years ago, DOW was sued by male Costa Rican banana workers who were showing up sterile after years of exposure to the highly toxic pesticide DBCP; women workers and family members who were also exposed were left out of the suit but are currently documenting their high rates of miscarriages, birth defects, and cancer in preparation for a suit of their own.

In 1991, ACPA opened its first "safe use" project to train growers in Guatemala, Thailand and Kenya. "We recognized we had to roll up our sleeves and get involved," says John McCarthy of ACPA's international division. The association's commitment to "safe use" is minuscule: $400,000 a year and one staff person in each country. But it makes good PR—as ACPA President Jay Vroom told Congress, these projects show industry's "advances" in "product stewardship and worker safety." "Three pilot projects four decades too late—how dare these fuckers make such claims?" [says] one health expert who has worked on pesticide safety programs in the Southern Hemisphere. "This 'safe use' is about buying companies another ten years" to export their goods, he says.

Little will change for either workers or consumers until farmers move away from an "agrochemical-intensive model of production," says PAN's Rosenthal. The right direction, say activists, is toward organic farming. The EPA's Browner agrees: "We know how to grow food with fewer chemicals, and that should be our goal." EWG's Richard Wiles, who directed a National Academy of Sciences study of alternative farming methods, says, "It's possible to grow an affordable, abundant food supply using few or no synthetic chemicals. For all major field crops—corn, soybean, wheat, barley—the science is there. You can eliminate pesticides that pose serious health risks and maintain current levels of production." What's missing, Wiles explains, is the incentive. "American farmers have very minimal regulatory or market incentive to cut back on pesticides. They see the chemicals as legal, loosely regulated, and a low-cost form of insurance, and farmers don't pay any of the cost of the environmental consequences. So what the hell? Why change?"

Contract with America Republicans are hell-bent on pushing through more deregulation and corporate perks. But they may be misreading the mood of the country. A poll commissioned by the National Wildlife Federation just after the 1994 elections found that 41 percent of people in the U.S. believe that existing regulations "don't go far enough in protecting the environment," that 46 percent agree that laws "do not require businesses to do enough to protect the environment," and that 64 percent say that government should pay subsidies to farmers for pesticide reduction.

The public's increasing health consciousness is reflected in organic food sales, which have skyrocketed over the past five years. And the emerging market is attracting a number of big food companies, a few of which have opened up organic divisions. Such rapid expansion—involving pesticide-happy companies—has prompted calls among some activists for federal regulation for the largely self-regulated organic food industry.

The growth of the organic market confirms what Betsy Lydon, of the New York City-based group Mothers and Others for a Livable Planet, has long maintained: "Change has to happen in the marketplace. Your food dollars *can* be very powerful." Her group, which has a mailing list of 25,000, is sponsoring a nationwide "shoppers' campaign" for healthier food choices. Members in Kentucky, Illinois, and New York are working with supermarket chains like D'Agostino's and Dominick's to encourage them to offer more organic food—which in many cases, Lydon says, is just slightly more expensive than nonorganic. When there is a real disparity, she says, "people need to talk to their retailer about price gouging. They should not be selling organic food as gourmet food." Lydon's group also spearheaded a project in Lexington, Kentucky, called a "buying club," involving 26 organic farmers and 100 families. The families give the farmers money in the early part of the season for seeds and supplies; come harvest, the farmers deliver their organic produce to the families at below-market rates.

Other groups, like the New York City-based Women's Environment and Development Organization (WEDO), are focusing on political action. WEDO is planning a series of nationwide "hearings" over the next year on the links between environmental factors, like pesticides, and breast cancer. WEDO is working in coalition with groups like One in Nine, a Long Island breast cancer awareness organization that is campaigning to get New York State to establish a pesticide registry that would be open to the public. "We found out that farmers have to register what they use and that information is supposed to go to the government. But they put the records into cartons and no one has access to them," says Geri Barish, head of One in Nine's Pesticide Project. "We want to know how much is used, where it's used, and what the studies say." A bill mandating such a registry made it through the state assembly last year, but the farm lobby killed it in the senate. Barish is determined to get it reintroduced. Although "we're just volunteers and many of us are not well," says Barish, "we decided we're not going to go away."

Internationally, the pesticide industry is running into roadblocks—any countries in the South[ern Hemisphere] have banned importation of the most deadly chemicals. And there are other advances: a United Nations-sponsored rice farmer training program in Southeast Asia has cut pesticide use in the region by 90 percent; in Sweden, pesticide use was reduced by 50 percent between 1985 and 1990; in Columbia, sugar growers use beneficial insects instead of pesticides; and some Cuban farmers, forced to go organic because of trade sanctions, now say that they don't want to go back to chemicals. "The global movement against pesticide misuse has grown fantastically in the last 10 to 15 years," says PAN's Rosenthal. "Today we have

thousands of organizations around the world pushing for sustainable and healthy agricultural techniques." But only the combined efforts of activists and consumers, working against official indifference to the public's health, can hope to one day repel the "chemical barrage that has been hurled against the fabric of life," in the words of Rachel Carson. Although life is "delicate and destructible," Carson wrote, it is also "tough and resilient, and capable of striking back in unexpected ways."

Critical Evaluation

1. Would a cost-benefit analysis show that pesticides are a necessary evil or a dispensable hazard?

2. The author states that pesticides are everywhere. But are they found "everywhere" in sufficient quantities for concern?

3. Based on the evidence she uses, and other information you have, does the author understate, overstate, or appropriately state her case? Why?

18

Can We Stop Global Warming?

John Harte

As with the problem of pesticides, the topic of global warming generates contradictory attitudes. Many people, including some experts, do not believe that global warming is truly a problem, or at least not a serious one. Their attitude appears reasonable because many are not aware of how warming affects climate (ironically, as John Harte notes, severe winter conditions are one of the consequences of global warming, not evidence against it). This attitude supports practices that help perpetuate the problem. The problem also continues because, at the macrolevel, Americans have not yet accepted the idea that sacrifices in the standard of living are necessary to safeguard the environment. Finally, even when there is agreement about ways to control global warming, the methods are often opposed by strong, vested interests such as corporations that view environmental protection laws as a threat to profits.

Still, many people are greatly concerned about global warming. Arguments like those provided by Harte strongly support this concern. In addition to his alarming account of the problem, Harte suggests possible ways to halt global warming.

Focus Questions

1. Why does global warming occur?
2. How soon will the warming threaten human well-being?
3. What are the effects of global warming?
4. How can we stop global warming?

By the middle of the 21st century, the Earth probably will be warmer than it has been at any time in human history—possibly since the age of dinosaurs ended 65,000,000 years ago. The projected increase in the average ground-level temperature ranges from three to eight degrees Fahrenheit. This may not seem like very much. After all, if tomorrow's temperature is eight degrees higher than today's, you might not notice it. Let us place this climate change in perspective, though. Over the several thousand years of emergence from the last ice age and poleward retreat of the glaciers, the average global temperature increased by just a little more than eight degrees. So, scientists are projecting a warming that could be comparable to the *total* rise since the last ice age! Because this warming will take place over a mere 50 to 100 years, its rapid pace could stress life on Earth far more than did the glacial pace of the prehistoric warming.

Why is the warming occurring? How much can the predictions be trusted? What will be the consequences to society and to life on Earth? What can be done to reduce impending climate change?

The warming is occurring because humanity is affecting the atmosphere. Each year, billions of tons of carbon dioxide are being loaded into it, an inevitable consequence of the burning of coal, oil, and natural gas. In the atmosphere, carbon dioxide acts like a blanket, trapping heat and radiating some of it back down to Earth. This process of heat trapping is called the greenhouse effect.

The level of atmospheric carbon dioxide has increased by more than 25% since the beginning of the Industrial Revolution. Most of that rise is due to fuel burning, but it also has resulted from the massive deforestation that has occurred during the past 200 years and continues today as, worldwide, an area of tropical forest nearly the size of Pennsylvania is cut and cleared each year. Carbon, which constitutes about half the weight of wood, converts to carbon dioxide when felled trees either rot or are burned.

Carbon dioxide is the main contributor to the warming, but other heat-trapping gases (known as "greenhouse gases") include nitrous oxide, methane, and chlorofluorocarbons. Nitrous oxide comes from excessive use of nitrogen fertilizers in agriculture.

Methane emanates from rice paddies and cattle feedlots. Chlorofluorocarbons, emitted from styrofoam manufacturing and other industrial processes, not only trap heat, but destroy the Earth's protective stratospheric ozone layer as well. Except for the internationally regulated chlorofluorocarbons, these gases are being emitted to the atmosphere at ever-increasing rates as the human population increases and the scale of energy use, industrial activity, and agriculture grows.

How fast will these greenhouse gases continue to build up in the atmosphere? The answer is not within the realm of scientific prediction—it depends entirely on human choices. Climatologists base their predictions of climate change on current knowledge of the physical behavior of the atmosphere and oceans. Not being good at predicting human behavior, they don't even try to do so.

Instead, they assume various possibilities, called scenarios, about the rate of buildup of the gases. For each scenario, a climate prediction is generated using climate models, that are run on the world's fastest computers.

Assuming that the current rates of growth of population and per capita fossil fuel use continue into the future, and that deforestation occurs at its current pace, greenhouse gases will build up extremely rapidly in the atmosphere—enough so that, about 40 years from now, a three to eight degree warming will occur. On the other hand, if the exponential growth of population and per capita energy use could be stopped, keeping total annual fuel consumption at current levels, this level of warming would be delayed by 50 years or more. If solar energy could be substituted expeditiously for fossil fuels, this warming need never occur.

Why should we believe these forecasts? There are several reasons. First, the same models used to predict the greenhouse effect describe Earth's current climate fairly reliably. While a weatherman cannot always predict tomorrow's rain, climatologists do understand the average properties of the planet's climate. Even before human intervention, there were natural greenhouse gases (primarily water vapor) in the atmosphere, without which the Earth would be about 50

degrees cooler than it is today. The models illustrate why it is not so cold. Second those same models reliably explain climate on other planets, such as Venus, which has far more carbon dioxide in its atmosphere and is hotter, and Mars, which has less greenhouse gas dioxide and is cooler. The models also describe well the observed summer-winter and day-night temperature differences on Earth.

Another reason for confidence in the models is that they indicate that the Earth should have warmed up about one degree during the past century as a result of human activity, and that is just what happened, according to climate data from all over the world. Until recently, it appeared that the climate models might be wrong, since the observed warming was not as great as the predicted warming. However, climate modelers now have realized that atmospheric soot has exerted a small, but significant, cooling effect. When soot as well as greenhouse gases are included, the models work well.

What will the warmer world feel like to our children and grandchildren? Warmer weather virtually is certain to occur in most locations, with a great increase in the number of days in which searing summer heat waves over 100 degrees afflict the cities. Sea level will rise, probably by as much as two or three feet during the 21st century as glacial and polar ice melt and the sea expands because of its higher temperature. This will cause massive coastline inundation in many areas, including, for instance, heavily populated coastal Bangladesh, island nations in the South Pacific, and south Florida. Evidence suggests that the seas already have risen an inch or two over the past century, an effect that is consistent with the reported global temperature increase.

Water supplies are likely to be affected. Tens and possibly hundreds of millions of people probably will lose their water supplies to salt water intrusion because of sea level rise. Hotter temperatures very likely will lead to drier summer soils in some areas, greatly stressing world food production.

The climate models cannot forecast reliably how the frequency and severity of droughts, intense hurricanes, or winter blizzards in particular locations will change. The January, 1996, blizzard in the eastern U.S. and the heat waves and droughts of the past few decades could be a preview of the *kinds* of climate stress to expect under global warming. Nevertheless, scientists cannot tell specific farmers the details of how their weather and therefore their crop yields will change, nor do they know whether or where to build new water storage facilities to cope with future drought. It strongly is suspected, though, that changing climate will disrupt food production even as the expanding human populations will require more.

Severe impacts on natural ecosystems can be anticipated, with symptoms that include the bleaching and death of coral reefs, loss of grasslands to invasive shrubs, a drop in waterfowl breeding sites, and severe stress on forests. Rising sea levels will flood productive and biologically diverse coastal wetlands, such as Everglades National Park, drowning a third or more of the present area. The biological extinction crisis the planet faces today, brought on by human encroachment on natural ecosystems, could pale compared to the devastating impacts of climate warming on the habitats of wild plants and animals.

As ecosystems are affected by warming, those changes are expected to influence the climate. Such circular effects are what scientists call feedback processes—changing climate changes ecosystems, which in turn changes climate. For instance, as soils warm, microbial processes might speed up, releasing carbon dioxide to the atmosphere. Because this would increase the amount of atmospheric carbon dioxide, and thus enhance the warming, it is called a positive feedback. If plant growth is stimulated by warming, thus increasing uptake of carbon dioxide from the atmosphere, the feedback would be negative because the ecosystem response would reduce the warming.

In addition, other feedbacks of a purely physical nature contribute to climate warming. For example, a warmer atmosphere can hold more water vapor; because water vapor is a greenhouse gas, this is a positive feedback. The most important physical feedbacks are incorporated into current climate models, but the ecological ones are ignored be-

cause their role still is very uncertain. Preliminary evidence, however, indicates that the ecological feedbacks triggered by global warming are likely to be predominantly positive. Hence, their neglect implies that scientists' models might be underestimating the magnitude of future warming. Until more research is carried out, it will not be possible to predict with much certainty the effect of these ecological feedbacks on future climate change. That uncertainty, combined with the inability to make detailed predictions about climate change at particular locations, means that knowledge of global warming will contain gaps and uncertainties for many years to come.

Some have suggested that these uncertainties provide an excuse to do nothing except wait for more scientific research to be carried out. Those who advocate procrastination often point to the possibility that, with better knowledge, the future rate of warming will not be as great as currently predicted. Uncertainty cuts two ways, though. The true magnitude of future warming is as likely to be more severe than currently predicted as it is to be less.

Seeking Solutions

The current dilemma is easily summarized: Humans are unleashing an unprecedented warming of the climate, with potentially severe human consequences, but the details of that warming can not be predicted accurately enough to suggest how to prepare for them. Even if the details could be predicted, the cost of preparing for the damage—for instance, by vacating the coastal zones and shifting agriculture to new, more favorable locations in the future—are likely to be staggering. What should be done?

One solution is to slow down the pace of climate change by reducing the rate the atmosphere is polluted with greenhouse gases. The technology exists; it is necessary only to muster the political will. Using energy more wisely could reduce fossil fuel burning greatly and therefore carbon dioxide emissions. Automobiles have been designed that are as safe as the ones driven today, yet achieve two to four times the fuel efficiency.

Refrigerators and lightbulbs exist that consume far less electricity than the ones now in use. Many homes easily can be retrofitted so that they leak less warmth and therefore consume less fuel for winter heating. These and other similar engineering innovations not only will reduce carbon dioxide emissions to the atmosphere, they greatly will reduce acid rain, a by-product of fossil fuel burning that is damaging lakes and forests, and urban smog, which is destructive to health.

As if that weren't enough reason to conserve energy, there is an economic payoff as well. Consumers who conserve energy save money by not paying for the energy they formerly wasted. While the initial cost of a more efficient lightbulb or refrigerator will be higher than that of an energy-wasteful one, numerous studies show that the higher cost is paid back within a few months or years of use, and after that the consumer saves money. Wise energy use also would reduce dependence on foreign sources of petroleum.

Americans already proved that they can save energy without jeopardizing the gross national product. From 1973 to 1986, U.S. GNP grew by 35% in real dollars without any increase in total energy consumption. The energy was saved, as well as the $150,000,000,000 that would have been spent if energy use had continued its historic lock-step with GNP. Many scientists and engineers maintain that the technology exists to do even better in the future. Total U.S. energy consumption per unit of GNP can be cut by 3.5% per year over the next two decades.

In the long run, however, the benefits of increasingly efficient energy use will be overtaken by rising population and the legitimate, inevitable demand of developing nations to achieve a higher standard of living. On this time frame, solar energy is the best strategy. It will be necessary to increase funding greatly for research and development of solar energy and reduce market barriers to the future deployment of this technology. Ironically, just as this need increases, Federal budgets for solar energy research are decreasing.

The developed nations have selfish reasons for setting a good energy example at home and then assisting the developing nations in the deployment of these technologies since their carbon dioxide will roast us just as effectively as ours will. Moreover, achieving a higher standard of living in poorer nations will be more likely if they do not repeat the same wasteful history that, in the industrialized world, fouled the air and water and squandered wealth.

Deforestation must be slowed and reforestation of previously forested land that has become agriculturally useless has to be promoted. That will require conservation incentive schemes and improvement of farm yields to reduce the pressure to clear new land. This will not be nearly as expensive as coping with the costs of global warming.

Finally, it is imperative to come to grips with human population growth, a major cause of increasing energy consumption and deforestation worldwide. Some nations in both the developing and developed world have made real progress controlling population growth; in others, such as many African countries, population still is growing rapidly and threatening a future calamity of unimaginable proportions. Population growth can be controlled by means that are perfectly compatible with civilization's precepts—for example, by raising the literacy rate for women and enhancing their status in society, providing people with the equipment needed to exercise choice over reproduction, and improving health care for children. Eventually, population growth will cease. The only question is whether it will be by such humane means or through massive starvation, disease, and war.

The U.S. population is not growing as rapidly as that of many developing nations and represents just five percent of the world population. Nevertheless, Americans are responsible for about 25% of the greenhouse gases emitted to the atmosphere and a huge share of global resource consumption. Controlling U.S. population growth is clearly necessary, as is cutting down on Americans' wasteful consumption of energy and other resources.

The prospect of climate warming confronts us with a choice. We can not predict the detailed future course of climate change, and so must make decisions under uncertainty. If we wait a few decades before taking action, we will know more about the details of the problem, but by then it will be far more difficult and expensive to forestall the warming. As knowledge of the impending disaster grows, the ability to prevent it shrinks. In some ways, we are like a parent on the sidewalk watching our little child dawdling while crossing the street. Should we wait and hope no car comes before she ambles across, or should we rush out and sweep her to safety? Is there really any doubt?

Critical Evaluation

1. Not everyone accepts the fact that global warming is occurring. Is the author convincing? Why?

2. There is also uncertainty about the effects of global warming. Are the effects the author notes realistic? Why?

3. Given the desire of people everywhere for economic growth and a higher standard of living, how realistic are the author's suggestions for a solution? Are there other possible solutions?

John Harte, "Can We Stop Global Warming?" In *USA Today*, March 1997, pp. 78-80. Copyright © 1997 by *USA Today*. Reprinted by permission of the Society for the Advancement of Education. ✦

19

Environmental Racism

Timothy Maher

At first, it might appear that environmental problems affect everyone equally. If, for example, one lives in a polluted urban area, are not all the people who live there affected by the pollution independently of their race or gender or social class? Actually, no. As Robert Bullard points out: "An abundance of documentation shows blacks, lower-income groups, and working-class persons are subjected to a disproportionately large amount of pollution and other environmental stressors in their neighborhoods as well as in their workplaces" (1990, 1). The point is, even if the area generally is polluted, it is not uniformly polluted throughout. The heaviest concentration of pollutants, and the most hazardous workplaces, are likely to be where minorities live and work.

In this selection, Timothy Maher notes another way in which environmental problems are distributed unequally—the location of toxic waste sites. At the microlevel, the attitudes of the well-to-do ("I don't want that near me") help keep the sites away from their areas. At the macrolevel, the attitudes influence government and corporate decisions about siting. The net result is environmental racism—the worst of the toxic waste sites are in African American and Latino communities.

Reference

Bullard, Robert D. 1990. *Dumping in Dixie: Race, Class, and Environmental Quality.* Boulder, Colo.: Westview Press.

Focus Questions

1. What is environmental racism?
2. What is the relationship between the location of toxic waste sites and race?
3. How can communities burdened with toxic waste sites be helped?

In many respects, Indiana is a very average state. Geographically, it is in the middle of the country; its income is about average, as is its unemployment rate and its ethnic composition. Both agriculture and industry are well represented; it is a mix of North and South. It is average—except when it comes to toxic wastes. In this category, Indiana outpaces most other states (all but seven others). It consistently ranks among the top 10 on most listings of hazardous waste sites, air pollution, and so on. Although the state as a whole is heavily polluted, there are large parts that are relatively unpolluted. Many other parts are polluted beyond use, the so-called sacrifice zones.

Public policy concerning allowable levels of pollution generally favors business interests. The regulatory agency, Indiana Department of Environmental Management (IDEM), is and has been severely underfunded and understaffed. A part of an unwritten public policy concerning toxics seems to have been that you dump it in someone else's backyard—but not just anyone's backyard. Toxic waste facilities have been regularly located in areas populated by African Americans, Latinos, Native Americans, or Asian Americans. Environmental racism is a very insidious form of discrimination, sometimes destroying whole communities, other times harming people in ways that will not appear for decades (i.e., cancer).

This article addresses the issue of environmental racism through a systematic analysis of the major toxic waste sites and toxic waste generators (i.e., industries, power plants) and the populations surrounding them. Because previous research has identified both race and class variables as being significantly related to the presence of serious toxic waste sites/generators, issues such as income, educational level, type of occupation, and ethnicity are included.

Review of Literature

Although environmental sociology is a relatively new field of study, there is an emerging literature that focuses on environmental equity issues. A number of studies have focused on social movement and community organizing aspects of environmental policy and waste disposal. Freudenberg's (1984) *Not in Our Backyard!*, Bullard's (1993) *Confronting Environmental Racism*, Boyte's (1984) *Community is Possible*, and Hofrichter's (1993) *Toxic Struggles* all analyze the dynamics of the social/collective reactions to hazardous wastes. They each identity significant components of successful challenges to corporate and governmental plans for locating toxic waste sites in various communities. They also stress the fact that these successful challenges are recent achievements; in the past, these kinds of facilities were located in communities with little opposition.

Another area of concern in the literature relates to the social characteristics of communities surrounding toxic waste sites. Although related to the issue of community organizing, these studies look at the past dumping and siting practices and policies of corporations and governments. Bullard's (1990) *Dumping in Dixie*, Bryant and Mohai's (1992) *Race and the Incidence of Environmental Hazards*, and the United Church of Christ Commission for Racial Justice's (1987) *Toxic Wastes and Race in the United States* are prime examples of this type of research. They have found a biased pattern of site placement practices by corporations and governments. Communities with significant African American and Latino populations appear to be favored as sites for toxic wastes. . . .

Other research (Maher, 1989, 1991, 1993) has also found a relationship between social class variables and toxic waste site placement. At the census-tract level, low income, low educational level, blue-collar occupations, and ethnicity were associated with hazardous waste sites. The more serious the hazardous waste problem, the more likely the surrounding populations were African American or Latino. This research differed from other studies in two ways; the first being its use of census-tract rather than county-level data. Census tracts allow for a more specific or targeted look at the population immediately surrounding toxic sites. Because counties are much larger than tracts, the entire population of a county may not be as directly affected by the toxins as are residents of the census tract where wastes are located. The second difference is that these three studies focused on all types of toxic sites, not just the most severe. As a result, relationships between the severity of the site and social factors were analyzed. In general, as sites got more severe and numerous (within census tracts), the populations got increasingly poorer, less well educated, more concentrated in blue-collar occupations, and more likely to be African American or Latino.

The present study is intended to link these previous smaller studies of urban areas in Indiana with a systematic statewide analysis of race and class characteristics. Because most rural areas are not tracked by the census, county-level data were used for comparative purposes. The use of county-level data makes this research somewhat more comparable to research being conducted in other parts of the country.

Theoretical Perspective

The basic premise of this study is that there has been a systematic practice or policy of locating the worst toxic waste sites in African American and Latino communities. This practice, termed *environmental racism*, has been demonstrated in parts of the southern United States (Bullard, 1990). Various other studies have focused on specific types of toxic sites (i.e., incinerators, landfills). The present study analyzes the worst known toxic waste sites and toxic waste generators in the state of Indiana and the social characteristics of their surrounding regions (county).

Environmental sacrifice zones, to some extent, become major obstacles to normal development. In fact, toxic pollution may make some areas unsuitable for any subsequent human use. Toxic pollution combined with community knowledge of the hazards will lead to negligible development or further contamination of an area due to its limited use for other social or economic activities.

The apparent concentration of the worst toxic waste sites in African American and Latino areas suggests a pattern of racism in the making and implementing of environmental policy. This pattern of toxic segregation has had three principal effects:

1. Whites, particularly decision makers, have been able to separate themselves from the worst environmental problems.

2. African American and Latino communities have had to suffer the health, social, and economic problems associated with toxic exposure.

3. Such pollution further restricts and endangers the available supply of safe, affordable, low-income housing.

These clearly discriminatory siting practices have been able to continue largely because of the White community's ability to control information concerning toxic pollution and its hazards. In the state of Indiana, very little reliable information has been made available to residents concerning hazardous pollution in their local areas. Neither the government nor the media have provided such information on local issues, although they have emphasized both pollution problems in eastern Europe and the radioactive pollution from Chernobyl.

There is an active relationship between human settlements and their natural environments, which is a basic premise of this research. There emerges in industrial societies a conflict over the diminishing supply of relatively unpolluted land, which is a second premise. The above conflict over desirable, relatively unpolluted land, which is manifested as a conflict between social classes and/or ethnic groups is the third basic premise underlying this investigation. The following hypotheses are drawn from the above conceptual approach.

Hypotheses

Toxic racism

Hypothesis 1a

The larger the proportion of African American and Latinos population, the greater the number of serious toxic waste sites.

Hypothesis 1b

Because the most serious side affects of acid rain occur hundreds of miles downwind from the generating site, these locations (primarily power plants) will not exhibit the above relationship with African American and Latino populations.

Toxic classism

Hypothesis 2a

The larger the proportion of people without a high school or college degree, the greater the number of serious toxic waste sites.

Hypothesis 2b

The larger the proportion of people with blue-collar occupations, the greater the number of toxic waste sites.

Hypothesis 2c

The lower the per capita income, the greater the number of toxic waste sites.

Hypothesis 2d

The higher the unemployment rate, the greater the number of toxic waste sites.

Data

Data for this project came from a number of sources, including (a) the Environmental Protection Agency (EPA) Superfund program, (b) IDEM, (c) the National Wildlife Federation (NWF) Toxic 500 list, and (d) the 1990 U.S. census (Bureau of the Census, 1990). Any single listing of toxic sites or toxic generators is invariably lacking in some regard. The use of multiple sources was meant to create an inclusive listing of the worst known toxic sites/generators in the state of Indiana. The sites/generators included here are ones for which sufficient information is available and that represent a serious area of toxic hazard (i.e., landfills, industrial generators, air/ground/water pollution, or acid rain).

There are, unfortunately, many more toxic sites/generators in Indiana than those included in this study. In some cases, the hazards these other sites pose may be less than those included; in other cases, less may be known about the particular site/generator.

The issue of environmental racism, however, has focused primarily on the placement of the most severe toxic problems in African American communities. For the purposes of this research, the 146 sites included represent the most severe toxic sites/generators in the state of Indiana.

Data Analysis

To systematically evaluate the social characteristics of areas seriously affected by toxic pollution, this research correlates county-level data from the 1990 U.S. census (Bureau of the Census, 1990) with the number and types of toxic sites within each county. The variables used in this analysis include ethnicity, per capita income, percentage of high school and college graduates, unemployment rate, and percentage of blue- and white-collar employees.

Because Indiana is a very diverse state with a mixture of urban, suburban, and rural areas, this research includes analyses within each type of area (urban, suburban, rural) as well as an analysis of the whole state. Are urban areas with particularly large African American and Latino populations targeted for toxic sites and urban areas with predominantly White populations not so targeted? Are suburban areas with larger African American and Latino populations targeted? Within metropolitan areas (urban and suburban combined), are counties with large African American and Latino populations targeted? In the state as a whole, are counties with the largest African American and Latino population targeted for excessive toxic pollution?

The argument that social class variables (income, education, and occupation) could explain the location of toxic waste sites (the toxic classism argument) is not at all supported by the data. Instead of toxic waste sites being concentrated in low-income, poorly educated, blue-collar areas, they appear to be disproportionately located in predominantly African American communities. . . .

There is some variation among the different types of sites (EPA Superfund, state superfund, NWF Toxic 500, and acid rain generators) and the communities they are located in. The main contributors to acid rain are coal-burning power plants. These cause serious environmental harm hundreds of miles downwind but very little in their home communities. Among this group of sites, there is no statistically significant relationship with African American and Latino populations. Conversely, the NWF sites tend to be active generators of many different pollutants, most of which do stay in the local community. This group of sites has the highest correlation with African American and Latino communities.

Overall, the data show a consistent relationship between ethnicity (African American/Latino) and the presence of toxic waste sites/generators (the only exception to this is in suburban counties, where there is a negative relationship). Social class variables either show no relationship or a relationship in the opposite direction from that hypothesized. The only exception is a correlation . . . in the urban/suburban grouping between unemployment and the presence of toxic sites/generators.

Conclusion

The results of this analysis of population characteristics at the county level differ somewhat from findings in previous studies at the census-tract level (Maher, 1989, 1991, 1993). In the earlier studies, the whole range of toxic sites (those with IDEM priority ratings of low, medium, and high) was correlated with the variables of race/ethnicity, income, education, and occupation. The social class variables were most consistently related to the presence of hazardous waste sites in particular census tracts. Race/ethnicity correlated highly with only the most serious sites (high and EPA Superfund).

In the present study, race/ethnicity are strongly related to the presence of Superfund, Toxic 500, and major acid rain sites in the state of Indiana. These results suggest a roughly parallel pattern of race and class discrimination in the site placement of toxic facilities. It is clear that for the most part, middle- and upper-income White communities are shielded by public and corporate policy from the worst hazardous by-products of modern industrial society. Counties with higher than average proportions of African Americans and Latinos in the population are significantly more likely than other counties to be home to highly polluting industries and toxic waste facilities. Within those affected counties, however, low income Whites frequently live closest to the actual sites (i.e., within the same census tract) and are clearly victimized much like the African American and Latino population. This pattern differs from results from studies of southern states (Bullard, 1990), where whole counties were segregated (nearly 100% African American). Counties in a northern state like Indiana are less likely to be so thoroughly segregated strictly by race, although they may house large populations of both impoverished Whites and African Americans or Latinos.

Regardless of whether racism or classism are at work in the toxic polluting of communities, public policy should focus on relieving the burden placed on already distressed communities. The following are some policy suggestions that would contribute to realizing that goal:

1. rigorous enforcement of environmental regulations;

2. expansion of civil rights laws to protect communities from discriminatory siting decisions;

3. more active public education programs to disseminate information to the public;

4. prompt relocation from dense urban neighborhoods of particularly abusive facilities (i.e., auto shredders, smelters, refineries);

5. development of regional environmental plans for safe removal and storage of locally generated wastes;

6. requirement of proof of environmental equity when licensing any new toxic generating or storage facility; and

7. improvement of public educational opportunities for poor people of all colors.

Researchers and activists would do well to concentrate their efforts on educating the public in victimized communities about toxic dangers in their midst and actions the public can take. Research has already established that past siting decisions have consistently favored the White middle and upper classes. Ironically, the White middle and upper classes generated the vast majority of toxic pollutants through high-consumption lifestyles unavailable to the poor. These same groups benefit financially through ownership and/or control over the corporations most involved in hazardous waste pollution.

Society has subsidized middle- and upper-class wealth by an unwritten tax on the environment. Each year, value is taken out of the collective natural environment by corporate profit making facilitated by pollution of the environment. The cost of this unwritten tax falls disproportionately on those who benefit the least from corporate profit-oriented environmental degradation. This tax represents a major transfer of wealth, including the reduced property values in contaminated areas and the enhanced values in the clean suburbs.

Future research would benefit from an analysis of this wealth transfer from poor and African American and Latino communities to affluent areas. The makeup of victimized communities is well established, but less is known about the communities that escape the worst of modern poisons.

Environmental equity must include protections for African American and Latino communities, but this must be accomplished without simply shifting all the wastes to impoverished White communities. For real change to occur and for a more sustainable future to be created requires a halt to the highly polluting lifestyles of middle- and upper-class Americans. Once poor and African American/Latino communities are unavailable for toxic dumping, the middle- and upper-class decision makers will be forced to accept wastes into their communities or switch to less polluting lifestyles and a more sustainable and equitable economy.

References

Boyte, H. C. (1984). *Community Is Possible*. New York: HarperCollins.

Bryant, B., & Mohai, P. (1992). *Race and the Incidence of Environmental Hazards: A Time for Discourse*. Boulder, CO: Westview.

Bulland, R. D. (1990). *Dumping in Dixie*. Boulder, CO: Westview.

Bulland, R.D. (Ed.). (1993). *Confronting Environmental Racism*. Boston: South End Press.

Bureau of the Census. (1990). *1990 United States Census*. Washington, DC: U.S. Government Printing Office.

Freudenberg, N. (1984). *Not In Our Backyard!* New York: Monthly Review Press.

Hofricter, R. (Ed.). (1993). *Toxic Struggles*. Philadelphia: New Society.

Maher, T. (1989). Communities as Victims: Social Impact of Toxic Pollution. *Proceedings of the Indiana Academy of the Social Sciences*, 24, 105-112.

Maher, T. (1991, April). Race, Class and Trash: Whose Backyard Do We Dump In? Paper Presented at the North Central Sociological Association annual meeting, Dearborn, MI.

——. (1993, April). Toxic Policies: Class and Race In Environmental Degradation. Paper Presented at the North Central Sociological Association annual meeting, Toledo, OH.

United Church of Christ Commission for Racial Justice. (1987). *Toxic Wastes and Race in the United States: A National Report on the Racial and Socio-Economic Characteristics of Communities with Hazardous Waste Sites*. New York: Author.

Critical Evaluation

1. Even though hazardous waste sites are likely to be in African American and Latino communities, how much of an actual health threat are they?

2. The author bases his conclusions on data from Indiana. Are the conclusions valid for the rest of the nation?

3. How realistic and how relevant are the author's suggestions for attacking the problem of environmental racism?

Timothy Maher, "Environmental Oppresion." In *Journal of Black Studies* 28:3, pp. 357–367. Copyright © 1998 by Sage Publications, Inc. Reprinted by permission. ✦

Project for Personal Application and Class Discussion: The Environment

Environmental problems are overwhelming. "What can one person do?" is a legitimate question to raise. Actually, if only one person is concerned, he or she can do little or nothing. But if millions of people accept personal responsibility to do something, significant progress can be made.

Think about what you personally can do to alleviate environmental problems. List as many specific actions as you can think of under each of the following categories:

- What I can do to reduce pollution?

- What I can do to cut back on the use of the earth's resources?

- What I can do to reduce the amount of waste and garbage?

- What I can do to reduce the amount of energy (electricity, gas, coal, etc.) I use?

- What I can recycle?

Look over your lists carefully. You will probably discover that most or all of your actions may add a little inconvenience to your life but will not substantially reduce your standard of living. In fact, the editors believe that substantial progress can be made in addressing environmental problems without any significant loss in living standard. ✦

PART II

Troubled Groups:
Problems of Inequality

Gender

The pursuit of happiness is one of the prerogatives asserted in the Declaration of Independence. For most Americans, this right translates into opportunities for education, careers, and income. In theory, each American has such opportunities. In practice, opportunities vary according to gender. For example, women tend to earn less than men. The U.S. Bureau of Labor reported that in 1996 the median weekly earnings of women 25 years and older were $444, compared to $599 for men of the same age (U.S. Bureau of the Census 1997: 431).

Moreover, these differences existed across various categories of occupations. For instance, the weekly median earnings for managers and professionals were $852 for men and $616 for women. For those in technical and support occupations, the median earnings were $650 for men and $498 for women. For service workers, the median earnings were $357 for men and $273 for women.

Of course, many factors—education, experience, number of hours worked, and job title—affect income. However, even when all these factors are taken into account, women still receive less income than men (Pfeffer and Ross 1990). The difference can only be explained on the basis of sex discrimination.

This section explores additional inequalities that hamper women's pursuit of happiness. These include stereotyped images of women, pressures to achieve a particular (and unrealistic) appearance, and impediments to career advancement.

References

Pfeffer, Jeffrey, and Jerry Ross. 1990. "Gender-Based Wage Differences." *Work and Occupations* 17:55–78.

U.S. Bureau of the Census. 1997. *Statistical Abstract of the United States*. Washington, DC: U.S. Government Printing Office. ✦

20

Sex Discrimination and Affirmative Action

Madeline E. Heilman

Why is there discrimination against women in such areas as education, occupation, and income? What can be done to rectify the situation? Madeline Heilman considers these two questions in the context of women attaining high corporate positions. She addresses the first question by showing how the social psychological factor of stereotyping perpetuates sex discrimination. She discusses the second by pointing out how affirmative action—a government program designed to reduce inequality—actually reinforced the stereotypes. A clear implication of Heilman's chapter is that the problem of sex discrimination must be attacked at both the macro- and microlevels. Laws and programs are needed, but so are changes in the attitudes and norms that develop in families and schools.

Focus Questions

1. What are sex stereotypes?

2. How do sex stereotypes affect women's advancement in the corporate hierarchy?

3. What has been the impact of affirmative-action programs on women's advancement in corporations?

There has been much discussion about when women will finally make it into the highest levels of American corporations. Although women have increasingly become represented in the corporate ranks, they are conspicuously absent at the very top. Thus, a *Fortune* magazine review of the proxy statements of the 1000 largest U.S. industrial and service companies indicated that less than one half of 1% of the highest paid officers and directors were women and a subsequent review of the annual reports of 255 major corporations revealed that only 5% of upper management positions were, as of 1990, held by women (Fierman, 1990). A recent report of a Federal panel, the Glass Ceiling Commission, based on a review of 1990 census reports, corroborates these figures; it states that while white males constitute only 43% of the labor force, they hold 95% of the senior management jobs (Holmes, 1995). Why are women so scarce at the top?

It is proposed here that stereotyped-based sex discrimination is a major cause, and that current organizational practices act to support and perpetuate it. Before developing this thesis, however, it is instructive to explore some commonly proposed alternative explanations for this phenomenon.

Some say that "it is simply a matter of time." Proponents of this point of view argue that women's absence from the top levels of management is a natural consequence of them not having been in managerial positions long enough for the natural career progression to take hold (Forbes, Piercy and Hayes, 1988). This is sometimes called the pipeline theory. But there is little evidence which supports this theory. According to the Feminist Majority Foundation (1991), a women's rights advocacy group, if the pipeline explanation were correct, women today should comprise at least 15% of those at the top levels of corporations. Others, too, find this explanation for women's lack of representation at the top ranks unsatisfactory (Fierman, 1990; Hymnowitz and Schellhardt, 1986; Salmons, 1987). Research on this issue has made evident that while women's representation in the workforce has burgeoned, and their numbers in the lower and middle ranks of management have swelled, few have advanced to the same levels or at the same pace as their male counterparts (Dipboye, 1987).

Another explanation for the dearth of women at the top places blame on women themselves. There long ha[ve] been assumptions about how women and men differ with regard to work-related skills and attitudes. And, in most cases, women are believed to be deficient. In fact, the popular literature is filled with self-help techniques to enable women to overcome the inherent deficits that result from being female. There are tips about succeeding at corporate gamesmanship (Harragan, 1977), about strategies for "breaking into the boys' club at the top" (Jardim and Hennig, 1990), and about improving one's communication style, supervising skills, and long term career perspective (Feuer, 1988). Each of these authors have inherently accepted the proposition that it is the weaknesses that women bring to the workplace which obstruct their advancement, weaknesses which must be overcome if women are to succeed.

But research evidence does not bear out this contention. Social and organizational psychologists who have investigated the nature and extent of sex related differences between women and men managers have come to a very different conclusion. Many ability differences that typically have been ascribed to men and women do not hold up under scientific scrutiny, and the idea that women are crippled by their lower aptitude is unwarranted (e.g., Maccoby and Jacklin, 1974). Moreover, the commonly accepted idea that men as compared to women do a better job in the leadership role in organizational settings because they are task-focused (focused on getting the work done) rather than interpersonally focused (focused on keeping people happy) is contradicted by data from recent literature reviews (Dobbins and Platz, 1986; Eagley and Johnson, 1990). Additionally, no scientific evidence has been reported validating the often made assumption that women lack the "drive" to get to the top. In fact, no differences between managerial men and women have been found in level of motivation (Morrison et al., 1987; Miner, 1977), nor in psychological needs and motives such as the need for achievement or need for power (Harlan and Weiss, 1982), and at least one researcher has concluded that women in management positions actually may be more motivated to succeed than their male counterparts because only the most motivated women would have continued on a career path fraught with so many obstacles (Powell, 1988). And, finally, there is no research evidence supportive of the commonly held idea that women managers are less committed to their careers because their primary commitment is to the family and home. In fact, a survey conducted by the American Management Association depicts women as compared to men managers as more committed to their careers, more willing to relocate, and more likely to make their jobs top priority when family-work conflicts occur (Hymnowitz and Schellhardt, 1986).

These research findings indicate that differences between men and women managers in abilities, attitudes and behavior are more apparent than real; most studies of practicing managers demonstrate no systematic differences between them (Powell, 1988; Howard and Bray, 1988). In fact, Donnell and Hall (1980), who conducted an expansive field study of almost 2000 matched pairs of men and women managers brought them to the conclusion drawn by many others—that the absence of women in upper management cannot be explained away by the idea that women "practice a different brand of management from that practiced by men" (p. 76). Thus, the argument that women are less equipped in skills or temperament to handle the arduous role of a senior manager, and consequently the current underrepresentation of women at the upper echelons is fair and equitable, seems highly questionable.

Despite this, however, beliefs that there are differences between men and women which profoundly affect their potential to succeed in the management role obstinately persist, justifying the underrepresentation of women and no doubt contributing to the problem. Why do such beliefs endure, even when they fly in the face of reality? The answer to this question, and a key factor in understanding the barriers confronting women in the corporate world, is the psychological phenomenon of sex stereotypes.

Sex Stereotypes

A stereotype is a set of attributes ascribed to a group and believed to characterize its individual members simply because they belong to that group. In the case of sex stereotypes, these are attributes which are imparted to individual men and women simply by virtue of their sex.

Stereotyping is at its core a categorization process, and can be a work-saving cognitive mechanism to simplify and organize the complex world we encounter. And, in many instances it is effective as well as efficient. Knowing that rocks are hard and do not melt when submerged in water enables us to act upon our environment far more effectively than if we had to establish these attributes every time we happened upon a rock. The problem is that stereotypes about groups of people often are inaccurate or they are overgeneralizations which do not apply to the individual group member who is targeted. In situations such as these, stereotypes become the basis for faulty reasoning, leading to biased feelings and actions, disadvantaging (or advantaging) others not because of what they are like or what they have done but because of the groups to which they are deemed to belong.

The stereotypes associated with the sexes are pervasive and widely shared. If asked to describe a "typical man" or a "typical woman," most people are able to do so. There also is remarkable agreement about the traits that characterize them. Whatever the age, religion, social class, marital status, educational background, or even mental health status of the research participants, researchers have consistently found great concurrence in the attributes ascribed to men and women (e.g. Broverman et al., 1972). Even the sex of the respondent makes no difference; men and women alike subscribe to sex stereotypic conceptions (Heilman, 1983).

The descriptions of men and women tend to differ dramatically, and are assumed to apply to nearly all men and women as members of their respective groups. In fact, investigations have revealed that men and women often are depicted as polar opposites (Broverman et al., 1972). Men are thought to be strong and active, and women are thought to be weak and passive. Thus, whereas men are described as decisive, independent, rational, objective and self-confident, women are described as indecisive, dependent, emotional, non-objective and insecure. Men and women also are described differently with respect to qualities of warmth and expressiveness, with women rated more favorably; they are viewed to be tender, understanding, concerned with others and comfortable with their feelings whereas men are described as just the opposite.

The traits associated with men and women not only are different but also are valued differently. Although each are credited with desirable traits, it is generally argued that those associated with men are more highly valued in Western culture than are those associated with women. That is, achievement oriented traits typically ascribed to men have been shown to be more highly valued than those concerning nurturance and affiliation typically ascribed to women. And one would expect this differential desirability of stereotypically masculine and feminine traits to be even more accentuated in achievement oriented settings such as the corporate world. Indeed, a number of investigations have demonstrated this to be so (Darley, 1976; Zellman, 1976).

But, do traditional stereotypic characterizations of women predominate even when women are managers? Are the differences in perceptions of men and women managers similar to the differences in perceptions of men and women more generally? If they are not, then invoking sex stereotypes as an explanation for the inhibition of women managers' career progress is in error.

Recent work in psychology attests to the importance of these questions. First, it has been shown that with the addition of job-relevant information stereotyping of women abates (Heilman, 1984; Tosi and Einbender, 1985). If the title of manager is considered to provide such job-relevant information, then it, too, should ameliorate stereotyping. Second, a compelling case has been made that the existence of a single and all-inclusive blanket stereotype of a social grouping may be faulty (Taylor, 1981). Instead, it has been suggested that these groupings are differentiated into a number of "subtypes," each characterized by a different cluster of attributes. Evidence of such subtypes of women has been provided (Deaux et al., 1985; Eagley and Steffon, 1984; Noseworthy and Lott, 1984). However, data collected in a recent study demonstrate quite vividly the fact that traditional sex stereotypes persist even when women are managers.

One hundred and fifty-two male managers from a range of industries and locations within the U.S. were asked to rate either men or women "in general" or men or women "managers" on an attribute inventory. Results of statistical tests indicated that although work-related characterizations of women were more favorable when they were said to be managers than when they were not, with only one exception (independence), these characterizations were still significantly more negative than those of men managers . . .: women managers were said to be less competent, active and potent, emotionally stable, and rational than men managers. . . . These findings attest to the powerful influence of sex stereotypes on perceptions and, specifically, document the fact that traditionally discrepant characterizations of men and women persist even when the men and women are said to be managers.

These data therefore do not challenge but instead fuel the idea that sex stereotypes are key elements in any consideration of why women's career advancement is inhibited. Regardless of their validity or their relevance when considering any one particular woman, sex stereotypes seem to be drawn upon, providing the basis for biased decision making which ultimately can thwart the upward progress of women managers. How this occurs, and the conditions under which stereotypes are apt to wield the most power, will be considered next.

The Lack of Fit Model

To fully explore how sex stereotypes might play a role in unfairly obstructing the advancement of women up the corporate hierarchy, it is critical to recognize that top management and executive level corporate jobs are considered to be "male" in character. This sex-typing of such positions has deep roots. Its origin is in the traditional view that paid work—especially if it is important, demanding and lucrative—is a man's domain. Women's absence from the work force, their lack of mobility and their failure to maintain career continuity all have reinforced that image. Now, when this no longer is the case, the image of paid employment as a man's activity tends to prevail.

Of course not all jobs are considered to be male in sex-type. Nurses, librarians, secretaries, elementary school teachers all are jobs which have traditionally been held by women. Such jobs also are notable for requiring the feminine skills and attributes which society attributes to women—sensitivity, nurture, and service. But the job of manager is quite different. It, apparently, is seen as "male," and thought to require an achievement-oriented aggressiveness and an emotional toughness that is distinctly male in character. Evidence for this has been provided by the work of Schein (1973, 1975) and more recently Powell and Butterfield (1989) and Heilman, Block and Martell (1989) in which the good manager has been shown to be described predominantly in masculine terms. Thus, not only are most managers men, but good management is also thought to be a manly business. It is believed to require skills and attributes imparted to men as a group.

How do stereotyped conceptions of women and the male sex-typing of corporate managerial positions in combination detrimentally affect women's career advancement? To answer this question it is important to understand the role played by "lack of fit," or perceived incongruity (Heilman, 1983).

Expectations about how successful an individual will be when working at a particular job are the driving force underlying personnel decisions. And these performance expectations are determined by the fit between the perception of the attributes the individual brings to the work setting and the perception of the job's requirements in terms of skills and orientation. If the fit is seen as a good one, then success will be expected; if the fit is seen as poor, then failure will be expected. These fit-derived performance expectations, whether positive or negative, play a key role in evaluation processes because there is a cognitive tendency to perpetuate and confirm them. Once expectations for an individual are in place, they create a predisposition toward negativity or positivity that colors subsequent perceptions and judgments. They serve as a filter for what information about an individual is attended to, affect how information that is made available is interpreted, and influence what information is remembered and subsequently recalled when critical decisions are being made.

Applying this reasoning to women in organizations it is clear that the skills and attributes presumed to be required to effectively handle male sex-typed upper management jobs do not correspond to the attributes believed to characterize women as a group. Forcefully taking a leadership role, making tough decisions, and actively competing for resources are simply not activities that are consistent with the prevailing view of what women are like. Thus one would expect that if a stereotyped view of women were taken when a woman was scrutinized for an executive role, expectations of failure would be a likely consequence. And these expectations of failure have profound consequences for the way in which women are evaluated, promoting a clear bias toward negativity. Women are not viewed as particularly suited for upper management roles, and information that they are indeed well equipped tends to be discredited and/or distorted to fit these negative performance expectations. The behavioral consequence is sex discrimination.

Sex Discrimination

The dynamics of sex discrimination in work settings have been heavily documented. What follows is a brief summary of the findings of many investigations in the psychology literature accumulated over a long period of years. Readers are referred to Heilman (1983) and Arvey and Campion (1982) for a more exhaustive treatment of this topic. Research has repeatedly demonstrated sex discrimination in employee selection processes; when the job in question is male sex-typed (and therefore a perceived lack of fit exists), women with identical credentials as male counterparts have been shown to be judged less qualified, are less likely to be hired and,

if they are hired, are compensated less generously. Sex bias also has been demonstrated in decisions about pay raises, promotions, employee utilization and training opportunities. This discriminatory treatment can be traced to two sources: sex bias in performance evaluation itself and sex bias in causal explanations of women's success. A myriad of investigations have pointed out that women's work is subjected to prejudiced evaluation—that the same product is judged more favorably if it is attributed to a man and therefore is rewarded more generously. Furthermore, even when successful performance is acknowledged (often because there is no way to deny it), it is attributed to factors such as luck or hard work rather than skill. The inconsistency with expectations is "fixed" by attributing the success to things other than competence, with the consequence that organizational rewards are unlikely to be bestowed nor advancement likely to occur on the basis of such successes (Heilman and Guzzo, 1978).

There are conditions which are particularly facilitative of stereotyping and the biased decision-making which it produces. Unfortunately, in many cases these are precisely the conditions that tend to abound in organizational contexts.

1. *The salience of sex is directly related to the degree stereotypes will be involved in forming impressions of any one specific woman.* When a woman's sex is distinctive and noticeable, sex is highly likely to be singled out as the critical inferential point about what she is like (Taylor et al., 1978). Furthermore, as Kanter (1977) so wisely pointed out, when they are numerically scarce, there is no challenge to stereotypic thinking—people are not confronted with the natural differences among women and are free to see each of them in monolithic terms. Since there rarely is a high concentration of women at upper management levels, the salience of sex is likely to be quite high, providing an impetus for stereotypic thinking.

Empirical justification for the idea that rarity can facilitate sex bias can be found in a study in which the sex composition of an applicant pool was systematically varied (Heilman, 1980). MBA students were found to evaluate a woman for a managerial position far more negatively in terms of qualifications, potential to succeed, and ultimate hiring recommendations when women comprised only one or two of the eight candidates under review than when they comprised a greater proportion of the applicant pool. Also, as expected, the woman candidate was depicted in far more stereotypic terms when women were scarce rather than well-represented in the pool.

2. *Stereotypes flourish in ambitious performance settings.* The tendency to distort performance information to conform with the expectations wrought by sex stereotypes is well documented. It has been shown that when performance information is ambiguous there is distortion of the outcome to conform to stereotype-consistent expectations about the lesser capability of women (e.g., Heilman, Martell and Simon, 1988). It is only when information of success is concrete, irrefutable, and/or objectively verifiable that such distortion is avoided (see Tosi and Einbender, 1985). Consistent with this, Nieva and Gutek (1980) propose that the more that inference is required to draw implications from performance information, the more stereotype-based bias is apt to creep into evaluations.

Since managerial-type positions are ones which often have few quantifiable or objective measures of success, they seem particularly vulnerable to distortion in the interpretation of outcomes. Stereotypes can, in such situations, provide structure and meaning to otherwise ambiguous data, and therefore are likely to weigh heavily in evaluations.

3. *The more unstructured the actual decision making procedure, the more apt are stereotypes to influence decision making.* Structured decision making forces the consideration of multiple sources of information about an individual and the paying of attention to a particular set of criteria, any one of which may be ignored without the constraint of having to attend to it. It ensures that particular attributes are assessed for everyone and that they are given equal weight in the decision process. Thus, structure in decision making precludes the automatic shorthand of using stereotypes to infer what the person

being evaluated is like, and the giving of biased emphasis to different attributes for different individuals. As we said earlier, stereotypes are efficient, and they are useful for the cognitively lazy. But structured decision making undercuts such laziness, forcing more attentive and systematic processing of greater amounts of relevant information.

There is not a great deal of consensus about what makes for effective senior management. In fact, very little is known about the process by which promotion decisions are made at the senior management level. Researchers have concluded that because of the complexity of these positions, promotion criteria tend to be subjective and vague (London and Stumpf, 1983; Stumpf and London, 1981). This absence of a structured decision making process is likely to foster the use of stereotypes in promotion decisions at executive levels, giving rise to erroneous inferences about women and prompting different aspects of their attribute profile to take precedence in decision making than would be the case for men. Thus, the potential for biased decision making is very high.

4. *The use of stereotypes is enhanced when performance cannot be unequivocally attributed to the individual.* It has long been accepted, based on the work of Deaux and her colleagues (e.g., Deaux, 1976), that because it is unexpected due to stereotypes of women and their talents, a woman's success on male tasks and jobs is explained away by factors other than her skill. It has been demonstrated that sometimes her success is attributed to luck (Deaux and Emswiller, 1974) or to hard work (Feldman-Summers and Kiesler, 1974). Similarly, a woman's success is sometimes attributed to someone else entirely, and she is not seen as the origin of the performance outcome. When this occurs, stereotypes about women are allowed free reign—the potentially disconfirming information is dismissed.

This phenomenon is of relevance given recent trends in organizations, and particularly given the current emphasis on teams as essential organizational units. Since the very notion of teams and team performance often obscures the visibility of individual contributions, they are likely to encourage, or at least not discourage, the use of sex stereotypes. An unintentional by-product may therefore be the promoting of biased evaluations of individual women and discriminatory treatment of them.

It has been argued here that corporate settings and the upper reaches of management in particular are fertile breeding grounds for sex bias because they facilitate the use of sex stereotypes in determining impressions of women. We now turn to consider the affirmative action policies and procedures that government and industry have embraced to facilitate the integration of women into the workforce. Underlying these policies and procedures is the idea that ensuring representation of women in nontraditional positions is key to solving the sex discrimination problem—that the rest will take care of itself. Unfortunately, however, this often is not the case.

In the following sections, I will report research I and my colleagues have done concerning the impact of affirmative action on reactions to its intended beneficiaries. Of particular interest to this discussion is the way in which such policies and procedures, because they heighten the salience of sex, can act to reaffirm and reinforce sex stereotypes and therefore, paradoxically, sometimes create additional basis for biased judgments and discriminatory actions.

The Impact of Affirmative Action

There are many individuals who themselves are members of the groups targeted to benefit from affirmative action efforts who have spoken out against such programs (e.g., Wilkerson, 1991; Wycliff, 1990). Many of these individuals agree that affirmative action stigmatizes their intended beneficiaries by causing inferences of substandard competence. Thus, Shelby Steele (1990), a prominent black professor, wrote in the *New York Times Magazine*, "the quality that earns us preferential treatment is implied inferiority"—the implication is that special treatment is needed. Similarly, Himmelfarb (1988), in the *New York Times*, claims that both women and minorities are likely to suffer the stigma of second-class citizenship as

a result of preferential treatment, because they will be subjected to the presumption that they were hired not because of their qualifications but because of their gender or race.

If these spokespeople are correct, then affirmative action taints its recipients with a stigma of incompetence (Nacoste, 1990). There is some empirical support for this point of view. Garcia, Erskine, Hawn and Casmay (1981) found that when commitment to an affirmative action policy was accentuated, more unfavorable evaluations were made about the qualifications of minority applicants to a graduate school program than when no mention of affirmative action was made. Furthermore, Heilman and Herlihy (1984) reported less occupational interest in a managerial job when the women incumbents projected to populate them were believed to have benefitted from preferential selection policies. Finally, Jacobson and Koch (1977) demonstrated that a woman's leadership performance was devalued when she was appointed leader on the basis of her sex.

Why might a stigma of incompetence derive from affirmative action efforts? . . . [I]f someone is thought to be hired or placed as a result of affirmative action efforts, then that supplies onlookers with a plausible and compelling explanation for the selection decision independent of the job incumbent's qualifications for the position. Consequently, the role of the individual's qualifications for the position—his/her skills and attributes—may well be "discounted," and the individual may be assumed to have been hired only because of his/her sex, with qualifications irrelevant to the selection process. And since it typically is assumed (on the basis of stereotypes) that women are not very well equipped to deal with the rigors of important traditionally male jobs, this assumption inevitably leads to another one—that the job incumbent does not really "have what it takes" to do the job well. After all, the reasoning goes, if this woman really were up to the task, she would not need help from affirmative action. Thus, the perception that ordinary and expected selection criteria were suspended heightens the salience of group membership. The consequence is that association with affirmative action spotlights her sex and therefore accentuates negative stereotypes in the evaluations of that particular woman beneficiary.

It is important to note here that assumptions about how affirmative action is implemented in organizations and the reality of how it actually is implemented may be far apart. It may be, for example, that sex is only taken into account after a consideration of qualifications. But, without information to the contrary, the widely shared view of affirmative action appears to be one involving preferential selection and treatment, often in the form of quotas (Holloway, 1989) based solely on group membership without regard for qualifications (Kravitz and Platania, 1993).

Based on this reasoning, we conducted a series of studies to directly examine the proposition that a stigma of incompetence arises from affirmative action initiatives. We also sought to obtain specific information about the degree to which being associated with affirmative action exacerbated stereotyped conceptions of women. It was our thesis that, under some conditions, affirmative action would create rather than alleviate problems for women by causing people to perceive them as possessing fewer of the characteristics deemed necessary for success in a traditionally male work context.

In the first study (Heilman, Block and Lucas, 1992, Study 1) we sought to determine not only whether those associated with affirmative action are stigmatized, but whether the negativity directed at them was appreciably above and beyond that which typically burdens women when they seek traditionally male jobs. Thus, we expected association with affirmative action not only to prompt an unfavorable evaluation of women generally, but to exacerbate the unfavorable evaluation which would have occurred even without the affirmative action label.

The study designed to test these ideas was quite straightforward. In what was described as research to help understand selection decisions, men and women college students reviewed the application materials of someone said to be recently hired for a job, and then both described what they thought the individual was like and made prognoses about his or her work effectiveness. Research participants received a job description in the form of a recruitment bulletin indicating job requirements and work responsibilities, and employment application materials containing information about educational background, work experience and general demographic information. The job was either highly male sex-typed (7% women) or more mildly male sex-typed (41% women). In all cases the information provided about the hiree was identical except for his/her sex, which was made evident by the name on the application materials and a photograph (which always depicted a white male or white female). Furthermore, when the hiree was female, she either was or was not linked to an affirmative action initiative by virtue of the handwritten commentary written on the application materials. We were interested not only in ratings of competence but in ratings on two central work related attributes considered part of the male stereotype: "potency" (e.g., strong-weak, tough-soft) and "activity" (e.g., persistent-gives up easily; assertive-passive).

Results indicated that, whatever the degree of sex-typing of the job, when there was an association with affirmative action, women not only were rated less favorably on all three evaluative dimensions than were men, but they also were rated less favorably than women hirees not associated with affirmative action. . . . In fact, the affirmative action label created problems for women even when their sex, by itself, did not result in more negative characterizations (mildly male-typed job) and clearly worsened problems for women when simply being a women already was problematic (competence and potency characterizations for the highly male-typed job). . . .

This study supports the idea that affirmative action can give rise to negativity and increased stereotyping. But, given the limited scope of this study, questions remained as to whether these results accurately represent the attitudes and sentiments of those actually in organizational settings. Indeed, the effects of the affirmative action label might be different in settings where individuals have more complete information about one another. They also may be different when the role affirmative action played in the individual's career path is inferred, as it typically is in organizations, rather than explicitly stated. We therefore conducted a second study (Heilman et al., 1992, Study 2) to determine whether the effects we found in the psychology laboratory would also be found in actual work settings when respondents could draw upon their personal experiences in providing research data. Our specific objective was to examine how beliefs about the role affirmative action played in an individual's career progress are related to negativity in perceptions of women (and in this case, other minority group members) employed in nontraditional positions.

Respondents were white males, ranging in age from 25–37 (mean age was 34), all of whom were currently employed in a wide range of industries. They were approached in airports, train stations, and outdoor lunch hour sitting areas near places of employment in Chicago and New York City, and asked to complete a brief questionnaire. The questionnaire's cover page informed them that the purpose of the research was to study working people's impressions of the changing composition of the work force. It instructed them to think of a specific co-worker, one who had joined their unit in recent years and who is a member of a group that in the past did not typically hold this type of position. They then were asked to respond to the questionnaire with this individual in mind. No names of respondents were obtained, and those who could not think of an individual who fit the description were asked to return their questionnaires.

The questionnaire was designed to assess both the perceived role of affirmative action in the decision to hire the co-worker, and the perception of the co-worker's competence, activity and potency. The resulting data demonstrated a strong correlation between the extent to which a nontraditional female co-worker is presumed to be an affirmative action hiree and the degree of negativity evidenced in respondents' descriptions. . . . The greater the role affirmative action was believed to have played, the lower her compe-

tence rating and the less active and potent she was thought to be. These correlations remained strong regardless of the length of time the respondent had worked with the co-worker or the co-worker's organizational level vis a vis the respondents. They also were strong regardless of whether the woman co-worker described was black or white.

The data from these two studies demonstrate not only a stigma of incompetence arising from association with affirmative action efforts, but also a heightening of stereotypic attributions. Whether respondents were students or working people, male or female, or the link with affirmative action was explicitly stated or merely inferred, a woman's association with affirmative action resulted in characterizations of greater passivity and less potency.

These studies make clear that affirmative action can, oddly enough, feed rather than quell the flames of sex bias in organizations. By focusing onlookers almost exclusively on group membership as the reason for selection and placement of women in formerly male dominated organizational positions, it apparently accentuates sex stereotypes. The first part of this paper explored the nature of these stereotypes and the way in which they can have detrimental consequences for women. If affirmative action promotes these conceptions, then there is a distinct possibility that rather than being a remedy for sex discrimination, it can be yet another contributor to the problem.

These ideas suggest that simply ensuring the presence of women in corporations should not be an acceptable societal or organizational objective. If these women are to be tainted by stereotypic attributions because of the process by which people presume them to have gotten access (whether or not the presumptions coincide with truth), there is a good chance that they will be crippled, never able to fully participate in the corporate world as equals with men. Indeed, it is no surprise that such women so often wind up in dead-end jobs or in staff and support positions which do not readily lead to the executive suite.

Concluding Comments

It would be gratifying to complete this paper with a flourish, and have THE ANSWER. I do not. Surely, we cannot dismantle affirmative action and other organizational initiatives aimed at promoting equality in the workplace, and assume that sex discrimination will not occur. Sex discrimination has a long history and has proved highly resistant to efforts to eliminate it. But it is equally clear that affirmative action, as it currently is construed, creates its own set of problems for those it is intended to help. It seems necessary to go back to the drawing boards, attending closely to the role of sex stereotypes in the sex discrimination process in designing further organizational interventions and in implementing ones that already are in place. For, without taking into account the psychological dynamics that allow detrimental inferences about women managers to be perpetuated, the battle against sex discrimination cannot be effectively waged.

References

Arvey, R. D. and J. E. Campion: 1982, "The Employment Interview: A Summary and Review of Recent Research," *Personnel Psychology* 35, 281-322.

Broverman, I. K., S. K. Vogel, D. M. Broverman, F.E. Clarkson and P. S. Rosenkrantz: 1972, "Sex-role Stereotypes: A Current Reappraisal," *Journal of Social Issues* 28, 59-78.

Darley, S.: 1976, "Big-time Careers for the Little Woman: A Dual-role Dilemma," *Journal of Social Issues* 32, 85-98.

Deaux, K.: 1976, "A Perspective on the Attribution Process," in J. Harvey, W. J. Ickes and R. F. Kidd (eds.), *New Directions in Attribution Research* (Vol. 1) (Lawrence Erlbaum Associates, New Jersey).

Deaux, K., W. Winton, H. Crowley and L. L. Lewis: 1985, "Level of Categorization and Content of Gender Stereotypes," *Social Cognition* 3, 145-167.

Deaux, K. and T. Emswiller: 1974, "Explanation of Successful Performance on Sex-linked Tasks: What Is Skill for the Male Is Luck for the Female," *Journal of Personality and Social Psychology* 29, 80-85.

Dipboye, R. L.: 1987, "Problems and Progress of Women in Management," in K. S. Koziara, M. H. Moskow and L. D. Tanner (eds.), *Working Women: Past, Present, Future* (BNA Books, Washington, DC), pp. 118-153.

Dobbins, G. H. and S. J. Platz: 1986, "Sex Differences in Leadership: How Real Are They?", *Academy of Management Review* 11, 118-127.

Donnell, S. M. and J. Hall: 1980, "Men and Woman as Managers: A Significant Case of No Significant Difference," *Organizational Dynamics* 8 (Spring), 60-76.

Eagley, A. H. and B. T. Johnson: 1990, "Gender and Leadership Style: A Meta-analysis," *Psychological Bulletin* 108, 233-256.

Eagley, A. H. and V. J. Steffon: 1984, "Gender Stereotypes Stem from the Distribution of Women and Men into Social Roles," *Journal of Personality and Social Psychology* 46, 735-754.

Feldman-Summers, S. and S. Kiesler: 1974, "Those Who Are Number Two Try Harder: The Effect of Sex on Attributions of Causality," *Journal of Personality and Social Psychology* 30, 846-855.

Feminist Majority Foundation: 1991, *Empowering Women in Business* (Washington, DC).

Feuer, D.: 1988, "How Women Manage," *Training* 25 (August), 23-31.

Fierman, J.: 1990, "Why Women Still Don't Hit the Top," *Fortune*, July 30, 40-62.

Forbes, J. B., J. E. Piercy and T. L. Hayes: 1988, "Women Executives: Breaking Down the Barriers?" *Business Horizons*, November-December, 6-9.

Garcia, L. T., N. Erskine, K. Hawn and S. R. Casmay: 1981, "The Effect of Affirmative Action on Attributions about Minority Group Members" *Journal of Personality* 49, 427-437.

Harlan, A. and C. L. Weiss: 1982, "Sex Differences in Factors Affecting Managerial Career Advancement," in P. A. Wallace (ed.), *Women in the Workplace* (Auburn House, Boston).

Harragan, B. L.: 1977, *Games Mother Never Taught You: Corporate Gamesmanship for Women* (Warner Books, New York).

Heilman, M. E.: 1980, "The Impact of Situational Factors on Personnel Decisions Concerning Women: Varying the Sex Composition of the Applicant Pool," *Organizational Behavior and Human Performance* 26, 386-395.

——. 1983, "Sex Bias in Work Settings: The Lack of Fit Model," in B. M. Staw and L. L. Cummings (eds.), *Research in Organizational Behavior* (Vol. 5) JAI Press, Greenwich, CT).

——. 1984, "Information as a Deterrent against Sex Discrimination: The Effects of Applicant Sex and Information Type on Preliminary Employment Decisions," *Organizational Behavior and Human Performance* 33, 174-186.

Heilman, M. E., C. J. Block and R. E Martell: 1995, "Sex Stereotypes: Do They Influence Perceptions of Managers?", *Journal of Personality and Social Behavior* 10(6), 237-252.

Heilman, M. E., C. J. Block, R. F. Martell and M. C. Simon: 1989, "Has Anything Changed?: Current Characterizations of Males, Females and Managers," *Journal of Applied Psychology* 74, 935-942.

Heilman, M. E. and J. M. Herlihy: 1984, "Affirmative Action, Negative Reaction? Some Moderating Conditions," *Organizational Behavior and Human Performance* 33, 204-213.

Heilman, M. E. and R. A. Guzzo: 1978, "The Perceived Cause of Work Success as a Mediator of Sex Discrimination in Organizations," *Organizational Behavior and Human Performance* 21, 346-357.

Heilman, M. E., R. F. Martell and M. Simon: 1988, "The Vagaries of Bias: Conditions Regulating the Undervaluation, Equivaluation and Overvaluation of Female Job Applicants," *Organizational Behavior and Human Decision Processes* 41, 98-110.

Heilman, M. E., C. J. Block and J. A. Lucas: 1992, "Presumed Incompetent?: Stigmatization and Affirmative Action Efforts," *Journal of Applied Psychology* 77, 536-544.

Himmelfarb, G.: 1988, "Universities Creating Second-class Faculties. Letter to the Editor," *New York Times*, May 15.

Holloway, F.: 1989, "What Is Affirmative Action?", in F. Blanchard and R Crosby (eds.), *Affirmative Action in Perspective* (Springer-Verlag, New York), pp. 9-19.

Holmes, S. A.: 1995, "Programs Based on Sex and Race Are Challenged," *New York Times*, March 16, first section, pp. 1, 22.

Howard, A. and D. W Bray: 1988, *Managerial Lives in Transition* (Guilford, New York).

Hymnowitz, C. and T. D. Schellhardt: 1986, "The Glass Ceiling: Why Women Can't Seem to Break Through the Invisible Barrier That Blocks Them from the Top Jobs," *Wall Street Journal*, March 24, pp. 1D-5D.

Jacobson, M. B. and W. Koch: 1977, "Women as Leaders: Performance Evaluation as a Function of Method of Leader Selection," *Organizational Behavior and Human Performance* 20, 149-157.

Jardim, A. and M. Hennig: 1990, "The Last Barrier: Breaking into the Boys' Club at the Top," *Working Woman*, November, 130-134.

Kanter, R. M.: 1977, *Men and Women of the Corporation* (Basic Books, New York).

Kravitz, D. and J. Platania: 1993, "Attitudes and Beliefs about Affirmative Action: Effects of Target and or Respondent Sex and Ethnicity," *Journal of Applied Psychology*.

London, M. and S. A. Stumpf: 1983, "Effects of Candidate Characteristics on Management Promotion Decisions: An Experimental Study," *Personnel Psychology* 36, 241-259.

Maccoby, E. E. and C. N. Jacklin: 1974, *The Psychology of Sex Differences* (Stanford University Press).

Miner, John: 1977, "Motivational Potential for Upgrading among Minority and Female Managers," *Journal of Applied Psychology* 62, 691-697.

Morrison, A. M., R. P. White and E. Van Velsor: 1987, *Breaking the Glass Ceiling: Can Women Reach the Top of America's Largest Corporations?* (Addison Wesley, Reading).

Nacoste, R. W.: 1990, "Sources of Stigma: Analyzing the Psychology of Affirmative Action," *Law and Policy* 12, 175-195.

Nieva, V. F. and B. A. Gutek: 1980, "Sex Effects on Evaluation," *Academy of Management Review* 5, 267-276.

Noseworthy, C. M. and A. J. Lott: 1984, "The Cognitive Organization of Gender-Stereotypic Categories," *Personality and Social Psychology Bulletin* 10, 474-481.

Powell, G. N. and D. A. Butterfield: 1989, "The 'Good Manager': Masculine or Androgynous?" *Academy of Management Journal* 22, 395-403.

Powell, G. N.: 1988, *Women and Men (Sage Publications, Newbury Park, CA).*

Salmons, S.: 1987, "Top Tiers Still Elude Women" *New York Times*, August 17, B4.

Schein, V. E.: 1975, "Relations between Sex-role Stereotypes and Requisite Management Characteristics among Female Managers," *Journal of Applied Psychology* 60, 340-344.

——. 1973. "The Relationship between Sex-role Stereotypes and Requisite Management Characteristics," *Journal of Applied Psychology* 57, 1)5-100.

Steele, S.: 1990, "A Negative Vote on Affirmative Action," *New York Times Magazine*, May 13, P. 46.

Stumpf, S. A. and M. London: 1981, "Management Promotions: Individual and Organizational Factors Influencing the Decision Process," *Academy of Management Review* 6, 539-549.

Taylor, S. E.: 1981, "A Categorization Approach to Stereotyping," in D. Hamilton (ed.), *Cognitive Processes in Stereotyping and Intergroup Behavior* (Erlbaum, Hillsdale, NJ), pp.83-114.

Taylor, S. E., S. T. Fiske, N. L. Etcoff and A. J.Ruderman: 1978, "Categorial and Contextual Bases of Person Memory and Stereotyping,"

Journal of Personality and Social Psychology 36, 778-793.

Tosi, H. L. and S. W. Einbinder: 1985, "The Effects of the Type and Amount of Information in Sex Discrimination Research: A Meta-analysis," *Academy of Management Journal* 28, 712-723.

Wilkerson, I.: 1991, "A Remedy for Old Racism Has a New Kind of Shackles," *The New York Times*, September 15, First Section, p. 1.

Wycliff, D.: 1990, "Blacks Debate the Costs of Affirmative Action," *The New York Times*, June 10, News of the Week Section, p. 3.

Zellman, G.: 1976, "The Role of Structural Factors in Limiting Women's Institutional Participation," *Journal of Social Issues* 32, 33-46.

Critical Evaluation

1. Do sex stereotypes reflect cultural beliefs or inherent differences between males and females?

2. Given that stereotypes can adversely affect female advancement, are stereotypes as important as other factors? Could the effects of stereotypes be neutralized by attending to those other factors?

3. The author notes the mixed results of affirmative action programs. How could the programs be retained without having the adverse consequences she notes?

Madeline E. Heilman, "Sex Discrimination and the Affirmative Action Remedy." In *Journal of Business Ethics* 16, pp. 877–889. Copyright © 1997 by Kluwer Academic Publishers. Reprinted by permission. ✦

21

How Beauty Myths Damage Women's Health

Jane Sprague Zones

Women face severe cultural pressures to measure up to current standards of beauty. Although, as Jane Sprague Zones notes, men also face norms about appearance, the pressures and influences on them are minuscule compared to those faced by women. At the macrolevel, economic factors (in the form of profits in varied beauty-care industries), a cultural value on beauty, and the traditional role of women as "ornaments" all contribute to the continuing pressures to achieve a look that few women possess naturally. The preferred look changes over time—from the wasplike waist and full breasts and hips of the 19th century to the slender, young, flawless ideal of the present. But whatever the ideal, it can be achieved chiefly by such measures as the liberal use of cosmetics, unhealthy clothing and eating habits, and surgery.

At the microlevel, the consequences of pressures to measure up to current standards of beauty include career impediments and dilemmas as well as adverse effects on both emotional and physical health. What can women do to avoid such consequences in the light of the powerful structural factors that pressure them to conform? Zones's suggestion may work for some women, but most will probably continue to be victimized. Structural changes as well as individual resistance are needed.

Focus Questions

1. What is the social significance of beauty?

2. What are the commercial aspects of the quest for beauty?

3. What are the health risks in the quest for beauty?

Of all the characteristics that distinguish one human being from the next, physical appearance has the most immediate impact. How a person looks shapes the kinds of responses she or he evokes in others. Physical appearance has similar effects on other social statuses. Those considered beautiful or handsome are more likely to accrue benefits such as attributions of goodness and better character, more desirability as friends and partners, and upward social mobility. Those considered unattractive receive less attention as infants, are evaluated more harshly in school, and earn less money as employees. The significance of physical appearance shifts in intensity as it interacts with other statuses, such as gender, race/ethnicity, age, class, and disability. For groups targeted for social mistreatment, such as women and racial or ethnic minorities, physical appearance has profound implications not only for the creation of first impressions but also for enduring influence on social effectiveness. The power of appearance pushes people to assimilate in order to avoid unwanted attention or to attract desired attention. The pushes and pulls to look "conventionally attractive" constitute assaults on diversity. . . .

Commonalities in Perception of Beauty

Many women concur that personal beauty, or "looking good," is fostered from a very early age. It is probably true that the ways in which people assess physical beauty are not naturally determined but socially and culturally learned and therefore "in the eye of the beholder." However, we tend to discount the depth of our common perception of beauty, mistakenly assuming that individuals largely set their own standards. At any period in history, within a given geographic and cultural territory, there are relatively uniform and widely understood models of how women "should" look. Numerous studies over time reinforce this notion (Iliffe 1960; Patzer 1985; Perrett, May, and Yoshikawa 1994).

Although there have always been beauty ideals for women (Banner 1983), in modern times the proliferation of media portrayals of feminine beauty in magazines, billboards, movies, and television has both hastened and more broadly disseminated the communication of detailed expectations. There are increasingly demanding criteria for female beauty in western culture, and women are strongly pressured to alter their appearance to conform with these standards.

Naomi Wolf, in her book *The Beauty Myth* (1991), contends that the effect of widespread promulgation of womanly ideals of appearance perpetuates the myth that the "quality called 'beauty' objectively and universally exists. Women must want to embody it and men must want to possess women who embody it. This embodiment is an imperative for women and not for men, which situation is necessary and natural because it is biological, sexual, and evolutionary" (12). Wolf declares that this is all falsehood. Instead, beauty is politically and economically determined, and the myth is the "last, best belief system that keeps male dominance intact" (12). She argues that as women have emerged successfully in many new arenas, the focus on and demand for beauty has become more intense, attacking the private sense of self and creating new barriers to accomplishment. In Wolf's view, the increasing obsession with beauty is a backlash to women's liberation.

Beauty's Social Significance for Individuals

Much of the evidence from studies done by experimental social psychologists shows why people assign such importance to their appearance. They have found that people judged to be physically attractive, both male and female, are assumed to possess more socially desirable personality traits and expected to lead happier lives (Dion, Berscheid, and Walster 1972). Social science research shows that "cute babies are cuddled more than homely ones; attractive toddlers are punished less often. Teachers give special attention to better-looking pupils, strangers offer help more readily to attractive people, and

jurors show more sympathy to good-looking victims" (Freedman 1986:7-8). This principle holds in virtually every aspect of our lives from birth to death and across racial and ethnic groups (Patzer 1985:232-33). The effects of these myriad positive responses to and assumptions about people who are considered attractive have self-fulfilling aspects as well. The expectations of others strongly shape development, learning, and achievement: people thought to be attractive become more socially competent and accomplished (Goldman and Lewis 1977). Appearance-based discrimination targets women more than men. Women's self-esteem and happiness are significantly associated with their physical appearance; no such relationship exists for men as a group (Allgood-Merten, Lewinsohn, and Hops 1990; Mathes and Kahn 1975). Women's access to upward mobility is also greatly affected by physical appearance, which is a major determinant of marriage to a higher status man. By contrast, potential partners evaluate men more for intelligence or accomplishment. The significance of beauty in negotiating beneficial marriages is particularly true for white working-class women (Elder 1969; Taylor and Glenn 1976; Udry 1977; Udry and Eckland 1984). Banner (1983), who has traced the shifting models of beauty and fashion over two hundred years of American history, concludes that although standards of beauty may have changed, and women have greatly improved their access to social institutions, many females continue to define themselves by physical appearance and their ability to attract a partner.

The preoccupation with appearance serves to control and contain women's ambitions and motivations to gain power in larger political contexts. To the degree that many females feel they must dedicate time, attention, and resources to maintaining and improving their looks, they neglect activities to improve social conditions for themselves or others. Conversely, as women become increasingly visible as powerful individuals in shaping events, their looks become targeted for irrelevant scrutiny and criticism in ways with which men in similar positions are not forced to contend (Freedman 1986; Wolf 1991). For example, Marcia Clark, the lead prosecutor in the O.J. Simpson trial, was the focus of unremitting media attention for her dress, hairstyle, demeanor, and private life.

The major difference between discrimination based on appearance and mistreatment based on gender, race, or other social attributes is that individuals are legally protected against the latter (Patzer 1985:11). In an eye-opening review of legal cases related to appearance and employment, Wolf documents the inconsistencies that characterize decisions to dismiss women on the basis of their looks. "Legally, women don't have a thing to wear" (1991:42). Requirements of looking both businesslike and feminine represent a moving target that invites failure. In *Hopkins v. Price-Waterhouse*, a woman who brought in more clients than any other employee was denied a partnership because, her employers claimed, she did not walk, talk, or dress in an adequately feminine manner nor did she wear makeup. In another court case, it was ruled "inappropriate for a supervisor" of women to dress "like a woman" (Wolf 1991:39). If one appears businesslike, one cannot be adequately feminine; if one appears feminine, one cannot adequately conduct business.

Beauty Myths and the Erosion of Self-Worth

Perhaps the biggest toll the "beauty myth" takes is in terms of women's identity and self-esteem. Like members of other oppressed groups of which we may also be part, women internalize cultural stereotypes and expectations, perpetuating them by enforced acceptance and agreement. For women, this is intensified by the interaction of irrational social responses to physical appearance not only with gender but with other statuses as well—race, class, age, disability, and the like. Continuous questioning of the adequacy of one's looks drains attention from more worthwhile and confidence-building pursuits . . .

Glassner argues that the dramatically increased attention to fitness, diet, and physical well-being in recent years has been accompanied by a plummeting of satisfaction with our bodies (1988:246). There seems to

be little relationship between actual physical attractiveness (conformance to culturally valued standards determined by judges) and individual women's satisfaction with their own appearance (Murstein 1972). Both men and women are unrealistic about how others perceive their bodies, but men tend to assume that people think they look better and women tend to assume that they look worse than they actually are perceived (Fallon and Rozin 1985). A recent poll of United States residents (Cimons 1990) found that fewer than a third of adults were happy with their appearance. Women were twice as likely as men to consider themselves to be fat.

Nagging self-doubts about weight emanate from the difference between projected images of women, many of which depict severely undernourished bodies, and our everyday reality. Half of the readers of *Vogue* magazine wear size 14 or larger (Glassner 1988:12), tormenting themselves with images of models with size 6 or smaller figures in every issue. Female models are 9 percent taller and 16 percent thinner than average women. Even the majority of women runners who are in good physical condition and fall within the ranges of weight and body fat considered desirable describe themselves as overweight (Robinson 1983). Research consistently shows that women not only overestimate their own size (Penner, Thompson, and Coovert 1991; Thompson and Dolce 1989) but they expect men to prefer thinner women than is the actual case (Rozin and Fallon 1988). . . .

The Commercial Imperative in the Quest for Beauty

Standards of beauty are continually evolving and proliferating, and as new standards develop, "bodies are expected to change as well" (Freedman 1986:6). Unlike race, gender, or age, attractiveness may be considered to some extent an "achieved" characteristic subject to change through individual intervention (Webster and Driskell 1983). As Wolf puts it, "The beauty myth is always actually prescribing *behavior* and not appearance" (1991:14; emphasis added). In her study of black and white Baltimore women of various ages, both working class and middle class, Emily Martin found a common theme in ways that women discussed their health, which she summarized as "your self is separate from your body" (1989:77). Participants in Martin's study saw the body as something that must be coped with or adjusted to.

To accommodate expectations for physical appearance, women are exhorted to invest large amounts of time, money, and physical and emotional energy into their physical being. "The closer women come to power, the more physical self-consciousness and sacrifice are asked of them. 'Beauty' becomes the condition for a woman to take the next step" (Wolf 1991:28). Geraldine Ferraro, who was the first female candidate for vice president of the United States nominated by a major political party, noted in her autobiography that there were more reports on what she wore than on what she said.

Although there are many compelling theories about how the cultural preoccupation with feminine appearance evolved, it is clear that at present it is held in place by a number of very profitable industries. The average person is exposed to several hundred to several thousand advertisements per day (Moog 1990). To pitch their products, advertisers create messages that cannot immediately be recognized as advertising, selling images in the course of selling products. Two-thirds of the models who appear in magazine ads are teenagers or young adults. Although we are now seeing greater diversity in models, older people, low-income people, and people with disabilities rarely show up in advertisements because they do not project the image that the product is meant to symbolize (Glassner 1988:37). In numerous ways, advertising attacks women's self-esteem so they will purchase products and services in order to hold off bad feelings (Barthel 1988).

Most women's magazines generate much of their revenue from advertisers, who openly manipulate the content of stories. Wolf (1991:81-85) documents incidents in which advertisers canceled accounts because of editorial decisions to print stories unsupportive of their products. *Ms.* magazine, for example, reportedly lost a major cosmetics account after it featured Soviet women on the cover who were not wearing makeup.

Americans spend an estimated $50 billion a year on diets, cosmetics, plastic surgery, health clubs, and related gadgets (Glassner 1988:13). A review of costs of common beauty treatments itemized in a 1982 newspaper story found that a woman of means could easily rack up the bulk of an annual salary to care for her physical appearance. This entailed frequent visits to the hair salon, exercise classes, regular manicures, a home skincare program with occasional professional facials, a monthly pedicure, professional makeup session and supplies, a trip to a spa, hair removal from various parts of the body, and visits to a psychiatrist to maintain essential self-esteem (Steger 1982). The list did not include the expense of special dietary programs, cosmetic surgery or dentistry, home exercise equipment, or clothing.

As new standards of beauty expectations are created, physical appearance becomes increasingly significant, and as the expression of alternative looks are legitimized, new products are developed and existing enterprises capitalize on the trends. Liposuction, developed relatively recently, has become the most popular of the cosmetic surgery techniques. Synthetic fats have been developed, and there is now a cream claimed to reduce thigh measurements.

Weight Loss

Regardless of the actual size of their bodies, more than half of American females between ages ten and thirty are dieting, and one out of every six college women is struggling with anorexia and bulimia (Iazzetto 1992). The quest to lose weight is not limited to white, middleclass women. Iazzetto cites studies that find this pervasive concern in black women, Native American girls (75 percent trying to lose weight), and high school students (63 percent dieting). However, there may be differences among adolescent women in different groups as to how rigid their concepts of beauty are and how flexible they are regarding body image and dieting (Parker et al. 1995). Studies of primary school girls show more than half of all young girls and close to 80 percent of ten- and eleven-year-olds on diets because they consider themselves "too fat" (Greenwood 1990; Seid 1989). . . .

Concern about weight and routine dieting are so pervasive in the United States that the weight-loss industry grosses more than $33 billion each year. Over 80 percent of those in diet programs are women. These programs keep growing even in the face of 90 to 95 percent failure rates in providing and maintaining significant weight loss. Congressional hearings in the early 1990s presented evidence of fraud and high failure rates in the weight-loss industry, as well as indications of severe health consequences for rapid weight loss (Iazzetto 1992). The Food and Drug Administration (FDA) has reviewed documents submitted by major weight-loss programs and found evidence of safety and efficacy to be insufficient and unscientific. An expert panel urged consumers to consider program effectiveness in choosing a weight-loss method but acknowledged lack of scientific data for making informed decisions (Brody 1992).

Fitness

Whereas in the nineteenth century some physicians recommended a sedentary lifestyle to preserve feminine beauty, in the past two decades of the twentieth century, interest in physical fitness has grown enormously. Nowhere is this change more apparent than in the gross receipts of some of the major fitness industries. In 1987, health clubs grossed $5 billion, exercise equipment $738 million (up from $5 million ten years earlier), diet foods $74 billion, and vitamin products $2.7 billion (Brand 1988). Glassner (1989) identifies several reasons for this surge of interest in fitness, including the aging of the "baby boom" cohort with its attendant desire to allay the effects of aging through exercise and diet, and the institution of "wellness" programs by corporations to reduce insurance, absentee, and inefficiency costs. A patina of health, well-toned but skinny robustness, has been folded into the dominant beauty ideal. . . .

Cosmetics

The average person in North America uses more than twenty-five pounds of cosmetics, soaps, and toiletries each year (Decker 1983). The cosmetics industry produces over twenty thousand products containing thousands of chemicals, and it grosses over $20 billion annually (Becker 1991; Wolf 1991). Stock in cosmetics manufacturers has been rising 15 percent a year, in large part because of depressed petroleum prices. The oil derivative ethanol is the base for most products (Wolf 1991:82, 307). Profit margins for products are over 50 percent (McKnight 1989). Widespread false claims for cosmetics were virtually unchallenged for fifty years after the FDA became responsible for cosmetic industry oversight in 1938, and even now, the industry remains largely unregulated (Kaplan 1994). Various manufacturers assert that their goods can "retard aging," "repair the skin," or "restructure the cell." "Graphic evidence" of "visible improvement" when applying a "barrier" against "eroding effects" provides a pastiche of some familiar advertising catchphrases (Wolf 1991:109-10).

The FDA has no authority to require cosmetics firms to register their existence, to release their formulas, to report adverse reactions, or to show evidence of safety and effectiveness before marketing their products (Gilhooley 1978; Kaplan 1994). Authorizing and funding the FDA to regulate the cosmetics industry would allow some means of protecting consumers from the use of dangerous products.

Cosmetic Surgery

In interviews with cosmetic surgeons and users of their services, Dull and West (1991) found that the line between reconstructive plastic surgery (repair of deformities caused congenitally or by injury or disease) and aesthetic surgery has begun to blur. Doctors and their patients are viewing unimpaired features as defective and the desire to "correct" them as intrinsic to women's nature, rather than as a cultural imperative.

Because of an oversupply of plastic surgeons, the profession has made efforts to expand existing markets through advertising and by appeals to women of color. Articles encouraging "enhancement of ethnic beauty" have begun to appear, but they focus on westernizing Asian eyelids and chiseling African American noses. As Bordo (1993:25) points out, this technology serves to promote commonality rather than diversity.

Plastic surgery has been moving strongly in the direction of making appearance a bona fide medical problem. This has been played out dramatically in recent times in the controversy regarding silicone breast implants, which provides plastic surgeons with a substantial amount of income. Used for thirty years in hundreds of thousands of women (80 percent for cosmetic augmentation), the effects of breast implants have only recently begun to be studied to determine their health consequences over long periods (Zones 1992). In a petition to the FDA in 1982 to circumvent regulation requiring proof of safety and effectiveness of the implants, the American Society of Plastic and Reconstructive Surgeons stated, "There is a common misconception that the enlargement of the female breast is not necessary for maintenance of health or treatment of disease. There is a substantial and enlarging body of medical information and opinion, however, to the effect that these *deformities* [small breasts] are really a disease which in most patients result in feelings of inadequacy . . . due to a lack of self-perceived femininity. The enlargement of the underdeveloped female breast is, therefore, often very necessary to insure an improved quality of life for the patient" (Porterfield 1982:4-5; emphasis added).

Cosmetic surgeon James Billie of Arkansas, who claims to have operated on over fifteen thousand beauty contestants in the past ten years, maintains that three-quarters of Miss USA pageant contestants have undergone plastic surgery (Garchik 1992). Cosmetic surgery generates over a third of a billion dollars per year for practitioners, some of whom offer overnight household financing for patients. The hefty interest rates are returned in part to the surgeons by the finance corporation (Krieger 1989). Although cosmetic surgery is the biggest commercial contender in the medical realm, prescription drugs are increasingly lucrative ventures

(such as Retin-A to reduce wrinkling skin, and hormones to promote growth in short boys and retard it in tall girls).

Health Risks in Quest of Beauty

Physicians and medical institutions have been quoted as associating beauty with health and ugliness with disease. Dr. Daniel Tostesen of Harvard Medical School, whose research is supported by Shiseido, an expensive cosmetics line, claims that there is a " 'subtle and continuous gradation' between health and medical interests on the one hand, and 'beauty and well-being on the other' " (Wolf 1991:227). The imperative to look attractive, while promising benefits in self-esteem, often entails both serious mental and physical health risks.

Mental Health

For most women, not adhering to narrow, standardized appearance expectations causes insecurity and distraction, but for many, concerns about appearance can have serious emotional impact. Up until adolescence, boys and girls experience about the same rates of depression, but at around age twelve, girls' rates of depression begin to increase more rapidly. A study of over eight hundred high school students found that a prime factor in this disparity is girls' preoccupation with appearance. In discussing the study, the authors concluded that "if adolescent girls felt as physically attractive, effective, and generally good about themselves as their male peers did, they would not experience so much depression" (Allgood-Merten, Lewinsohn, and Hops 1990:61). Another study of the impact of body image on onset and persistence of depression in adolescent girls found that whereas a relatively positive body image does not seem to offer substantial protection against the occurrence of depression, it does seem to decrease the likelihood that depression will be persistent (Rierdan and Koff 1991; Rierdan, Koff, and Stubbs 1989).

Physical Health

Perceived or actual variation from society's ideal takes a physical toll, too. High school and college-age females who were judged to be in the bottom half of their group in terms of attractiveness had significantly higher blood pressure than the young women in the top half. The relationship between appearance and blood pressure was not found for males in the same age group (Hansell, Sparacino, and Ronchi 1982).

Low bodyweight has been heavily promoted as a life-prolonging characteristic. There is evidence to support this contention, but the effect of advocating low weight in collusion with the heavy cultural prescription for a very slender look has led people into cycles of weight loss and regained weight that may act as an independent risk factor for cardiovascular disease (Bouchard 1991). A recent review of the medical literature on weight fluctuation concludes that the potential health benefits of moderate weight loss in obese people, however, is greater than the known risks of "yo-yo dieting" (National Task Force 1994). Women constitute 90 percent of people with anorexia, an eating disorder that can cause serious injury or death. The incidence of anorexia has grown dramatically since the mid-1970s, paralleling the social imperative of thinness (Bordo 1986).

There are direct risks related to using commodities to alter appearance. According to the Consumer Products Safety Commission, more than 200,000 people visit emergency rooms each year as a result of cosmetics-related health problems (Becker 1991). Clothing has its perils as well. In recent years, meralgia paresthetica, marked by sciatica, pain in the hip and thigh region, with tingling and itchy skin, has made an appearance among young women in the form of "skin-tight jean syndrome" (Gateless and Gilroy 1984). In earlier times, the same problems have arisen with the use of girdles, belts, and shoulder bags. The National Safety Council revealed that in 1989 over 100,000 people were injured by their clothing and another 44,000 by their jewelry (Seligson 1992,). These figures greatly underestimate actual medical problems.

Approximately 33 to 50 percent of all adult women have used hair coloring agents. Evidence over the past twenty-five years has shown that chemicals used in manufacturing hair dyes cause cancers in animals (Center 1979). Scientists at the National Cancer Institute (NCI) recently reported a significantly greater risk of cancers of the lymph system and of a form of cancer affecting bone marrow, multiple myeloma, in women who use hair coloring (Zahm et al. 1992). In the last twenty years, the incidence of non-Hodgkin's lymphoma in the United States increased by more than 50 percent largely as a result of immune deficiency caused by HIV. However, the NCI researchers conclude that, assuming a causal relationship, hair coloring product use accounts for a larger percentage of non-Hodgkin's lymphoma among women than any other risk factor. These conclusions have been challenged, however, by more recent research (Fackelmann 1994).

Because no cosmetic products require follow-up research for safety and effectiveness, virtually anything can be placed on the market without regard to potential health effects. Even devices implanted in the body, which were not regulated before 1978, can remain on the market for years without appropriate testing. During the decade of controversy over regulating silicone breast implants, the American Society of Plastic and Reconstructive Surgeons vehemently denied any need for controlled studies of the implant in terms of long-term safety. The society spent hundreds of thousands of dollars of its members' money in a public relations effort to avoid the imposition of requirements for such research to the detriment of investing in the expensive scientific follow-up needed (Zones 1992). Although case reports indicate a potential relationship between the implants and connective tissue diseases, recent medical reports discount the association. Definitive research will take more time to assuage women's fears.

Health consequences of beauty products extend beyond their impact on individuals. According to the San Francisco Bay Area Air Quality Management District, aerosols release 25 tons of pollution every day. Almost half of that is from hairsprays. Although aerosols no longer use chlorofluorocarbons (CFCs), which are the greatest cause of depletion of the upper atmosphere ozone layer, aerosol hydrocarbons in hairsprays are a primary contributor to smog and ground pollution.

The Beauty of Diversity

Both personal transformation and policy intervention will be necessary to allow women to present themselves freely. Governmental institutions, including courts and regulatory agencies, need to accord personal and product liability related to appearance products and services the attention they require to ensure public health and safety. The legal system must develop well-defined case law to assist the court in determining inequitable treatment based on appearance discrimination.

Short of complete liberation from limitations imposed by appearance expectations, women will continue to attempt to "improve" appearance to better social relations. Ultimately, however, this is a futile struggle because of the depth and intensity of feelings and assumptions that have become attached to physical appearance. The predominant advice given to women in the body-image literature is to seek therapeutic assistance to transform damaged self-image into a more positive perspective on oneself. Brown (1985) recommends a social context in which such transformation can take place, as does Schwichtenberg (1989), who suggests that, failing women's unified rejection of costly and potentially dangerous beauty products and processes, women should band together into support networks. Lesbian communities have led the way, showing how mutual support can diminish the effects of the dominant society on women. By using supportive relationships as an arena to experiment with physical presence, women create a manageable and enjoyable social situation. The Black Women's Health Project has successfully modeled the formation of local support groups to encourage members to lead healthier lives. Having a small group as referents reduces the power of commercial interests to define beauty standards. Overweight women have created such resources in the form of national alliances (such as the National Association to Advance Fat Acceptance), magazines (such as *Radiance*), and regional support systems (Iazzetto 1992).

The personal solution to individual self-doubt or even self-loathing of our physical being is to continuously make the decision to contradict the innumerable messages we are given that we are anything less than lovely as human beings. Pinkney (1994) suggests several ways to reshape "a raggedy body image" by improving self-perception: respect yourself, search for the source of the distress, strut your strengths, and embrace the aging process. In a passage from *Beloved*, Toni Morrison demonstrates the way: "Love your hands! Love them. Raise them up and kiss them. Touch others with them, pat them together, stroke them on your face 'cause they don't love that either. *You* got to love it, *you!*" (1994:362).

References

Allgood-Merten, Betty, Peter M. Lewinsohn, and Hyman Hops 1990. "Sex Differences and Adolescent Depression." *Journal of Abnormal Psychology* 99:55-63.

Banner, Lois W. 1983. *American Beauty*. Chicago: University of Chicago Press.

Barthel, Diane. 1988. *Putting on Appearances: Gender and Advertising*. Philadelphia: Temple University Press.

Becker, Hilton. 1991 "Cosmetics: Saving Face at What Price?" *Annals of Plastic Surgery* 26:171-73.

Bordo, Susan. 1986. "Anorexia Nervosa: Psychopathology as the Crystallization of Culture." *Philosophical Forum* 17:73-104.

———. 1993. *Unbearable Weight: Feminism, Western Culture and the Body*. Berkeley: University of California Press.

Bouchard, Claude. 1991. "Is Weight Fluctuation a Risk Factor?" *New England Journal of Medicine* 324:1887-89.

Brand, David. 1988. "A Nation of Health Worrywarts?" *Time*, 25 July, 66.

Brody, Jane E. 1992. "Panel Criticizes Weight-Loss Programs." *New York Times*, 2 April, A10.

Brown, Laura S. 1985. "Women, Weight, and Power: Feminist Theoretical and Therapeutic Issues." *Women and Therapy* 4:61-71.

Cimons, Marlene. 1990. "Most Americans Dislike Their Looks, Poll Finds." Los Angeles Times, 19 August, A4.

Decker, Ruth. 1983. "The Not-So-Pretty Risks of Cosmetics." *Medical Self-Care* (Summer):25-31.

Dion, Karen, Ellen Berscheid, and Elaine Walster. 1972. "What Is Beautiful Is Good." *Journal of Personality and Social Psychology* 24:285-90.

Dull, Diana, and Candace West. 1991. "Accounting for Cosmetic Surgery: The Accomplishment of Gender." *Social Problems* 38:54-70.

Elder, Glen H., Jr. 1969. "Appearance and Education in Marriage Mobility." *American Sociological Review* 34:519-33.

Fackelmann, K. A. 1994. "Mixed News on Hair Dyes and Cancer Risk." *Science News* 145 (5 Feb.):86.

Fallon, April E., and Paul Rozin. 1985. "Sex Differences in Perceptions of Desirable Body Shape." *Journal of Abnormal Psychology* 94:102-5.

Freedman, Rita. 1986. *Beauty Bound*. Lexington, MA: Lexington Books.

Garchik, Leah. 1992. "Knife Tricks Come to the Rescue." *San Francisco Chronicle*, 1 September, C5.

Gateless, Doreen, and John Gilroy. 1984. "Tight-Jeans Meralgia: Hot or Cold?" *Journal of the American Medical Association* 252:42-43.

Gilhooley, Margaret. 1978. "Federal Regulation of Cosmetics: An Overview." *Food Drug Cosmetic Law Journal* 33:231-38.

Glassner, Barry. 1988. *Bodies: Why We Look the Way We Do (And How We Feel about It)*. New York: Putnam.

——. 1989 "Fitness and the Postmodern Self" *Journal of Health and Social Behavior* 30:180-91.

Goldman, William, and Philip Lewis. 1977. "Beautiful Is Good: Evidence that the Physically Attractive Are More Socially Skillful." *Journal of Experimental and Social Psychology* 13:125-30.

Greenwood, M. R. C. 1990 "The Feminine Ideal: A New Perspective." *UC Davis Magazine* (July):8-11.

Hansell, Stephen, J. Sparacino, and D. Ronchi. 1982. "Physical Attractiveness and Blood Pressure: Sex and Age Differences." *Personality and Social Psychology Bulletin* 8:113-21.

Iazzetto, Demetria. 1988. "Women and Body Image: Reflections in the Fun House Mirror." Pp. 34-53 in Carol J. Leppa and Connie Miller (Eds.), *Women's Health Perspectives: An Annual Review*. Volcano, CA: Volcano Press.

——. 1990 "What's Happening with Women and Body Image?" *National Women's Health Network News*: 1, 6, 7.

Iliffe, A. H. 1960. "A Study of Preferences in Feminine Beauty." *British Journal of Psychology* 51:267-73.

Kaplan, Sheila. 1994. "The Ugly Face of the Cosmetics Lobby." *Ms.* (Jan.-Feb.):88-89.

Krieger, Lisa M. 1989. "Fix Your Nose Now, Pay Later." *San Francisco Examiner*, 30 October, 1.

Martin, Emily. 1989. *The Woman in the Body: A Cultural Analysis of Reproduction*. Boston: Beacon Press.

Mathes, Eugene W, and Arnold Kahn. 1975. "Physical Attractiveness, Happiness, Neuroticism, and Self-Esteem." *Journal of Psychology* 90:27-30.

Mathes, Eugene W, Susan M. Brennan, Patricia M. Haugen, and Holly B. Rice. 1985. "Ratings of Physical Attractiveness as a Function of Age." *Journal of Social Psychology* 125:157-68.

Mcknight, Gerald. 1989. *The Skin Game: The International Beauty Business Brutally Exposed*. London: Sidgwick and Jackson.

Moog, Carol. 1990. *Are They Selling Her Lips? Advertising and Identity*. New York: William Morrow.

Morrison, Toni. 1994. "We Flesh." P. 362 in Evelyn C. White (Ed.), *The Black Women's Health Book*, Rev. Ed. Seattle: Seal Press.

Murstein, Bernard 1. 1972. "Physical Attractiveness and Marital Choice." *Journal of Personality and Social Psychology* 22:8-12.

National Task Force on the Prevention and Treatment of Obesity. 1994. "Weight Cycling." *Journal of the American Medical Association* 272(15):1196-1202.

Parker, Sheila, Mimi Nichter, Mark Nichter, Nancy Vuckovic, Colette Sims, and Cheryl Ritenbaugh. 1995 "Body Image and Weight Concerns Among African American and White Adolescent Females: Differences that Make a Difference." *Human Organization* 54(2):103-13.

Patzer, Gordon L. 1985. *The Physical Attractiveness Phenomena*. New York: Plenum Press.

Penner, Louis A., J. Kevin Thompson, and Dale L. Coovert. 1991. "Size Overestimation Among Anorexics: Much Ado About Very Little?" *Journal of Abnormal Psychology* 100:90-93.

Perrett, D. I., K. A. May, and S. Yoshikawa. 1994. "Facial Shape and Judgments of Female Attractiveness." *Nature* 368:239-42.

Pinkney, Deborah Shelton. 1994. "Body Check." *Heart and Soul* (Summer):50-55.

Porterfield, H. William. 1982. Comments of the American Society of Plastic and Reconstructive Surgeons on the Proposed Classification of Inflatable Breast Prosthesis and Silicone Gel-Filled Breast Prosthesis, Submitted to the Food and Drug Administration. Washington, 1 July.

Rierdan, Jill, and Elissa Koff. 1991. "Depressive Symptomatology Among Very Early Maturing Girls." *Journal of Youth and Adolescence* 20:415-515.

Rierdan, Jill, Elissa Koff, and Margaret L. Stubbs. 1989. "Timing of Menarche, Preparation, and Initial Menstrual Experience: Replication and Further Analyses in a Prospective Study." Journal of Youth and Adolescence 18:413-26.

Robinson, Jennifer. 1983. "Body Image in Women over Forty." *Melpomene Institute Bulletin* 2:12-14.

Rozin, Paul, and April E. Fallon. 1988. "Body Image, Attitudes to Weight, and Misperceptions of Figure Preferences of the Opposite Sex: A Comparison of Men and Women in Two Generations." *Journal of Abnormal Psychology* 97:342-45.

Schwichtenberg, Cathy. 1989. "The 'Mother Lode' of Feminist Research: Congruent Paradigms in the Analysis of Beauty Culture." Pp. 291-306 in Brenda Dervin, Lawrence Grossberg, Barbara J. O'Keefe, and Ellen Wartella (Eds.), *Rethinking Communication*. Newbury Park, CA: Sage.

Seid, Roberta Pollack. 1989. *Never Too Thin: Why Women Are at War with Their Bodies*. New York: Prentice Hall.

Seligson, Susan. 1992. "The Attack Bra and Other Vicious Clothes." *San Francisco Chronicle*, 13 January, D3-D4.

Steger, Pat. 1982. "The Making Of A BP: How To Diet, Polish and Pay Your Way To Well-Groomed Perfection." *San Francisco Chronicle*, 3 August, 15.

Taylor, Patricia Ann, and Norval D. Glenn. 1976. "The Utility of Education and Attractiveness for Females' Status Attainment through Marriage." *American Sociological Review* 41:484-98.

Thompson, J. Kevin, and Jefferey J. Dolce. 1989. "The Discrepancy between Emotional vs. Rational Estimates of Body Size, Actual Size, and Ideal Body Ratings: Theoretical and Clinical Implications." *Journal of Clinical Psychology* 45:473-78.

Udry, J. Richard. 1977. "The Importance of Being Beautiful: A Reexamination and Racial Comparison." *American Journal of Sociology* 83:154-60.

Udry, J. Richard, and Bruce K. Eckland. 1984. "Benefits of Being Attractive: Differential Payoffs for Men and Women." *Psychological Reports* 54:47-56.

Webster, Murray, Jr., and James E. Driskell Jr. 1983. "Beauty as Status." *American Journal of Sociology* 89:1404-65.

Wolf, Naomi. 1991. *The Beauty Myth: How Images of Beauty Are Used Against Women*. New York: William Morrow.

Zahm, Sheila Hoar, Dennis D. Weisenburger, Paula A. Babbitt, Et Al. 1992. "Use of Hair Coloring Products and the Risk of Lymphoma, Multiple Myeloma, and Chronic Lymphocytic Leukemia." *American Journal of Public Health* 82:990-97.

Zones, Jane Sprague. 1992. "The Political and Social Context of Silicone Breast Implant Use in the United States." *Journal of Long-Term Effects of Medical Implants* 1:225-41.

Critical Evaluation

1. The author asserts that "appearance-based discrimination targets women more than men." Do you agree? Why or why not?

2. The author suggests that high profits drive advertisers to influence women to invest heavily in their beauty. Do the advertisers create a need or respond to a demand?

3. There are health risks, as the author notes, in the quest for beauty. What are the health risks (including emotional and social) of rejecting the quest for beauty?

Jane Sprague Zones, "Beauty Myths and Realities and Their Impact on Women's Health." In S. Ruzek et al., eds., *Women's Health*, pp. 249–75. Copyright © 1997 Ohio State University Press. Reprinted by permission. ✦

22

Running in Place

Virginia Valian

Even if a person has a good job, he or she may find that the payoff depends on sex, race, or both. Women, for example, are still rarely found in high corporate positions. The reason for this situation depends upon whom you ask. A survey of female senior executives and CEOs at Fortune 1000 companies found that the most common reason given by women was their exclusion from informal networks (or, in common terms, the old-boy network). In contrast, the most common reason given by men was the women's lack of significant management or line experience (Crittenden 1996).

In this selection, Virginia Valian addresses the issue of women's rise in the corporate structure, noting how women confront obstacles to advancement. She particularly stresses the importance of a social psychological factor—gender schemas—in affecting people's perceptions. The result is differential treatment of males and females—to the detriment of females. Unfortunately, gender schemas will not change easily because they are rooted in longstanding cultural practices. Still, as Valian suggests, steps can be taken to counter the negative effects of the schemas on women's careers.

Reference

Crittenden, Ann. 1996. "Up the Corporate Ladder: A Progress Report." *Working Woman*, May.

Focus Questions

1. What is a gender schema?
2. How do people learn gender schemas?
3. How do gender schemas affect women's advancement in their careers?

In 1980, as part of a school economics project, a group of fifth and sixth graders bought six shares of stock in the Mohasco Corporation, a carpet and furniture manufacturer then based in New York City. The fledgling investors later attended a Mohasco shareholders' meeting, where an eleven-year-old girl asked the company's president and chief executive officer: "What are you doing to improve the role of women in your company?"

"Learning very young, isn't she?" the CEO replied. "As a company we have promoted—that didn't come out quite like I intended—we have encouraged the expanded use of young ladies in various parts of our company. We have no officers who are young ladies, though we have them moving up the ranks. We have very brilliant young ladies in management roles, in the area of computer programming. We'll have a place for you in a few years."

Whatever one might think about the ingenuousness of the CEO's response, his company's subsequent record of promoting women to upper-management jobs cannot be examined. Mohasco suffered several financial setbacks in the 1980s and is now a privately held company. One can, however, look at the overall figures for corporations in the United States. In 1978, two years before the eleven-year-old asked her question, there were two women heading Fortune 1000 companies; in 1994 that number had not changed. In August 1996, sixteen years after the question, there were four. Perhaps even more telling, a 1996 review of the 1,000 largest firms in the United States showed that only 1 percent of the top five jobs in those corporations—sixty posts out of 5,000—were filled by women.

The story is similar in academe. According to a major study published in 1996 by the National Science Foundation, 60 percent of the women in science and engineering in 1993 had tenure or tenure-track positions, compared with 77 percent of men. And women were overrepresented in non-tenure-track positions: 14 percent held those jobs, compared with 8 percent of men. (The remainder of each sex held jobs to which tenure does not apply; women were more likely to find themselves in that category as well.)

The women in the study also lagged behind in salary. The median income of women from all scientific disciplines combined—including mathematics, computer specialties, psychology, the social sciences, physics, chemistry, biology and engineering—was 78 percent of the men's: $48,400, compared with $61,500 for men. And within each of those fields, women earned less: from 93 percent of men's salaries in mechanical engineering to 76 percent in environmental science.

In virtually every profession I have examined—business, academe, medicine, law, sports—the picture looks the same: men earn more money and achieve higher status than women do. After more than three decades of struggles for gender equality, the progress of women continues to be slow and slight. Differences in education and experience sometimes explain part of the disparity in pay and rank, but gender always explains another, more subterranean, part.

From the first day women set foot on a career path, they are required to meet a higher standard.

At a restaurant in Manhattan near the end of the lunch hour I sit watching the manager's child, not quite two, toddling among the mostly empty tables. The child is wearing a jacket and pants of bright red, blue and yellow fabric. A baseball cap worn back-to-front partly covers the child's ear-length curly blond hair. Is the child a girl or a boy? The baseball cap and pants suggest a boy, but the hair length suggests a girl. The toddler's adventurousness might signal a boy, but its looks are androgynous and I cannot make up my mind.

The first thing adults want to establish about a child—even a newborn—is its sex. But what does sex, which is largely independent of a baby's behavior, tell an adult about the child? The answer is that the label "girl" or "boy" gives the adult a starting point from which to interpret the child's behavior, even its physical features. The label allows the adult to categorize an attractive baby as pretty, if it is a girl, or handsome, if it is a boy. The label brings into play the adult's preexisting beliefs about differences between the sexes. Those beliefs—some conscious and some not—make up an intuitive concept or schema of gender.

In white, Western, middle-class society, the gender schema for men includes being independent, assertive and task-oriented. Men act. The gender schema for women is different; it includes being nurturant, expressive and concerned about others. Women take care of people and express emotions.

The social consensus about basic differences between males and females can be gleaned from the greeting cards people send to congratulate parents on a new baby. A 1993 study by the psychologist Judith S. Bridges of the University of Connecticut in Hartford found, as expected, no pink ones for boys and no blue ones for girls. Pictures of toys, rattles and mobiles appear more often on girls' cards, and balls, sports equipment and vehicles show up more often on boys' cards. Female babies are pictured sleeping or immobile more often than male babies are, whereas boys are shown more often in active play.

Decorative elements on the cards show gender biases, too. Frills, lace, ribbons, flowers and hearts are all used more for girls than for boys. Verbal descriptions of infants also differ; the term *sweet*, for instance, crops up far more often for girls than for boys. The most striking difference is that expressions of happiness or joy are found more often on cards for boys—64 percent of cards—than for girls—49 percent of cards. People expect parents to be happier about the birth of a boy than about the birth of a girl. Greeting cards thus project babies as already embodying gender schemas. One class of babies is decorative; the other is physically active—and brings the greater joy.

Men and women carry around similar gender schemas for both sexes. In one study investigators asked college students to rate the behavior of a baby who had been videotaped crying. Some students were told that the baby was a boy and others that it was a girl. Regardless of their own gender, students described the baby labeled as male as angrier than the same infant labeled as female.

In another study parents were asked to rate their newborns on several different attributes when the babies were no more than twenty-four hours old. By objective measures, there were no differences in weight, height, color, muscle tone, reflex responses, heart rate or respiratory rate between the girls and the boys. Yet the parents of the baby boys saw their sons as bigger than the parents of daughters saw their baby girls. Furthermore, fathers of sons judged their babies to be better coordinated, more alert, stronger and hardier than did fathers of daughters. Knowing a child's sex skews perceptions.

But do such faulty concepts of gender have any real consequences? To answer that question, ask another one: Which baby seems better suited to an active and successful professional life—the baby who is better coordinated, more alert, hardier and stronger, or the one who is less coordinated, less alert, less hardy and weaker? Which baby is better suited for housework and child care? Just as it is unfair to picture one child as less capable than she is, it is also unfair to see the other as more capable than he is. From the first child too little will be expected; from the second too much.

As children grow up, they learn the gender schemas of their parents. Those schemas will affect their own performance as professionals, not to mention their expectations of other men and women, and their evaluations of other people's work. The most important consequence of those gender schemas for professional life is that men are consistently overrated and women are underrated. Whatever helps people focus on a man's gender gives him a small advantage, a plus mark. Whatever accentuates a woman's gender results in a small loss for her, a minus mark.

That consequence emerges in sharp relief in the results of a 1991 survey of U.S. professionals working in international business. The economists Mary Lou Egan and Marc Bendick Jr. of Bendick & Egan Economic Consultants in Washington, DC, analyzed the contributing factors in determining men's and women's salaries: number of graduate degrees, range of occupations pursued, number of years' experience, kinds of strategies used for career advancement, whether or not the person is designated "fast track," number of hours worked per week and the like. The investigators found that favorable marks on such factors typically helped both men and women make higher salaries, but they helped

the women to a lesser extent; fourteen of the seventeen factors examined benefited men more. The result is just what gender schemas would lead one to expect: women's achievements, qualifications and professional choices are worth less than men's are.

A bachelor's degree, for instance, contributed $28,000 to men's salaries but only $9,000 to women's. A degree from a high-prestige school contributed $11,500 to men's salaries but *subtracted* $2,400 from women's. Not holding back one's career for the benefit of a spouse's was worth $21,900 a year for men but only $1,700 a year for women. Being designated "fast track" added $10,900 for men but only $200 for women. Experience living outside the United States added $9,200 to men's salaries but, like high-prestige education, subtracted from women's—$7,700 a year. Similarly, deliberately choosing international work added $5,300 for men but subtracted $4,200 for women. Finally, speaking another language added $2,600 for men but took away $5,100 for women.

Egan and Bendick conjectured that the assets of speaking another language and having lived outside the United States are interpreted differently for men than for women. A man is seen as choosing to live abroad or learn a language not for fun but for the professional benefits such activities can bring. The choice signals a commitment to his career. In the gender schema for women, on the other hand, a woman goes abroad or learns a language simply for pleasure. Such a woman telegraphs indifference to her career.

Gender schemas are usually unarticulated. Their content may even be disavowed. Most men and women in the professions and academe explicitly, and sincerely, profess egalitarian beliefs. But conscious beliefs and values do not fully control the workings of gender schemas. Egalitarian beliefs help, but they do not guarantee objective and fair evaluation and treatment of other people.

A true story about a science department at a prestigious university, circa 1990, illustrates how expectations that arise out of gender schemas can drag down a woman's career. A newly hired young woman Ph.D. has a conference with the chair of her department, a man, about the courses she will teach. She is eager to teach a large introductory lecture course. The chair refuses, saying the students will not accept a woman instructor in that role. The woman presses a bit, saying she thinks she can do it and would like to try. The chair does not want to take a chance, and he assigns her instead to a laboratory course. The woman is not happy with the substitution, because laboratory courses eat up time. As a young faculty member, she needs to spend as much time as possible developing her research and writing for publication, so that she will be able to earn promotion and tenure. And as circumstances have it, the competition for such promotion will be both direct and unfair. A male peer, also a new Ph.D., is assigned to the lecture course, and he will thereby have more time for research than she will.

The example captures the many different forces—particularly the gender expectations—that merge to put a woman on swampy ground. The chair thinks he is being objective about the students' preferences and is shielding an important course from risk. Nothing about the meeting causes him to think his decision might have been unfairly guided by gender schemas. The conference has also set a bad precedent. It has activated the chair's nonconscious views about women and tied them to the new faculty member. In the future he is likely to reactivate those views whenever he evaluates her. In a way, she has already failed, because he has already labeled her to himself as an unacceptable lecturer.

The glass ceiling—the popular term for subtle biases that keep women from reaching the top levels of organizations—is held up in part by gender schemas. But another force is also at work keeping the glass intact: the long-term buildup of small differences in the evaluation and treatment of men versus women.

A useful concept in sociology is the accumulation of advantage and disadvantage. It suggests that, like the interest on invested capital, advantages accrue, and that, like the interest on debt, disadvantages also pile up. Very small differences in treatment can, over time, give rise to large disparities in salary, promotion rates and prestige. It is unfair to neglect even minor instances of group-based bias, because they add up to major inequalities.

A computer model of promotion practices at a hypothetical company convincingly shows the powerful cumulative effects of even small-scale bias. In 1996 the psychologists Richard F. Martell of Columbia University in New York City, David M. Lane of Rice University in Houston, Texas, and Cynthia Emrich of the University of Otago in Dunedin, New Zealand, simulated a company with an eight-level hierarchy staffed at the bottom level by equal numbers of men and women. The model assumed that over time a certain percentage of employees would be promoted from one level to the next. It also assumed a minuscule bias in favor of promoting men, a bias accounting for only 1 percent of the variability in promotion. After many series of simulated promotions, the highest level in the hierarchy was 65 percent male.

Statistics on women's progress in the professions back up the idea that a series of small setbacks, such as not getting a good assignment, results in widening chasms in advancement. Women at each rank of academe, regardless of their subject, have lower average salaries than men do. Moreover, the inequalities are progressive: the disparity is smaller at the assistant professor level than at the full professor level.

In academe, as well as in business and law, the interaction between salary and rank can lead to fuzzy comparisons between men's and women's earnings. A more informative picture would compare peers. But if male full professors—like male law partners—are on average older than female full professors, they will have more experience and earn higher salaries. Comparisons within the upper ranks, therefore, can overestimate income disparities.

In junior ranks, however, comparing apparent peers can have the opposite effect: it can cause an underestimation of income disparities. Since male assistant professors are promoted at a faster rate than female assistant professors, the people in a lower rank will include not only young men and women but also older women who should have been promoted out of that rank. Data on the incomes of men and women who are the same number of years post-degree, or who have the same number of years' experience, regardless of rank, make the fairest comparisons.

The 1996 National Science Foundation study tabulated such data from 1993. It found that among the newest Ph.D.'s in science and engineering—those with degrees earned in 1991 or 1992—women scientists at universities and four-year colleges earned 99 percent of the median salary of their male counterparts. For more experienced women, though, the slope got icy. Women academics whose degrees were awarded between 1985 and 1990 earned 92 percent of men's salaries; women with degrees from between 1980 and 1982 earned 90 percent; and those with degrees from between 1970 and 1979 earned 89 percent. Thus the most recent female graduates start out on a roughly equal salary footing with their male counterparts, but are likely to lose that equality as early as three years after earning their Ph.D.'s.

A different sample of male and female scientists, intended to represent those who show high achievement early in their careers, was followed from 1987 to 1990 by the sociologist Gerhard Sonnert and the physicist Gerald Holton, both of Harvard University. The participants had won postdoctoral fellowships from either the National Science Foundation or the National Research Council between 1952 and 1985. Because those national fellowships are prestigious, the men and women who earn them are roughly equal in education, experience and performance at the start of their academic careers. Nevertheless, except for biologists, women with such fellowships had less success climbing through the ranks than men did. For example, women who had earned their doctorates in the physical sciences, mathematics and engineering after 1978 languished almost a full rank behind their male peers; women in the social sciences were more than three-quarters of a rank behind.

The women in Sonnert and Holton's sample were somewhat less productive than the men, but even when productivity was considered, the women (again, except the biologists) held lower ranks than comparable men. Thus, even women who have a prestigious credential profit from it less than men do.

Why young female and male biologists fare equally well is not known. One possible explanation comes from a 1995 study by Sonnert, in which senior biologists rated a small group of junior biologists on a four-point scale. Although not asked to do so, the senior biologists implicitly took quality, as well as quantity, of publications into account. Their ratings of the women were slightly higher than those of the men, a difference that vanished when citation rates were not considered. Taken together, the data suggest that biologists' assessments are more sensitive to quality than those of other scientists and that the difference helps women gain equal ground.

What is true for academe holds even more strongly in the corporate world. A 1990 Fortune magazine survey of 799 of the largest U.S. industrial and service companies showed that only nineteen women—less than one-half of 1 percent—were listed among the more than 4,000 highest-paid officers and directors. In business as in academe, women earn less than men (two of those nineteen women had cash compensation under $85,000 a year), are promoted more slowly and work in less prestigious institutions.

On the positive side, women's earnings have improved. In a 1996 survey of the twenty highest-paid women in U.S. corporations, the lowest total compensation was $833,350. But 615 men earned more than the twentieth woman on the list. And again, as in academe, to the extent that performance can be accurately measured, men and women appear to perform equally well. Independent of all other factors, gender appears to play a key role in people's ability to get ahead.

The inequality in status between men and women professionals will not go away by itself. It will not be smoothed by normal economic tides or by women's acquisition of more and better work skills. Excellent work skills are necessary for success, but they are not enough to guarantee equality.

So where do we go from here? Affirmative-action policies, legislation and court action remain important roads to change in the workplace. But the elusive nature of gender schemas demands more subtle remedies as well. The most important remedy is learning about gender schemas in the first place: how they develop, how they work, how they are maintained and how they skew hopes and expectations. With that knowledge, men and women can begin to find ways to neutralize them.

One successful long-term program was developed recently at the Johns Hopkins University School of Medicine in Baltimore, Maryland. At medical schools throughout the United States, women are underrepresented in the top professorial rank. After an internal report documented lower pay and slower rates of promotion for women faculty in the Johns Hopkins department of medicine, the (male) chair of the department appointed a committee to design procedures for improving women's status. The committee members found that women were put up for promotion later than their male peers. The problem seemed to have many facets, ranging from the failure of evaluators to identify qualified women, to ignorance on the part of the women themselves of the criteria for promotion. The solution aimed to change all those facets. Each female faculty member (and later, each male faculty member) was evaluated annually and given an explicit progress report. A monthly meeting was established to give women faculty concrete information about how to move through their professional careers and to handle problems that might arise. Those meetings were needed in part because mentors of male junior faculty were more likely to pass along that advice informally than were mentors of female junior faculty.

Another change was to teach senior faculty to act as mentors, in an effort to level unequal treatment of junior men and junior women. The committee members had learned, for instance, that mentors invited male junior faculty to chair conferences (and thereby receive public exposure) six times as often as they invited female junior faculty.

Within five years, the program became extremely successful. In 1990 there were only four women associate professors; by 1995 there were twenty-six. The improvement did not spring from changes in promotion criteria. What did change was women's knowledge of what was required for promotion. In 1990 only 26 percent of the women reported that they were advised about the criteria, but in 1993, 46 percent reported being advised. It is likely that knowledge of promotion requirements helps candidates mold their behavior accordingly. One must notice too, however, that slightly more than half the women still had not gotten the facts about how to climb through the ranks.

The Johns Hopkins program shows that institutions can, with major efforts, keep their female employees from getting stuck in the marshy bottoms of their professions. Yet the limits of the program also suggest the need for remedies that take more direct aim at gender schemes, such as those that would train evaluators in reasoning and judging.

Unless everyone—women and men alike—understands how gender schemas hobble women professionally, women will not get the positive evaluations their work merits. They will get less than their fair share—and their progress will continue to be painfully slow.

Critical Evaluation

1. The author acknowledges that education and experience can explain part of the inequality women face. How much can those factors explain?

2. The author asserts that women are expected to meet higher standards than men. Is that true? What evidence is there?

3. Gender schemas help explain male-female inequality. What other factors are important, and how do they relate to the schemas?

Virginia Valian, "Running In Place," *The Sciences,* Jan/Feb, 1998. Adapted from Virginia Valian, *Why So Slow? The Advancement of Women.* Copyright © 1997 by the MIT Press. Reprinted by permission. ✦

Project for Personal Application and Class Discussion: Gender

Most Americans say they believe in equality between men and women. In your own experience (including your observation of others and your reading), how much inequality have you noted? Write down the kinds of inequality you have observed or read about in each of the areas below (you can include examples of males as well as females being unequal and also examples where you think the inequality is harmless or even appropriate):

1. dating

2. the classroom

3. family life

4. the workplace

5. small-group discussions

Which of the inequalities do you believe should be eliminated? What can you do to help? ◆

Race and Ethnicity

Like gender, race and ethnicity are ascribed characteristics that affect how much people can achieve in American society. In theory, it is only competence and performance that matters. In practice, race and ethnicity have long been handicaps to aspirations. Consider income. In 1996 the median weekly earnings for white workers was $506; for African Americans it was $387, and for Hispanic Americans it was $339 (U.S. Bureau of the Census 1997:431).

As with women, income disparities among racial and ethnic minorities cannot be fully accounted for by such factors as differences in education and work experience. Like women, racial and ethnic minorities also face hurdles that white males do not face in their efforts to obtain a high-quality education and pursue a rewarding career. For example, Sharon Collins (1997) interviewed 76 black executives and concluded that they were channeled into positions (such as affirmative-action manager) that were peripheral to the core goals of the company. This treatment meant that they never achieved the powerful, decision-making positions that white male executives filled.

This section examines various ways in which race and ethnicity are handicaps to the efforts of minorities to achieve the American dream. As the various readings demonstrate, prejudice and discrimination continue to dog the steps of minorities at every turn despite the progress made over the past four decades of civil-rights activism.

References

Collins, Sharon M. 1997. "Black Mobility in White Corporations: Up the Corporate Ladder but Out on a Limb." *Social Problems* 44:55–67.

U.S. Bureau of the Census. 1997. *Statistical Abstract of the United States*. Washington, DC: U.S. Government Printing Office. ✦

23

'The Land That Never Has Been Yet'

Anthony M. Platt

The civil-rights movement gathered momentum in the late 1950s and considerable progress seemed to occur in subsequent years. Yet by the 1990s, some of the gains had been lost and race relations remained severely troubled. Anthony Platt identifies four changing conditions and challenges that hamper the quest for equality. At the macrolevel, a changed economy, difficulties with educational opportunities, and a retreat from governmental support for affirmative action are important factors impeding the progress of minorities. The structural hurdles are supported by changed attitudes on the part of whites, including working-class and middle-class whites who face some new impediments of their own. Like Madeline Heilman (Chapter 20), Platt sees the role of affirmative action as a crucial part of the struggle.

Focus Questions

1. What does the author mean by the "precariousness of racial equality?"

2. What are the changing conditions and challenges that make the achievement of racial equality difficult?

3. Why may a "non-racialized democracy" in the United States be impossible?

Introduction

The Nation has not yet found peace from its sins.

—W.E.B. Du Bois (1903)

An American looks like a wounded person whose wound is hidden from others, and *sometimes from herself. An American looks like me.*

—Alice Walker (1992)

If you believe, as I do, in racial equality as a matter of moral principle and in the incompatibility of political democracy with racial hierarchy, then you will no doubt agree that we live in very difficult times, and that the end of this millennium represents a sorrowful rather than celebratory occasion. It is difficult to remain optimistic when so many visions remain unrealized and so much ground has been lost. Because race is such a deep and enduring wound in the body politic, the struggle for racial equality, even at its most optimistic moments (which have been few), requires us to always keep a sharp lookout for that "hellhound on my trail," to quote bluesman Robert Johnson (quoted in Litwack, 1991: 25). . . .

Living with Inequality

The precariousness of racial equality is evident when we look at the profound shift that has taken place in the cultural-political climate of the United States in the last 25 years. In 1968, the Kerner Report—perhaps the most important liberal statement about race ever to be issued by the federal government—provided seemingly unassailable moral authority for the conclusion that we live in a "separate and unequal" society; it was an indictment of the hypocrisy of American democracy. The Kerner Report represented the most optimistic aspect of liberalism, namely, that racial antagonisms are non-rational legacies of early modern society that will wither away under the relentless pressure of Reason, Science, and Progress imposed by an interventionist, technocratic state (Gerstle, 1994; Wallerstein, 1991). By 1994, however, liberalism was dead, replaced by the pessimism of neoliberal pseudoscience like Richard Herrnstein and Charles Murray's *The Bell Curve* (1994: 551), with its repudiation of social reform. "Trying to eradicate inequality with artificially manufactured outcomes has led to disaster," they conclude. "It is time for America once again to try living with inequality, as life is lived."

The Bell Curve is neither the work of cranks nor an anomaly. It is representative of an influential genre of neoliberal and neoconservative literature that is taken seriously in Washington, DC, and resonates widely in the commercial media (Platt, 1996). Liberal and radical views about race are all but absent from public and political discourse, having been marginalized to universities and intellectuals without a power base. This abrupt change is due to a variety of complex, interrelated, national and international events. In the last two decades we have witnessed the rapid growth of a globalized, transnational economy and a corresponding weakening of states. This has created internal fiscal crises within the nation-state, even one as powerful and seemingly stable as the United States. With economic instabilities within nation-states have come political crises, as reflected in the rise to power of the Reagan wing of the Republican Party, the defeat of liberalism within the Democratic Party, and the collapse of mass activism.

With respect to issues of racial equality, the reversals too have been fast and furious. In some respects, we have returned to (or maybe never left) the racialized formations of the 1950s. The suburban housing boom of the 1960s perpetuated segregation through Federal Housing Authority policies and redlining by the banks, while public housing authorities maintained segregation by building projects within *barrios* and ghettos (Sacks, 1994). Efforts to integrate the public schools have largely been undermined by white flight to the suburbs, by a deepening economic polarization and tax cuts that have seriously damaged the quality of public life, and by the hands-off policies of a federal judiciary that is stamped with the sensibilities of Reagan-Bush appointees.

Laws and policies have little meaning if they are not regulated and enforced with urgency and conviction. For example, the Equal Employment Opportunity Commission, the main federal agency that investigates complaints of bias in employment, has a backlog of more than 90,000 cases (Holmes, 1995a: 1, C22). Similarly, the Johnson administration's contract-compliance program, which had a significant impact in both awarding contracts to minority-owned businesses and compelling federal contractors to hire workers of color, "virtually ceased to exist in all but name after 1980" (researcher Jonathan Leonard, cited in McMillen, 1995:7-8). Not surprisingly, union membership is back to over 80% white.

In the last 20 years, all levels of government have lost a large cadre of civil servants who not only supported affirmative action, but also worked enthusiastically to breathe life into the policy. Long before the judicial and executive branches began to dismantle civil rights legislation, the policy of affirmative action shifted to one of benign neglect, then malign opposition. The kind of affirmative action policy that compelled institutions to make profound changes in organizational priorities and culture is long gone. It has already been whittled away to a shadow of its former self. In a series of cases involving federal contracts, electoral districts, race-based scholarships, and public school integration plans, the Supreme Court has turned a political, social, and moral mandate into a compressed tunnel of opportunity. Now, affirmative action must be "narrowly tailored," "serve a compelling national interest," and be "subject to strict scrutiny." Race can no longer be used, for example, as a "predominant factor" in drawing district voter lines and, when used, must be based on compelling evidence of a specific pattern of previous discrimination.

Some may understand this retreat from racial equality as simply a nostalgic return to the good old days of the 1950s, made possible by the absence of a mass movement. But there are also some significant new conditions at work that add both complexity and difficult new challenges. We will need to reinvent our movement in new ways in order to meet these challenges. I will comment on four of these changing conditions and challenges.

First, economic conditions have changed profoundly since the 1950s. With deindustrialization and restructuring, a growing gulf between public and private education, a decline in union jobs, and a contraction in public sector employment, it is not surprising that we have witnessed a growing concentration of populations of color in places where unemployed adults typically find themselves—in public ghettos, *barrios*, and reservations, on welfare, in public housing projects, in jails and prisons, and in the military. Much of the economic ground gained by affirmative action in the decades of the 1960s and 1970s has been lost, with no sign of recovery in the near future. For the overwhelming majority of African Americans, Chicanos, Central Americans, black Cubans, Southeast Asians, Haitians, Puerto Ricans, American Indians, and poor whites, the job future looks very bleak, alternating between seasonal work or low-paying, mostly part-time service jobs or entrepreneurial hustles in the irregular and illegal economy. The relationship between racism and imprisonment has been widely observed (Platt, 1995), so here I will comment on another aspect of the racialization of America that requires our attention.

Many African American men and women and Latinos have chosen the military as a job and refuge from a hostile economy. Between 1970 and 1990, blacks in the military almost doubled. Populations of color now comprise 42% of the Army, 32% of the Navy, and 25% of the Air Force. Of all women in the service, about one-third are black (Wood, 1996: 3; Graham, B., 1995: 1, 10-11; *New York Times*, 1995: E4). In the past, the military was a route of upward mobility for the working class. After the Civil War, the Grand Army of the Republic lobbied and received relatively generous pension benefits; and after World War II, millions benefited from the GI Bill to get low-interest loans, education subsidies, and technical training. The beneficiaries in both cases were overwhelmingly white men. As men and women of color flooded into the military during and after the Korean War, there were no similar rewards. For many, military service now is close to the poverty line and the GI Bill no longer offers adequate incentives for college or a route into professional careers (Sacks, 1994).

Second, even middle-class professionals, who made considerable gains after World War II, are at risk of returning to a segregated world. According to a recent study by the Southern Education Foundation, the leading public universities in the South remain more than 80% white. In Mississippi, where college tuition costs represent about 40% of the annual income of an average black family, fewer African Americans earned bachelor's degrees in 1991 than in 1979 (Applebome, 1995: 16). Nationwide, the proportion of African Americans with a bachelor's degree in education decreased one percent between 1972 and 1992 (*Ibid*.: 22-24) and the production of African Americans with doctorates has been stagnant since the late 1970s.

In 1994, three times as many doctorates were awarded to non-U.S. citizens (primarily from China, Taiwan, Korea, and India) as were awarded to all American doctoral recipients of color (Simmons and Thurgood, 1995). Moreover, with the likely abandoning of all race-specific scholarships, as ordered by the Supreme Court in the *Banneker* case and quickly implemented by universities in Texas, Colorado, and California, this situation can only get worse (Holmes, 1995d: 11; Associated Press, 1995). American Indians are absent from most university faculties, Latinos barely have a toehold, and the majority of African American intellectuals are back teaching in historically black colleges and universities. Walk onto any campus these days and you will see a large number of employees of color, but over 80% of them work in clerical, support, or maintenance positions (Schultz, 1993: 51-52). It may be that we have seen the high point of faculty diversity.

Third, the United States has always been a multiracial, multicultural society, but we are in the midst of an historic shift to the kind of heterogeneity that has never existed in the past. By the year 2050, according to the Census Bureau, the Anglo population of the United States will be about 53%, compared to 74% today. Latinos will increase the most, from 10.2 to 24.5%, Asians from 3.3 to 8.2%, and African Americans will remain relatively stable, from 12 to 13.6% (Holmes, 1996: 8). These changing racial demographics present a major challenge for an anti-racist movement that must encompass a complicated array of social, economic, cultural, and identity constituencies. Racism, like ethnicity, is not monolithic. If it was difficult in the 1950s and 1960s to build unities between urban African Americans fighting for citizenship, rural and urban Chicanos with divided national loyalties, and American Indians struggling for sovereignty (not to mention the interests of middle-class, white women and students), then imagine the difficulties before us now. To our already complex mix, we must add the extraordinary diversity of "Latinos" (Zavella, 1994); an "Asian" population that stretches from well-trained Korean professionals to uneducated peasants from Cambodia; an immigrant population from Mexico and Central America that includes both migrant workers and political refugees; an American Indian population that includes a tiny minority of millionaires (as a result, mostly, of providing casinos to non-Indians) and a huge majority that lives in wretched poverty; and a fast-growing population of biracial and multiracial families who represent the kind of cultural hybridity that typifies an increasingly interdependent, mobile world. Defining the unities of our movement will be no small task. "Was there no common denominator on which we could all meet?" asked Carlos Bulosan (1973: 147) in the 1940s. It is the same question we must ask ourselves in the 1990s.

Fourth, affirmative action was initially put into practice when higher education and the public sector were still expanding, and there was growth in middle-class professions. White, middle-class youth supported the civil rights struggle out of a sense of idealism and political commitment. It did not hurt that progress for blacks and Chicanos, for example, did not mean losses for Anglos. In the 1990s, we face very different circumstances. Affirmative action in times of cutbacks and contraction means a more racially equitable distribution of misery, as more and more Anglos begin to experience their whiteness as a color they can no longer take for granted. White working-class men and their families have lost economic ground, and their sons and daughters face a very precarious future. The aspiring white middle class must pay more to go to college, must compete more to get in, and has no guarantee that a degree will lead to upward mobility. This economic uncertainty, combined with 20 years of a right-wing political culture, has produced a fierce backlash. Just as the Irish did in the 19th century and Jews did after World War II,

many Euro-Americans are asserting their whiteness out of a sense of defensiveness and insecurity, but this time they are downwardly mobile.

Twilight

To return to the question I raised at the beginning of this article, I do not think that we are heading back to the days of . . . a formal system of white supremacy. The past rarely reproduces itself so precisely. Yet I do think that our era and our movement share a great deal in common with the aftermath of Reconstruction. They both represent moments of transition when it is possible to see more clearly and feel more deeply the "twoness"—the possibility and its negation— that Du Bois described so vividly in *The Souls of Black Folk*. We made ground, then lost it. Our generation experienced a sense of optimism and the possibility of achieving a vision of racial equality, only to be overwhelmed, in the words of historian Leon Litwack (1991:25), by the "terrifying sense of personal betrayal and anguish" that comes from living in a society that is "impossible to overcome— or to escape." We went from a struggle that drew upon the most progressive traditions of activism—what Langston Hughes calls the "dream" that "lies deep in the heart of me"— to one that now, as so often in the past, draws upon the most mean-spirited, populist traditions of racism and white supremacy. "So kind and yet so cruel," is how Carlos Bulosan (1973: 147) summed up his experience in the United States.

There is much evidence to confirm the impression that race is a sufficiently deep wound to make the patient fatally ill, that democracy may not be possible in the United States. After all, we live on a continent whose pre-Columbian population of six or seven million (maybe as many as 12.5 million by some accounts) was reduced to not even one-quarter of one million by 1900 (Edmunds, 1995). Slaughter, disease, kidnapping, and starvation took its toll on this very land, here in Alta California where, by 1910, over 60% of the original Californian tribes were extinct or close to extinction (Almaguer, 1994: 130). Since then there has been a long trail of sorrows for many people in this country, the majority, in fact, if we also include the experience of immigrants from Ireland, southern and eastern Europe and the Middle East, most women of all colors, and the many victims of sexual bigotry.

At moments like this, when all that we fought for seems so tenuous, it is difficult to stay the course. However, this is not the time to retreat from affirmative action and the principles of racial equality. The more we concede, the more they will take. We can learn this lesson from McCarthyism, when the majority of intellectuals, liberals, and university officials refused to defend unpopular ideas. We need to face this crisis—"bring this thing out to the light," as Fannie Lou Hamer (1986: 326) liked to say—rather than bury it in amnesia or pretense. In the twilight, to use Anna Deavere Smith's metaphor for our racial crisis, it is important that we sharpen our vision. "We might not like what we see," she says, "but in order to change it, we have to see it clearly" (Smith, 1993: xii; 1994).

Also, we need to revisit the issue of integration. Politically, it is not a concept that is advocated very much these days, as we are presumably learning to live, once again, with inequality and segregation. Intellectually, the idea is also out of fashion. The teaching of "multiculturalism," with its respect for difference and uniqueness, typically accepts the basic premises of segregation and apartness. "It is too often forgotten," observes Eric Foner (1995: 488), "that integration is a very radical idea." Integration is not necessarily the same as assimilation, that is, the "absorption" of the other into a preexisting, hegemonic social system. Integration of economic and political institutions also can promise "a vision of a nation transformed, one in which equality is a reality for all Americans." Minimally, we need to reconnect the relationship between culture, power, and economic structures (Hall, 1994; Wood, 1996).

Our most difficult challenge is to imagine the struggle for racial justice as a project that can potentially reach the majority of Americans. Despite the history of institutionalized racism and its continual reproduction in new forms, despite public opinion polls that confirm the worst, I share James Baldwin's hope that beneath the arrogance of white American racism we can also find "power and sorrow, both unadmitted [and] unrealized, the power of inventors, the sorrow of the disconnected" (Baldwin 1957:119).

I started this talk with Du Bois trying to free the nation of the sin of racism and Alice Walker speaking of our collective wound. Let me close with a couplet from a prayer-poem written by Primo Levi in 1982:

This year in fear and shame,
Next year in virtue and justice.

References

Almaguer, Thomas. 1994. *Racial Fault Lines: The Historical Origins of White Supremacy in California*. Berkeley: University of California Press.

Applebome, Peter. 1995. "College Segregation Persists, Study Says." *New York Times* (May 18).

Associated Press. 1995. "Ethnic Scholarships Reported Restricted." *San Francisco Chronicle* (December 26).

Baldwin, James. 1957. *Giovanni's Room*. London: Michael Joseph.

Bulosan, Carlos. 1973. *America Is in the Heart: A Personal History*. Seattle: University of Washington Press.

Du Bois, W.E.B. 1993. "The Souls of Black Folk" (originally published in 1903). New York: Alfred A. Knopf.

Edmunds, David R. 1995. Native Americans, New Voices: American Indian History, 1895-1995. *American Historical Review* 100, 3 (June).

Foner, Eric. 1995. "The Great Divide." *The Nation* (October 30).

Gerstle, Gary. 1994. "The Protean Character of American Liberalism." *American Historical Review* 99, 4 (October).

Graham, Bradley. 1995. "Military Short of Victory in War on Bias." *Washington Post* (April 29).

Hall, Stuart. 1994. "Cultural Studies: Two Paradigms." Nicholas B. Dirks, Geoff Eley, and Sherry B. Ortner (eds.), *Culture/Power/History: A Reader in Contemporary Social Theory*. Princeton: Princeton University Press.

Hamer, Fannie Lou. 1986. "To Praise Our Bridges." Dorothy Abbott (ed.), *Mississippi Writers: Reflections of Childhood and Youth*, Vol. 2. Jackson: University Press of Mississippi.

Herrnstein, Richard J. and Charles Murray. 1994. *The Bell Curve: Intelligence and Class Structure in American Life*. New York: The Free Press.

Holmes, Steven A. 1996. "Census Sees a Profound Ethnic Shift in U.S." *New York Times* (March 14).

——. 1995a. "Programs Based on Sex and Race Are Under Attack." *New York Times* (March 16).

——. 1995b. "U.S. Issues New, Strict Tests for Affirmative Action Plans." *New York Times* (June 29).

——. 1995c. "As Affirmative Action Ebbs, A Sense of Uncertainty Rises." *New York Times* (July 6).

——. 1995d. "Minority Scholarship Plans Are Dealt Setback by Court." *New York Times* (May 23).

Levi, Primo. 1988. *Collected Poems*. Translated by Ruth Feldman and Brian Swann. London: Faber and Faber.

Litwack, Leon. 1991. "Hellhound on My Trail: Race Relations in the South from Reconstruction to the Civil Rights Movement." Harry J. Knopke et al., *Opening Doors: Perspectives on Race Relations in Contemporary America*. Tuscaloosa:University of Alabama Press.

McMillen, Liz. 1995. "Berkeley Professor Sees No Economic Erosion for Whites, and Modest Effects for Blacks." *Chronicle of Higher Education* (November 17).

New York Times 1995. "Black and White: Career by Career." *New York Times* (June 18).

Platt, Anthony M. 1996. "'Living with Inequality': Race and the Changing Discourse of Victimization in the United States." *Comparative Law Review* 29, 4.

——. 1995. "Crime Rave." *Monthly Review* 47, 2 (June).

Rampersad, Arnold (ed.). 1995. *The Collected Poems of Langston Hughes*. New York: Alfred A. Knopf.

Sacks, Karen. 1994. "How Did Jews Become White Folks." Steven Gregory and Roger Sanjek (eds.), *Race*. New Brunswick: Rutgers University Press.

Schultz, Debra L. 1993. *To Reclaim a Legacy: Analyzing the 'Political Correctness' Debates in Higher Education*. New York: The National Council for Research on Women.

Simmons, Robert O. and Delores H. Thurgood. 1995. Summary Report 1994: Doctorate Recipients from United States Universities. Washington, DC: National Academy Press.

Smith, Anna Deavere. 1994. *Twilight Los Angeles, 1992*. New York: Anchor Books.

——. 1993. *Fires in the Mirror*. New York: Anchor Books.

Walker, Alice. 1992. *Possessing the Secret of Joy*. New York: Harcourt, Brace, Jovanovich.

——. 1967. "The Civil Rights Movement: What Good Was It?" *The American Scholar* (Autumn).

Wallerstein, Immanuel. 1991. *Unthinking Social Science: The Limits of Nineteenth Century Paradigms*. Cambridge, U.K.: Polity Press.

Wood, Ellen Meiksins. 1996. "Issues of Class and Culture: An Interview with Aijaz Ahmad." *Monthly Review* (October).

Wood, David. 1996. "Military a Magnet for Black Women." *San Francisco Examiner* (February 11).

Zavelia, Patricia. 1994. "Reflections on Diversity Among Chicanas." Steven Gregory and Roger Sanjeck (eds.) *Race*. New Brunswick: Rutgers University Press.

Critical Evaluation

1. The author notes the various reversals in the effort to achieve racial equality. How much progress has been made, and how much of that progress continues?

2. The author writes of "returning to a segregated world." Some African Americans advocate a certain amount of separation in order not to be oppressed by the white majority. Would racial minorities profit by some carefully selected areas of segregation? Why or why not?

3. The author's solution to the racial problem is to continue with some policies and principles that resulted in some progress in the past. Is there a need, instead, for some creative new approaches to the race problem? What might they be?

Anthony M. Platt, "'The Land That Never Has Been Yet': U.S. Race Relations at the Crossroads." In *Social Justice* 24:1, pp. 7–23. Copyright © 1997 by *Social Justice*. Reprinted by permission. ✦

24

The Hispanic Dropout Mystery

Susan Headden

Education is usually a necessary foundation for attaining higher socioeconomic status. But minorities (except for Asian Americans) tend to acquire less education than whites. And of all the minority groups, Hispanic Americans have the lowest educational achievement. Among adults in 1996, 82.8 percent of whites, 74.3 percent of African Americans, and 53.1 percent of Hispanic Americans had completed four years of high school or more (U.S. Bureau of the Census 1997:159). Hispanics, then, have unusually large dropout rates from high school. Susan Headden discusses the Hispanic dropout rate, noting how it is influenced both by structural factors (poverty) and social psychological factors (interaction with peers and parents).

Reference

U.S. Bureau of the Census. 1997. *Statistical Abstract of the United States*. Washington, DC: U.S. Government Printing Office.

Focus Questions

1. How does the Hispanic dropout rate compare with that of whites and African Americans?

2. What are the reasons for the high Hispanic dropout rate?

3. How can the problem be addressed?

The atmosphere at Denver's North High School is electric with the start of a new school year. On a warm autumn morning, teenagers are storming the hallways, all blue nail polish, baggy pants, and promise. Principal Joe Sandoval plays the traffic cop, lassoing a kid here, feinting a punch there, urging one and all to "Apurate! Hurry up!" The air at this nearly all-Hispanic school is so charged that it effectively conceals a grim fact: Of the 1,500 students expected to register for school this week, more than 350 have failed to show up. Sandoval has launched an ambitious effort to find them. The odds are great, however, that most of them will never come back.

North High School illustrates one of the most serious and stubborn problems in U.S. public education. The dropout rate for Hispanic students nationwide is 30 percent—nearly three times the rate for whites and twice the rate for blacks. It crosses income lines, transcends language ability, and persists despite a dramatic decline in the dropout rates for other groups. Most discouraging, the dropout rate for children of American-born Hispanics is even higher than for those born to immigrants, suggesting that the longer a family lives in the United States, the more entrenched the problem becomes.

In an upcoming report, the Department of Education is expected to call for heightened legislative and public attention to Hispanic dropouts. Last week, New Mexico Sen. Jeff Bingaman proposed spending $100 million on prevention programs and designating a federal "dropout czar." The issue is of concern not only to Hispanics. In just eight years, according to the U.S. Census Bureau, Hispanics will surpass blacks as the nation's largest minority group. Already they fill nearly half the desks in many of the nation's urban public schools.

Divergent Opinions

Hispanic teens say they leave school for reasons common to troubled students from all ethnic groups: They're failing, they're bored, they're working to support a family. But beyond these factors, opinions diverge about why Latino dropout rates have been persistently high for the past 25 years. Hispanics say that the public schools marginalize them, disrespecting their culture, neglecting their language problems, and setting standards so low that kids can't help but reduce expectations. Others insist it is Hispanics themselves who are giving up on education.

Language is one obvious barrier to Hispanic academic success. Forty-three percent of Hispanic dropouts are foreign born, and many of them don't get special language help. Bilingual-education advocates cite the dropout rate when arguing that more courses should be taught in Spanish; opponents hold it up as proof of the failure of bilingualism to make students learn English.

But language difficulty is not the only reason Hispanics leave school. Contrary to popular perception, most Hispanic dropouts were born here and speak English fluently. The greater problem—particularly among poor Hispanics, where the dropout rate is close to 41 percent—may be handicaps to learning in any language. One third of Hispanic children live in poverty, and like many inner-city children, they start school at a substantial disadvantage: They rarely attend preschool, and their parents, often ill-educated or illiterate, don't read to them.

Poverty also goes a long way toward explaining why Mexican-Americans, Central Americans, and Puerto Ricans drop out of school at rates far higher than, say, Cuban-Americans, who tend to be wealthier and immigrate for political reasons. Schools in rural Mexico are apt to be remote, overcrowded, and limited to the primary grades. Partly because of this weak academic tradition, many Hispanic parents don't demand as much of American schools as whites and blacks do.

Peer pressure to drop out can be nearly overwhelming in the Hispanic community, as DeAnza Montoya, a pretty Santa Fe teen, can attest. In her neighborhood, it was considered "Anglo" and "nerdy" to do well in school. So DeAnza cruised in wildly painted cars with her "low rider" friends and didn't worry about the future. She claims she was simply doing what was expected of her. "In school they make you feel like a dumb Mexican," she says, adding that the slights only bring Hispanics closer together. That fierce Latino loyalty, particularly when applied to family, is an ethic that teachers find hard to challenge. A sound instinct in most circumstances, it can nevertheless prompt a student to leave school for reasons as seemingly flimsy as the one offered by the North High dropout who insisted on working full time to pay for wrecking his brother-in-law's car.

Addressing the Problem

Even if blame for the dropout crisis lies with the students, a solution is likely to come from the schools. The black dropout rate plummeted once schools focused on it; to have a similar impact on Hispanics, reformers say, teachers must go beyond the classroom to counsel at-risk students and their families. Teachers may have to speak Spanish and schedule conferences around parents' jobs. Most important, reformers call for more Hispanic role models. The U.S. public-school population is 13.5 percent Hispanic, yet Latinos account for only 3 percent of the teachers.

Programs that target the Hispanic dropout rate are showing promise around the country. Former dropout Shileene Martinez, 14, is thriving at Colorado High School in Denver, which schedules small classes to accommodate students' work hours. In Santa Fe, a mentoring program matches members of the Hispanic business community with at-risk youth. And a nationwide effort sponsored by Coca-Cola enlists would-be dropouts as tutors for younger children.

Should the alternatives fail, administrators might take a cue from Joe Sandoval at North High School. Here, students intent on quitting school must sign a waiver reading: "By signing this, I realize I will not have the skills to survive in the 21st century." They are then presented with a "Certificate of Dropping Out." Occasionally, it achieves the intended effect. One teen, Sandoval recalls, threw the document back in Sandoval's face, shouting "I don't want this piece of s---!" Far from being insulted, the principal welcomed the wayward student back to school.

Critical Evaluation

1. Hispanics are a very diverse group. For example, what would the results on dropout rates look like if one compared Puerto Ricans with Mexican Americans and with Cuban Americans?

2. If Hispanic groups were considered separately by national origin, would some different factors emerge to explain the dropout rates?

3. The author notes things that schools could do to address the problem. What could other institutions, such as the family, the government, and religion, do to alleviate the problem?

25

The Covert War: Stealth Racism in America

Jerelyn Eddings

Interaction patterns both reflect and tend to perpetuate racial prejudice and discrimination. Surveys show that far more whites than minorities believe that the race problem is much less severe than it was a few decades ago. Whites tend to minimize the amount of prejudice and discrimination in society and even to talk about "reverse discrimination" in which they are the victims of government efforts to help minorities. Nevertheless, the attitudes that both flow from and support the kind of structural inequalities discussed in previous selections are far from dead.

In earlier research, Joe Feagin reported on 37 in-depth interviews with African Americans in a number of cities in various sections of the country. He found that middle-class blacks faced ongoing experiences of humiliation and discrimination in their encounters with whites. In this selection, Jerelyn Eddings calls such experiences examples of "stealth racism." He notes various kinds of stealth racism in black-white relationships.

Reference

Feagin, Joe R. 1991. "The Continuing Significance of Race: Antiblack Discrimination in Public Places." *American Sociological Review* 56: 101–16.

Focus Questions

1. What is stealth racism?

2. How does stealth racism show up in everyday experiences of African Americans?

3. What does stealth racism suggest about equality between the races?

For Roy Johnson, a senior editor at *Money* magazine, the latest indignity came after a recent dinner at a fancy restaurant in the wealthy New York City suburb where he and his family live. First the parking valet handed him the keys to his Jaguar instead of fetching the car. Then an elderly white couple came out and handed him the keys to their automobile, with the instruction: "It's a black Mercedes-Benz." Johnson responded that his own car was a black Jaguar, but the Mercedes-Benz owner didn't seem to understand. "It took him a while to realize that I was not a valet," says Johnson. "It didn't matter that I was dressed for dinner and had paid a handsome price for the meal, just as he had. What mattered was that I didn't fit his idea of someone who could be equal to him."

Such incidents, which are depressingly familiar to African-Americans of all ages, incomes and social classes, help explain why black and white attitudes often differ so starkly—not only toward the O. J. Simpson verdict and Nation of Islam leader Louis Farrakhan but also toward each other, toward the country and toward almost all of America's institutions. A recent *Washington Post* survey found that 68 percent of blacks believe racism is still a major problem in America. Only 38 percent of whites agreed.

Many Americans find the gulf between blacks and whites perplexing. After all, official racial segregation is a bad memory and 40 years of laws, policies and court decisions have helped African Americans make significant progress toward equal opportunity. Indeed, a black man born in Harlem could be the nation's next president.

Simmering Anger

But a kind of stealth racism persists, unmistakable to every black but largely invisible to many whites who are appalled by a . . . cross burning. It is evident in the everyday encounters African-Americans have with racial prejudice and discrimination, like the valet parking incident. Such encounters often strike whites as trivial misunderstandings. But they remind blacks that they are often dismissed as less intelligent, less industrious, less honest and less likely to succeed. Some insults are patently racist; others may be evidence of insensitivity or bad manners rather than racial prejudice. But the accumulation of affronts feeds the simmering anger described in books such as Nathan McCall's bestseller *Makes Me Wanna Holler* or Ellis Cose's chronicle of the injuries suffered by middle-class blacks, *The Rage of a Privileged Class.*

"What is amazing to me is the number of whites who express surprise that any of this happens," observes Mary Frances Berry, chairperson of the U.S. Commission on Civil Rights, who says she has been kept under surveillance at shopping malls and recently was forced to wait for a table at a restaurant until a group of whites who arrived after she did was seated. "We are not the melting pot we pretend to be."

"There are isolated cases of racism daily for African-Americans. I am not surprised at anything I see or hear," says Myrlie Evers-Williams, chair of the NAACP, who says a white man accidentally bumped into her in a hotel lobby on the day of the Simpson verdict and called her a "black bitch" before stomping off. "This country is saturated with examples of racism—blatant and subtle, and that is nothing new to African-Americans and it is nothing new to me."

A few stealth racism staples:

- *Taxis that never stop.* Andrew Barrett, a commissioner of the Federal Communications Commission, says that on days when he's not wearing a suit and tie but needs to catch a cab home he calls the taxi company and identifies himself to the dispatcher as a black man not wearing a suit. "If I stay for dinner late, I walk to a hotel and ask the doorman to get a cab," he says. "Quite often a driver will jump out of line to avoid taking me."

U.S. News photographer Brian Palmer phoned for a taxi to pick him up at the White House at 2 a.m. after an out-of-town trip with the president. "I called the taxi service from the Secret Service kiosk. They assured me one was coming. I stood out on the street and attempted to hail empty taxis right in front of the White House. Nothing. Over 20 cabs zipped by me," including one from the service Palmer called. Finally Palmer called back to tell the dispatcher the fare is the black man with camera equipment and press credentials around his neck. The next cab stopped.

- *Suspicious shoppers.* Thomas McCrary Jr. and a friend went bargain shopping for a new computer at a strip mall in a predominantly white suburb of Chicago. After comparing prices at different stores, they got the best buys and loaded the equipment into their car, only to be blocked by two police squad cars. The officers checked their licenses, asked about their credit cards and questioned why the two had gone to so many stores. The process took 20 minutes and left McCrary wondering, "When did it become against the law to go shopping?"

Victoria Roberts, a black lawyer from Detroit, tells a similar story about her 16-year-old daughter. A few years ago, Rachel Gehrls and four white and six black girlfriends had a slumber party at a hotel in suburban Detroit. The next morning she and three of the black girls went to the hotel gift shop for candy, but the white owner refused to serve them, complaining that there were too many people in the store and demanding that they leave. Rachel persuaded her four white girlfriends to visit the shop. The owner sold them candy with no problem.

- *Shopping slights.* Bebe Moore Campbell, author of *Brothers and Sisters*, a novel that examines racial tensions among a group of co-workers and friends, says she believes whites are in denial about prejudice in America and instances of subtle racism. "I often run into the 'What are you doing in Saks?' attitude from white salespeople, who watch me as I go around the store," she says. "At a jewelry store, they approach me early on and say, 'Well now, that costs $2,500,' as if it's just assumed that I can't afford to pay for nice things."

Campbell also describes going to a white dentist who refused to let her insurance company pay the bill, demanded payment up-front and treated her rudely. "I know these things happen to white people, too, but I doubt with the same frequency or degree of disrespect," she says. "These things begin to have a cumulative effect, until you find yourself angry and perplexed."

- *Fear of black men.* Robert Mackey, a 31-year-old accountant, got into an elevator in an Atlanta office building last August with two other black men, all on their way to work. In the instant before the door closed, a white office worker on the elevator jumped out leaving the black men stunned. "We were three well-dressed, well-groomed men going to work, and it is outrageous that this woman would act as if she was unsafe in the presence of three black men going to work," says Mackey. "I'm 5 foot 10 and 240 pounds, and I try to see myself as others see me, but I don't think a white man the same size would have been perceived as threatening."

- *Unequal service.* Margaret Bush-Ware, a professional fund-raiser who recently moved to Washington, DC, from Los Angeles, was on standby for a TWA flight from St. Louis to Los Angeles. She was next in line but watched helplessly as the airline agents put white passengers on ahead of her and four other black standbys. She missed two flights. "It was only when I finally found a black ticket agent and told her what happened that I got a flight," she says. "But I had been there all day."

- *The unwelcome mat.* Robert Lawrence, 73, is a retired deputy superintendent of education in California and one of the original Tuskegee Airmen, the first black Army Air Corps pilots. He and his wife, Ernestine, went shopping for a new home in an upscale subdivision of Santa Fe, N.M., a few months ago, but he says the agent made it clear they were not welcome. "On more than one occasion during the visit, we were made to feel, 'Why are you looking here?'"

Lawrence says. "I had the gut feeling they didn't want me there even if I could afford it."

- *No respect.* Carolyn Harraway, a third-year resident at the Medical College of Virginia, is offended every time she goes to her bank. "They refer to me as 'Carolyn' but they always call white women by their last name," she says. "I'm young, but I'm still very offended, especially because I've watched very carefully and they always call white women Mrs. or Miss or even Ms. . . . Sometimes I think it's just part of that Southern girl thing where whites think they can call African Americans anything."

- *Surprised by success.* Harriet Richardson Michel, who with her husband owns parking garages and medallion taxicabs in New York, was on vacation in Costa Rica when she was approached at poolside by a white woman from Idaho. "Oh, you speak such good English," the woman said. When Michel said she was an American, the response was amazement. "I'm just amazed that you could afford the same vacation as I can," the woman said. "Maybe being from Idaho she was less sophisticated, I don't know," says Michel. "But I think there are a lot of whites that are amazed that any of us can afford the same cars and addresses if we're not entertainers. Some may have no conscious notion of it, but some others must know how many indignities they visit upon black people every day because of their attitudes and actions."

"With the aftermath of the Simpson case we have clear documentation that we are a divided society," says Evers-Williams, whose husband, civil rights worker Medgar Evers, was murdered in Mississippi three decades ago. "Those who thought we were doing extremely well . . . are wrong." Indeed, the banality of prejudice in America today suggests that the battle for equal rights—and for better communication between whites and blacks—is far from over.

Critical Evaluation

1. The chapter gives illustrative examples of stealth racism rather than evidence from a large sample. How pervasive are such experiences?

2. Could some instances of perceived stealth racism actually be a misinterpretation of the white person's intent?

3. Does this chapter accurately portray, overstate, or understate the amount of racism which African Americans typically encounter?

Jerelyn Eddings, "The Covert Color War." In *U.S. News & World Report*, Oct. 1995. Copyright © 1995 by *U.S. News & World Report*. Reprinted by permission. ✦

26

Affirmative Action Works!

Robert C. Davidson and Ernest L. Lewis

For many years, affirmative action programs were regarded as essential for dealing with racial inequalities. In the 1990s these programs came under vigorous attack, and various states began to disband them. We have already seen a strong defense of the program in Chapter 23. The defenders believe that affirmative action programs are a necessary structural factor in the fight against inequality. These programs, they argue, require educational and business organizations to open their doors to those who have been disadvantaged by an impoverished background but who, given the chance, can carve out successful careers. Further evidence in support of the programs is offered by Robert Davidson and Ernest Lewis, who found that affirmative action had positive outcomes for minority students at the University of California, Davis School of Medicine.

Focus Questions

1. What are some arguments for and against affirmative action programs in medical schools?

2. What kind of academic progress did students admitted under affirmative action make?

3. How well did affirmative action students function in their careers?

Affirmative action admission programs have recently become increasingly controversial. The regents of the University of California recently established a new policy, by a narrow majority of the members, prohibiting the use of race as a factor in admission decisions at all the University of California campuses.[1] One argument used against affirmative action programs is that they allow less qualified applicants to be admitted. Standard preapplication test scores, such as the Medical College Admission Test (MCAT) in the case of medical education, are cited as more objective measurements of academic capability. Combined with the previous record of academic accomplishment measured by the grade point average (GPA), these 2 numerical measurements are recommended as the major or even sole criteria for admission decisions. Supporters of affirmative action programs argue that other criteria should be used in conjunction with test scores and GPAs to admit a student population with certain characteristics that are deemed to be socially important. The most common social characteristic proposed as an additional criterion for admission policies is ethnicity. Arguments for the use of ethnicity as a criterion for admission include equity as compensation for past societal discrimination as well as a utilitarian argument that these students are needed to better serve certain underserved populations. While the body of data is not large, several studies have indicated that underrepresented minority graduates from medical school are more likely to practice in areas that are medically underserved and have higher percentages of minority patients and patients without private medical insurance coverage. These studies also have documented that communities with a high percentage of minority residents are likely to be the communities where medical services are least available.[2,3,4] Thus, proponents of affirmative action support ethnicity as a positive characteristic for admission to medical school.

The debate regarding affirmative action admission policies is usually centered on the issue of ethnicity and, to a lesser extent, sex. However, admissions committees routinely use a variety of applicant characteristics beyond objective test scores and GPA. Examples of unique qualities that may influence the committee to offer admission to a candidate with lower test scores and GPA include unique life experiences, leadership qualities, evidence of overcoming barriers such as poverty or physical disability, and fluency in multiple languages. The uniqueness of ethnicity as a criterion appears to be the emotional response it engenders in many who believe that its use disadvantages majority applicants. Even the term majority becomes confusing in a state in which dynamic changes in the ethnic population will soon place the traditional non-Hispanic white in a minority position regarding population percentages.

Previous studies have addressed the validity of the use of MCAT score and GPA as predictors of medical student success.[5, 6, 7, 8] These studies confirm the positive predictive value of these measures with regard to performance in preclinical courses and in the scores obtained in the basic science portion (Part I) of the National Board of Medical Examiners (NBME) examination. This examination was the predecessor to the current US Medical Licensure Examination (USMLE). These studies confirm that students who perform better in formal examinations prior to medical school will continue to do so in medical school. However, their predictive value for success in clinical course work is less clear, and very little is known regarding their ability to predict practice competency.

The University of California, Davis, School of Medicine is 1 of 5 medical schools in the University of California system. It was founded in the mid 1960s and accepted its first class in 1968. From its inception, it has maintained a commitment to the enrollment of a diverse student population. The admission requirements for the school were set by the faculty through its executive committee and included a minimum undergraduate GPA and MCAT score. . . . An earlier affirmative action program of the school was successfully challenged in a famous reverse discrimination suit, Regents of the University of California vs Bakke.[9] Alan Bakke brought suit against the university after being denied admission to the University of California, Davis, School of Medicine. The court agreed with his complaint and ordered his admission to the school. The university appealed this decision, and the case was ultimately decided by the US Supreme Court. The "Bakke decision" declared that the school's policy of setting aside a specific number of places in its first-year class for underrepresented minority applicants was unconstitutional. However, the court's decision affirmed that race could be one of a number of applicant characteristics considered in the acceptance of students for admission. Alan Bakke was admitted to the School of Medicine in 1978 and successfully graduated with the MD degree. Since the Bakke case, the school has continued to offer admission to select applicants with certain characteristics deemed important to the admissions committee but whose MCAT score and GPA have been less than the recommended minimum and were less than that of other applicants who were not offered admission. For purposes of this study, we have labeled these students as "special consideration admissions." This cohort of special consideration admissions includes minority students admitted under a traditional affirmative action race-based preference. It also includes students with characteristics other than race that were deemed important enough to offer preferential admission despite lower objective scores. This study was designed to examine the effect of this special consideration admission policy on the composition of the student population of the school of medicine and the experience of this cohort of affirmative action and other special consideration admissions in medical school, postgraduate training, and professional activities after training.

Methods

Study Population

The special consideration admissions study population consisted of all students admitted to the University of California, Davis, School of Medicine with an undergraduate GPA of less than 3.0 (4.0 scale) and/or an MCAT average score of less than 10 for the 4 numerically reported test subscores from the entering class of 1968 through the entering class of 1987 who either graduated with the class of 1991 or earlier classes or terminated study prior to graduation. We used MCAT scoring distribution curves for the study years prior to the current scoring methods to identify comparable admissions scoring below an average of 10 or less.

Each student in the study population was prospectively matched with a student who was accepted in the same year under the regular admission criteria. The matched student was the next alphabetical name on the admissions list who was of the same sex and whose age at admission was within 2 years difference of the study subject.

Data Sources

The study consisted of 4 sections. The first of these was a review of the admissions data on all students admitted to the school during the 20-year study period. . . . The data collected in this portion of the study included undergraduate GPA, admission MCAT score defined as the highest test score prior to admission, sex of the student, age on entry to the school, and ethnicity. Ethnicity was self-reported by the applicant and cross-checked with annual reports on the student body composition to the AAMC. From this master file, the study population and matched cohort were derived.

The second part of the study was a review of the academic progress of the study and match students. Information was obtained from the individual student files maintained by the school. . . . The third part of the study consisted of a mailed evaluation questionnaire to the residency director of the program in which the graduates of both the study group and the matched control group began their postgraduate clinical training. The residency director evaluated the graduate on completion of the residency program, any evidence of academic difficulty during the program, honors accorded the graduate during the residency program, and an overall rating comparing the graduate to all other residents in the program.

The final part of the study consisted of a mailed questionnaire to the graduates in the study and control populations. Addresses were obtained from the alumni association of the school and were cross-checked with the American Medical Association Physician Master File. Information collected in this portion of the study consisted of residency and fellowship experience, other postgraduate academic training at the master's or doc-

toral level American Board of Medical Specialties certification status, professional employment characteristics, clinical practice characteristics, patient population served, health professions student teaching activities, and a satisfaction rating of their career choices to date.

Results

Admissions Data

From the school's first entering class in 1968 through the entering class of 1987, there were 1784 students admitted into the MD program. Of these students, 356 (20%) met the study criteria for a special consideration admission. . . .

The ethnicity of the study population was very different from that of regular admission students. Majority (non-Hispanic white) students constituted 74% of all entrants but only 46% of the special consideration study population. . . . There were 152 underrepresented minority applicants admitted through the special consideration process, which constituted 42.7% of all such admissions. Without the affirmative action effect of the special consideration admission process, only 58 (4.0%) of regular admission students would have been from these underrepresented minority groups. . . .

Academic Progress

For the second part of the study, the study group was compared with the matched cohort control group. The control group was analyzed to ensure that they represented the population of all students admitted under the regular admissions criteria. There was no statistical difference between the matched control population and all regular admission students when analyzed for sex, age on admission, undergraduate GPA, MCAT score, or ethnicity. Thus, the remainder of the study compared the study population with the matched control population.

The mean undergraduate GPA of the study population was 3.06 on a 4.00 scale. This was significantly lower than the 3.50 mean of the control population. The MCAT scores were also significantly lower for the study population. Students in the entering classes from 1968 through 1981 were evaluated on an earlier MCAT scoring method then in use. The study population from these years had a mean MCAT score of 544, while the control students' mean score was 613. For the entering classes beginning in 1982 through the end of the study period in 1991, the new MCAT scale was used with a range from 1 to 15. On this scale, the study population had a mean score of 9.0 while the control population had a mean of 11.0. As expected on all these measures, the study group was significantly lower as this population was defined by lower GPA and MCAT scores.

Both groups had a high rate of successful graduation from medical school, although the matched control group had a statistically significant higher rate. The study population had a graduation rate of 94% while the control group rate was 98%. The graduates of both groups had an identical mean time from matriculation to graduation of 4.2 years. However, of those students who did not graduate, the study population had a longer time from matriculation to dismissal (2.8 years) than the control group (1.7 years). . . .

To measure academic progress in medical school, the grades obtained in 2 required preclinical and 2 clinical core rotations were compared. The preclinical courses selected as representative were molecular and cell biology and pathology, and the clinical courses were the required third-year clerkships in internal medicine and surgery. In 1978, halfway through the study period, the school changed its grading procedures from a pass/fail system to a standard letter grade. To facilitate analysis, we assigned a numerical value to the pass/fail grade system with an honors grade equal to 2.0, satisfactory equal to 1.0, and failure equal to 0.0. With the exception of the pass/fail grade system on the pathology course and the surgery clerkship, all the course scores were significantly higher for the regular admission matched control population. . . .

Residency Training

The study and matched cohort group numbers were reduced for this portion of the study by entrants who did not graduate or did not elect to enter residency training. Two graduates in the study group and 10 in the matched control group elected to pursue other options such as advanced degree academic programs. Thus, 331 surveys were mailed to the residency directors of the initial postgraduate training program of the study population and 335 for the control population graduates. The overall return rate for the surveys was 76% with a 73% return rate for the study population and a 79% return rate for the control group. The percentage of graduates in both groups who completed their initial choice of residency program was identical at 82%. Most of the graduates in both groups who did not complete their initial residency program switched to another program in the same discipline or changed to a different residency discipline. One study graduate and 2 control group graduates were asked to leave their program. There was no difference between the 2 populations in residents who were identified as having academic difficulty in their program. . . . There was also no significant difference in the percentage of residents in both groups who received special honors such as best resident or chief resident. The study group had a rate of 16%, with honors, while the control group had slightly higher but not significant rate of 21%. The residency directors' evaluations of the residents' performance showed no difference in the 2 populations. . . .

The study graduates showed a similar pattern to the control group in the residency discipline they selected. The most popular selection for both groups was family practice, with 89 (25%) of the study graduates and 86 (24%) of the control group selecting this discipline. Of the study graduates, 264 (74%) chose primary care disciplines, which, for purposes of the study, we defined as family practice, internal medicine, pediatrics, obstetrics and gynecology, and rotating internships. The control group showed a similar pattern, with 270 (76%) selecting primary care residencies.

Graduate Survey

The populations for this part of the study were slightly different because of a reduction of study number by attrition. Eight of the study graduates and 5 in the control group were deceased. We could not find addresses for 14 of the graduates. Of the remaining graduates, 185 (58%) of the study group and 225 (67%) of the control group returned their surveys for an overall response rate of 63%.

Both groups showed a similar pattern of obtaining certification by their respective specialty boards. Of the study group respondents, 148 (80%) were board certified, while 187 (85%) of the control group were board certified. The most common reason given for not being board certified was the delay between completion of residency and completion of requirements for certification. Two graduates in the control group and none of the study group responded that they failed the certifying examination.

The self-described practice characteristics of the 2 groups were remarkably similar. Private practice was the most common style of practice for both groups. . . . The size of the graduates' practices, defined as number of physicians in the practice, was also similar for the 2 populations. When asked to estimate the ethnicity of their patient population, the study group estimated that 55% of their patients on average were white compared with 59% in the control group. Similarly, the study group estimated that 17% of their patients did not speak English compared with 13% in the control group. These estimated averages could not be tested by statistical measures. Both groups showed a similar pattern of involvement in health professions, student teaching activities, with 51% of the study group and 57% of the control group responding that they teach on a regular basis.

The final question of the survey asked the graduates to rate their level of satisfaction in 4 areas. Three of these related to their professional career to date and the fourth to a more general satisfaction rating of their life. There was no difference between the study graduates and the control group graduates on their satisfaction level for their decision to pursue medicine as a career, their choice of a medical specialty, and their current practice. However, when asked to rate their overall satisfaction with their life, the study graduates responded that they were more satisfied than the control graduates.

Comment

This study was prompted in large part by a controversial decision of the Board of Regents of the University of California to bar ethnicity as a criterion for admission at all their schools and campuses. Our purpose was to study the effect of a special consideration admission process that used ethnicity as one criterion at one of the medical schools of the University of California on the composition of the students admitted to the school and to follow these students through the longitudinal process of medical education, postgraduate residency training, and their professional activities after training. . . .

Since our criteria for inclusion in the study population did not include ethnicity, we expected some special consideration admissions not to be ethnic minorities. We were surprised to find that nearly half of the special consideration admissions were not from minority groups. However, the affirmative action intent of the special consideration admissions process is evident in the finding that 75% of all underrepresented minority admissions came through the special consideration process. The records of the admissions committees did not allow identification of the factors other than ethnicity that were used in granting special consideration admissions. The fact that affirmative action has become the controversial issue should be viewed in the context that many other characteristics are routinely factored into admission decisions.

Although there was a difference in graduation rates between the study students and the matched control students, the 94% graduation rate of the special consideration admission students confirmed that the admissions committee was able to accurately predict success in the ability of the applicants to complete the academic requirements for graduation. In our experience, it is not uncommon in the discussion of the admissions committee that an applicant will be viewed as an outstanding individual but his or her ability to meet the rigorous academic workload and content of medical education will be questioned by some. Comments are often made that we do not want to do a disservice to the applicant by admission to a program in which they are likely to fail. At this medical school, the process worked well to produce an ethnically and experientially diverse population with a high probability of successfully completing medical school.

The differences found in the study between the special consideration admission students and the regular admission students were more prominent in the basic science courses in the first and second years of the curriculum. The clinical courses in the third year of the curriculum continued to show differences but the 2 populations began to merge in their achievements in class work and test scores. After graduation, the residency experiences of the 2 populations were quite similar, with both population equally likely to receive honors evaluations and no detectable difference in academic difficulty in their residency training program. By the time they had completed residency, the practice characteristics of the 2 populations were nearly identical. Thus, there appears to be a convergence of academic progress between the special consideration admission physicians and their regular admission colleagues as the process of their training lengthens. There is also a convergence in career decisions and practice characteristics between the 2 populations.

This study will not stop the debate regarding affirmative action programs. We have shown that a special consideration admissions process with a major emphasis on cultural diversity in the student population at one school of medicine has been very successful in selecting students with the academic capability to succeed in medical school and provide a student population with broad cultural diversity.

Notes

1. Affirmative Action: Undergraduate Admissions and Graduate and Professional School Admissions: Special Report 1 to the Regents of the University of California Committee on Educational Policy and the Special Committee on Affirmative Action Policies. Oakland: University of California Office of the President; 1995.

2. Davidson R, Montoya R. The distribution of services to the underserved: a comparison of minority and majority medical graduates in California. West J Med. 1987; 146:114-117.

3. Moy E, Bartman BA. Physician race and care of minority and medically indigent patients. JAMA. 1995; 173:1515-1520.

4. Komaromy M, Grumbach K, Drake M, et al. The role of black and Hispanic physicians in providing health care for underserved populations. N Engl J Med. 1996; 334:1305-1310.

5. Mitchell KJ. Traditional predictors of performance in medical school. Acad Med. 1990; 65:149-158.

6. Hall FR, Bailey MA. Correlating students undergraduate science GPAs, their MCAT scores, and the academic caliber of their undergraduate colleges with their first-year academic performances across five classes at Dartmouth Medical School. Acad Med. 1991; 67:121-123.

7. Hall ML, Stocks MT. Relationships between quality of undergraduate science preparation and preclinical performance in medical school. Acad Med. 1995; 70:230-235.

8. Meleca CB. Traditional predictors of academic performance in a medical school's independent study program. Acad Med. 1995; 70:59-63.

9. Regents of the University of California v. Bakke, 438 US 265.

10. Council on Graduate Medical Education. Council on Graduate Medical Education, Second Report: The underrepresentation of minorities in medicine. Washington, DC: U.S. Dept of Health and Human Sevices; 1990. DHHS Pulication HRS-P-DM 90-1.

11. American Medical Association, Instituions, Programs and Issues. Washington, DC: Association of American Medical Colleges; 1992:9.

Critical Evaluation

1. The authors base their study on one medical school. Would research on all medical schools yield similar results? Why or why not?

2. No data were gathered on patient evaluations of their physicians. How would affirmative-action physicians compare with other physicians if patients evaluated them?

3. Would additional data underscore the continuing need for affirmative-action programs? For example, are minority physicians more likely to serve minority populations?

Robert C. Davidson and Ernest L. Lewis, "Affirmative Action Works!" In *Journal of the American Medical Association* 178, pp. 1153–9. Copyright © 1997 by the American Medical Association. Reprinted by permission. ✦

Project for Personal Application and Class Discussion: Race and Ethnicity

The materials in this section focus on various troublesome aspects of race and ethnic relations in the United States. You need to know about such things. The editors believe there is also value in taking a positive look at the issue of race and ethnicity. Let us celebrate our commonalities and our diversity.

First, think about our commonalities. Independent of race or ethnicity, in what ways are Americans alike? Make a list of values, aspirations, and beliefs that you think are typical of Americans whatever their race or ethnic background.

Second, celebrate diversity. Think about the major racial and ethnic groups in the United States: European Americans, African Americans, Hispanic Americans, Asian Americans, and Native Americans. Make a list of what you believe are the distinctive contributions and strengths of each of these groups.

If possible, share your thoughts with members of racial or ethnic groups different from your own. As a result, you may want to modify your list.

Whenever you encounter someone from another race or ethnic group, use your list to remind yourself of your commonalities and of the distinctive contributions and strengths of such people. Does the reminder make a difference in how you initially feel about that person and how you initially relate to him or her? ✦

Poverty

More than 36 million Americans live in poverty (U.S. Bureau of the Census 1997:476). Although poverty afflicts all types of Americans, percentages are disproportionately high for women (particularly single mothers) and minorities. In terms of numbers, there are more poor whites than poor African Americans or Hispanics. But the percentages are much higher for African Americans and Hispanics than for whites.

Poverty affects the totality of life; the poor have less of everything valued in American society. And this economic deprivation has negative consequences for their overall well-being. For example, three researchers studied over 1,000 economically-marginal adults in California (Lynch, Kaplan, and Shema 1997). Not all of these adults were below the poverty line, but all were in the lower income brackets. The researchers found that their subjects suffered physically, psychologically, and mentally because of their economic hardship. Compared to those with higher incomes, the subjects were more likely to have problems with such activities as cooking, shopping, and managing money, and were more likely to be clinically depressed.

This section explores a number of issues surrounding poverty and efforts to alleviate it. The issues necessarily include the nonpoor as well as the poor: as Chapter 1 pointed out, the recipients of most government welfare are not poor individuals but U.S. corporations.

References

Lynch, John W., George A. Kaplan, and Sarah J. Shema. 1997. "Cumulative Impact of Sustained Economic Hardship on Physical, Cognitive, Psychological, and Social Functioning." *New England Journal of Medicine* 337:1889–1895.

U.S. Bureau of the Census. 1997. *Statistical Abstract of the United States*. Washington, DC: U.S. Government Printing Office. ✦

27

Images of Poverty: The Disreputable Poor

Judith A. Chafel

Negative attitudes toward the poor are an important social psychological factor that help
perpetuate poverty by casting blame on the
poor themselves. After all, if the poor are responsible for their situation, why should the
rest of society feel any responsibility for helping
them? Judith Chafel reviews research over the
past three decades and finds that the poor have
been, and continue to be, disparaged by large
numbers of nonpoor. These attitudes are found
in children as well as adults, and they support
inaction on behalf of the poor.

Chafel draws on research that shows that
these negative attitudes are not consistent with
the data we have on poverty and the poor. She
also points out some structural and social psychological changes that are needed for a realistic attack on the problem.

Focus Questions

1. What, according to adults, are the
   causes of poverty?

2. What do these adult beliefs affect support for social welfare policies?

3. What do children believe about the
   causes and cure of poverty?

In the United States today, a large proportion
of children and families live in poverty. In
1992, the most recent year for which estimates are available, 21.1 % of all related children younger than age 18 in families and 25%
of those younger than age 6 were poor (U.S.
Bureau of the Census, 1993). Over the past
decade and a half, these numbers have risen.
In the next few years, unless specific steps are

taken to alleviate poverty, the proportion of
poor children is expected to remain high
(Scarbrough, 1993).

Why are so many children and families in
the United States today impoverished? The
reasons for economic privation are varied
and complex (Bianchi, 1993). One factor that
has contributed to its persistence emanates
from existing societal images of the poor. To
explain, poverty is a social reality that profoundly influences a large number of lives. As
individual members of society seek to understand the reasons for its existence, they form a
conceptual framework (cognitive metatheory)
through which they perceive experience, and
their attitudes and actions are influenced by
the causal view of poverty that they adopt
(Hartman, 1984; Kluegel & Smith, 1986).
These conceptions shape society's response
to the problem (Blank, 1989; Cook & Barrett,
1992; Corcoran, Duncan, Gurin, & Gurin,
1985; Hartman, 1984; Kluegel & Smith,
1986), and negative images (e.g., "the undeserving poor") serve to restrict the formation
of a viable policy designed to ameliorate the
aversive effects of poverty (Blank, 1989, p.
158; Feagin, 1975; Hendrickson & Axelson,
1985; Kluegel & Smith, 1986). Of the many
factors influencing support for social welfare
policy, images of program recipients have a
decided and important effect (Cook & Barrett, 1992).

This article reviews literature on the conceptions that children and adults have about
poverty. Adult findings are analyzed first to
provide a context for illuminating the child
findings. The latter are emphasized for three
reasons. First of all, the ideas of children have
received only scant attention and have not
been systematically analyzed by comparison
with those of adults. Second, when children
are consistently socialized into beliefs early
in their lives, these beliefs form a perspective
that is resistant to change (Kluegel & Smith,
1986). Third, the beliefs of children indicate
whether existing societal ideas are being perpetuated into the next generation. If societal
images of poverty inaccurately characterize
the poor and constrain policy on their behalf,
then it is imperative to influence these misconceptions when they are most amenable to
change. . . .

Research on Adult Conceptions

Historical Roots

Feagin (1975) explained that negative images of the poor have historical roots. Medieval Christianity espoused an ethic of "benevolent paternalism" toward the indigent, but it was replaced by the "usually harsh, morality of Protestantism" with its work ethic (p. 15). Hard work was highly valued, and those unwilling to engage in it were believed to demonstrate a "lack of grace" (p. 22). Economic inequality was viewed as being dictated by God and necessary due to differences in human character and virtue. Both the cause and cure of poverty, then, resided with the individual. Achievement-oriented values such as these have been widely espoused throughout our country's history (Feagin, 1975).

The ideology of individualism, as Feagin (1975, p. 34) explained, received further affirmation during the 19th century with the adoption of the evolutionary ideals of Social Darwinism (namely, the struggle for survival, survival of the fittest). The ideals corresponded well with the entrepreneurial expansion of the nation as it exploited resources and developed industry. Beliefs included the assumption that the best would compete successfully against their opposition, and that social and economic inequality resulted when the superior were rewarded with success, the inferior with failure. Fierce competition was natural, poverty inevitable, and government was not to meddle with the system (Feagin, 1975). As Feagin put it, social Darwinism "further sanctified the work ethic," shifting the source of its legitimacy from God to the laws of nature (pp. 36-37). Similarly, the conditions of the American frontier contributed to the development of this belief system by making essential for survival "a dependence on individual effort, and self-reliance" (p. 37). Historically, then, as Feagin's analysis points out, an ethos of individualism, a work ethic, and a view that the poor require moral reform has influenced American thinking about poverty.

Beliefs About Causes

In an article aptly titled "Poverty: We Still Believe That God Helps Those Who Help Themselves," Feagin (1972) presented findings of a nationwide survey conducted in 1969 that examined American attitudes toward poverty. Findings indicated that a majority of Americans sampled believed that the poor themselves were responsible for their plight. When asked about the causes of poverty, about half of the sample offered individualistic reasons (e.g., lack of effort, loose morals), fewer emphasized structural ones (e.g., low wages, exploitation by the rich), and the number of fatalistic reasons (e.g., bad luck) varied greatly. Half of the lowest and highest income groups scored high with respect to individualistic factors; those in between were somewhat more likely to do so (Feagin, 1975). Greater weight was assigned to both structural and fatalistic reasons by the low-income group than the affluent one; the other groups offered responses in between the two extremes (Feagin, 1975).

Drawing on a national survey and other available data sets to examine the basic beliefs held by Americans about social and economic inequality, Kluegel and Smith (1986) obtained findings consistent with those of Feagin (1972, 1975). Their data were collected in 1980 through interviews conducted with a large nationally representative sample of respondents 18 years of age and older. The results were comprehensively analyzed in a variety of ways; only selected findings are presented here.

First, the beliefs of participants about perceived economic opportunity were assessed. Percentage distributions indicated that approximately 70% of the respondents replied affirmatively to the statement that "everyone who works hard can get ahead" (Kluegel & Smith, 1986, p. 44), whereas about 90% perceived opportunity with respect to themselves even more positively, considering it to be the same as or better than the average American. When asked to rate the opportunity to get ahead for various socioeconomic groups, 83% believed that children of the rich have an edge over the average person; most rated children of the working class as having an equal chance; and most considered the poor, Blacks, and women as having equal or better opportunity. Whereas a substantial margin regarded education as the most effective way of attaining economic advancement, a majority of respondents failed to believe that everyone has an equal chance of securing a higher education.

Second, the beliefs of respondents about causal explanations for a variety of economic outcomes were analyzed. . . . When asked about the causes of poverty, Kluegel and Smith's (1986) respondents considered individual factors much more important than structural ones. Fifty percent considered the individualistic items (e.g., lack of effort, ability, talent; lack of thrift and proper money management skills) as being very salient, whereas 34% considered the structural ones (e.g., wages, jobs, schools) to be very salient. Detailed over-time comparisons revealed that in the more than a decade of time that had elapsed since Feagin's (1972) study, the ranking of reasons for poverty was virtually unchanged.

Kluegel and Smith (1986) . . . found structuralist rather than individualistic causes espoused by low-income respondents. From their data, they concluded that sociodemographic factors predicted the former more than the latter, which are far more widely ascribed to across social strata. Structural beliefs, when they are espoused, tend to result in what Kluegel and Smith (1986) termed compromise images (e.g., "the idea that barriers to opportunity exist but can be overcome by strenuous individual efforts") (p. 101). In other words, they are appended to the prevailing ideology; they do not supplant it.

Summary

To sum up, there is considerable agreement reflected in the above findings about the beliefs of adults concerning the causes of poverty. Poverty was attributed more to individual than to societal factors by participants in both studies reviewed in this section. When structural barriers to opportunity were acknowledged in the case of Kluegel and Smith's (1986) study, such recognition did not significantly alter the belief that "everyone who works hard can get ahead" (p. 44). Causal attributions for poverty did not shift from the individual to society. Instead, as Kluegel and Smith (1986) pointed out, the admission resulted in compromise images.

Overall, these findings reflect an unflattering view of the poor as morally deficient and personally responsible for their plight. That so much agreement is to be found in these studies is indicative of the degree of consensus with which prevailing societal views about poverty are held.

Support for Social Welfare Policy

Not surprisingly, given their beliefs about the causes of poverty, Feagin's (1972) respondents were disinclined to endorse new social policy to alleviate poverty. When Feagin (1972) asked them to evaluate public assistance programs for the poor, a plurality of respondents showed themselves to be antiwelfare. The probability of holding an unfavorable view of welfare climbed as income rose. Individualistic explanations of poverty and antiwelfarism were positively correlated; antiwelfarism and structural explanations were negatively related. When questioned about a guaranteed-job plan and a guaranteed-income plan as possible ways to alleviate poverty, nearly two thirds of the respondents supported the former, but this number was reduced to half when participants' commitment was assessed by asking them whether they would endorse it, even if it meant higher taxes. Lower income groups displayed the most inclination to favor the remedies. The measures were less likely to be supported by those scoring high on individualistic explanations of poverty than those scoring low; but the opposite was true for respondents espousing structural or fatalistic explanations.

Surprisingly, when asked whether poverty would ever be eradicated, three quarters of the respondents advocated "an all-out Federal effort to get rid of poverty" (Feagin, 1972, p. 108). In Feagin's (1972) words, "Apparently ending poverty is like finding truth—an unattainable but worthy goal" (p. 108). Overall, Feagin concluded that the attitudes and values illuminated in his survey served to sustain the status quo.

Kluegel and Smith (1986) also examined the views of their respondents concerning redistributive types of social policy for the poor. Government-guaranteed jobs for all persons willing to work was supported by 47% and guaranteed incomes for all workers was supported by 61% of their respondents. Of the policies surveyed, the least favored was welfare, with none of its items receiving a majority of positive responses. Stereotypes of welfare recipients as "lazy" and "dishonest about their need" were supported by 70% to 80% of the respondents (p. 152). The welfare items were the same as those asked by Feagin in his (1972) survey. By comparison with Feagin's findings, the 1980 data, as Kluegel and Smith pointed out, showed respondents as more likely to agree that too much money was expended on it and to say that those on welfare did not attempt to work to support themselves. But respondents also believed that welfare did not afford its recipients sufficient support. That finding, as well as the one pertaining to the dishonesty of welfare recipients, differed little from 1969. Overall, one can discern from these findings that Kluegel and Smith's respondents appeared to be even more antiwelfare than those sampled by Feagin (1972). . . .

An implicit assumption behind individualistic explanations of poverty reflected in the above findings is that only those worthy of assistance should be supported by social welfare. A study by Cook and Barrett (1992) extended Feagin's (1972, 1975) and Kluegel and Smith's (1986) work by directly examining so-called recipient deservingness as an explanation for program support. Cook and Barrett drew on a nationally representative sample of the public at large as well as a smaller representative sample of members of Congress. Data were collected through interviews conducted in 1986. Findings revealed that their respondents (the public and members of Congress) viewed program recipients as deserving and supported social welfare policy on their behalf. The data were comprehensively analyzed; only selected results are reported here.

First, the beliefs of the public were assessed. Participants were asked to respond to the following statements about recipients of Aid to Families with Dependent Children (AFDC), Medicaid, and Social Security (all federally funded social programs) (Cook & Barrett, 1992): First, "most people now receiving [benefits] really need the [benefit] provided"; and second, "most people who get [the benefit] have no sources of income other than government benefits" (p. 97). More than half of the respondents agreed with the first statement (expressing less agreement for AFDC than the other programs); and half or more replied affirmatively to the second (with AFDC once again showing the least agreement). Then, participants were presented with assertions designed to assess the following: (a) whether recipients were accountable for their need, (b) desired independence, and (c) employed their benefits wisely. Most disagreed with the first statement; an overwhelming majority agreed with the second statement; and, finally, the last statement elicited the most divergence. In each case, AFDC was viewed the least favorably. But as Cook and Barrett (1992) put it, "There is no universal belief that AFDC recipients are undeserving" (p. 102). To sum up, respondents generally viewed program recipients positively, although their support of AFDC was less than that expressed for the other programs.

Cook and Barrett (1992) found that five aspects of deservingness (needing benefits, possessing no other sources of assistance, taking personal responsibility for need, desiring independence, and employing benefits wisely) were important variables in predicting public support for AFDC and Medicaid, although this was not the case for Social Security, whose support was shaped by only three of the above aspects. The three aspects affecting support for all three programs listed in order of influence were recipient need, desire for independence, and wise employing of benefits. Demographic characteristics of the participants sampled (age, education, gender, income, and race) were examined to ascertain whether they confounded these findings, but they were not predictive of the data. One significant result (among the few mentioned) is that the poor were more supportive of all three programs than the more affluent, not a surprising finding and one consistent with Feagin's (1972) and Kluegel and Smith's (1986) data showing rising support of welfare as income declined.

These findings are not directly comparable with those of Feagin (1972) and Kluegel and Smith (1986). Different questions were asked of participants and the views respondents expressed may have differed accordingly. But these results do suggest a possible shift in public attitudes about those participating in social welfare programs. Like the earlier studies, public skepticism of welfare is apparent.

Members of Congress were also questioned concerning their beliefs about recipient deservingness, and its relationship to support for programs was studied. Because the question format differed between the two groups (the public and members of Congress), the data, as Cook and Barrett (1992) pointed out, are not entirely comparable. Recipient deservingness was employed as a justification for federally funded public assistance programs (AFDC, Medicaid) by approximately half but for social insurance programs (Social Security, Medicare) by only a third of the respondents. Need was the most frequently cited aspect of recipient deservingness; it was mentioned by about two thirds of the respondents employing deservingness as a justification for their support of public assistance programs. Nearly all comments made by respondents about deservingness as a justification were positive, and need was declared to be valid by every respondent citing it.

As Cook and Barrett (1992) emphasized in the conclusion to their study:

> When recipients are seen as being in need, as having no other sources of help, as wanting to be independent, and as not being at fault for their condition, support will be forthcoming. Support for public assistance programs depends a great deal on images of program recipients. (p. 212)

Both sets of respondents (the public at large and members of Congress) subscribed to this view. . . .

Building on the work of Cook and Barrett (1992), Will (1993) drew on . . . a nationally representative sample to analyze public perceptions of the poor and circumstances when they are perceived to be deserving of public assistance. To ascertain respondents' perceptions of need as being legitimate or not legitimate, they were asked to respond to various vignettes illustrating hypothetical families requiring government support.

Although Will's (1993) respondents discriminated between the circumstances portrayed in the vignettes, they supported public assistance, even when need was not entirely legitimate. They believed that the poor deserve a minimally acceptable standard of living, but their perceptions of deservingness influenced levels of support. They were most supportive when problems appeared to be extrapersonal or structural in nature—that is, stemming from conditions outside immediate control (e.g., large family composition, a father's physical disability) and not easily amenable to personal volition. Greater generosity was elicited for those families seeking to better their circumstances than those who were not. As Will (1993) put it, "all families 'deserve' support, but some are more deserving than others, depending on the extent to which an honest effort is being made" (p. 317).

Summary

In sum, findings of the four studies just critiqued agree as well as disagree. Both Feagin's (1972) and Kluegel and Smith's (1986) research illustrate that societal conceptions of the causes of poverty are linked with support for social welfare policy. Of the causes of poverty surveyed, individualistic conceptions were more popular than any other. Participants espousing individualistic conceptions were more reluctant than those holding structural views to support a variety of measures to alleviate poverty. By contrast, Cook and Barrett's (1992) findings suggest a possible shift in public attitudes toward the poor—namely, a greater willingness to endorse policy on their behalf. But like the studies just cited, their data underscore the significance of deservingness as an explanation for program support. So does Will's (1993) study, which examined specific circumstances under which the poor are seen to be deserving. The participants in that study adhered to a belief in a minimally acceptable standard of living for those in poverty, but their perceptions of recipient worthiness influenced levels of support. Viewed as a whole, these findings indicate that a predisposition to impute personal responsibility for poverty shapes as well as restricts support for social welfare policy.

Conceptions of Justice

Of the studies cited so far in this review, only Kluegel and Smith (1986) evaluated their participants' beliefs about the justice of economic inequality. This was done in two ways: in principle and in fact. When asked about economic inequality in principle, percentage distributions showed (a) that respondents believed that the unequal ability and talents of people cause income inequality and it cannot be altered, (b) that disparity of wealth prompts hard work, and (c) that human nature dictates that some will inevitably desire to possess more than others. They rejected the notion of need as the basis for a just appropriation of income among all who contribute equally to society. Income inequality was viewed positively by respondents, but a considerable number also believed that equality was beneficial. Somewhat over half of them agreed that greater equality would bring about a more conflict-free society. . . .

From their analyses, Kluegel and Smith (1986) concluded that actual economic inequality was viewed less fairly by those of lower socioeconomic status than others and that there were fewer socioeconomic differences in beliefs about the justice of economic inequality in principle than those in fact. . . .

Summary

In sum, the findings of Kluegel and Smith (1986) about adult conceptions of justice reflect support for a social system characterized by economic inequality. A number of beliefs are highlighted in the data reviewed in this section: first, the inevitability of economic inequality; second, its usefulness for society; third, the need to "control one's own outcomes by one's own efforts," to borrow Kluegel and Smith's (1986, p. 114) words; and finally, equity as the basis for allocating societal resources. These beliefs are all consistent with findings cited earlier. They provide a rationale for adhering to the status quo, mitigating against any meaningful social change on behalf of the poor.

Conclusions

The literature just reviewed spans nearly a quarter of a century from 1972 to 1993. "During that time, the nation experienced a social revolution (e.g., the Civil Rights Movement, the War on Poverty) that profoundly influenced popular thinking about issues, such as wealth and privation, and the incorporation of disenfranchised groups into the mainstream" (Chafel, 1995). Nonetheless, an ideology of individualism prevailed in American society. That ideology emphasized a number of beliefs: first, the personal responsibility of each individual for his or her place in life; second, the opportunity afforded by the "system" to improve one's circumstances; third, the social utility of economic inequality in motivating achievement; and finally, the existing system as equitable and fair (Kluegel & Smith, 1986). The causes of poverty were seen by the American public as being individualistic in nature, and support for social welfare policy reflected a punitive attitude toward the poor as being deserving of their plight. Work by Feagin (1972) and Kluegel and Smith (1986) support this view. At the same time, the work of Cook and Barrett (1992) and Will (1993) suggest that whereas Americans adhere to recipient deservingness as "a controlling concept of social welfare" (Cook & Barrett, 1992, p. 37; cited in Macarov, 1978, p. 98), they also espouse a social right's perspective, believing that the poor are worthy of assistance as dictated by some degree of need, a point that is corroborated by some of Kluegel and Smith's data. Finally, not all socioeconomic groups are equally sanguine about the system, those of lower socioeconomic status view it less fairly than others (Cook & Barrett, 1992; Feagin, 1972; Kluegel & Smith, 1986). . . . In sum, the findings reviewed here reveal a substantial degree of support for the status quo.

Stated differently, they reflect little, if any, dissent against the status quo. Conspicuously absent is any shared vision of social possibilities other than what already exists. Concepts opposing those described are necessary if the existing social order is to be challenged: in place of poverty's inevitability, the ability of society to remedy it; rather than its utility, its destructiveness; instead of an ethos of individualism ("every woman for herself"), a sense of community; and, finally, as a substitute for the fairness of economic privation, its injustice. These conceptions diverge radically from those espoused. . . .

Research on Children's Conceptions

Do children of elementary school age or younger have beliefs about poverty? The answer is yes. Even children as young as preschool age are conscious of social and economic inequality in society, although the ideas they display are quite embryonic. As children grow older, their concepts take on greater complexity; they are also parallel to adult views (Chafel, 1995). The work cited here supports these assertions (Furby, 1979; Harrah & Friedman, 1990; Leahy, 1981, 1983a, 1983b; Ramsey, 1991; Simmons & Rosenberg, 1971).

Early Awareness

Ramsey (1991) examined whether preschoolers are cognizant of social class differences. The children studied were White, 3-, 4-, and 5-year-olds, equally drawn from low- and middle-socioeconomic status families. They were shown photographs of rich and poor people and asked to classify them. Respondents did not spontaneously talk about social class; but they did correctly identify rich and poor when they were asked. Open-ended descriptions of the people depicted in the pictures revealed that there were only two class-related attributes cited by Ramsey's participants: attire (by 27%) and job (by 25%).

Employing a Piagetian framework and the methodology of a clinical interview, Leahy (1981) investigated children's conceptions of wealth and poverty. Participants ranged in age from 5 to 18 years and were representative of upper-, upper middle-, middle-, working-, and lower-class families. They were asked about questions describing people who are rich (poor) and commenting about their similarities and differences. The descriptions offered by Leahy's (1981) respondents varied with age. Typical responses of the youngest children pertained to peripheral conceptions (appearances, behaviors,

possessions). Illustrative examples provided by Leahy (1983b) are, "The rich 'have clothes . . . money . . . food to eat,' whereas the poor 'don't have no food to eat . . . they don't have a place to live' " (p. 96). The comments of older respondents referred to psychological or sociocentric ideas (traits, thoughts; life chances, class consciousness). Examples of the former include these: "The rich are 'smart' . . . they have 'different personalities' . . . poor people are 'lazy. They are poor because they don't want to work' " (p. 96). Finally, sociocentric concepts were reflected by such comments as "poor people 'are not being recognized as part of the system. They are neglected, ignored, treated wrong' " (p. 96). . . .

Summary

In sum, studies by Ramsey (1991) and Leahy (1981) verify that children of elementary school age or younger are cognizant of social and economic inequality in society. Even as young as preschool age, they are able to discern rich and poor as different and to recognize a few observable class-related attributes. As they grow older, they become more perceptive of rich and poor as being members of society belonging to different social strata. Leahy's (1981, 1983a) studies, based on the methodology of a clinical interview, present data documenting that the ideas of older children are qualitatively different from those of younger ones.

Beliefs About Causes

As one might expect, children's understandings about the causes of poverty become increasingly more sophisticated with age. Whereas preschoolers are aware of wealth and poverty, Ramsey (1991) found only a limited comprehension of the nature and causes of economic inequality among the sample of children she studied. Most respondents were unable to say "why some people had more money than others" (p. 78). When responses were made, the children's understandings reflected concrete monetary transactions ("They [the poor people] forgot to go to the store to get their money") (p. 79).

In his comprehensively conceived study, Leahy (1983a, 1983b) analyzed the explanations that his (1981) respondents gave for wealth and poverty. Participants were asked, for example, "Why are some people rich, while others are poor?" (Leahy, 1983a, p. 113). The youngest participants (6 to 11 years of age) were unable to think causally about class differences. . . . For example, a characteristic reply was, "Because they have more money (or no money)" (Leahy, 1983a, p. 114). Older participants (11 to 14 years of age) displayed more complex ideas . . . they believed that economic inequality emanated from individual merit; that is, from differences that people displayed with respect to the level of education they attained, the effort they set forth, the work undertaken by them, or the intelligence they possessed. Similarly, people could better their circumstances as a result of equity factors (work, effort, education, investment). For example, they said that "poor don't have jobs. Rich have good jobs" (Leahy, 1983a, p. 114). . . . Because an equity conception was increasingly employed by participants with age, irrespective of social class, Leahy (1990) concluded that his respondents adhered to "a belief in a just world where the 'losers' are viewed as obtaining their just due" (p. 119).

Leahy's (1983a, 1983b) findings are consistent with those of Harrah and Friedman (1990) and Furby (1979). Harrah and Friedman asked middle-class children, ages 8, 11, and 14, about the causes of wealth and poverty. The researchers cautioned that the findings they obtained may not be generalizable inasmuch as the small sample of children they studied resided in a small community afflicted by economic hardship. Yet, the similarity of their results to Leahy's (1983a, 1983b) data suggests that the former do have some generality. Effort was mentioned by 55 of the 87 respondents as the main cause of wealth and poverty. Personal factors, such as ability, intelligence, and effort, were frequently cited by children in the sample as an explanation for unemployment.

Furby (1979) asked White participants from a middle- and upper middle-class location about reasons for the unequal distribution of wealth. The replies provided by them revealed variations with age in their understandings. When asked about why some possess more than others, the youngest children (kindergarten, 2nd, and 5th graders) uttered as major reasons differences pertaining to the availability of money, the passive acquisition of possessions, and preferences and needs. These factors were cited by the children as major reasons for the ownership of more possessions. By 11th grade, respondents' replies reflected (with moderate frequency) more active acquisition of wealth as a causal factor for economic inequality; that is, their statements displayed the belief that "some people work hard and achieve," an equity conception (Furby, 1979, p. 187). With age—that is, by 11th grade—they became increasingly cognizant of the inevitability of economic inequality, perceiving it to be beyond individual control due to factors related to the environment or to chance. Findings for adults in Furby's (1979) sample are consistent with the developmental trend for adolescents just noted, although inheritance (i.e., passive acquisition of possessions) was also mentioned with moderate frequency. The adults also gave circumstances beyond individual control as one of two most often cited reasons for economic inequality. That the oldest participants in Furby's (1979) study stressed external factors as causes of economic inequality contrasts with work cited earlier by Feagin (1972, 1975) and Kluegel and Smith (1986) and may possibly be explained by the fact that the latter research drew on nationally representative samples of respondents across various socioeconomic groups, whereas the former did not.

Simmons and Rosenberg (1971) did not question children directly concerning their beliefs about the causes of economic inequality, but they did ask them about their understandings of equality of opportunity. Third- to 12th-grade children residing in a large, metropolitan area, "heavily Negro" (to use the researchers' words), and somewhat more representative of the working class, were queried about whether all American children "have the same chance to grow up and get the good things in life" (p. 239). Not every child was able to respond to the question; 70% of the children of elementary school age who did answered negatively. Socioeconomic, racial, or ethnic disadvantage was given as an explanation by some participants in Simmons and Rosenberg's sample as to why some children are not granted an equal opportunity. With age, the children became increasingly able to reply, again conveying their skepticism that equal opportunity existed for all. These findings differ from those of Kluegel and Smith (1986) cited earlier. In that study, adult respondents replied affirmatively to the statement (by Kluegel & Smith, 1986) that "everyone who works hard can get ahead" (p. 44). The different findings may possibly be explained by the different way that the questions in the two studies were asked.

When participants in Simmons and Rosenberg's (1971) study were asked about their own life chances, they were optimistic, regardless of their socioeconomic status and age; and with age, their aspirations rose. One reason why the children possibly were more sanguine about themselves is that they were unaware of their own social class identification—when asked, only 15 % of the elementary school-age children knew what the term *social class* meant and tended to rate themselves higher than the class to which they belonged. Thus, the children's optimism may have stemmed from a lack of social awareness. . . . At any rate, the children's optimistic view of their own life chances resembles Kluegel and Smith's (1986) findings on adults, noted previously.

To highlight just a few of their results with respect to socioeconomic differences, Simmons and Rosenberg (1971) found that barriers to opportunity were discerned by more advantaged than disadvantaged children of elementary school age. Both groups of children became more class conscious with age, but variations appeared according to status: Black and working- or lower-class children were less aware than Whites and middle-class ones. These findings as well as those pertaining to the children's optimistic view of their life chances serve to mitigate against the emergence of class conflict. If those with less to gain from the existing order are less aware of its social barriers, and participants are optimistic at every age and socioeconomic level about their life chances, then support is provided for the status quo (Simmons & Rosenberg, 1971).

Summary

To sum up, the findings indicate that young children have only a vague understanding of the reasons for economic inequality. But children do engage in causal thinking about class differences. Surprisingly, the ideas of older children resemble adult concepts, as equity is increasingly employed with age to explain economic inequality. That children draw on equity as an explanation for wealth and poverty represents a consistent finding across several studies (Furby, 1979; Harrah & Friedman, 1990; Leahy, 1983a, 1983b, 1990), although Furby (1979) also noted an increasing awareness with age of factors beyond individual control. Viewed as a whole, these results point to the pervasiveness with which a dominant ideology about poverty exists in American society and the efficacy of the socialization process.

Ideas About Alleviating Poverty/Notions of Justice

Like adults, children do cognize about ways to remedy economic hardship and think about social justice. Leahy (1983a) asked his participants, "What would have to happen so that there would be no poor people?" and "Should some people be rich, while others be poor?" (p. 113). Lacking causal reasoning to explain wealth and poverty, the youngest children displayed an egocentric view of the economy, believing that it functioned to serve the child's interests or that it acted on behalf of the poor (Leahy, 1990). These views are exemplified by the statements, " 'You can go to the bank and ask them for money' " or " 'The waiter could give me money' " (p. 117). One could better one's circumstances in this way. Possessing more advanced ideas, older children believed that social mobility occurs as a result of equity. They employed equity conceptions to justify economic inequality (e.g., the poor could better themselves by working hard and securing education and jobs), and the principle of equality to oppose it (e.g., social change could occur when the wealthy shared their resources). With even more sophisticated ideas, the oldest of Leahy's (1990) respondents increasingly spoke about altering the system as a way of dealing with poverty but acknowledged the difficulty of doing so. Their comments highlighted class conflict, or its fruitlessness. But, as Leahy (1990) pointed out, use of sociocentric ideas to challenge poverty was rare; equity continued to characterize responses at this level.

According to Leahy (1983a, 1990), there was more evidence for agreement than disagreement with the existing social system, although the findings, as he pointed out, unequivocally confirmed neither notion (Chafel, 1995). Evidence for the legitimacy of economic inequality derived, for example, from the increasing use with age of equity conceptions and infrequent allusion to external-structural factors as causes of wealth and poverty (namely, race and the political and social system) (Leahy, 1983a). By adolescence, fatalistic justifications for poverty increased (e.g., "There's always going to be poor people—that's human nature") (Leahy, 1990, p. 116). As Leahy (1990) put it, "The fatalism of inequality is not based on a view that classes would actively resist change; rather, it reflects a view that human nature and complex society require stratification" (pp. 116-117). Evidence for the illegitimacy of economic inequality stemmed, for example, from the higher likelihood of middle-class participants drawing on equity to account for poverty more than other classes and the lesser fatalism of some groups (e.g., Blacks, working-class males) about the certitude of economic inequality (Leahy, 1983a). But, as Leahy (1983a, 1990) emphasized, broad consensus existed by socioeconomic status in the children's conceptions and little class consciousness appeared to be reflected in the data. . . .

Furby's (1979) participants were asked the question, "How do you feel about some people having a lot more things than other people?" (p. 192). . . . To summarize Furby's (1979) findings, kindergarten and second graders found it difficult to offer evaluative judgments in reply to the question. Nonevaluative sentiments expressed by the children included "the deprivation and unhappiness of those with less, the fact that

those with more are well-off, and a norm of sharing (sharing either does or should occur)" (p. 193). Some second graders communicated explicit indifference to the unequal distribution of wealth, a neutral evaluative judgment. Most of the replies elicited from the fifth-grade children were nonevaluative, but they more readily evaluated than the younger children, including in their negative responses (which were more frequent than positive ones) the hardship and unhappiness experienced by those less well-off, along with a norm of equality. Their nonevaluative statements reflected the idea that inequality entails waste, along with sentiments similar to those of the second graders.

Also worthy of note here are Furby's (1979) findings pertaining to high school-age youth and adults. When they were asked how they felt about the unequal distribution of possessions, the high schoolers offered more evaluative judgments than the younger children but, like the younger children, expressed more negative than positive statements. Differential work ("some people work harder than others") (Furby, 1979, p. 194) represented the salient positive evaluation offered by respondents of this age. By comparison, adults offered a more equal distribution of positive and negative evaluations and more frequently expressed indifference to inequality than the younger age groups. Positive judgments expressed by the adults included differential work and ability and the legitimate accumulation of different quantities of belongings. These findings for adults are consistent with those of Kluegel and Smith (1986) noted earlier; both sets of results reflect endorsement of the existing social order.

Summary

To sum up the findings reviewed in this section, children do possess ideas about ways to alleviate poverty and have rudimentary notions of justice. Increasingly with age, equity conceptions are employed to explain economic inequality and to account for social mobility (Furby, 1979; Leahy, 1983a, 1983b, 1990). With age, children become increasingly accepting of poverty and view it as an inevitable aspect of the social system (Leahy, 1990). According to Leahy (1983a), external structural factors (such as race and the political and social system) are infrequently mentioned as causes of wealth and poverty. Once again, these conceptions mirror adult views about poverty.

Conclusions

Like the work cited earlier on adults, the literature just reviewed spans nearly a quarter of a century, from 1971 to 1991. That work is sparse, but it does confirm that children primarily of elementary school age or younger do have conceptions about wealth and poverty. Further, as one might expect, their understandings become qualitatively different with age (Leahy, 1981, 1983a, 1983b, 1990). With age, children increasingly draw on equity conceptions to explain and justify poverty (Furby, 1979; Leahy, 1981, 1983a, 1983b, 1990) and to account for social mobility (Leahy, 1983a, 1983b, 1990). They consider economic inequality legitimate (Leahy, 1990) and perceive it to be an inevitable aspect of the social system (Furby, 1979; Leahy, 1990). Sociodemographic variables influence children's ideas about social and economic inequality, but their effect is not profound: Across varying socioeconomic strata, children agree more than they disagree (Leahy, 1981, 1983a, 1983b, 1990; Simmons & Rosenberg, 1971) The absence of competing class perspectives reflected in the children's ideas attests to their allegiance to the status quo (Leahy 1983a, 1983b, 1990; Simmons & Rosenberg, 1971).

Contrasting Images

Although sparse, when viewed as a whole, the studies just cited reveal remarkable consistency in the thinking of adults and children about poverty. To borrow Leahy's (1983b) query, "Could one imagine that as children or adolescents become more similar to adults in age that they would become less like adults in their social concepts?" (p. 89). Like adults, children come to view poverty as emanating from individual differences in merit. Moreover, like them, the ideas of some about social justice and ways to remedy economic privation are generally consistent with the causal

views of equity they hold about poverty. These beliefs belie the facts.

The Panel Study of Income Dynamics Findings

To illustrate briefly, Corcoran et al. (1985) tracked the economic status of a nationally representative sample of low-income individuals over a 10-year period (from 1969 to 1978). The Panel Study of Income Dynamics (PSID) investigated the nature, extent, and duration of long-term poverty among these families. The data contradicted the notion that poverty results from individual psychological attributes of the poor. Corcoran et al. (1985) found that "the characteristics of the persistently poor do not conform to the conventional wisdom" (p. 516). The study (Corcoran et al., 1985) asked, "Do the poor differ from the non-poor in the components of motivation measured in the study? Do these components of motivation cause people to enter or remain in poverty, or to become or remain dependent on welfare?" (p. 527). Briefly, the PSID data showed that first, psychological dispositions did not appear to precipitate poverty; second, whereas the poor may be dissimilar from the nonpoor on some personality and motivational measures, these variations seem to stem from their economic status; third, subsequent achievement (either within or across generations) was not influenced by the motivational and psychological attributes assessed by the study; and finally, there was only a weak relationship found between the poverty/welfare status of parents and their children. As a result of their findings, Corcoran et al. (1985) concluded that antipoverty policy should focus not on the psychological dispositions of the poor but on events and their consequences (e.g., family composition changes, labor market events).

Diversity of the Poverty Population

In her 1989 article, Blank argued that the term the poor, although suggestive of a cohesive population, denotes a group characterized by great diversity. The causes of poverty vary from subgroup to subgroup within the population (e.g., the elderly, women with children). According to Blank, the dominant images of poverty that characterize the thinking of many Americans about poverty simply are not consistent with demographic data on the poor. As she advised, "The emphasis in this country on encouraging the poor to work harder ignores evidence that the vast majority of the poor either cannot participate in the labor market, are already looking for more work and not finding it, or are already working full-time" (p. 160). Acknowledging that some subset of the poor may be "less industrious" than the rest of society, she emphasized that the notion was definitely not tenable for the vast majority of those afflicted by economic hardship (p. 166).

The Working Poor

Citing data based on the 1988 Current Population Survey reported by Bane and Ellwood (1989), Chafel (1993) has explained that of two-parent families living in poverty, approximately 45% have a full-time worker year-round. Of those with two healthy parents, more than 50% have at least one worker. Furthermore, data from the 1991 Current Population Survey reported by Lamison-White (1992) verified that in 1990, nearly 45.4% of poor female-headed families with children worked, as compared with 69.4% of nonpoor female-headed families with children (Chafel, 1993). The chief reason for not working provided by both groups was family responsibility (Chafel, 1993).

A Job Ceiling

Ogbu (1978) has employed the concept of a job ceiling to describe the inferior position of many groups, which he refers to as "castelike minorities" (p. 29), in our society. According to Ogbu, these minorities are prevented from competing freely for employment and are largely restricted to the least desirable occupations. Occupations above the job ceiling are more worthwhile with respect to pay, prestige, and other benefits, whereas those below are less so. Data support Ogbu's interpretation that discrimination acts as a barrier to advancement for some groups. To illustrate briefly, the poverty rate differs by race and ethnicity: for Whites, 11.6%; for persons of Hispanic origin (any race), 29.3%; and for Blacks, 33.3% (1992 figures, U.S. Bureau of the Census, 1993). Further, some groups are more likely to exit out of poverty than others: Between 1990 and 1991, 23.3 % of Whites, 17.4% of Blacks, and 14.3% of Hispanics; and to enter into poverty: in 1991, 2.5% of Whites, 6.5% of Blacks, and 8.3% of Hispanics (U.S. Bureau of the Census, 1993).

In sum, evidence provided by these sources suggests that the responsibility for poverty does not entirely belong to the poor themselves. As a causal explanation for poverty, the predisposition for blaming the victim so prevalent in American society and reflected in the literature on the conceptions of adults and children about poverty reviewed here is not supported by the facts. Instead, much of the responsibility for poverty belongs elsewhere: namely, with social structural factors and barriers to opportunity.

Empirical and Pedagogical Implications

Viewing poverty as a self-inflicted condition ignores the social forces that give rise to poverty, and policy premised on this assumption will inevitably be misguided (Ryan, 1984). By deflecting attention away from the real causes, existing societal images of poverty (blaming the victim) leave the problem unresolved (Ryan, 1984). The inequity of capitalism as an economic system, as suggested earlier, is responsible in part for the problem of poverty (*World Book Encyclopedia* 1994). Acknowledging that inequity exists shifts the responsibility for poverty away from the individual to society at large and implies the need for economic reform, which is essential in a variety of areas: to designate a few, national income and welfare policy, employment, and education. The economic status quo works well for some members of our society, who have a stake in preserving it and adhere to beliefs that support it. The difficulty of dismantling conceptions of poverty that serve the interests of a powerful segment of our society should not be underestimated, although such a revision may be necessary to affect any meaningful social change.

Ethical considerations warrant an attempt to revise existing images about the poor. If prevailing images inaccurately characterize the economically dispossessed and affect them in negative ways, then society has an obligation to challenge these misconceptions (Blank, 1989). From the perspective of child development, at least two avenues of activity can be pursued: (a) examining the processes whereby children are socialized into conventional ways of thinking about economic privation and (b) designing educational interventions to counter stereotypes about poverty. . . . Pursuing the activities suggested next will not solve the problem of poverty, which is exceedingly complex; they should only be construed as a part of a much larger whole.

Socialization

First, understanding the origins of these beliefs may enable us to change them. What socialization factors are the acquisition of negative stereotypes about poverty, and how do socialization and cognition interact to explain the "developmental pathway and departures from it" (McLoyd, 1990, p. 338)? Prime sources of enculturation are parents, peers, school settings, and the media. What messages are being conveyed by these sources, and how do children interpret them (Ramsey, 1991)? Do socialization processes vary for children of different socioeconomic status and, as McLoyd has suggested, ethnicity? In what ways does direct experience with wealth and poverty shape children's perceptions?

To elaborate, what role do peers play in the socialization process? Hall and Jose (1983) have raised the question of "whether a child's peers corroborate, oppose, or exert little influence on the acquisition of a coherent belief system about equality from the adult culture" (p. 254). Ethnographic studies conducted in socioeconomically diverse classroom settings can provide rich descriptive portrayals of the dynamics of school life and investigate the extent to which pressure is exerted by peers to adopt certain views.

Similarly, the content of children's literature should be examined. What do books at various age levels (e.g., picture books for young children) say about poverty? Are the images presented accurate, varied, and posi-

tive? Do they broaden understandings or promote stereotypes? Do they encourage cultural conformity in thinking about the poor or stimulate divergent points of view?. . . .

Education

Second, educational experiences should be created to counter prevailing stereotypes about the poor, although such intervention is likely to engender controversy inasmuch as it is designed to challenge the status quo. Whereas the potential for controversy should not discourage educators from pursuing this step, they should be aware of its disputatious nature and duly prepared for any conflict that might arise. Angry parents may surface to contest ideas that run counter to their own about poverty and those of the children they socialize.

The objective of any course of study should be to help children think critically about poverty and the existing economic system. Important topics to address in the design of curricula concern such basic questions as, What causes poverty? Is it inevitable and just? Can it be alleviated? What obligations does it entail for society? and What kinds of economic and social remedies are desirable (Hartman, 1984)? Through a variety of experiences (e.g., field trips, simulations, and role-plays) children can be educated to broaden their perspectives and acquire more favorable constructs about those who live in poverty and their circumstances. . . .

Conclusion

This article has reviewed literature on the conceptions that children and adults have about poverty. What emerges from the review is a portrait of a society content with the status quo, whereby a predisposition to blame the victim provides moral justification for the disenfranchisement of millions from the economic mainstream. There is remarkable similarity in the thinking of adults and children about poverty, with both displaying conformist ways of thinking about the poor. Whether the problem of poverty is resolved depends, at least in part, on developing ideologies that question negative stereotypes and that counter rather than legitimate the status quo. Individualistic explanations must be replaced with structural ones that acknowledge the need for economic reform. Contemporary misconceptions that inaccurately depict the poor and limit policy on their behalf should be challenged when they are most amenable to change: during childhood.

References

Bane, M. J., & Ellwood, D. (1989). "One Fifth of the Nation's Children: Why Are They Poor?" *Science* 245, 1047-1053.

Bianchi, S. (1993). "Children Of Poverty: Why Are They Poor? In J. Chafel (ed.), *Child Poverty and Public Policy* (Pp. 91-125). Washington, DC: Urban Institute Press.

Blank, R. (1989). "Poverty and Policy: The Many Faces of the Poor." In C. R. Strain (ed.), *Prophetic Visions And Economic Realities* (Pp. 156-168). Grand Rapids, MI: Erdman.

Chafel, J. (1993). "Conclusion: Integrating Themes About Child Poverty in Search of a Solution." In J. Chafel (ed.), *Child Poverty and Public Policy* (Pp. 327-345). Washington, DC: Urban Institute Press.

Chafel, J. (1995). "Children's Conceptions of Poverty." In S. Reifel (ed.), *Advances in Early Education and Day Care* (vol. 7). Greenwich, CT. JAI.

Children's Britannica (vol. 4). (1989). Chicago: Encyclopedia Britannica.

Cook, E, & Barrett, E. (1992). *Support for the American Welfare State: The Views of Congress and the Public*. New York: Columbia University Press.

Corcoran, M., Duncan, G., Gurin, G., & Gurin, P. (1985). "Myth and Reality: The Causes and Persistence of Poverty." *Journal of Policy Analysis and Management* 4, 516-536.

Feagin, J. (1972). "Poverty: We Still Believe that God Helps Those Who Help Themselves." *Psychology Today* 6, 101-110, 129.

Feagin, J. "Subordinating the Poor." Englewood Cliffs, NJ: Prentice Hall.

Furby, L. (1979). "Inequalities in Personal Possessions: Explanations for and Judgements about Unequal Distribution." *Human Development* 22, 180-202.

Furby, L., Harter, S., & John, K. (1975). The Nature and Development of Possession and Ownership: A Cognitive-Attitudinal Study of 5- to 21-Year-Olds (Monograph 15, No. 4). Oregon Research Institute.

Hall, W., & Jose, P. (1983). "Cultural Effects on the Development of Equality and Inequality." In R. Leahy (ed.), *The Child's Construction of Social Inequality* (Pp. 253-285). New York: Academic Press.

Harrah, J., & Friedman, M. (1990). "Economic Socialization in Children in a Midwestern American Community." *Journal of Economic Psychology* 11, 495-513.

Hartman, R. (ed.). (1984). *Poverty and Economic Justice*. New York: Paulist.

Hendrickson, R., & Axelson, L. (1985). "Middle-Class Attitudes Toward The Poor: Are They That Changing?" *Social Service Review* 59, 295-304.

Hoggart, R. (ed.). (1992). *Oxford Illustrated Encyclopedia of Peoples and Cultures*. New York: Oxford University Press.

Kluegel, J., & Smith, E. (1986). *Beliefs about Inequality: Americans' Views of What Is and What Ought to Be*. New York: Aldine De Gruyter.

Lamison-White, L. (1992). "Income, Poverty, and Wealth in The United States: A Chart Book." In *U.S. Bureau of the Census, Current Population Reports* (Series P-60, No. 179). Washington, DC: Government Printing Office.

Leahy, R. (1981). "The Development of the Conception of Economic Inequality: I. Descriptions and Comparisons of Rich and Poor People." *Child Development* 52, 523-532.

——. (1983a). "Development of the Conceptions of Economic Inequality: II. Explanations, Justifications, and Concepts of Social Mobility and Change." *Developmental Psychology* 19, 111-125.

——. (1983b). "The Development of the Conception of Social Class." In R. Leahy (ed.), *The Child's Construction of Social Inequality* (Pp. 79-107). New York: Academic Press.

——. (1990). "The Development of Concepts of Economic and Social Inequality." *New Directions for Child Development* 46, 107-120.

Macarov, D. (1978). *The Design of Social Welfare*. New York: Holt, Rinehart & Winston.

Mcloyd, V. (1990). "The Impact of Economic Hardship on Black Families and Children: Psychological Distress, Parenting, and Socioemotional Development." *Child Development* 61, 311-346.

Ogbu, J. (1978). *Minority Education and Caste: The American System in Cross-Cultural Perspective*. New York: Academic Press.

Ramsey, P. (1991). "Young Children's Awareness and Understanding of Social Class Differences." *Journal Of Genetic Psychology* 152, 71-82.

Ryan, B. (1984). "Blaming the Victim." In R. Hartman (ed.), *Poverty and Economic Justice* (Pp. 173-187). New York: Paulist.

Scarbrough, W. (1993). "Who Are the Poor?: A Demographic Perspective." In J. Chafel (ed.), *Child Poverty and Public Policy* (Pp. 55-90). Washington, DC: Urban Institute Press.

Simmons, R., & Rosenberg, M. (1971). "Functions of Children's Perceptions of the Stratification System." *American Sociological Review* 36, 235-249.

U.S. Bureau Of The Census. (1993). Current Population Reports, Series P60-185, *Poverty In The United States 1992*. Washington, DC: Government Printing Office.

Will, J. (1993). "The Dimensions of Poverty: Public Perceptions of the Deserving Poor." *Social Science Research* 22, 312-332.

World Book Encyclopedia. (vol. 3). (1994). Chicago: World Book.

Critical Evaluation

1. Do adults and children still hold the attitudes described by Chafel? Why or why not?

2. How would a political conservative respond to this chapter? A political liberal?

3. How adequate and practical are the author's suggestions for changing existing images of the poor?

28

A Profile of the Working Poor

Samantha Quan

Some well-to-do Americans criticize the poor for not working themselves out of poverty. They assume that if a person is poor, he or she is able to work but refuses to do so. But a great many poor Americans do work. In this selection, Samantha Quan provides detailed information about the kind of people who comprise the working poor. Her profile underscores some of the structural factors involved, including lack of education, wage differentials between occupational categories, family structure, and the labor market.

This selection shows the inadequacy of simplistic solutions to poverty, such as "let them work." Those who attribute poverty to a lack of motivation or laziness not only unfairly malign the poor but hinder the development of programs and policies that could help people out of their poverty.

Focus Questions

1. How many Americans are working but poor?

2. What kind of education and occupation do the working poor have?

3. What kind of labor market problems adversely affect the working poor?

In 1996, 36.5 million persons, 13.7 percent of the population, lived at or below the official poverty level. Although the Nation's poor were primarily children and adults who were not in the labor force, 1 in 5, or 7.4 million persons were classified as "working poor." This level was about the same as in 1995. The working poor are individuals who spent at least 27 weeks in the labor force (working or looking for work), but whose income fell below the official poverty threshold. The poverty rate—the ratio of the working poor to all persons in the labor force for at least 27 weeks—was 5.8 percent, little changed from the 5.9 percent reported in 1995. (See table A.)

A majority of the working poor (58 percent) usually worked full time, although full-time work substantially lowers a person's probability of being poor. Among persons in the labor force for 27 weeks or more, the poverty rate for those usually employed full time was 4.1 percent compared with 12.4 percent for usual part-time workers. Only 5 percent of the working poor were actively looking for a job for more than 6 months in 1996, but ended up not working at all.

Table A
Poverty Status of Persons and Primary Families in the Labor Force for 27 Weeks or More, 1994–96
(Number in Thousands)

Characteristic	1994	1995	1996
Total persons[1]	124,303	126,020	128,320
in poverty	7,660	7,484	7,421
Poverty rate	6.2	5.9	5.8
Unrelated individuals	23,622	24,207	25,539
In poverty	2,322	2,312	2,423
Poverty rate	9.8	9.5	9.5
Primary families[2]	56,789	57,262	58,087
In poverty	4,111	4,008	4,084
Poverty rate	7.2	7.0	7.0

1. Includes persons in families, not shown separately.
2. Primary families with at least one member in the labor force for more than half of the year.

This report presents data on the relationships between labor force activity and poverty in 1996 for individual workers and their families. The data were collected in the March 1997 supplement to the Current Population Survey, a nationwide monthly survey of about 50,000 households conducted by the Bureau of the Census for the Bureau of Labor Statistics. . . .

Demographic Characteristics

Of all persons in the labor force for at least 27 weeks during 1996, slightly more women than men were poor (3.8 and 3.6 million, respectively). The poverty rate was much higher for working women, however, as fewer

Table B

**Persons in the Labor Force for 27 Weeks or More Who Worked During the Year: Poverty
Status by Occupation of Longest Job Held, 1996
(Numbers in Thousands)**

Occupation	Persons who worked	Total below poverty level	Poverty rate
Total who worked	127,486	7,037	5.5
Percent	100.0	100.0	
Service occupations	13.4	29.	12.3
Technical, sales, and administrative support	29.4	23.0	4.3
Operators, fabricators, and laborers	14.5	20.6	7.8
Other occupations	42.7	26.5	3.4

of them were in the labor force for more than half of the year. Specifically, the proportion of working women living in poverty during the year (6.5 percent) remained relatively unchanged from 1995, while that for men fell by 0.4 percentage point to 5.2 percent.

Although nearly three-fourths of the working poor were white workers, black and Hispanic workers continued to experience poverty rates that were more than twice the rates of whites. White working women and men in the labor force for more than half of the year were about equally likely to be poor. By contrast, black working women had a poverty rate of 14.2 percent—almost twice the rate of black working men (8.6 percent). As in earlier years, younger workers were most vulnerable to being poor, particularly minority teenagers. High poverty rates among younger workers largely reflect the lower earnings and higher rates of unemployment associated with having relatively little education and work experience.

Educational Attainment

In general, the risk of living in poverty falls rapidly as individuals attain higher educational levels. Out of all persons in the labor force for at least half of 1996, those with less than a high school diploma had a higher poverty rate (16.2 percent) than high school graduates (6.3 percent). Workers with an associate degree or 4-year college degree reported the lowest poverty rates, 3.2 and 1.5 percent, respectively. Poverty rates generally are higher for black workers than for white

workers at both higher and lower education levels.

Poverty rates of white men and women were fairly similar at all educational levels; however, among black men and women, there were marked disparities, especially at lower education levels. The poverty rate for black women workers with less than a high school diploma was 30.6 percent compared to 18.1 percent for black men. Moreover, among high school graduates, the poverty rate of black women (18.0 percent) was almost twice that of black men (9.3 percent). Among college graduates, these differences disappear.

Occupation

During 1996, nearly three-fourths of the working poor were employed in one of the following three occupational groups: service; technical, sales, and administrative support; or operators, fabricators, and laborers. (See table B.) Persons employed in managerial and professional specialty occupations had the lowest probability of being poor. In all occupational groups, women are generally more likely than men to be poor, and blacks are more likely to be below the poverty level than whites.

The poverty rate for those employed in service occupations was 12.3 percent. Female service workers had a higher poverty rate than did their male counterparts. Household service workers (i.e., housekeepers, childcare workers, and cooks), almost all of whom were women, had a poverty rate of 21.8 percent. Protective service providers, such as firefighters, policeman, and guards, two-thirds of whom were men, reported a poverty rate of only 3.6 percent. The poverty rate among service providers other than private household or protective—which includes bartenders, waiters and waitresses, dental assistants, janitors, and hairdressers—was 13.2 percent. Although the number of white service providers living in poverty was more than twice that of blacks, the overall poverty rate for black service providers was 6.6 percentage points higher than that for whites (17.7 versus 11.1 percent).

The number of women employed in technical, sales, and administrative support occupations was nearly twice that of men. This was due largely to the fact that women outnumbered men by over 3 to 1 in administrative support occupations. In technical and sales occupations, the proportion of working men and women was relatively equal. The poverty rates for women and men employed in administrative support occupations were about the same at 3.2 and 3.1 percent, respectively; similarly, there were no marked disparities between the rates for working women and men in technical occupations (2.5 versus 1.8 percent). However, the poverty rate for women employed in sales occupations was nearly two and a half times more than their male counterparts, largely because women tend to hold very different types of sales jobs than men. In fact, the earnings difference between men and women in sales is larger than it is in any other major occupational group.

Approximately 8 percent of operators, fabricators, and laborers in the labor force for 27 weeks or more were poor. Although the total number of men in these occupations outnumbered women by 3 to 1, the poverty rate for women was 3 percentage points higher (10.1 versus 7.1 percent). Similarly, while three fourths of the working poor in these occupations were white, their poverty rate was 4.5 percentage points lower than that for blacks (7.1 versus 11.6 percent).

Workers in managerial and professional specialty occupations reported the lowest rate of poverty (1.6 percent). About 580,000 out of the 36.7 million persons employed in managerial and professional specialty occupations had incomes below the poverty level. Of those, 302,000 were in professional specialty occupations, such as engineers, architects, scientists, and teachers. Pre-kindergarten and kindergarten teachers had a particularly high poverty rate (7.9 percent) among professional workers.

Family Structure

In 1996, nearly 4.1 million families lived below the poverty level despite having at least one member in the labor market for 27 weeks or more, little changed from the 1995 total. Of these, nearly half were families maintained by women. The poverty rate for families—the ratio of poor families with workers to all families with workers—was 7.0 percent in 1996, the same as that reported in 1995.

The poverty rate for families with just one member in the labor force was over seven times more than that of families with two or more members in the workforce (14.6 versus 1.9 percent). Families maintained by women with only one member in the labor force were nearly two times more likely to be poor than were such families maintained by men. Married-couple families with two or more members in the labor force had the lowest poverty rate (1.6 percent).

The poverty rate was even higher in families with children. The poverty rate for families with children under age 18 that were maintained by a woman, who was the sole supporter, was 26.6 percent in 1996. Similarly, families maintained by men had a 13.7-percent poverty rate. Married-couple families with children had a poverty rate of only 6.0 percent, similar to the 1995 rate.

Working women who were the sole supporters of their families had the highest poverty rate in 1996 (20.2 percent), more than twice the rate for their male counterparts (9.4 percent). Workers in married-couple families were the least likely to be poor; in fact, working wives reported the lowest rate of poverty, 1.9 percent in 1996. Working husbands had a rate of 3.9 percent.

Unrelated Individuals

In 1996, 25.5 million unrelated individuals were in the labor force for more than half the year; of those, 2.4 million lived below the poverty level. Unrelated individuals are those persons who live by themselves or with others not related to them. Their poverty rate was 9.5 percent in 1996, the same as in 1995.

Teenagers were most vulnerable to being poor; in 1996, more than half of the teenagers living on their own or with others not related to them lived below the poverty level. The poverty rate was higher for women than for men (10.7 versus 8.5 percent). The number of white unrelated individuals living in poverty far exceeded the number of blacks or Hispanics; however, the poverty rates for the latter two groups were 12.4 and 18.0 percent, respectively, compared with only 9.1 percent for whites.

Of the 2.4 million unrelated individuals who lived below the poverty level, 67.1 percent lived with others. These individuals reported a poverty rate more than twice that of individuals who lived alone. Many unrelated individuals with below poverty earnings may live with others out of necessity. Conversely, many of those who live alone do so because they have sufficient incomes to support themselves. However, unrelated individuals' poverty status is determined by each person's resources. The pooling of resources and sharing of expenses may allow some individuals in this category who are technically classified as poor to live above the poverty level.

Labor Market Problems

Three primary labor market problems frequently experienced by workers whose incomes fall below the poverty threshold are: unemployment, low earnings, and involuntary part-time employment. . . . Among those who participated in the labor force for more than half the year and usually worked in full-time wage and salary positions, 3.9 million, or 3.9 percent, lived in poverty in 1996, little changed from the prior year. This analysis is restricted to full-time wage and salary workers.

Nearly 90 percent of the working poor that usually worked full time experienced at least one of the major labor market problems in 1996. Low earnings continued to be the most common problem; 7 in 10 poor workers were subject to low earnings alone, or in combination with other labor market problems. Nearly 40 percent of the working poor experienced unemployment, either alone or in combination with other problems. Only 6.2 percent of the working poor experienced all three problems—low earnings, unemployment and involuntary part-time work.

Some 488,000 of these working poor, or 12.5 percent, did not experience any of the three labor market problems in 1996. Their poverty status may be associated with other factors, including short-term employment, some weeks of voluntary part-time work, or a family structure that increases the risk of poverty.

Critical Evaluation

1. What would be the economic consequences of requiring employers to pay all workers wages sufficient to keep them out of poverty?

2. Since female-headed families have the highest rate of poverty of any group, shouldn't more attention be paid to preventing family breakup than to wages?

3. What kinds of governmental and educational action to reduce poverty are suggested by this chapter?

Samantha Quan, *A Profile of the Working Poor, 1996.* U.S. Department of Labor, Washington, DC: Government Printing Office, 1997. ✦

29

Education as a Weapon in the Hands of the Restless Poor

Earl Shorris

Workfare was a reaction, in part, to the frustration of many Americans with the failure of welfare and other government programs to eradicate poverty. People continue to search for the answer to the problem. But because the causes of poverty are many and varied, the solution is not likely to be found in any single program or effort. Rather, innovative new measures must be sought and tried. Earl Shorris describes one such effort that originated with the observation of a poor woman. As he realized, it is not the answer for all the poor. But it made a remarkable difference in the lives of some.

Although Shorris did not investigate exactly what went on with the people helped by the program, it is reasonable to assume at least one crucially important social psychological factor: the program somehow engendered hope in those who previously could see none. The deprivations and dilemmas associated with living in poverty can result in learned helplessness, a condition in which people believe that they cannot make a difference in themselves or their situations no matter what they do. Consequently, they no longer try to bring about change, convinced that all efforts are pointless. Whatever breaks people out of learned helplessness thereby enables them to take the steps necessary to improve their situation.

Focus Questions

1. What is meant by a "moral alternative to the street?"

2. What kind of innovative program did the author set up at The Door?

3. How did the program affect the participants?

Next month I will publish a book about poverty in America, but not the book I intended. The world took me by surprise—not once, but again and again. The poor themselves led me in directions I could not have imagined, especially the one that came out of a conversation in a maximum-security prison for women that is set, incongruously, in a lush Westchester suburb fifty miles north of New York City.

I had been working on the book for about three years when I went to the Bedford Hills Correctional Facility for the first time. The staff and inmates had developed a program to deal with family violence, and I wanted to see how their ideas fit with what I had learned about poverty.

Numerous forces—hunger, isolation, illness, landlords, police, abuse, neighbors, drugs, criminals, and racism, among many others—exert themselves on the poor at all times and enclose them, making up a "surround of force" from which, it seems, they cannot escape. I had come to understand that this was what kept the poor from being political and that the absence of politics in their lives was what kept them poor. I don't mean "political" in the sense of voting in an election but in the way Thucydides used the word: to mean activity with other people at every level, from the family to the neighborhood to the broader community to the city-state.

By the time I got to Bedford Hills, I had listened to more than six hundred people, some of them over the course of two or three years. Although my method is that of the bricoleur, the tinkerer who assembles a thesis of the bric-a-brac he finds in the world, I did not think there would be any more surprises. But I had not counted on what Viniece Walker was to say.

It is considered bad form in prison to speak of a person's crime, and I will follow that precise etiquette here. I can tell you that Viniece Walker came to Bedford Hills when she was twenty years old, a high school dropout who read at the level of a college sophomore, a graduate of crackhouses, the streets of Harlem, and a long alliance with a brutal man. On the surface Viniece has remained as tough as she was on the street. She speaks bluntly, and even though she is HIV positive and the virus has progressed during her time in prison, she still swaggers as she walks down the long prison corridors. While in prison, Niecie, as she is known to her friends, completed her high school requirements and began to pursue a college degree (psychology is the only major offered at Bedford Hills, but Niecie also took a special interest in philosophy). She became a counselor to women with a history of family violence and a comforter to those with AIDS.

Only the deaths of other women cause her to stumble in the midst of her swaggering step, to spend days alone with the remorse that drives her to seek redemption. She goes through life as if she had been imagined by Dostoevsky, but even more complex than his fictions, alive, a person, a fair-skinned and freckled African-American woman, and in prison. It was she who responded to my sudden question, "Why do you think people are poor?"

We had never met before. The conversation around us focused on the abuse of women. Niecie's eyes were perfectly opaque—hostile, prison eyes. Her mouth was set in the beginning of a sneer.

"You got to begin with the children," she said, speaking rapidly, clipping out the street sounds as they came into her speech.

She paused long enough to let the change of direction take effect, then resumed the rapid, rhythmless speech. "You've got to teach the moral life of downtown to the children. And the way you do that, Earl, is by taking them downtown to plays, museums, concerts, lectures, where they can learn the moral life of downtown."

I smiled at her, misunderstanding, thinking I was indulging her. "And then they won't be poor anymore?"

She read every nuance of my response, and answered angrily, "And they won't be poor no *more.*"

"What you mean is—"

"What I mean is what I said—a moral alternative to the street."

She didn't speak of jobs or money. In that, she was like the others I had listened to. No one had spoken of jobs or money. But how could the "moral life of downtown" lead anyone out from the surround of force? How could a museum push poverty away? Who can dress in statues or eat the past? And what of the political life? Had Niecie skipped a step or failed to take a step? The way out of poverty, was politics, not the "moral life of downtown." But to enter the public world, to practice the political life, the poor had first to learn to reflect. That was what Niecie meant by the "moral life of downtown." She did not make the error of divorcing ethics from politics. Niecie had simply said, in a kind of shorthand, that no one could step out of the panicking circumstance of poverty directly into the public world.

Although she did not say so, I was sure that when she spoke of the "moral life of downtown" she meant something that had happened to her. With no job and no money, a prisoner, she had undergone a radical transformation. She had followed the same path that led to the invention of politics in ancient Greece. She had learned to reflect. In further conversation it became clear that when she spoke of "the moral life of downtown" she meant the humanities, the study of human constructs and concerns, which has been the source of reflection for the secular world since the Greeks first stepped back from nature to experience wonder at what they beheld. If the political life was the way out of poverty, the humanities provided an entrance to reflection and the political life. The poor did not need anyone to release them; an escape route existed. But to open this avenue to reflection and politics a major distinction between the preparation for the life of the rich and the life of the poor had to be eliminated.

Once Niecie had challenged me with her theory, the comforts of tinkering came to an end; I could no longer make an homage to the happenstance world and rest. To test Niecie's theory, students, faculty, and facilities were required. Quantitative measures would have to be developed; anecdotal information would also be useful. And the ethics of the experiment had to be considered: I resolved to do no harm. There was no need for the course to have a "sink or swim" character; it could aim to keep as many afloat as possible.

When the idea for an experimental course became clear in my mind, I discussed it with Dr. Jaime Inclan, director of the Roberto Clemente Family Guidance Center in lower Manhattan, a facility that provides counseling to poor people, mainly Latinos, in their own language and in their own community. Dr. Inclan offered the center's conference room for a classroom. We would put three metal tables end to end to approximate the boat-shaped tables used in discussion sections at the University of Chicago of the Hutchins era,[1] which I used as a model for the course. A card table in the back of the room would hold a coffeemaker and a few cookies. The setting was not elegant, but it would do. And the front wall was covered by a floor-to-ceiling blackboard.

Now the course lacked only students and teachers. With no funds and a budget that grew every time a new idea for the course crossed my mind, I would have to ask the faculty to donate its time and effort. Moreover, when Hutchins said, "The best education for the best is the best education for us all," he meant it: he insisted that full professors teach discussion sections in the college. If the Clemente Course in the Humanities was to follow the same pattern, it would require a faculty with the knowledge and prestige that students might encounter in their first year at Harvard, Yale, Princeton, or Chicago.

I turned first to the novelist Charles Simmons. He had been assistant editor of *The New York Times Book Review* and had taught at Columbia University. He volunteered to teach poetry, beginning with simple poems, Housman, and ending with Latin poetry. Grace Glueck, who writes art news and criticism for *The New York Times*, planned a course that began with cave paintings and ended in the late twentieth century. Timothy Koranda, who did his graduate work at MIT, had published journal articles on mathematical logic, but he had been away from his field for some years and looked forward to getting back to it. I planned to teach the American

history course through documents, beginning with the Magna Carta, moving on to the second of Locke's Two Treatises of Government, the Declaration of Independence, and so on through the documents of the Civil War. I would also teach the political philosophy class.

Since I was a naif in this endeavor, it did not immediately occur to me that recruiting students would present a problem. I didn't know how many I needed. All I had were criteria for selection:

- Age: 18–35.

- Household income: Less than 150 percent of the Census Bureau's Official Poverty Threshold (though this was to change slightly).

- Educational level: Ability to read a tabloid newspaper.

- Educational goals: An expression of intent to complete the course.

Dr. Inclan arranged a meeting of community activists who could help recruit students. Lynette Lauretig of The Door, a program that provides medical and educational services to adolescents, and Angel Roman of the Grand Street Settlement, which offers work and training and GED programs, were both willing to give us access to prospective students. They also pointed out some practical considerations. The course had to provide bus and subway tokens, because fares ranged between three and six dollars per class per student, and the students could not afford sixty or even thirty dollars a month for transportation. We also had to offer dinner or a snack, because the classes were to be held from 6:00 to 7:30 P.M.

The first recruiting session came only a few days later. Nancy Mamis-King, associate executive director of the Neighborhood Youth & Family Services program in the South Bronx, had identified some Clemente Course candidates and had assembled about twenty of her clients and their supervisors in a circle of chairs in a conference room. Everyone in the room was black or Latino, with the exception of one social worker and me.

After I explained the idea of the course, the white social worker was the first to ask a question: "Are you going to teach African history?"

"No. We'll be teaching a section on American history, based on documents, as I said. We want to teach the ideas of history so that—"

"You have to teach African history."

"This is America, so we'll teach American history. If we were in Africa, I would teach African history, and if we were in China, I would teach Chinese history."

"You're indoctrinating people in Western culture."

I tried to get beyond her. "We'll study African art," I said, "as it affects art in America. We'll study American history and literature; you can't do that without studying African-American culture, because culturally all Americans are black as well as white, Native American, Asian, and so on." It was no use; not one of them applied for admission to the course.

A few days later Lynette Lauretig arranged a meeting with some of her staff at The Door. We disagreed about the course. They thought it should be taught at a much lower level. Although I could not change their views, they agreed to assemble a group of Door members who might be interested in the humanities.

On an early evening that same week, about twenty prospective students were scheduled to meet in a classroom at The Door. Most of them came late. Those who arrived first slumped in their chairs, staring at the floor or greeting me with sullen glances. A few ate candy or what appeared to be the remnants of a meal. The students were mostly black and Latino, one was Asian, and five were white; two of the whites were immigrants who had severe problems with English. When I introduced myself, several of the students would not shake my hand, two or three refused even to look at me, one girl giggled, and the last person to volunteer his name, a young man dressed in a Tommy Hilfiger sweatshirt and wearing a cap turned sideways, drawled, "Henry Jones, but they call me Sleepy, because I got these sleepy eyes—"

"In our class, we'll call you Mr. Jones."

He smiled and slid down in his chair so that his back was parallel to the floor.

Before I finished attempting to shake hands with the prospective students, a waif-like Asian girl with her mouth half-full of cake said, "Can we get on with it? I'm bored."

I liked the group immediately.

Having failed in the South Bronx, I resolved to approach these prospective students differently. "You've been cheated," I said. "Rich people learn the humanities; you didn't. The humanities are a foundation for getting along in the world, for thinking, for learning to reflect on the world instead of just reacting to whatever force is turned against you. I think the humanities are one of the ways to become political, and I don't mean political in the sense of voting in an election but in the broad sense." I told them Thucydides' definition of politics.

"Rich people know politics in that sense. They know how to negotiate instead of using force. They know how to use politics to get along, to get power. It doesn't mean that rich people are good and poor people are bad. It simply means that rich people know a more effective method for living in this society.

"Do all rich people, or people who are in the middle, know the humanities? Not a chance. But some do. And it helps. It helps to live better and enjoy life more. Will the humanities make you rich? Yes. Absolutely. But not in terms of money. In terms of life.

"Rich people learn the humanities in private schools and expensive universities. And that's one of the ways in which they learn the political life. I think that is the real difference between the haves and have-nots in this country. If you want real power, legitimate power, the kind that comes from the people and belongs to the people, you must understand politics. The humanities will help.

"Here's how it works: We'll pay your subway fare; take care of your children, if you have them; give you a snack or a sandwich; provide you with books and any other materials you need. But we'll make you think harder, use your mind more fully, than you ever have before. You'll have to read and think about the same kinds of ideas you would encounter in a first-year course at Harvard or Yale or Oxford.

"You'll have to come to class in the snow and the rain and the cold and the dark. No one will coddle you, no one will slow down for you. There will be tests to take, papers to write. And I can't promise you anything but a certificate of completion at the end of the course. I'll be talking to colleges about giving credit for the course, but I can't promise anything. If you come to the Clemente Course, you must do it because you want to study the humanities, because you want a certain kind of life, a richness of mind and spirit. That's all I offer you: philosophy, poetry, art history, logic, rhetoric, and American history.

"Your teachers will all be people of accomplishment in their fields," I said, and I spoke a little about each teacher. "That's the course. October through May, with a two-week break at Christmas. It is generally accepted in America that the liberal arts and the humanities in particular belong to the elites. I think you're the elites."

The young Asian woman said, "What are you getting out of this?"

"This is a demonstration project. I'm writing a book. This will be proof, I hope, of my idea about the humanities. Whether it succeeds or fails will be up to the teachers and you."

All but one of the prospective students applied for admission to the course.

I repeated the new presentation at the Grand Street Settlement and at other places around the city. There were about fifty candidates for the thirty positions in the course. Personal interviews began in early September.

Meanwhile, almost all of my attempts to raise money had failed. Only the novelist Starling Lawrence, who is also editor in chief of W. W. Norton, which had contracted to publish the book; the publishing house itself; and a small, private family foundation supported the experiment. We were far short of our budgeted expenses, but my wife, Sylvia, and I agreed that the cost was still very low, and we decided to go ahead.

Of the fifty prospective students who showed up at the Clemente Center for personal interviews, a few were too rich (a postal supervisor's son, a fellow who claimed his father owned a factory in Nigeria that employed sixty people) and more than a few could not read. Two home-care workers from

Local 1199 could not arrange their hours to enable them to take the course. Some of the applicants were too young: a thirteen-year-old and two who had just turned sixteen.

Lucia Medina, a woman with five children who told me that she often answered the door at the single-room occupancy hotel where she lived with a butcher knife in her hand, was the oldest person accepted into the course. Carmen Quinones, a recovering addict who had spent time in prison, was the next eldest. Both were in their early thirties.

The interviews went on for days.

Abel Lomas shared an apartment and worked part-time wrapping packages at Macy's. His father had abandoned the family when Abel was born. His mother was murdered by his stepfather when Abel was thirteen. With no one to turn to and no place to stay, he lived on the streets, first in Florida, then back in New York City. He used the tiny stipend from his mother's Social Security to keep himself alive.

After the recruiting session at The Door, I drove up Sixth Avenue from Canal Street with Abel, and we talked about ethics. He had a street tough's delivery, spitting out his ideas in crudely formed sentences of four, five, eight words, strings of blunt declarations, with never a dependent clause to qualify his thoughts. He did not clear his throat with badinage, as timidity teaches us to do, nor did he waste his breath with tact.

"What do you think about drugs?" he asked, the strangely breathless delivery further coarsened by his Dominican accent. "My cousin is a dealer."

"I've seen a lot of people hurt by drugs."

"Your family has nothing to eat. You sell drugs. What's worse? Let your family starve or sell drugs?"

"Starvation and drug addiction are both bad, aren't they?"

"Yes," he said, not "yeah" or "uh-huh" but a precise, almost formal "yes."

"So it's a question of the worse of two evils? How shall we decide?"

The question came up near Thirty-fourth Street, where Sixth Avenue remains hellishly traffic-jammed well into the night. Horns honked, people flooded into the street against the light. Buses and trucks and taxicabs threatened their way from one lane to the next where the overcrowded avenue crosses the equally crowded Broadway. As we passed Herald Square and made our way north again, I said, "There are a couple of ways to look at it. One comes from Immanuel Kant, who said that you should not do anything unless you want it to become a universal law; that is, unless you think it's what everybody should do. So Kant wouldn't agree to selling drugs or letting your family starve."

Again he answered with a formal "Yes."

"There's another way to look at it, which is to ask what is the greatest good for the greatest number: in this case, keeping your family from starvation or keeping tens, perhaps hundreds of people from losing their lives to drugs. So which is the greatest good for the greatest number?"

"That's what I think," he said.

"What?"

"You shouldn't sell drugs. You can always get food to eat. Welfare. Something."

"You're a Kantian."

"Yes."

"You know who Kant is?"

"I think so."

We had arrived at Seventy-seventh Street, where he got out of the car to catch the subway before I turned east. As he opened the car door and the light came on, the almost military neatness of him struck me. He had the newly cropped hair of a cadet. His clothes were clean, without a wrinkle. He was an orphan, a street kid, an immaculate urchin. Within a few weeks he would be nineteen years old, the Social Security payments would end, and he would have to move into a shelter.

Some of those who came for interviews were too poor. I did not think that was possible when we began, and I would like not to believe it now, but it was true. There is a point at which the level of forces that surround the poor can become insurmountable, when there is no time or energy left to be anything but poor. Most often I could not recruit such people for the course; when I did, they soon dropped out.

Over the days of interviewing, a class slowly assembled. I could not then imagine who would last the year and who would not.

One young woman submitted a neatly typed essay that said, "I was homeless once, then I lived for some time in a shelter. Right now, I have got my own space granted by the Partnership for the Homeless. Right now, I am living alone, with very limited means. Financially I am overwhelmed by debts. I cannot afford all the food I need. . . ."

A brother and sister, refugees from Tashkent, lived with their parents in the farthest reaches of Queens, far beyond the end of the subway line. They had no money, and they had been refused admission by every school to which they had applied. I had not intended to accept immigrants or people who had difficulty with the English language, but I took them into the class.

I also took four who had been in prison, three who were homeless, three who were pregnant, one who lived in a drugged dreamstate in which she was abused, and one whom I had known for a long time and who was dying of AIDS. As I listened to them, I wondered how the course would affect them. They had no public life, no place; they lived within the surround of force, moving as fast as they could, driven by necessity, without a moment to reflect. Why should they care about fourteenth-century Italian painting or truth tables or the death of Socrates?

Between the end of recruiting and the orientation session that would open the course, I made a visit to Bedford Hills to talk with Niecie Walker. It was hot, and the drive up from the city had been unpleasant. I didn't yet know Niecie very well. She didn't trust me, and I didn't know what to make of her. While we talked, she held a huge white pill in her hand. "For AIDS," she said.

"Are you sick?"

"My T-cell count is down. But that's neither here nor there. Tell me about the course, Earl. What are you going to teach?"

"Moral philosophy."

"And what does that include?"

She had turned the visit into an interrogation. I didn't mind. At the end of the conversation I would be going out into "the free world"; if she wanted our meeting to be an interrogation, I was not about to argue. I said, "We'll begin with Plato: the *Apology*, a little of the *Crito*, a few pages of the *Phaedo* so that they'll know what happened to Socrates. Then we'll read Aristotle's *Nicomachean Ethics*. I also want them to read Thucydides, particularly Pericles' Funeral Oration in order to make the connection between ethics and politics, to lead them in the direction I hope the course will take them. Then we'll end with *Antigone*, but read as moral and political philosophy as well as drama."

"There's something missing," she said, leaning back in her chair, taking on an air of superiority.

The drive had been long, the day was hot, the air in the room was dead and damp. "Oh, yeah," I said, "and what's that?"

"Plato's Allegory of the Cave. How can you teach philosophy to poor people without the Allegory of the Cave? The ghetto is the cave. Education is the light. Poor people can understand that."

At the beginning of the orientation at the Clemente Center a week later, each teacher spoke for a minute or two. Dr. Inclan and his research assistant, Patricia Vargas, administered the questionnaire he had devised to measure, as best he could, the role of force and the amount of reflection in the lives of the students. I explained that each class was going to be videotaped as another way of documenting the project. Then I gave out the first assignment: "In preparation for our next meeting, I would like you to read a brief selection from Plato's *Republic:* the Allegory of the Cave."

I tried to guess how many students would return for the first class. I hoped for twenty, expected fifteen, and feared ten. Sylvia, who had agreed to share the administrative tasks of the course, and I prepared coffee and cookies for twenty-five. We had a plastic container filled with subway tokens. Thanks to Starling Lawrence, we had thirty copies of Bernard Knox's *Norton Book of Classical Literature*, which contained all of the texts for the philosophy section except the *Republic* and the *Nicomachean Ethics*.

At six o'clock there were only ten students seated around the long table, but by six-fifteen the number had doubled, and a few minutes later two more straggled in out of the dusk. I had written a time line on the blackboard, showing them the temporal progress of thinking—from the role of myth in Neolithic societies to *The Gilgamesh Epic* and forward to the *Old Testament, Confucius*, the Greeks, the New Testament, the Koran, the *Epic of Sonjara*, and ending with Nahuatl and Maya poems, which took us up to the contact between Europe and America, where the history course began. The time line served as context and geography as well as history: no race, no major culture was ignored. "Let's agree", I told them, "that we are all human, whatever our origins. And now let's go into Plato's cave."

I told them that there would be no lectures in the philosophy section of the course; we would use the Socratic method, which is called maieutic dialogue. "'Maieutic' comes from the Greek word for midwifery. I'll take the role of midwife in our dialogue. Now, what do I mean by that? What does a midwife do?"

It was the beginning of a love affair, the first moment of their infatuation with Socrates. Later, Abel Lomas would characterize that moment in his no-nonsense fashion, saying that it was the first time anyone had ever paid attention to their opinions.

Grace Glueck began the art history class in a darkened room lit with slides of the Lascaux caves and next turned the students' attention to Egypt, arranging for them to visit the Metropolitan Museum of Art to see the Temple of Dendur and the Egyptian Galleries. They arrived at the museum on a Friday evening. Darlene Codd brought her two-year-old son. Pearl Lau was late, as usual. One of the students, who had told me how much he was looking forward to the museum visit, didn't show up, which surprised me. Later I learned that he had been arrested for jumping a turnstile in a subway station on his way to the museum and was being held in a prison cell under the Brooklyn criminal courthouse. In the Temple of Dendur, Samantha Smoot asked questions of Felicia Blum, a museum lecturer. Samantha was the student who had burst out with the news, in one of the first sessions of the course, that people in her neighborhood believed it "wasn't no use goin' to school, because the white man wouldn't let you up no matter what." But in a hall where the statuary was of half-human, half-animal female figures, it was Samantha who asked what the glyphs meant, encouraging Felicia Blum to read them aloud, to translate them into English. Toward the end of the evening, Grace led the students out of the halls of antiquities into the Rockefeller Wing, where she told them of the connections of culture and art in Mali, Benin, and the Pacific Islands. When the students had collected their coats and stood together near the entrance to the museum, preparing to leave, Samantha stood apart, a tall, slim young woman, dressed in a deerstalker cap and a dark blue peacoat. She made an exaggerated farewell wave at us and returned to Egypt—her ancient mirror.

Charles Simmons began the poetry class with poems as puzzles and laughs. His plan was to surprise the class, and he did. At first he read the poems aloud to them, interrupting himself with footnotes to bring them along. He showed them poems of love and of seduction, and satiric commentaries on those poems by later poets. "Let us read," the students demanded, but Charles refused. He tantalized them with the opportunity to read poems aloud. A tug-of-war began between him and the students, and the standoff was ended not by Charles directly but by Hector Anderson. When Charles asked if anyone in the class wrote poetry, Hector raised his hand.

"Can you recite one of your poems for us?" Charles said.

Until that moment, Hector had never volunteered a comment, though he had spoken well and intelligently when asked. He preferred to slouch in his chair, dressed in full camouflage gear, wearing a nylon stocking over his hair and eating slices of fresh cantaloupe or honeydew melon.

In response to Charles's question, Hector slid up to a sitting position. "If you turn that camera off," he said. "I don't want anybody using my lyrics." When he was sure the red light of the video camera was off, Hector stood and recited verse after verse of a poem that belonged somewhere in the triangle formed by Ginsberg's *Howl*, the Book of Lamentations, and hip-hop. When Charles and the students finished applauding, they asked Hector to say the poem again, and he did. Later Charles told me, "That kid is the real

thing." Hector's discomfort with Sylvia and me turned to ease. He came to our house for a small Christmas party and at other times. We talked on the telephone about a scholarship program and about what steps he should take next in his education. I came to know his parents. As a student, he began quietly, almost secretly, to surpass many of his classmates.

Timothy Koranda was the most professorial of the professors. He arrived precisely on time, wearing a hat of many styles—part fedora, part Borsalino, part Stetson, and at least one-half World War I campaign hat. He taught logic during class hours, filling the blackboard from floor to ceiling, wall to wall, drawing the intersections of sets here and truth tables there and a great square of oppositions in the middle of it all. After class, he walked with students to the subway, chatting about Zen or logic or Heisenberg.

On one of the coldest nights of the winter, he introduced the students to logic problems stated in ordinary language that they could solve by reducing the phrases to symbols. He passed out copies of a problem, two pages long, then wrote out some of the key phrases on the blackboard. "Take this home with you," he said, "and at our next meeting we shall see who has solved it. I shall also attempt to find the answer."

By the time he finished writing out the key phrases, however, David Iskhakov raised his hand. Although they listened attentively, neither David nor his sister Susana spoke often in class. She was shy, and he was embarrassed at his inability to speak perfect English.

"May I go to blackboard?" David said. "And will see if I have found correct answer to *zis* problem."

Together Tim and David erased the blackboard, then David began covering it with signs and symbols. "If first man is earning this money, and second man is closer to this town . . ." he said, carefully laying out the conditions. After five minutes or so, he said, "And the answer is: B will get first to Cleveland!"

Samantha Smoot shouted, "That's not the answer. The mistake you made is in the first part there, where it says who earns more money."

Tim folded his arms across his chest, happy. "I shall let you all take the problem home," he said.

When Sylvia and I left the Clemente Center that night, a knot of students was gathered outside, huddled against the wind. Snow had begun to fall, a slippery powder on the gray ice that covered all but a narrow space down the center of the sidewalk. Samantha and David stood in the middle of the group, still arguing over the answer to the problem. I leaned in for a moment to catch the character of the argument. It was even more polite than it had been in the classroom, because now they governed themselves.

One Saturday morning in January, David Howell telephoned me at home. "Mr. Shores," he said, Anglicizing my name, as many of the students did.

"Mr. Howell," I responded, recognizing his voice.

"How you doin', Mr. Shores?"

"I'm fine. How are you?"

"I had a little problem at work."

Uh-oh, I thought, bad news was coming. David is a big man, generally good-humored but with a quick temper. According to his mother, he had a history of violent behavior. In the classroom he had been one of the best students, a steady man, twenty-four years old, who always did the reading assignments and who often made interesting connections between the humanities and daily life. "What happened?"

"Mr. Shores, there's a woman at my job, she said some things to me and I said some things to her. And she told my supervisor I had said things to her, and he called me in about it. She's forty years old and she don't have no social life, and I have a good social life, and she's jealous of me."

"And then what happened?" The tone of his voice and the timing of the call did not portend good news.

"Mr. Shores, she made me so mad, I wanted to smack her up against the wall. I tried to talk to some friends to calm myself down a little, but nobody was around."

"And what did you do?" I asked, fearing this was his one telephone call from the city jail.

"Mr. Shores, I asked myself, 'What would Socrates do?' "

David Howell had reasoned that his co-worker's envy was not his problem after all, and he had dropped his rage.

One evening, in the American history section, I was telling the students about Gordon Wood's ideas in *The Radicalism of the American Revolution*. We were talking about the revolt by some intellectuals against classical learning at the turn of the eighteenth century, including Benjamin Franklin's late-life change of heart, when Henry Jones raised his hand.

"If the Founders loved the humanities so much, how come they treated the natives so badly?"

I didn't know how to answer this question. There were confounding explanations to offer about changing attitudes toward Native Americans, vaguely useful references to views of Rousseau and James Fenimore Cooper. For a moment I wondered if I should tell them about Heidegger's Nazi past. Then I saw Abel Lomas's raised hand at the far end of the table. "Mr. Lomas," I said.

Abel said, "That's what Aristotle means by incontinence, when you know what's morally right but you don't do it, because you're overcome by your passions."

The other students nodded. They were all inheritors of wounds caused by the incontinence of educated men; now they had an ally in Aristotle, who had given them a way to analyze the actions of their antagonists.

Those who appreciate ancient history understand the radical character of the humanities. They know that politics did not begin in a perfect world but in a society even more flawed than ours: one that embraced slavery, denied the rights of women, practiced a form of homosexuality that verged on pedophilia, and endured the intrigues and corruption of its leaders. The genius of that society originated in man's re-creation of himself through the recognition of his humanness as expressed in art, literature, rhetoric, philosophy, and the unique notion of freedom. At that moment, the isolation of the private life ended and politics began.

The winners in the game of modern society, and even those whose fortune falls in the middle, have other means to power: they are included at birth. They know this. And they know exactly what to do to protect their place in the economic and social hierarchy. As Allan Bloom, author of the nationally best-selling tract in defense of elitism, *The Closing of the American Mind*, put it, they direct the study of the humanities exclusively at those young people who "have been raised in comfort and with the expectation of ever increasing comfort."

In the last meeting before graduation, the Clemente students answered the same set of questions they'd answered at orientation. Between October and May, students had fallen to AIDS, pregnancy, job opportunities, pernicious anemia, clinical depression, a schizophrenic child, and other forces, but of the thirty students admitted to the course, sixteen had completed it, and fourteen had earned credit from Bard College. Dr. Inclan found that the students' self-esteem and their abilities to divine and solve problems had significantly increased; their use of verbal aggression as a tactic for resolving conflicts had significantly decreased. And they all had notably more appreciation for the concepts of benevolence, spirituality, universalism, and collectivism.

It cost about $2,000 for a student to attend the Clemente Course. Compared with unemployment, welfare, or prison, the humanities are a bargain. But coming into possession of the faculty of reflection and the skills of politics leads to a choice for the poor—and whatever they choose, they will be dangerous: they may use politics to get along in a society based on the game, to escape from the surround of force into a gentler life, to behave as citizens, and nothing more; or they may choose to oppose the game itself. No one can predict the effect of politics, although we all would like to think that wisdom goes our way. That is why the poor are so often mobilized and so rarely politicized. The possibility that they will adopt a moral view other than that of their mentors can never be discounted.

And who wants to run that risk?

On the night of the first Clemente Course graduation, the students and their families filled the eighty-five chairs we crammed into the conference room where classes had been held. Robert Martin, associate dean of Bard College, read the graduates' names. David Dinkins, the former mayor of New York City, handed out the diplomas. There were speeches and presentations. The students gave me a plaque on which they had misspelled my name. I offered a few words about each student, congratulated them, and said finally, "This is what I wish for you: May you never be more active than when you are doing nothing. . . ." I saw their smiles of recognition at the words of Cato, which I had written on the blackboard early in the course. They could recall again too the moment when we had come to the denouement of Aristotle's brilliantly constructed thriller, the *Nicomachean Ethics*—the idea that in the contemplative life man was most like God.

One or two, perhaps more of the students, closed their eyes. In the momentary stillness of the room it was possible to think.

The Clemente Course in the Humanities ended a second year in June 1997. Twenty-eight new students had enrolled; fourteen graduated. Another version of the course will begin this fall in Yucatan, Mexico, using classical Maya literature in Maya.

On May 14, 1997, Viniece Walker came up for parole for the second time. She had served more than ten years of her sentence, and she had been the best of prisoners. In a version of the Clemente Course held at the prison, she had been my teaching assistant. After a brief hearing, her request for parole was denied. She will serve two more years before the parole board will reconsider her case.

A year after graduation, ten of the first sixteen Clemente Course graduates were attending four-year colleges or going to nursing school; four of them had received full scholarships to Bard College. The other graduates were attending community college or working full-time. Except for one: she had been fired from her job in a fast-food restaurant for trying to start a union.

Note

1. Under the guidance of Robert Maynard Hutchins (1929-1951), the University of Chicago required year-long courses in the humanities, social sciences, and natural sciences for the Bachelor of Arts degree. Hutchins developed the curriculum with the help of Mortimer Adler, among others; the Hutchins courses later influenced Adler's Great Books program.

Critical Evaluation

1. How many poor people would be helped by the kind of program described in this chapter? Why?

2. Would this kind of program work in other parts of the nation? Why or why not?

3. Are there alternative ways to use such a program, e.g., making it a part of public school education?

Project for Personal Application and Class Discussion: Poverty

What is it like to live in poverty? Sometimes students smile when they hear the question; they respond with: "I know what it's like because I live in poverty now." In most cases, the response comes not from their having an impoverished background but from their present circumstances as a student. Moreover, even if their perception of their current situation is accurate, none of those students expect to continue in poverty indefinitely.

Do you believe you are currently living in poverty? Make a rough estimate of your annual living expenses. Whether or not you personally pay for them, include housing, food, clothing, books and tuition, transportation, entertainment/recreation, and insurance. Then look up the latest poverty threshold in the *Statistical Abstract of the United States*. For example, for 1995, the poverty level for an individual was $7,929.

Does the cost of your current lifestyle fall above or below the poverty level? If you had to live at the poverty level, what would you cut out of your budget? If your income remained at or below the poverty level indefinitely, what would be your prospects for marriage? A family? A satisfying life? ✦

PART III

Troubled Behavior: Problems of Deviance

Abuse of Alcohol and Other Drugs

The extent of alcohol and other drug abuse has varied over time in the United States. Such abuse peaked in 1979 and has declined somewhat since then. However, the problem remains severe. There are more than 14 million problem drinkers, 60 million smokers, and 13 million users of illegal drugs.

Drug abuse is one type of self-destructive behavior. According to the Centers for Disease Control (1996), six kinds of behavior contribute to the leading causes of illness and death: use of tobacco, use of alcohol and other drugs, behavior that results in accidents and injuries, sexual behavior that results in unintended pregnancy or a sexually transmitted disease, unhealthy eating habits, and lack of exercise. Interestingly, these behaviors tend to cluster together—that is, people who engage in one are likely to engage in a number of the others as well. Moreover, the behaviors tend to begin in adolescence and extend into adulthood.

Readings in this section examine various facets of the drug problem. Like the other problems examined in this book, there is no single cause and there are no simple solutions.

Reference

Centers for Disease Control. 1996. "Youth Risk Behavior Surveillance: United States, 1995." *Morbidity and Mortality Weekly Report* 45 (March 8). ✦

30

Perceived College Drinking Norms and Alcohol Abuse

H. Wesley Perkins and Henry Wechsler

Social norms are an important structural factor that influences individual behavior. But what if people misperceive the norms? This is the question that H. Wesley Perkins and Henry Wechsler raise in their study of alcohol abuse among college students. Campus norms about drinking behavior are not sufficiently clear and precise to the bulk of students. As a result, students react to their own perceptions of the norms. Perkins and Wechsler do not deal with how individual perceptions arise and why they differ. Undoubtedly a combination of social-psychological factors (drinking patterns of friends and perhaps pre-enrollment attitudes about the norms) and structural factors (such as students' economic resources and media portrayals of college life as free-wheeling and partying) contribute to the perceptions.

In any event, these misperceptions legitimate abuse, particularly when combined with an existing personal permissiveness towards drinking. The recommendations of Perkins and Wechsler for dealing with the problem are important in light of the fact that alcohol use and abuse is high on campuses, with one study reporting that 44 percent of students are binge drinkers (five drinks in a row on at least one occasion in the two weeks prior to the survey) (Wechsler et al. 1994).

Reference

Wechsler, H.A., A. Davenport, G. Dowdall, B. Moeykens, and S. Castillo. 1994. "Health and Behavioral Consequences of Binge Drinking." Journal of the American Medical Association 272:1672–77.

Focus Questions

1. Why are perceived norms important?

2. How do perceived college drinking norms vary?

3. How do perceived norms affect drinking behavior?

Introduction

Alcohol abuse among college students has been highly linked to the influence of peers in the peer intensive environment of college campuses for several decades (cf. Gusfield 1961; Perkins 1985; Orcutt 1991). Classic theories and research in social psychology have long argued that friendship affiliation needs and social comparison processes (Festinger 1954), pressures toward peer group conformity (Asch 1951, 1952), and the formation and acquisition of reference group norms (Newcomb 1943; Newcomb and Wilson 1966; Sherif 1936, 1972) typically coalesce to produce a strong desire within (or force upon) individuals to adopt and maintain peer group attitudes and to act in accordance with their peers' expectations and behaviors. Even if behavior such as heavy alcohol use is viewed as deviant by the larger society, youths may socially learn and continue abusive drinking in response to peer groups that provide models and rewards for such behavior and perpetuate a definition of it as desirable (Akers et al. 1979).

Yet the influence of peers in terms of what those peers actually think and do is only part of the problem. What students believe to be the attitudes and behaviors of their peers is just as crucial and may have its own independent influence on college student drinking. Indeed, the strongest effect of peers may occur through the impression one develops of peer norms, but that perception may be significantly distorted for many students. Research in a variety of college settings including large universities and small colleges and in different regions of the United States has found that most students do not accurately perceive the real norms regarding peer alcohol use (cf. Baer and Carney 1993; Baer et al. 1991; Perkins and Berkowitz 1986; Prentice and Miller 1993). Instead, students tend to perceive an exaggerated level of use and more permissive attitudes than actually exist. This phenomenon of misperceptions does not mean that alcohol abuse is not a major problem in most colleges. The crucial point is that the actuality of widespread alcohol abuse on many campuses may be fueled, at least in part, by some students thinking that their peers are even heavier users and that their peers hold even more permissive attitudes than is the reality. . . .

The subjective perceptions, be they accurate or inaccurate, must be taken as important in their own right, because people act on their perceptions of their world in addition to acting within a real world. Ultimately, this misperception of student norms may serve as a self-fulfilling prophecy encouraging more alcohol abuse than would otherwise be the case following the classic sociological dictum that things that are perceived as real are real in their consequences (Thomas and Thomas 1928).

Regardless of any tendency overall to perceive an exaggerated norm, all students on any particular campus are not likely to identically perceive the campus norms about drinking. Various social constituencies and friendship networks may affect peer conversations about alcohol use as well as actual exposure to student drinking. Thus variation in individual students' perceptions of campus permissiveness or restraint in drinking norms may be an important consideration. Students who perceive a more moderate campus norm in a specific college environment may be more constrained to act in accordance with that relatively moderate perception of peer expectation and practice (Agostinelli et al. 1995; Perkins and Berkowitz 1986). In contrast, those students who think that their campus peers desire and expect heavy alcohol consumption and frequent intoxication may be at greater risk for personal alcohol abuse as they feel pressured to conform to this perceived norm. Thus, the primary purpose of this study is to examine variation in the perceived drinking norms of college students and explore the relationship between perceived campus norms and personal alcohol abuse.

Of course the student's personal attitude regarding alcohol consumption should not be ignored here. How permissive one is in one's own attitude about drinking will undoubtedly have a substantial impact on personal alcohol abuse. One's personal attitude about drinking may also have an influence on and be partially the result of one's perception of the campus drinking norm. Independent of personal attitudes, however, the question remains about the potential impact of a perceived norm. That is, do students consume alcohol in a fashion that, to some degree, reflects their perceptions of the normative standards even independently of their personal drinking codes? Do their perceptions of the norm make a difference in their behavior apart from their personal beliefs about appropriate behavior?

The interactive effect of perceived norms and personal attitudes may also be an important consideration. Several studies have suggested that the influence of one's attitude on behavior is most salient in a context of supportive peer norms, although research results have varied somewhat by the nature and extent of the behavior (cf. Andrews and Kandel 1979; Grube and Morgan 1990; Grube et al. 1986; Liska 1974; Rabow et al. 1987). Thus, someone who personally believes that abusive intoxication is acceptable and *simultaneously* perceives a very permissive peer norm may be far more encouraged to abuse alcohol than she or he would be simply by the independent influence of one's personal attitude or a perception of a permissive environment. A student whose own attitude is favorable to heavy drinking, for example, may only act on that inclination, or act more readily on it, if he or she perceives peers to be accepting of such behavior (Perkins and Berkowitz 1986). Otherwise, the student may not feel comfortable acting on his or her desire to drink or drink heavily in a social environment perceived as incompatible with that personal desire. Thus, a secondary purpose of this study is to examine the degree of relationship between perceived campus norms and personal alcohol abuse that exists independent of and interactively with personal attitudes about drinking.

In short, the objectives of this study are to address four specific questions about college students' perceptions of drinking norms in their campus environment by analyzing data gathered in a study of college drinking at 140 colleges and universities nationwide. First, in addition to variation in perceptions of the campus drinking norms based on differences in actual campus environments, to what extent can variation be observed in perceptions of the norms among students attending the same school? Second, do students' perceptions of the drinking norm predict personal alcohol abuse patterns independent of each school's contribution to a students' predicted alcohol abuse? Third, do perceptions of the drinking norm contribute to the prediction of personal alcohol abuse even when personal attitudes about drinking are controlled? Fourth, if more permissive perceptions of the campus norm do predict greater personal alcohol abuse, does this pattern vary by the personal attitudes students hold about drinking?

Methods

Sample

The data for this research are drawn from a survey of undergraduates at 140 colleges and universities in 40 states and the District of Columbia representing a cross section of American four-year undergraduate institutions of higher education. . . . The final student sample contained more women than men (58% vs 42%), owing in part to the inclusion of six all-women's institutions. The sample was predominantly White (81%); other students include Asians and Pacific Islanders (7%), Spanish and Hispanic Americans (7%) Blacks (6%), and Native Americans (1%). Forty-five percent of the students were younger than 21 years, 38% were aged 21 to 23 years, and 17% were aged 24 years or more.

Measures

Personal Alcohol Attitude. Respondents were asked the following question: "In your own opinion, how much do you think is appropriate for a college student to drink in each of the following situations?" Nine situations were provided (at a party, in an off-campus bar, in an on-campus pub, before driving a car, on a date, with friends, alone, before noon, and on a week night) along with four response categories for each item (no alcohol at all, only 1 to 2 drinks, enough to get high but not drunk, or enough to get drunk). . . .

Perceived Campus Alcohol Norm. An index of the student's perception of the campus norms about alcohol use was created based on students' responses to five items. Respondents were asked to indicate their degree of agreement with each of five items described as "advice for a new student at your school" using four categories (strongly agree, agree, disagree, and strongly disagree). Specifically the five items were: (1) Students here admire non-drinkers, (2) it's important to show how much you can drink and still hold your liquor, (3) you can't make it socially at this school without drinking, (4) drinking is an important part of the college experience, and (5) school rules about drinking are almost never enforced. . . .

Personal Alcohol Abuse. An index of personal alcohol abuse based on negative consequences of drinking was constructed from students' responses to a list of 12 potential hazards of intoxication. Specifically, respondents were asked to indicate which of the following had occurred once or multiple times during the academic year as aconsequence of their own drinking: (1) had a hangover, (2) missed a class, (3) got behind in school work, (4) did something you later regretted, (5) forgot where you were or what you did, (6) argued with friends, (7) engaged in unplanned sexual activity, (8) did not use protection when you had sex, (9) damaged property, (10) got into trouble with the campus or local police, (11) got hurt or injured, and (12) required medical treatment for an alcohol overdose. . .

Results

Variation in Perceived Norms

Students' actual scores on the perceived campus environment ranged from the lowest possible score (0) indicating very little perceived permissiveness or importance of alcohol use on campus to the highest possible score (15) indicating perceptions that alcohol use was perceived as an integral part of the normative campus culture. The overall mean of this measure was 5.48 with a standard deviation of 2.63. About one-quarter of the overall sample scored 3 or lower and about one-quarter reported perceptions resulting in scores of 8 or higher indicating considerable variation in the perceived norm. Of course variation would be expected among students from different campuses participating in the survey as the alcohol cultures at different schools sampled may vary a great deal. Indeed, when the average perception score was calculated for students responding from each of the 140 schools that were sampled, the mean scores ranged from a low of .75 where presumably very little alcohol is used on campus to 7.94 where alcohol consumption presumably is consumed heavily and relatively frequently in the social life of students. There was also considerable variation, however, in the perceived norm scores of respondents within each of the 140 schools that were sampled. . . . Thus, individual students' perceptions of the norm are diverse and relatively little of this variation in how permissive the drinking norm on campus is perceived to be can be accounted for simply as the direct product of accurate perceptions of differing campus cultures that exist across the country.

Effect of Perceived Alcohol Norm

The question remains as to whether these differing perceptions of the campus norm among students within each campus context will actually have an impact on their own drinking. Thus, the student's score for his or her perception of the campus norm was entered as an independent variable predicting one's score on the index of personal alcohol abuse . . . Several social background characteristics identified as influencing students' alcohol abuse in other research (Wechsler et al. 1995) were also included in this analysis . . . [including] the student's age, year in school, and number of close friends . . . gender, religious background (Protestant, Catholic, Jewish, other religion, and no religion), race (Asian, Black, White, and other), fraternity or sorority membership, and living environ-

ment (single sex residence hall, coed residence hall, fraternity or sorority house, or off-campus private residence). . . .

The results . . . indicate that perceptions of the campus alcohol norm clearly have the largest effect on personal alcohol abuse, an effect much greater than that of any of the social background factors. When alcohol is perceived as a more prominent aspect of the local campus culture, drinking problems were much more likely to have been encountered during the academic year. Greek social membership and having a relatively large social network of friends are next in contributing to personal drinking problems with gender, age, Greek housing, and categories of race and religion making marginal, but statistically significant, contributions. . . .

As initially discussed it may be that personal attitudes are interrelated with how one perceives the environment; perceived norms may contribute to one's personal attitudes and the attitudes one holds may color one's perceptions of the cultural norms. Because it is also quite likely that personal attitudes directly affect how one behaves to some degree, it is useful to examine whether perceived norms have any influence on personal drinking completely independent of the personal attitudes about drinking held by students. . . . Results here indicate, as might be expected, that personal alcohol attitude holds the lion's share of effect on personal alcohol abuse. . . . Nevertheless, the perceived campus alcohol norm retains a significant effect on personal alcohol abuse independent of personal attitude about drinking, an effect that is still larger than that found for any of the social background factors.

In the final portion of this investigation we examined the interactive effect of normative perceptions in combination with different personal attitudes. As argued initially, perceptions of less restraint in the drinking environment may be more influential, perhaps, when they reinforce already permissive personal attitudes. . . . [The results suggest] that perceiving a permissive norm can encourage alcohol abuse among students whose own drinking attitudes are conservative or very permissive . . . [but that] perceptions of the norm become relatively more important in explaining alcohol abuse among students with more liberal predispositions. . . .

Conclusions

The results of this survey representing colleges and universities nationwide demonstrate that students' perceptions of the normative climate concerning campus alcohol use do vary considerably. Only a small portion of this variation in how permissive the norms of the institution are believed to be can be accounted for by differences in perceptions created by the particular institutions involved in the study. Thus, although variation in actual student drinking cultures will certainly affect what a student sees as the norm, much more of the variation in perceptions reflects the fact that at any school students will typically exhibit a wide range of beliefs about the norms of alcohol consumption that takes place on their campus.

Caution is warranted in interpretations of additional results in this study, given the use of cross-sectional data. Nevertheless, the analyses do suggest that, independent of the influence of actual local campus norms, a student's perception of the campus norm significantly contributes to his or her own drinking behavior. When the norm on a specific campus is perceived by a student as quite permissive, he or she is more likely to abuse alcohol, even apart from the influence of his or her own attitude. Thus, if a student believes that heavy alcohol use is the norm and is expected by most students, then regardless of the accuracy of the perception, he or she is more likely to become involved in alcohol abuse, even after taking his or her own attitude about drinking into account.

Finally, the data suggest that if a student personally believes in abstinence or very restrained drinking, then what she or he thinks about the campus norms has only a relatively weak impact on her or his own drinking behavior. In contrast, if a student personally believes that drinking enough to get intoxicated is acceptable in many circumstances, then his or her perception of the larger campus' standards becomes much more important. The individual with a permissive attitude is either constrained to conform to his or her perception of a less permissive norm or encouraged to act on personal tendencies toward destructive alcohol use by the comfortably supportive perception of widespread and frequent intoxication in the larger campus culture.

This research, based on nationwide data, suggests that alcohol abuse prevention efforts on college and university campuses may be more effective in reducing problem drinking by including a proactive strategy that addresses perceived norms in campus initiatives (Perkins 1994). If students' misperceptions that exaggerate their peer norms are exposed and replaced with a more accurate perception of peer expectations and practices, their own drinking behavior is likely to become less problematic especially among students with permissive personal attitudes about drinking who would be highly encouraged by their misperceptions to drink abusively. An emphasis on correcting misperceptions of drinking norms can be introduced at primary, secondary, and tertiary levels of intervention in prevention programs (Berkowitz and Perkins 1987). Mass media campaigns, orientation programs, and curricular initiatives can be designed to inform entire campus populations of the true norms based on accurate survey research. Workshops using techniques to reveal actual peer expectations can be targeted at groups who are high risk for drinking problems on campus. Individual and group counseling sessions for alcohol abusers can give attention to these students' distorted impressions of the peer environment that reinforce their problematic behavior. In each instance, there exists the possibility that the power of peer influence can be positively engaged to constrain drinking problems as students internalize less exaggerated perceptions of peers.

References

Agostinelli, G., J.M. Brown, and W. Miller. 1995. "Effects of Normative Feedback on Consumption Among Heavy Drinking College Students." *Journal of Drug Education* 25:31-40.

Akers, R.L., M.D. Krohn, L. Lanza-Kaduce, and M. Radosevich. 1979. Social Learning and Deviant Behavior: A Specific Test of a General

Theory. *American Sociological Review* 44:636-655.

Andrews, Norman K., and D. B. Kandel. 1979. "Attitude and Behavior: A Specification of the Contingent Hypothesis." *American Sociological Review* 44:298-310.

Asch, S. E. 1951. "Effects of Group Pressure on the Modification and Distortion of Judgements." *Groups, Leadership And Men*, ed. H. Guetzkow, Pittsburgh: Carnegie Press.

———. 1952. *Social Psychology*. Englewood Cliffs, N.J.: Prentice-Hall.

Baer, J. S., and M. M. Carney. 1993. "Biases in the Perceptions of the Consequences of Alcohol Use Among College Students." *Journal of Studies on Alcohol* 54:54-60.

Baer, J. S., A. Stacy, and M. Larimer. 1991. "Biases in the Perception of Drinking Norms Among College Students." *Journal Of Studies On Alcohol* 52:580-586.

Berkowitz, A. D., and H. W. Perkins. 1987. "Current Issues in Effective Alcohol Education Programming." In *Alcohol Policies and Practices on College and University Campuses*, ed. J. S. Sherwood, 69-85. NASPA Monograph Series, Volume 7, National Association of Student Personnel Administrators, Inc.

Fesfinger, L. 1954. "A Theory of Social Comparison Processes." *Human Relations* 7:117-140.

Grube, J. W., and M. Morgan. 1990. "Attitude—Social Support Interactions: Contingent Consistency Effects in the Prediction of Adolescent Smoking, Drinking, and Drug Use." *Social Psychology Quarterly* 53:329-339.

Grube, J. W., M. Morgan, and S. T. McGree. 1986. "Attitudes and Normative Beliefs as Predictors of Smoking Intentions and Behaviours: A Test of Three Models." *British Journal Of Social Psychology* 25:81-93.

Gusfield, J. R. 1961. "The Structural Context of College Drinking." *Quarterly Journal of Studies on Alcohol* 22:428-443.

Liska, A. E. 1974. "The Impact of Attitude on Behavior: Attitude—Social Support Interaction." *Pacific Sociological Review* 17:83-97.

Newcomb, T. M. 1943. *Personality and Social Change: Attitude Formation in a Student Community*. New York: Holt, Rinehart And Winston.

Newcomb, T. M., and E. K. Wilson. 1966. *College Peer Groups*. Chicago: Aldine Publishing Company.

Orcutt, J. D. 1991. "The Social Integration of Beers and Peers: Situational Contingencies in Drinking and Intoxication." In *Society, Culture, and Drinking Patterns Reexamined*, eds. D. J.

Pittman and H. R. White, 198-215. New Brunswick, N.J.: Rutgers Center of Alcohol Studies.

Perkins, H. W. 1985. "Religious Traditions, Parents, and Peers as Determinants of Alcohol and Drug Use Among College Students." *Review Of Religious Research* 27:15-31.

———. 1994. "Confronting Misperceptions of Peer Drug Use Norms Among College Students: An Alternative Approach for Alcohol and Other Drug Education Programs." In *FIPSE Drug Prevention Programs in Higher Education Training Institute Manual*, 4th ed., edited by L. M. Grow, 453-473. Fund for the Improvement of Post Secondary Education, U.S. Department of Education.

Perkins, H. W., and A. D. Berkowitz. 1986. "Perceiving the Community Norms of Alcohol Use Among Students: Some Research Implications for Campus Alcohol Education Programming." *International Journal of the Addictions* 21:961-976.

Prentice, D. A., and D. T. Miller. 1993. "Pluralistic Ignorance and Alcohol Use on Campus: Some Consequences of Misperceiving the Social Norm." *Journal of Personality and Social Psychology* 64:243-256.

Rabow, J., C. A. Neuman, and A. C. R. Hernandez. 1987. "Contingent Consistency in Attitudes, Social Support and the Consumption of Alcohol: Additive and Interactive Effects." *Social Psychology Quarterly* 50:56-63.

Sherif, M. 1936. *The Psychology Of Social Norms*. New York: Harper.

———. 1972. "Experiments on Norm Formation." In *Classic Contributions To Social Psychology*, eds. E. P. Hollander and R. G. Hunt, 320-329. New York: Oxford University Press.

Thomas, W. I., and D. S. Thomas. 1928. *The Child in America*. New York: Alfred A. Knopf, Inc.

Wechsler, H. A. Davenport, G. Dowdall, B. Moeykens, and S. Castillo. 1994. "Health and Behavioral Consequences of Binge Drinking in College: A National Survey of Students at 140 Campuses." *Journal of the American Medical Association* 272:1672-1677.

Wechsler, H., G. W. Dowdall, A. Davenport, and S. Castillo. 1995. "Correlates Of College Student Binge Drinking." *American Journal of Public Health* 85:921-926.

Critical Evaluation

1. Is alcohol abuse by collegians simply a phase or an indication of a continuing problem?

2. How do you react to this chapter on the basis of your experiences as a student?

3. What are the implications of the findings for reducing the amount of alcohol abuse on campuses?

H. Wesley Perkins and Henry Wechsler, "Variation in Perceived College Drinking Norms and Its Impact on Alcohol Abuse." In *Journal of Drug Issues* 26:4, pp. 961–974. Copyright © 1996 by *Journal of Drug Issues*. Reprinted by permission. ✦

31

Women Who Smoke

Centers for Disease Control

Tobacco use generally begins in adolescence. More than 70 percent of high school students have smoked, and more than a third identify themselves as current users (Centers for Disease Control 1996). Nationally, about a fourth of adult Americans use tobacco.

Although more men than women smoke, the rate of men's smoking has declined more than that of women. The report from the Centers for Disease Control furnishes important data on smoking among women. As the report points out, women suffer even more health consequences from smoking than men do because women jeopardize their reproductive processes. They also put their children at risk in a number of ways. Why do they do it? The report notes one structural factor that makes a difference in whether or not women smoke—education. Another factor at the macrolevel is the effective ads that portray the female smoker as sophisticated, happy, and in control of her own life. At the microlevel, most females begin smoking because of peer pressure and/or parental example. No matter what their reasons were for beginning, however, quitting (for men as well as women) is very difficult. Most people fail one or more times before they are able to free themselves of the habit. Many never can.

Reference

Centers for Disease Control. 1996. "Youth Risk Behavior Surveillance: United States, 1995." Morbidity and Mortality Weekly Report 45:No. SS-4.

Focus Questions

1. How does education affect the rate of women smoking?

2. How does smoking affect a woman's health?

3. What happens to women who quit smoking?

In the United States, about 22 million adult women and at least 1.5 million adolescent girls currently smoke cigarettes. Among women, use of tobacco has been shown to increase the risk of cancer, heart and respiratory diseases, and reproductive disorders. More than 140,000 women die each year from smoking-related diseases—the most preventable cause of premature death in this country.

Women Who Smoke

Despite our knowledge about the death, disease, and addiction caused by smoking, in 1993, 22 percent of U.S. women 18 years of age and older were current cigarette smokers. Female smokers typically begin to smoke during adolescence—usually before high school graduation. The earlier a young woman begins to use tobacco, the more heavily she is likely to use it as an adult. Cigarette use is somewhat less common among African American than among white women (21 percent as compared to 24 percent). Smoking is much more common among women with fewer years of education (table 1).

Table 1
Smoking Rates Among Women 18–44 Years Old, by Educational Attainment (1991)

Educational Group	Current smokers
Some high school education	40%
Graduated from high school	32%
Some college education	24%
Graduated from college	12%

A Slow Decline

The prevalence of smoking among women decreased by about 11 percent between 1965 and 1993. From 1965 to 1983, the decline in smoking prevalence was greater among men than among women. Since 1983, however, the decline has been comparable for women and men.

Health Effects

Using tobacco increases a woman's risk of chronic health problems and premature death.

Cancers

Tobacco use accounts for nearly one third of all cancer deaths. An estimated 62,000 women die each year from lung cancer, which has surpassed breast cancer as the leading cause of cancer deaths among women. These deaths are largely due to smoking. The lung cancer death rate among women has increased by more than 400 percent over the last 30 years and is continuing to increase.

In addition to increasing the risk of lung cancer, tobacco use is a major risk factor for cancers of the cervix, mouth, throat, esophagus, kidney, pancreas, and bladder.

Heart Disease and Stroke

Women who smoke greatly increase their risk of heart attack and stroke. Each year approximately 34,000 deaths from ischemic heart disease among women are attributed to smoking. In addition, about 8,000 deaths from stroke among women are attributed to smoking. Most of these deaths are in women who are past menopause—however, smoking increases the risk more in younger women than in older women. Some studies suggest that smoking cigarettes dramatically increases the risk of heart disease among premenopausal women who are also taking birth control pills.

Reproductive Health

Tobacco use has a damaging effect on women's reproductive health. Smoking is associated with complications of pregnancy, early menopause, and reduced fertility.

Tobacco Use During Pregnancy

An estimated 18 to 20 percent of pregnant women smoke throughout their pregnancies. According to the Office of the Surgeon General, smoking is probably the most important modifiable cause of poor pregnancy outcomes among women in the United States. Tobacco use is associated with an increased risk of miscarriage, stillbirth, preterm delivery, and infant death, and is a cause of low birth weight in infants.

Low Birth Weight

Recent estimates suggest that eliminating smoking during pregnancy could prevent about 20 percent of cases of low birth weight and about 8 percent of preterm deliveries in the United States. Tobacco use during pregnancy slows fetal growth, often causing babies to have health problems as a result of low birth weight.

SIDS

Research also suggests that infants are more likely to die from Sudden Infant Death Syndrome (SIDS) if their mothers smoke during and after pregnancy, compared to infants whose mothers do not smoke. Although the risk is somewhat less, infants are also more likely to die from SIDS if their mothers stop smoking during pregnancy and resume smoking after delivery.

Children's Health

Tobacco use by mothers can also adversely affect children after birth. It's estimated that U.S. mothers who smoke at least ten cigarettes a day cause from 8,000–26,000 new cases of asthma among their children, annually. In addition, each year between 200,000 and one million children with asthma have their condition worsened by exposure to "second-hand" smoke. Exposing an infant to second-hand smoke also increases the child's risk of pneumonia, bronchitis, and fluid in the middle ear.

Health Risks

Tobacco use in women increases the risk of:

- cancer
- heart disease and stroke
- reproductive disorders
- emphysema
- bronchitis
- pneumonia

Quitting Smoking

Women who quit smoking tend to gain weight; however the health benefits of quitting are considerable, while health risks related to a small amount of weight gain are very minor. Research shows the average weight gain after quitting smoking is only about 5 pounds, which can be controlled through diet and exercise.

Critical Evaluation

1. Does education discourage women from smoking or is there some other reason for the inverse relationship between smoking and years of education?

2. How much likelier is a smoker than a nonsmoker to suffer the various health problems?

3. The chapter is designed to discourage women from starting to smoke or to encourage them to stop smoking. Is the information on the health hazards of smoking sufficient for that purpose or is something more needed?

Centers for Disease Control, "Women Who Smoke." Centers for Disease Control Website, 1997. ✦

32

Adolescence: The Danger Zone Years for Substance Abuse

The National Center on Addiction and Substance Abuse at Columbia University

In the mid-1990s, concern arose over adolescent use of illegal drugs. Although overall drug use continued to decline, use had increased among some adolescents and was beginning at earlier ages. Interaction patterns are one of the strongest predictors of drug use among adolescents: those with friends who are users are far more likely to be users themselves than those whose friends do not use drugs. The changes occurring in adolescence, noted in the report from the National Center on Addiction and Substance Abuse at Columbia University (CASA), make youth more vulnerable to experimenting with drugs and to yielding to peer pressure when their friends use drugs.

In other words, there is a large potential market for drugs in the adolescent population. At the structural level, such widely accepted norms as "you deserve to be happy" and "you should do your own thing" contribute to the willingness to experiment with drugs.

Not all adolescents are equally likely to use drugs. Use varies both by gender and by race or ethnicity. The variations in use by adolescents noted in the CASA report are similar to those found for adults generally.

Focus Questions

1. What are the recent trends in drug use by adolescents?

2. What characteristics of adolescence affect the decision to experiment with drugs?

3. What are the effects of drug use on adolescents?

4. How is drug use by adolescents related to age, gender, racial or ethnic background, and geographic region?

The hope for a drug-free America rests with America's adolescents and those who influence their attitudes and activities.

In five years of intensive research, The National Center on Addiction and Substance Abuse at Columbia University (CASA) has found that an individual who makes it through age 21 without smoking, using drugs or abusing alcohol is virtually certain never to do so. There will of course be exceptions—often stemming from tragedies such as the loss of a child or spouse, perhaps from latent genetic characteristics. But it is during the teen years that the overwhelming majority of Americans make the decisions that will determine whether they have lives free of substance abuse and addiction.

The Carnegie Corporation of New York's landmark report, *Great Transitions: Preparing Adolescents for a New Century,* marks adolescence as the "crucially formative phase [that] can shape an individual's life course and thus the future of a whole society." Nowhere does that statement resonate with greater force than with respect to substance abuse and addiction.

That is why this Commission applauds the Clinton Administration's decision this year to make teenagers the focus of the national drug control strategy and to expand the goals of the strategy to include educating teens to reject alcohol and tobacco, as well as illegal drugs. The critical importance of adolescence also explains why the Commission finds so disturbing the recent, often sharp increases in substance use and abuse among American adolescents. Since 1992, daily smoking has been rising among teens. Use of marijuana, which had declined steadily from 1979 until 1991, has since jumped sharply. The percentage of 8th graders who have tried crack, powder cocaine or heroin, though small, has been creeping up since 1991. Beer and other alcohol continue to be the substances teens use most: in 1996, 55 percent of 8th graders, 72 percent of 10th graders, and four out of five 12th graders (79 percent) said they had tried alcohol. Inhalants, though often overlooked in discussions of adolescent substance abuse, are easily accessible to teens and are used particularly by younger adolescents and in poor neighborhoods. In 1996, more than 20 percent of 8th graders said they had used an inhalant at some point during their life. Steroid use continues to be a problem, particularly among male athletes such as football players and wrestlers, but also among other adolescent males.

Of even more concern is that youngsters are using and abusing substances at earlier and earlier ages. According to the University of Michigan's Monitoring the Future Study, "[t]he peak ages for initiation of cigarette smoking appear to be in the sixth and seventh grades (24 percent)—or between ages 11 and 12—but with a considerable number initiating smoking even earlier. In fact, 17% of the 1995 eighth grade respondents reported having their first cigarette by fifth grade." More young teens are smoking and using marijuana and inhalants: between 1992 and 1996, the proportion of 8th graders who reported smoking during the past 30 days jumped by more than a third, from 15.5 percent to 21 percent; during the same four-year period, the proportion of 8th graders who said they had used marijuana during or before 7th grade rose from 7.7 percent to 12.7 percent, while the proportion of 8th graders who reported using inhalants during or before 7th grade grew from 14.5 percent to 17.7 percent. The average age of first marijuana use has also dropped. In 1963, the mean age of individuals who tried marijuana for the first time was 24.2. By 1979, the mean age had dropped to 17.6 and in 1994, the average age of individuals trying marijuana for the first time was 16.3. Between 1990 and 1994, for first alcohol use, the average age fell from 16.5 years to 15.9 years; for daily cigarette use, from 18.9 years to 16.8 years.

The 1996 survey of 9- to 12-year olds conducted by The Partnership for a Drug-Free America reflects this increased use of drugs at younger ages. It shows that from 1995 to 1996, the proportion of 9- to 12-year-olds trying marijuana doubled from two to four percent and from 1993 to 1996, the proportion who tried cocaine rose from two to three percent. Significantly, more of these children were offered drugs in 1996 than in 1993. And these 9- to 12-year-olds are less likely than their predecessors to believe that "using drugs is dangerous" and less likely to say they "don't want to hang around people who use drugs." All of this signals big trouble ahead as these pre-teens move into their adolescent years, unless their attitudes change.

Teenage girls are smoking, drinking and using drugs at the same early ages as teenage boys and with comparable frequency.

If drug use among teenagers continues at recent rates or even if such use is slightly reduced, America will enter the new Millennium with more teenagers using drugs, since the number of adolescents is rising and continues to rise throughout the early years of the next century. The number of teens age 12 to 17 will increase from 20.1 million to 23.6 million between 1990 and the year 2000, rising to 25 million by 2010.

Several factors present today lead us to be concerned about the persistence of adolescent drug use. The 9- to 12-year old tracking survey of The Partnership for a Drug-Free America reveals sharp increases in marijuana and other drug use among this age group and a decline in the group's sense that using drugs is risky. The University of Michigan's *Monitoring the Future Study* reflects a decline in teens' perception of risk of using drugs. CASA's 1997 survey reveals an enormous jump—from 39 percent in 1996 to 56 percent in 1997—in the proportion of teens with friends and classmates using drugs like cocaine, heroin and acid. Marijuana is more widely available to teens than ever before and most of it is more potent than it was 20 years ago. There are far more drugs, particularly pills and inhalants, available today. Smoking is up among teens, as is binge drinking, both associated with the likelihood of drug use.

However effective the efforts of national and local law enforcement in interdicting illegal drugs at the border and arresting drug dealers, a wide variety of substances are likely to be available to American adolescents. As a society we have had little success in keeping cigarettes and alcohol out of the hands of 12- to 17-year-olds even though it is illegal for them to purchase these products. In focus groups and responses to surveys conducted by CASA, older teens make it clear that they can get their hands on marijuana in a matter of hours or at most a day. Drugs are so widely available in and around most high schools that the term drug-free school has become an oxymoron in America. Numerous household and automotive products contain chemicals that teens may inhale in order to get high. This means that both outside and inside teenagers' homes and schools, alcohol, tobacco, illegal drugs and inhalants are easily accessible to teenagers looking for a high.

Taken together, the rising substance use among America's teens, the younger ages at which such use begins, the closing of the gender gap between boys and girls and the ready availability of so many substances constitutes a profound threat to American adolescents. And they know it. CASA's surveys consistently reveal that 12- to 17-year-olds consider drugs the biggest problem they face....

It is time for adults to stop asking what's gone wrong with America's teens and instead begin asking what adults can do to help adolescents negotiate the treacherous rapids of alcohol, nicotine and illicit drugs into which we have tossed them. Unless adults take more responsibility, we will deny millions of adolescents the chance to develop their talents to the fullest, confine hundreds of thousands to lives of addiction, crime and poor mental and physical health, and condemn thousands to death during their teen years from drug overdoses, alcohol poisoning, violence and accidents.

What Is Adolescence?

There is no standard definition of adolescence. For purposes of this report, we have selected the years from 12 through 17. Most people identify age 12 as the beginning of adolescence because this is typically when children begin to undergo physical and developmental changes associated with puberty. Because the legal system generally recognizes 18-year-olds as adults, the seventeenth year is often viewed as the end of adolescence. There are more than 20 million adolescents between the ages of 12 and 17, and extensive and reliable data are available for those years. The 1995 and 1996 surveys of The National Center on Addiction and Substance Abuse at Columbia University focus on those years, as does the National Household Survey on Drug Abuse of the National Institute on Drug Abuse. *The Monitoring the Future Study* of the University of Michigan surveys students in their schools and categorizes them according to grade level: 8th, 10th and 12th graders, largely 12- to 17-year-olds.

As we will discuss, there are distinct differences among adolescents of varying ages. The sharpness of these differences becomes apparent when the attitudes of 12- and 13-year-olds are compared with those of 16- and 17-year-olds, with ages 14 and 15 as a time of transition.

Adolescence is a time of significant physical, intellectual, emotional and social change. The experiences of younger teens are quite different from those of older teens and the experiences of boys differ from those of girls. These distinctions are especially important as they relate to the choices teens make about smoking, drinking and using drugs.

Physical Changes

A central feature of adolescence, puberty is a series of biological changes that physically transform a child into a reproductively mature adult. These changes which take about four years are the hallmark of early adolescence, with girls beginning the process about a year and a half earlier than boys. A boy's image of his own body normally improves as physical maturation occurs. Many girls experience a conflict between the normal processes of puberty and the high value society places on being thin. Particularly for girls who mature at early ages, this conflict can set the stage for low self-esteem, substance abuse and eating disorders.

Intellectual Changes

Adolescents concentrate on learning, discover how to think logically, grapple with abstract concepts, and come to understand consequences of behavior. But during times of stress—for example when teens feel pressured to join in drug use with peers—emotions may prevail over logic and judgment. Teens tend to have a sense of immortality and invulnerability that makes them think they can use attractive but dangerous substances with impunity.

Social and Emotional Changes

Adolescents think about how they compare to other teens and to images of adulthood they see in their families and communities and through the fashion, music and entertainment industries. This can be affirming or debilitating depending on the comparisons the teens draw. Early adolescence often involves a decline in self-esteem, particularly for girls, possibly making them more susceptible to substance abuse, depression, suicide, and delinquent behavior. As teens become less inclined to conform to the opinions of parents, they increasingly conform to those of their peers. A teen associating with a peer group whose members use dangerous substances is more likely to do the same.

Many teens begin to experiment with sex when they are emotionally immature. Substance use can both increase the likelihood and lower the age of such experimentation and hike the likelihood of adverse health and even life-threatening consequences. . . .

For all teens, substance use and abuse presents serious hazards. It can interfere with their ability to learn, their social, intellectual and physical development, and in the most tragic cases it can lead to serious accidents and even death. . . .

Adolescence and Alcohol, Tobacco and Other Drugs: A Dangerous Mix

Adolescent experimentation with cigarettes, illegal drugs and other dangerous substances, which declined during the 1980s, has been rising in the 1990s.

Alcohol is the drug of choice among teenagers, the one they use and abuse most frequently. The percentages of teens who have tried alcohol have remained steadily high since 1990 and the percentage of 8th graders who are binge drinking seems to be increasing. At the same time, teen use of marijuana (lifetime, annual, past month, and daily use) has shown a marked increase among 8th, 10th, and 12th graders. In other areas as well, illicit drug use has shown some disturbing trends. Overall, from 1992 to 1996, the percentage of 12th graders using any illicit drug in the past year rose from 27 percent to more than 40 percent; the percentage who had used any illicit drug other than marijuana within the past year climbed from 15 to nearly 20 percent.

Use of Dangerous Substances Interferes With Adolescent Growth and Development

Use of alcohol, tobacco and illicit drugs, particularly in early and mid-adolescence, interferes with the physical, intellectual and emotional development of adolescents. Even experimental use increases the chances of accidents, illness and death.

Teen abuse of alcohol and drugs can impair judgment, coordination and motor skills and inhibit short term memory and ability to concentrate at a time when adolescents most need these skills, when they are learning in school.

Over the long run, drug and alcohol use impairs intellectual development. Scientific research suggests that adolescent substance use may alter the behavior of neurotransmitters in the brain. With greater long-term use, the risk of cancer, liver disease, heart disease, and other life threatening and debilitating conditions increases.

As a teen's drug use increases, social relationships with family members and friends may deteriorate. Drinking and smoking marijuana engage a teen with peer groups that are more likely to become involved with drugs like cocaine and heroin. Because drug use and drunk driving are illegal activities and because of the strong links between drug use and increased criminal behavior, use of alcohol, marijuana or other illicit drugs may put a teen into the juvenile justice system, which in turn may tilt the teen toward more criminal activity. Certain drugs may also trigger aggressive behavior and schizophrenic-like symptoms.

The Earlier and More Often the Teen Uses, the Greater the Risk and Progression of Drug Use

For many teens, a progression towards using increasingly dangerous substances starts with cigarettes and alcohol, moves to marijuana, and then on to other illicit drugs such as cocaine, heroin and acid. When teens first use tobacco and alcohol, no one can predict who among them will go on to use marijuana. Most don't. For teens who use tobacco, alcohol and marijuana, no one can predict who will go on to use other illicit drugs. Most don't. But, adolescents who play with the fire of nicotine, alcohol and marijuana increase their risk of getting burned by the flames of acid, cocaine and heroin.

In 1994, The National Center on Addiction and Substance Abuse at Columbia University published a report, *Cigarettes, Alcohol, Marijuana: Gateways to Illicit Drug Use,* which analyzed the relationship of use of cigarettes, alcohol and marijuana to use of other illicit drugs. From its examination of available data, surveys of teens and responses from focus groups, CASA has uncovered strong statistical relationships between the use of cigarettes, alcohol and marijuana and the subsequent use of cocaine.

Two important conclusions came out of this work:

- The earlier a teen starts using cigarettes, alcohol and marijuana, the greater the likelihood that teen will use other illicit drugs.

- The more frequently a teen uses cigarettes, alcohol and marijuana, the greater the likelihood that teen will use other drugs.

For these reasons, alcohol and tobacco are often referred to as gateways to marijuana use and alcohol, tobacco and marijuana are referred to as gateway drugs to other illicit drug use. . . .

The 1994 CASA study analyzed data from the National Household Survey on Drug Abuse (NHSDA) of the National Institute on Drug Abuse and concluded that regardless of gender, race or ethnicity, the probability of illicit drug use was considerably higher for those who had used a gateway drug as a child.

CASA's findings were consistent with a number of other studies. Work by Kandel and Yamaguchi, for instance, indicates that most cocaine users begin their drug use with cigarettes or alcohol and then progress to marijuana before moving on to cocaine. Their work also suggests that adolescent cocaine users begin using gateway drugs an average of two years earlier than those adolescents who do not use cocaine. Ellickson, Hays, and Bell found evidence that weekly smoking may precede the initial use of hard drugs and that marijuana use accompanies hard drug use. Welte and Bames, as well as other researchers, have argued that cigarettes play a larger role as a gateway drug for women than men.

In this report, using the Centers for Disease Control and Prevention's (CDC) data from the 1995 Youth Risk Behavior Survey of 10,900 9th to 12th graders, for the first time, CASA has analyzed the statistical relationship between use of gateway substances and use of other illicit drugs, controlling for a variety of other risk factors such as fighting, carrying a weapon, attempting suicide, having multiple sexual partners, [and] driving drunk. The findings reveal a stunning statistical link between smoking, drinking and using pot—in and of themselves—and the use of harder drugs.

Among teens who did display some of these other risk behaviors, the probability of marijuana use was influenced by these behaviors. Nevertheless, looking at these risk factors independently (holding all others constant), alcohol and cigarette use demonstrated a more powerful statistical relationship to marijuana use than any of these other behaviors. For instance, among kids who reported being in three or more fights in the previous year, those who reported having smoked a cigarette in the past month were five times more likely to have reported using marijuana than those who reported fighting but not smoking.

These are the stunning findings of statistical correlation:

- Among 12- to 17-year-olds who report no other problem behaviors, those who report drinking alcohol and smoking cigarettes at least once in the past month are 30 times more likely to have also smoked marijuana than those who report neither smoking nor drinking alcohol. These correlations are more pronounced for girls than boys: for girls, 36 times likelier; for boys, 27 times likelier.

- Among 12- to 17-year-olds who report no other problem behaviors, those who report using all three gateway drugs (cigarettes, alcohol, marijuana) in the past month are almost 17 times likelier to have used a harder drug like cocaine. Here, the relationship of gateway drug use to use of other illicit drugs is stronger for boys than girls. Teenage boys who report using all three substances (cigarettes, alcohol, marijuana) at least once in the past 30 days are 29 times more likely to have used a harder drug than boys who report using none of these substances. Teenage girls who report using all three substances are 11 times more likely to have used a harder drug.

These relationships between use of gateway substances and other illegal drug use are more potent than early statistical relationships found between smoking and lung cancer (nine to ten times likelier in the 1964 Surgeon General's report) and between high cholesterol and heart disease (two to four times likelier in the early phases of the Framingham Heart Study).

While these data demonstrate only statistical (not causal) correlations, neuroscience research may help to explain the relationship between use of alcohol, cigarettes and marijuana and use of harder drugs. Two recently released studies suggest a biomedical basis for the link between use of alcohol and use of marijuana, as well as between use of marijuana and use of drugs like cocaine and heroin. Research by Gaetano DiChiara of the University of Cagliari in Italy and his colleagues indicates that THC (delta-9-tetrahydrocannabinol, the primary psychoactive ingredient in marijuana) may trigger the brain's reward system to release dopamine, a chemical which gives users the sensation of pleasure. It is dopamine and the brain's reward system which researchers have sug-

gested make drugs like heroin and cocaine so addictive. Gaetano DiChiara suggests that marijuana may prime the brain to seek substances like heroin that act in a similar way. Earlier studies demonstrated that nicotine and cocaine have a similar impact on dopamine levels in the brain.

Up until this time, researchers have disagreed on whether marijuana was physically addictive. Studies have suggested psychological dependence, but because cannabis stays in the body for so long after use, physical dependence has been a matter of debate. In another recent study conducted by Koob and Weiss and published in *Science* magazine, however, researchers used an antagonist to induce immediate cannabis withdrawal in rats. The rats exhibited symptoms of emotional stress and anxiety like those associated with withdrawal from cocaine, alcohol and opiates. According to *Science*, "the results, experts say, provide the first neurochemical basis for a marijuana withdrawal syndrome, and one with a strong emotional component that is shared by other abused drugs." Koob and Weiss believe that the stress and anxiety brought on by marijuana withdrawal might nudge a user toward harder drugs. These two studies suggest that marijuana operates on the brain in a manner similar to alcohol, cocaine and heroin, both to induce pleasure during use and to cause anxiety following cessation in use. . . .

The Addiction Continuum

No teen who experiments with tobacco, alcohol or drugs expects to become addicted. With the exception of crack cocaine users, most teens who experiment do not get hooked. For an increasing number, however, experimentation progresses to more regular use. Initial use may be motivated by curiosity, thrill seeking or peer pressure. Eager to appear cool and be one of the group, a teen may begin using dangerous substances socially as a way to be accepted by peers.

Teens using drugs or alcohol quickly learn that particular substances can produce certain pleasurable effects. Many then use alcohol, marijuana or other illicit drugs to feel good, to relieve stress or cope with difficult situations. This type of use is considered "instrumental": teens are intentionally using certain substances to manipulate their emotions and behavior.

These teens are in dangerous territory. From here, it's a short step to habitual use and then into the stage of compulsive use or addiction. No clear line separates these final stages of addiction where substance use becomes the predominant means of recreation and coping. Former interests drop away. New friends who use substances replace old ones who don't. Activities center on getting and using drugs. Teens in these later stages of the addiction continuum continue to use drugs and alcohol despite negative legal, social, physical, and academic consequences.

In the "compulsive" or final stage of addiction, teens lose control over their substance use. The addicted teen is preoccupied with getting drunk or high. Mood altering substances control the teen's life. The teen becomes isolated from family and friends. . . .

The Demographics of Teen Substance Use

While substance use is an issue for all adolescents, patterns may be related to age, gender, racial and ethnic background and geographic region.

Age Makes a Difference

In general, younger teens use illicit drugs less than older teens. However, younger adolescents do use alcohol, tobacco, marijuana and inhalants—gateway substances that they perceive to be less risky and are easier to acquire than other substances. Most drug abusers report that they began using such gateway substances before age 14. Alcohol, tobacco and marijuana are also the substances most likely to be used by older teens; most teens who use steroids, LSD, cocaine and amphetamines do not begin use of these substances until 9th grade.

A noticeable change in patterns of drug use occurs between middle school and high school—at about age 14 through 15. As teens go from 12 and 13 to 16 and 17, their proximity to dangerous substances increases and their antipathy to such substances decreases.

Drugs become perceived as more benign, less of a "big deal"; they are ubiquitous, easier to get; there is less fear of using drugs, more peer pressure to use them and such use often comes to be regarded as normal.

The Closing of the Gender Gap

CASA's 1996 report, *Substance Abuse and The American Woman*, found that among teenagers, the gender gap in smoking, drinking and drug use has largely disappeared. Girls and boys are often indistinguishable in their rates of alcohol and drug use. Since 1975, adolescent girls have been equally or more likely than boys to smoke. Today, girls and boys are just as likely to be current daily smokers (21 percent vs. 22 percent among 12th graders) or to have never smoked (37 percent vs. 36 percent among 12th graders). Boys and girls are also equally likely to quit smoking.

Adolescent girls and boys are also almost as likely to be current drinkers (47 percent vs. 56 percent among 12th graders). Though girls are still less likely than boys to binge drink, the gap has narrowed since 1975. Twelfth grade girls are less likely than boys to binge on beer (20 percent vs. 37 percent) and hard liquor (16 percent vs. 25 percent), but equally likely to binge on wine (6 percent).

The gap between girls' and boys' illicit drug use has closed in the last 30 years, but boys are still more likely to become regular users. Girls are almost as likely as boys to have used illicit drugs other than marijuana (17 percent vs. 21 percent).

Experimentation at young ages is a concern for all adolescents, but it is most ominous for girls. In older generations, women were more likely to try their first cigarette, drink or illicit drug at a later age than men. This is one reason women were less likely to become regular users; they started when they were more mature and less vulnerable to the temptation and pressure to smoke and get high or drunk. But over the last 30 years, this protective factor has vanished. Girls and boys are now wading into drugs, alcohol and tobacco at the same early ages.

Teen boys and girls exhibit different symptoms of substance abuse. Boys tend to be outer-directed, displaying symptoms such as drunk driving, fighting and truancy. Girls are likelier to be inner-directed, displaying anxiety, depression and lack of self-esteem as signals of substance abuse. Girls who abuse drugs are more likely to have suffered sexual abuse than boys. The rate of substance abuse among boys and girls is becoming increasingly similar. Women become intoxicated more quickly than men and addicted more rapidly than men. Tragically, girls who are high on alcohol and drugs increase their risk of being raped and most teen pregnancy occurs when one or both teens are high or drunk.

Race and Ethnicity

Different ethnic and racial groups show different patterns of initiation and use of various substances. Hispanic 12- to 15-years olds report the highest lifetime and past month use of all drugs. Forty-two percent of Hispanic males have been offered or sold illegal drugs on school property. Only 29 percent of white non-Hispanic males and 20 percent of black non-Hispanic males report similar experiences.

By 12th grade, white students have the highest rate of use for almost all substances except cocaine, crack and steroids. Hispanics report the highest rates of use for cocaine, crack and steroids.

The highest rate of cigarette use on school property is among white teens. White teens start smoking two years earlier than black teens—age 12 for whites compared to age 14 for blacks. Black teens show the lowest percentages of substance use, regardless of gender or age, though these figures may be skewed because of higher school dropout rates of blacks and the failure of surveys to account adequately for dropouts.

Blacks also tend to be slightly older when they initiate alcohol and marijuana use. Black teens are more affected by their perception of immediate negative consequences of substance use than white students and by their expectation of punishment for drug use. Since 1992, however, African-American teens have narrowed the gap in marijuana use.

Geography

The use of particular substances varies by geography, but no area is immune. For the most part, illicit drug use tends to be highest among 12th graders in the Northeast. However, marijuana use is somewhat higher among young teens in the West, where 18 percent of 8th graders admitted trying marijuana. The West also ranked first in LSD use for 8th graders, and for cocaine, crack and methamphetamine use among 12th graders. The South had the highest teen rates of use for heroin, barbiturates and tranquilizers. The Northeast and North Central regions had highest daily smoking and alcohol use.

Critical Evaluation

1. Is the proportion of adolescents who try drugs a problem or only the proportion that become regular users?

2. The report states that adolescents have easy access to alcohol, tobacco, and illegal drugs in their homes and schools. Is this true? Just how accessible are drugs?

3. Does the report accurately portray, understate, or overstate the dangers of adolescent drug use?

Project for Personal Application and Class Discussion: Abuse of Alcohol and Other Drugs

Chapter 30 reports Perkins and Wechsler's research on perceived and personal drinking norms. As you read it, did you think about your own school? What are the norms about drug usage? How do they compare with your personal standards? How do your standards compare with those of your parents and your friends?

Answer the following questions, which are similar to those used in the research of Perkins and Wechsler, indicating your opinion, your perception of your school norms, and your perception of your parents' and friends' opinion.

1. For each of the following situations, how much is it appropriate to drink? (1 = no alcohol at all; 2 = one to two drinks; 3 = enough to get high but not drunk; 4 = enough to get drunk):

	myself	school	parents	friends
a. on a date				
b. at a party				
c. alone at home				
d. at an off-campus bar				

2. For each of the following drugs, how much usage is appropriate? (1 = don't even try it; 2 = okay to try, but don't use regularly; 3 = use whenever you want):

	myself	school	parents	friends
a. marijuana				
b. inhalants				
c. other illegal drugs				

Ask your parents and friends to respond to the questions as a check against your perceptions. Check your perceptions of the school by the average response of all members of your class.

How accurate were your perceptions? How did they compare with those of your parents and friends? What effect does all of this have on your drug usage? ✦

Crime and Delinquency

W hen asked what they regard as the nation's most serious problems, Americans consistently put crime near the top of the list. Reports of crime waves generate fear and demands for action. Even people who live in relatively crime-free areas express fears about being victimized.

Crime rates vary over time (Rand, Lynch, and Cantor 1997). In 1995, rates of rape, robbery, and aggravated assault were at or near their lowest point in 23 years. Rates of theft and household burglary declined fairly steadily from the late 1970s to the mid-1990s. In 1995, the burglary rate was about half the 1973 rate. By contrast, computer crime has grown rapidly (McCollum 1997). Some police departments now have special units that deal with computer crime. People who engage in computer crime do so for a variety of reasons, ranging from the criminal who engages in fraud to make money to the hacker who enjoys securing private information to the employee who uses the computer against an employer because of financial problems or conflict with the boss.

In spite of declines in some specific crimes, the overall rate of crime is still high. Virtually everyone will be a victim of some kind of crime during his or her lifetime. And if recent incarceration rates remain unchanged, about one out of every 20 people—about one out of every 11 men and one out of every 91 women—will serve time in prison during their lifetime (Bonczar and Beck 1997).

Crime, in other words, continues to be a social problem of major dimensions and intense concern. In this section we examine some of the many faces of crime.

References

Bonczar, Thomas P., and Allen J. Beck. 1997. "Lifetime Likelihood of Going to State or Federal Prison." *Bureau of Justice Statistics Special Report*. Washington, DC: Government Printing Office.

McCollum, Tim. 1997. "Computer Crime." *Nation's Business*, November.

Rand, Michael R., and James P. Lynch. 1997. "Criminal Victimization 1973-95." *National Crime Victimization Survey*. Washington, DC: U.S. Government Printing Office. ✦

33

Sex Offenses and Offenders

Lawrence A. Greenfeld

Violent crimes are the most feared. Although men are more likely than women to be victims of a violent crime, women are vulnerable to one of the most traumatic kinds of crime— rape. Lawrence Greenfeld reports federal data on rape and sexual assault, including information on offenders. Note that while the rate of sex offenses declined, the number of those incarcerated for such offenses continued to increase. In other words, compared to the past, more offenders are being caught and convicted.

A substantial proportion of all crime, including sexual assault, is committed by young males (see Table 1). An important structural factor in understanding crime rates, then, is the age composition of the society. Crime rates tend to fluctuate in accord with the proportion of males in their 20s and 30s in the population. Another important factor is the family—those who come from dysfunctional families are more likely than others to engage in crime. Sexual offenders, in particular, tend to have a history of childhood abuse. At the microlevel, this abuse generates attitudes of disdain for conventional morality and rage against an abusive world. As many social scientists have pointed out, rape is more a crime of hatred than it is of sexual desire.

Focus Questions

1. How do the number of sex offenses reported by victims compare with those reported by law enforcement agencies?

2. How many sex offenders are there?

3. How are sex offenses connected with other crimes?

Measuring the Extent of Sex Offending

The Reports from Victims

In 1995 persons age 12 or older reported experiencing an estimated 260,300 attempted or completed rapes and nearly 95,000 threatened or completed sexual assaults other than rape.

- The number reported by victims age 125 declined significantly from 1993:
  1993—1 violent sex offense for every 435 residents.
  1995—1 violent sex offense for every 625 residents.

- In 1994 and 1995 a third of the victims said that the rape/sexual assault victimization was reported to a law enforcement agency.

The Law Enforcement Response

In 1995 the number of forcible rapes reported to the police nationwide was 97,460, the lowest total since 1989.

- The highest rate of forcible rape recorded by law enforcement agencies since 1976 was in 1992—84 per 100,000 women, or about 1 forcible rape for every 1,200 women. By 1995 the rate had decreased over 14%.

- In 1995 law enforcement agencies reported that about half of all reported forcible rapes were cleared by an arrest—an estimated 34,650 arrests for forcible rape. There were 94,500 arrests for other sex offenses.

The per capita rate of arrest for forcible rape or sexual assault in 1995, 50.3 per 100,000 residents, was the same as that in 1983.

Federal statistical series obtaining data on arrested or convicted persons—Uniform Crime Reports, National Judicial Reporting Program, and National Corrections Reporting Program—show a remarkable similarity in the characteristics of those categorized as rapists: 99 in 100 are male, 6 in 10 are white, and the average age is the early thirties.

Pretrial Release and Adjudication of Rape Offenders

About half of rape defendants are released prior to trial. Among those released, half had to post a financial bond. The median bond amount was $23,500.

- About 1 in 20 filings for a violent felony in the 75 largest counties in 1992 were for rape.

- In 1992 an estimated 21,655 felony defendants nationwide were convicted of rape; 8 in 10 had pleaded guilty.

- Over two-thirds of convicted rape defendants received a prison sentence.

- For rape defendants sentenced to prison, the average term imposed was just under 14 years. About 2% of convicted rapists received life sentences.

Corrections and the Convicted Sex Offender

On a given day about 234,000 offenders convicted of rape or sexual assault are under the care, custody, or control of corrections agencies. About 60% of these sex offenders are under conditional supervision in the community.

Rape and sexual assault offenders account for just under 5% of the total correctional population in the United States:

- Among 906,000 offenders confined in state prisons in 1994, 88,000, or 9.7%, were violent sex offenders.

- Since 1980 the average annual growth in the number of prisoners has been about 7.6%. The number of prisoners sentenced for violent sexual assault other than rape increased by an annual average of nearly 15%—faster than any other category of violent crime and faster than all other categories except drug trafficking.

- While the average sentence of convicted rapists released from State prisons has remained stable at about 10 years, the average time served has increased from about 3 1/2 years to about 5 years; for those released after serving time for sex-

ual assault, the sentence has been a stable 6 1/2 years, and the average time served grew about 6 months to just under 3 years.

- Rapists and sexual assaulters serving time in State prisons were less likely to have had a prior conviction history or a history of violence than other incarcerated violent offenders, though they were substantially more like history of convictions for violent sex offenses.

- Sexual assault offenders were substantially more likely than any other category of offenders to report having experienced physical or sexual abuse while growing up.

- Violent sex offenders were substantially less likely than other violent offenders to have committed their crime with a weapon; however, rapists were about as likely as all violent offenders to report having used a knife.

- In two 3-year BJS (Bureau of Justice Statistics) followups of samples of felons placed on probation and of felons released from prison, rapists had a lower rate of rearrest for a new violent felony than most other categories of offenders convicted of violence. Yet, rapists were more likely than others to be rearrested for a new rape.

Sex Offenses and Murder

After the latter half of the 1980's, the percentage of all murders with known circumstances in which investigators identified rape or another sex offense as the principal circumstance of the murder has declined from about 2% of murders to less than 1%.

- Between 1976 and 1994 there were an estimated 405,089 murders in the United States. Of these, the circumstances surrounding the murder are known in 317,925, or 78.5%. Among the cases with known circumstances, an estimated 4,807, or 1.5%, were classified as involving rape or another sex offense.

- Offenders in sexual assault murders are about 6 years younger on average than other murderers. Youth under 18 have accounted for about 10% of the sexual assault murders since 1976.

Table 1

Characteristics of Known Offenders in Murders Involving Sexual Assault, 1976–94

Offender characteristic	Murders	
	All	Sexual assault
Sex		
Male	86.6%	95.0%
Female	13.4	5.0
Race		
White	47.8%	58.0%
Black	50.3	39.9
Other	1.9	2.1
Age		
12 or younger	.2%	.1%
13–17	8.1	9.9
18–24	30.1	39.1
25–29	18.0	22.5
30–39	23.1	21.1
40–49	11.1	5.4
50–59	5.4	1.5
60 or older	3.9	.4
Average	31 yrs	26 yrs

Source: "Sex Offenses and Offenders," *Bureau of Justice Statistics: Executive Summary,* January (Washington, DC: U.S. Government Printing Office, 1997).

Critical Evaluation

1. Are some victims' reports of sex offenses an overstatement of the situation? Why?

2. Are the activities of law-enforcement agencies noted in this report adequate for sex offenses?

3. What could be done to reduce the number of sex offenses?

Lawrence A. Greenfield, "Sex Offenses and Offenders." Washington, DC: U.S. Government Printing Office, 1997. ✦

34

Controlling Crime Before It Happens

J. David Hawkins

Not only is a substantial proportion of crime committed by young people, but offenses by the young have also been increasing while the overall rate of violent crime has been going down. What can be done? Traditionally, the juvenile justice system has used a combination of punishment, treatment, and rehabilitation. J. David Hawkins discusses another way to deal with juvenile crime—prevent it before it happens. A first step is to identify the reasons that young people resort to crime. Hawkins discusses various structural and social psychological factors that increase the chances that young people will resort to violent behavior. It is these factors that must be addressed in a risk-focused prevention program if juvenile crime is to be reduced. Moreover, to the extent that juvenile crime is reduced, adult crime rates will also go down. For nearly all adult offenders were also offenders as children or adolescents.

Focus Questions

1. What is the public-health model of crime prevention?

2. What factors put young people at risk for violence?

3. What factors protect young people from the risk?

Traditionally, the juvenile justice system has employed sanctions, treatment, and rehabilitation to change problem behaviors after they have occurred. Advocates of a prevention-based approach to crime control invite the scorn of critics who believe prevention amounts to little more than "feel-good" activities. Yet the practitioner—the probation officer confronted daily with young people in trouble—is often aware of the need for effective prevention. As a probation officer in the early 1970's working with delinquent teenagers, I found myself asking, "Couldn't we have prevented these youngsters from getting to this point? Couldn't we have interceded before they were criminally referred to the courts?"

Once they have experienced the reinforcing properties of drugs and are convinced of crime's profitability, young people are difficult to turn around. Once invested in the culture of crime, they reject the virtues attributed to school and family, for reasons that are all too clear. For them, school is not a place of attachment and learning, but of alienation and failure; family is not a source of love and support, but of unremitting conflict.

Dealing with these youths as a probation officer, I saw my job as something akin to operating an expensive ambulance service at the bottom of a cliff. The probation staff were the emergency team patching up those who fell over the edge. Many of us who have worked in juvenile corrections have come to realize that to keep young people from falling in the first place, a barrier is needed at the top of the cliff. In short, we believe that prevention is more effective and less costly than treatment after the fact. David Mitchell, chief judge of the juvenile court for Baltimore County, once observed, "It is of no value for the court to work miracles in rehabilitation if there are no opportunities for the child in the community. Until we deal with the environment in which they live, whatever we do in the courts is irrelevant."

Effective Prevention Based on the Public Health Model

In prevention, where action precedes the commission of crime, it is wise to heed the admonition that guides physicians: "Above all, do no harm." Hard work and good intentions, by themselves, are not enough to ensure that a program to prevent violence or substance abuse will succeed, let alone that it will not make things worse.

Early prevention efforts in the "War on Drugs" serve to illustrate this point. Well-meaning people were concerned about substance abuse and decided to do something about it by introducing prevention programs in the schools. They collected information, pictures, and even samples of illicit drugs, took these materials to the schools, and showed them to students; they talked about the behavioral and health effects of drugs and warned of the risks associated with their use. Contrary to intention and expectation, these drug information programs failed to reduce or eliminate drug use and, in some instances, actually led to its increase. The real lesson learned in the schools was that information, which is neutral, can be employed to the wrong end, producing more harm than good. These early prevention workers had not envisioned drug information in the context of a comprehensive prevention strategy.

Increasingly, the preventive approach used in public health is being recognized as appropriate for use as part of a criminal justice strategy. It is instructive to review an example of how the model has been applied to disease control. Seeking to prevent cardiovascular disease, researchers in the field of public health first identified risk factors; that is, the factors whose presence increased a person's chances of contracting the disease: tobacco use, high-fat diet, sedentary lifestyle, high levels of stress, and family history of heart disease. Equally important, they determined that certain protective factors (e.g., aerobic exercise or relaxation techniques) helped prevent the development of heart problems.

These public health researchers were concerned with halting the onset of heart disease in order to avoid risky, invasive, and costly interventions, such as angioplasty or bypass surgery, after the disease had taken hold. Their goal was to reduce or counter the identified risk factors for heart disease in the population at large; their strategy was to launch a massive public advocacy campaign, conducted in multiple venues (e.g., the media, government, corporations, schools), aimed at elimination of "at risk" behaviors (and the attitudes supporting them). If risk could not be avoided altogether, the campaign could at least promote those behaviors

and attitudes that reduce risk of heart disease. Proof that this two-pronged strategy has been effective is in the numbers: a 45-percent decrease in the incidence of cardiovascular disease, due in large measure to risk-focused prevention. Application of the same prevention principles to reduce the risks associated with problem behaviors in teenagers, including violence, can work as well.

Identifying Risk Factors for Violence

Using the public health model to reduce violence in America's communities calls for first identifying the factors that put young people at risk for violence in order to reduce or eliminate these factors and strengthen the protective factors that buffer the effects of exposure to risk.

Over the past few years, longitudinal research (that is, studies that follow youngsters from the early years of their lives into adulthood) has identified factors associated with neighborhoods and communities, the family, the schools, and peer groups, as well as factors residing in the individual that increase the probability of violence during adolescence and young adulthood. These factors . . . also have been shown to increase the probability of other health and behavior problems, including substance abuse, delinquency, teen pregnancy, and dropping out of school. . . .

In Neighborhoods

Five risk factors arising from the community are known to increase the probability that a young person will engage in violence:

- *Availability of guns.* The United States has one of the highest rates of criminal violence in the world, and firearms are implicated in a great number of these crimes. In recent years, reports of gun-toting youths in inner-city schools and of violent incidents involving handguns in school environs have created mounting concern. Given the lethality of firearms, the increased likelihood of conflict escalating into homicide when guns are present, and the strong association between availability of firearms and homicide rates, a teenager having ready access to firearms through family, friends, or a source on the street is at increased risk of violence.

- *Community laws/norms favorable to crime.* Community norms are communicated through laws, written policies, informal social practices, and adult expectations of young people. Sometimes social practices send conflicting messages: for example, schools and parents may promote "just say no" themes while alcohol and substance abuse are acceptable practices in the community. Community attitudes also influence law enforcement. An example is the enforcement of laws that regulate firearms sales. These laws have reduced violent crime, but the effect is small and diminishes as time passes. A number of studies suggest that the reasons are community norms that include lack of proactive monitoring or enforcement, as well as the availability of firearms from jurisdictions having no legal prohibitions on sales or illegal access. Other laws related to reductions in violent crime, especially crime involving firearms, include laws governing penalties for licensing violations and for using a firearm in the commission of a crime.

- *Media portrayals of violence.* The highly charged public debate over whether portrayals of violence in the media adversely affect children continues. Yet research over the past 3 decades demonstrates a clear correlation between depictions of violence and the development of aggressive and violent behavior. Exposure to media violence also teaches violent problem-solving strategies and appears to alter children's attitudes and sensitivity to violence.

- *Low neighborhood attachment/community disorganization.* Indifference to cleanliness and orderliness, high rates of vandalism, little surveillance of public places by neighborhood residents, absence of parental involvement in schools, and low rates of voter participation are indicative of low neighborhood attachment. The less homogeneous a community in terms of race, class, religion, or mix of industrial to residential areas, the less connected its residents may feel to the overall community and the more difficult it is to establish clear community goals and identity. Higher rates of drug problems, juvenile delinquency, and violence occur in such places.

- *Extreme economic deprivation.* Children who live in deteriorating neighborhoods characterized by extreme poverty are more likely to develop problems with delinquency, teen pregnancy, dropping out of school, and violence. If such children also have behavior and adjustment problems early in life, they are also more likely to have problems with drugs as they mature. The rate of poverty is disproportionately higher for African American, Native American, or Hispanic children than for white children; thus, children are differentially exposed to risk depending on their racial or cultural backgrounds.

In Families

Obviously, the home environment, family dynamics, and parental stability play a major role in shaping children. Three risk factors for violence are associated with the family constellation: poor family management practices, including the absence of clear expectations and standards for children's behavior, excessively severe or inconsistent punishment, and parental failure to monitor their children's activities, whereabouts, or friends; family conflict, either between parents or between parents and children, which enhances the risk for all of the problem behaviors; and favorable parental attitudes and involvement in violent behavior, which increase the risk that children witnessing such displays will themselves become violent.

At School

Two indicators of risk for violence are associated with a child's experiences at school. Antisocial behavior of early onset (that is, aggressiveness in grades K–3, sometimes combined with isolation or withdrawal or sometimes combined with hyperactivity or attention-deficit disorder) is more frequently found in boys than girls and places the child at increased risk for problems, including violence, during adolescence. The risk factor also includes persistent antisocial behavior first exhibited in adolescence, such as skipping school, getting into fights, and misbehaving in class. Young people of both genders who engage in these behaviors during early adolescence are at increased risk for drug abuse, juvenile delinquency, violence, dropping out of school, and teen pregnancy. Academic failure, if it occurs in the late elementary grades and beyond, is a second school-related risk factor that is likely to result in violence and other problem behaviors. Specifically, it is the experience of failure that appears to escalate the risk, rather than ability per se.

In Peer Groups and Within the Individual

If youngsters associate with peers who engage in problem behaviors (for example, drug abuse, delinquency, violence, sexual activity, or dropping out of school), they are much more likely to do the same. Further, the earlier in their lives that young people become involved in these kinds of experiences—or take their first drink of alcohol or smoke their first marijuana cigarette—the greater is the likelihood of prolonged, serious, and chronic involvement in health and behavior problems. Even when a young person comes from a well-managed family and is not burdened with other risk factors, associating with friends who engage in problem behaviors greatly increases the child's risk. In addition, certain constitutional factors—those that may have a biological or physiological ba-

sis—appear to increase a young person's risk. Examples of constitutional factors include lack of impulse control, sensation seeking, and low harm avoidance.

Protective Factors

It is well known that some youngsters, even though they are exposed to multiple risk factors, do not succumb to violent, antisocial behavior. Research indicates that protective factors reduce the impact of negative risk factors by providing positive ways for an individual to respond to these risks. Three categories of protective factors have been identified:

- Individual characteristics: A resilient temperament and positive social orientation.
- Bonding: Positive relationships with family members, teachers, or other adults.
- Healthy beliefs and clear standards: Beliefs in children's competence to succeed in school and avoid drugs and crime coupled with establishing clear expectations and rules governing their behavior.

Critical Evaluation

1. Has the author identified all the risk factors for violence? Does genetics play any role?

2. Are some of the risk factors identified more important than others?

3. What can be done to increase the protective factors?

J. David Hawkins, "Controlling Crime Before It Happens." In *National Institute of Justice Journal*, August 1995, pp. 10–18. Washington, DC: U.S. Government Printing Office. ✦

35

The Impact of Federal Sentencing Reforms on African Americans

Marvin D. Free, Jr.

In theory, everyone is treated equally in the criminal justice system. In point of fact, the system and even some of the laws do not treat all people fairly. As a result, "liberty and justice for all" is an ideal rather than a reality for millions of Americans, particularly for women and for racial and ethnic groups.

Marvin D. Free, Jr. shows how African Americans are disproportionately penalized by certain federal sentencing reforms. A macrolevel change (new legislation dealing with drug offenses) has microlevel consequences (punishment of offenders) that do not affect all offenders equally. The point, of course, is not that offenders should not be punished, but that the punishment for one group should not be more severe than that of another group for the same type of offense.

Focus Questions

1. Why has sentencing reform occurred?
2. How do mandatory minimums discriminate against African Americans?
3. How have sentencing guidelines increased the proportion of minority defendants processed in federal court?

African Americans are disproportionately found in the inmate population of federal penal institutions. Although composing 12.1%

of the total United States population (U.S. Bureau of the Census, 1992, p. 17), African Americans constituted 33.8% of all federal inmates in 1993 (Maguire & Pastore, 1994, p. 628). The overrepresentation of African Americans in federal prisons raises an interesting question: What effect have the U.S. sentencing guidelines, which emerged from the Sentencing Reform Act of 1984, and mandatory minimum statutes had on African Americans? . . .

Sentencing Reform in the United States

Recent changes in federal sentencing are the result of two simultaneous and related forces. First, "mandatory minimums" (i.e., statutory requirements that a person convicted of a specific offense shall receive at least the minimum sentence prescribed by that statute), which, until lately, were used sparingly, have today been expanded to include entire classes of offenses (U.S. Sentencing Commission, 1991b). Second, the Sentencing Reform Act of 1984 has altered the processing of federal defendants. This act created the U.S. Sentencing Commission and charged it with the responsibility of developing sentencing guidelines for federal offenses. The guidelines, submitted to Congress in April 1987, became effective on November 1, 1987 (Heaney, 1991). . . .

Sentencing Reform and Racial Discrimination

As indicated . . . sentencing reform in the United States came packaged as either the U.S. Sentencing Commission's sentencing guidelines, which applied to *all* federal crimes committed on or after November 1, 1987, or legislatively mandated minimum sentences, which applied to only specified *classes* of crimes. Thus, to the extent possible, an evaluation of sentencing reform should analyze separately these two alterations in sentencing policy. . . .

Mandatory Minimums and Racial Bias

Using data for fiscal year 1990, the U.S. Sentencing Commission (1991b) observed that African Americans were more likely than Whites to be convicted under mandatory minimum provisions, even though they constituted a much smaller percentage of all federal defendants than their White counterparts. African Americans, who constituted 28.2% of all federal defendants, accounted for 38.5% of all federal defendants convicted under mandatory minimum provisions. Comparable figures for Whites were 46.9% and 34.8%, respectively.

The study also found that African Americans were more likely than either Whites or Hispanics to be sentenced at or above the indicated mandatory minimum. More than two thirds (67.7%) of all Black federal defendants convicted under the mandatory minimum provisions received sentences that were at or above the indicated mandatory minimum. In contrast, 54% of the White and 57.1% of the Hispanic federal defendants convicted under the mandatory minimum provisions received these sentences (U.S. Sentencing Commission, 1991b, p. 80).

Why are African Americans disproportionately convicted under the mandatory minimum provisions and why are they more likely than Whites and Hispanics to receive severe sentences under the mandatory minimum provisions? Much of the disparity can be attributed to the emphasis on drug offenses. This is readily seen by analyzing data from pre- and postguidelines periods, in that the guidelines reflected the increasingly severe penalties required under the mandatory minimum provisions. In 1986, the last full year prior to the implementation of the guidelines, only 19% of all African Americans convicted in federal court were convicted of drug trafficking. By the first half of 1990, however, this figure had risen to 46%. The comparable White rates were 26% in 1986 and 35% for the first 6 months of 1990 (McDonald & Carlson, 1993, p. 10). Thus, prior to the implementation of mandatory minimum provisions for drug offenses, Whites were more likely than Blacks to be convicted of drug trafficking, whereas the reverse was true after these provisions went into effect.

The dramatic increase in drug convictions for African Americans mirrors the harsher

sanctions attached to crack cocaine offenses. With the law equating 1 gram of crack cocaine with 100 grams of powder cocaine, even relatively modest quantities of crack cocaine can lead to rather severe penalties. A serious user of crack cocaine, for instance, could require 5 or more grams of the substance for the weekend. Yet, this amount presently carries a mandatory minimum prison term of 5 years (Vincent & Hofer, 1994, p. 23). Prior to this, federal judges typically placed first-time offenders on probation (Alschuler, 1991).

Not only are crack cocaine offenses more heavily sanctioned, they are also somewhat more likely than offenses involving powder cocaine to be sentenced at or above the indicated mandatory minimum. Data analyzed by the U.S. Sentencing Commission (1991b, p. 72) revealed that 67.5% of the offenses involving crack cocaine, compared to 64.9% of the offenses involving powder cocaine, were sentenced at or above the indicated mandatory minimum.

The significance of the harsher sanctions attached to crack cocaine offenses is disclosed in an investigation by Douglas McDonald and Kenneth Carlson (1993). They conclude that the single most important difference that contributed to the longer sentences for Black federal offenders was their overrepresentation in crack cocaine trafficking. Examining the potential impact of sentencing crack and powder cocaine traffickers the same for identical amounts of the drug, McDonald and Carlson (1993, p. 21) report that instead of African Americans receiving sentences that averaged 30% longer than that of Whites, the average sentence for African American cocaine traffickers would have been 10% *shorter* than that of their White counterparts. In addition, it would have reduced by half the Black/White difference in average prison sentence for all federal crimes.

Evidence of potential racial bias in the charging of Black defendants in federal court with the selling of crack cocaine has been detected by Richard Berk and Alec Campbell (1993). Analyzing data sets from Los Angeles, they observed that although state charges for the sale of crack cocaine were similar to the sheriff's department arrest patterns, African

Americans were overrepresented in federal cases when compared to their patterns of arrest by the sheriff's department. Also indicative of possible racial bias was the finding that over a 4-year period in federal court, no Whites were charged with the sale of crack cocaine.

Arguments in favor of maintaining a legal distinction between crack and powder cocaine frequently center on the assumption that crack is more dangerous because it is instantly addicting and is related to violence. Contradictory evidence, nonetheless, is beginning to surface. Data from the Careers in Crack Project tend to refute the notion that crack is any more instantly addicting than powder cocaine. Additionally, crack use did not appear to substantially alter the involvement of men in nondrug offending. Moreover, whereas the use of crack was unrelated to violent behavior, the sale of crack was strongly related to violence, thereby suggesting that the violence associated with inner-city crack culture is probably the result of systemic violence involved in the sale of illicit drugs, rather than the pharmacological properties of the drug itself (Johnson et al., 1995).

The continuation of a legal distinction between the two types of cocaine can also be challenged on other grounds. First, the mood-altering ingredient is the same in both. Second, powder cocaine, if dissolved in water and injected intravenously, has a similar effect to that of smoking crack cocaine. Finally, powder cocaine can be converted into crack cocaine by using baking soda and water to remove the hydrochloride from the powder cocaine (see State v. Russell, 1991).

Sentencing Guidelines and Racial Bias

Because the sentencing guidelines are anchored by mandatory minimum sentences, any discussion of the impact of the guidelines on African Americans is somewhat arbitrary. Though numerous studies have attempted to evaluate the effect of the new system on sentencing, few have specifically analyzed racial differences. Accordingly, care must be exercised when assessing the extant research.

Data analyzed by the U.S. Sentencing Commission (1991a) disclosed little sentencing disparity under the guidelines if offenders with similar criminal records are compared. When the commission limited the analysis to four major offenses (bank robbery, powder cocaine distribution, heroin distribution, and bank embezzlement), race was a factor . . . in sentencing outcome only for heroin distribution. Whereas 92.3% of all Whites convicted of heroin distribution were given sentences at the bottom of the guideline range, the comparable figures for African Americans and Hispanics were 82.6% and 56.7%, respectively (U.S. Sentencing Commission, 1991a, p. 310). Nonetheless, the small samples employed in the analyses of different offenses make any generalizations uncertain (for a critique of the study, see Tonry, 1993). The report further revealed that across all offense categories for the last half of fiscal year 1990, African Americans were more likely than either Whites or Hispanics to be sentenced at the bottom of the guidelines range.

An investigation by McDonald and Carlson (1993) found that substantial racial disparity in sentencing occurred after the guidelines were implemented. During the period 1986 to 1988, prior to full implementation of the new system, White, African American, and Hispanic defendants received similar sentences in federal district courts. Average maximum prison sentences ranged from 51 months for Whites and Hispanics to 55 months for African Americans (p. 3). However, between January 20, 1989, and June 30, 1990, racial disparities in sentencing appeared. African Americans and Hispanics convicted of federal offenses and subject to the provisions of the Sentencing Reform Act of 1984 were more likely than Whites to be sentenced to prison. Further, African Americans received longer average prison sentences (71 months) than either Whites (50 months) or Hispanics (48 months) (p. 4). These disparities, the investigators note, were primarily the result of differences in the characteristics of the offenses and offenders that the law recognizes as legitimate for sentencing purposes. McDonald and Carlson (1993) conclude that the sentencing disparities they observed were generally not a consequence of the guidelines themselves with the exceptions of "the mandatory minimum sentencing laws passed for drugs, especially crack cocaine, and the particular way the Sentencing Commission arrayed guideline ranges above the statutory minima" (p. 21).

A study conducted by the U.S. General Accounting Office (1992) revealed that the effect of race on sentencing was not consistent under the guidelines. There were, nevertheless, some situations in which African Americans were at a disadvantage. Bank robbery and larceny, for instance, are offenses in which African Americans and Whites were less likely than Hispanics to have their counts reduced or dismissed and consequently received longer sentences for these crimes. Additionally, the data disclosed that African Americans were less likely than Whites and Hispanics to have their counts reduced or dismissed before going to trial for heroin distribution. And, though the reasons are unclear, African Americans were less likely than Whites to plead guilty, despite the fact that offenders convicted by plea generally received shorter sentences than those convicted at trial.

It additionally appears that the sentencing guidelines have increased the proportion of minority defendants processed in federal court. Methodological criticisms aside (see Schulhofer, 1992; Wilkins, 1992), Gerald Heaney's (1991, 1992) comparison of offenders sentenced under the guidelines to those sentenced under preguidelines law disclosed that African Americans accounted for 22.3% of the preguidelines defendants but composed 26.2% of the guidelines defendants. Hispanics fared even worse, going from 8.5% of the defendants under the preguidelines to 26.3% of the defendants under the guidelines (Heaney, 1991, p. 204; 1992, p. 781). In other words, Black representation increased by almost 4% and Hispanic representation grew by nearly 18% under the guidelines.

The investigator contends that two factors are primarily responsible for these changes (Heaney, 1991). First, he asserts, many law enforcement officials pursued their cases through federal court instead of state court believing that the defendants would be imprisoned longer under the new federal standards. The second factor attributed to the changes involves the filing of marginal cases.

According to Heaney, some cases were filed in federal court that would otherwise not have been filed in either state or federal court because the guidelines now made the prosecution worth the effort.

Heaney (1991) also observed that under the guidelines, the average sentence increased most dramatically for African Americans. Although the average sentence for African Americans under preguidelines law in 1989 was 27.8 months, this figure swelled to 68.5 months for cases sentenced the same year under the guidelines. To be sure, the average sentence for Whites and Hispanics expanded as well under the guidelines, but the increases of 19 months for Whites and 13.7 months for Hispanics (p. 207) pale in comparison to that experienced by African Americans.

What accounts for the greater Black/White disparity under the new system? Heaney (1991) suggests that the emphasis on curtailing crack cocaine traffic, accompanied with the stiffer penalties attached to crack cocaine, contributed to the expansion of the average sentence for African Americans. Moreover, being more likely than Whites to possess a criminal record, African Americans are at a greater disadvantage in sentencing.

The negative impact of the guidelines on African Americans is apparently not confined to longer sentences: On average, African Americans are less likely than Whites to be given a probation-only disposition in federal court cases prosecuted under the new system (Heaney, 1991, 1992). The probability of receiving straight probation, of course, varies depending on the offense. For instance, Whites are over 3 times more likely than African Americans under the new standards to receive probation-only for offenses involving drugs and violence. On the other hand, African Americans are slightly more likely than Whites to receive a straight probation disposition for property crimes and have a 6% greater chance than Whites to receive this disposition in immigration cases (Heaney, 1991, p. 207; 1992, p. 780).

Most recently, *The Tennessean* newspaper in Nashville conducted a study of all 1992–1993 federal convictions using data furnished by the U.S. Sentencing Commission.

The analysis of approximately 80,000 cases controlled for offense severity and prior record. Overall, the investigation revealed that African Americans received sentences that averaged 10% longer than those of comparable Whites (p. 1A). Although Hispanics received sentences similar to those of Whites, in 74 of the 90 federal court districts, African Americans received longer sentences than Whites charged with the same crimes (p. 6A). The amount of disparity, however, varied from one federal district to another, with the largest disparity occurring in the East Missouri district where, on average, African Americans were given sentences that were 40% longer than those of Whites (p. IA). Additionally, the disparity was not due to the imposition of mandatory minimum sentences as the disparity remained even after omitting drug convictions.

Discussion and Conclusion

That mandatory minimum statutes have had an adverse effect on African Americans is corroborated by the literature. Research shows that African Americans are more likely than Whites to be convicted under mandatory minimum provisions and more likely than Whites to be sentenced at or above the indicated mandatory minimum. Much of the disparity is apparently a consequence of the differential treatment accorded crack cocaine offenders.

The disparity between sentences involving crack and powder cocaine has recently been investigated by the U.S. Sentencing Commission. In a 220-page report submitted to Congress in February 1995, the Commission revealed its plans to modify the sentencing guidelines to remedy this disparity (Locy, 1995). Whether the sentencing standards will undergo alterations is unclear, though, as the Justice Department has exhorted Congress to reject the commission's proposal to make the penalty for crack cocaine the same as that for powder cocaine ("Justice Agency Urges," 1995).

Sentencing guidelines research suggests that racial disparities have been enhanced under the new sentencing structure. Investigators have observed that African Americans are more likely that Whites, under the guidelines, to be sentenced to prison and to receive longer sentences. Overall, African Americans are less likely than Whites to receive a disposition of probation only. They are also less likely than other groups to have their counts reduced or dismissed for certain crimes. Furthermore, since the guidelines have become effective, minority representation in federal court has grown substantially.

Explanations of the inefficacy of sentencing reform to alleviate racial disparity focus on several areas largely concealed from empirical analysis. According to Heaney (1991, 1992), the guidelines have created the possibility of additional sentencing disparity by giving greater power to prosecutors. With judges having carefully circumscribed discretion in sentencing decisions under the new standards, prosecutors now have greater influence on sentencing outcomes. As prosecutors decide who and what to charge, prosecutorial decisions, in effect, establish the appropriate sentencing guideline range. Moreover, prosecutors control the flow of information about the offense that will be used by probation officers in their presentence investigation reports. To the extent that racial bias might enter into prosecutorial decision making, additional disparity is possible.

Another source of disparity involves the decision regarding the court of jurisdiction (Heaney, 1991, 1992). The decision to prosecute in state court or federal court can have important consequences for defendants, particularly in drug cases, because mandatory minimum statutes have influenced the sentencing guidelines in cases prosecuted under federal law. The possibility of more severe sentences in federal court can be readily seen by examining background data from United States v. Williams (1990). In this U.S. District Court case, the defendants, who were African American, had been referred to federal court where their crack cocaine distribution carried a sentencing range of 188 to 235 months under the guidelines. In contrast, conviction of the same offense by the state would result in a sentence of under 2 years.

Sentencing guidelines are additionally unlikely to eliminate racial disparity because sentence length is tied to the defendant's criminal history and Black defendants are more likely than their White counterparts to have prior criminal records ("Developments in the Law," 1988; Heaney, 1992). Any previous racial bias in enforcement of the law is, therefore, amplified under the new standards.

The investigative and preprosecution practices of law enforcement officials can further lead to hidden sentencing disparities. This is especially evident in the enforcement of drug laws. Because sentence severity increases as the quantity of drugs bought or sold increases, some drug enforcement agents have encouraged their suspects to purchase or sell larger quantities to impose stiffer penalties when they are apprehended (see United States v. Rosen, 1991). Another practice leading to a longer sentence is to postpone the arrest until the cumulative amount purchased results in a statutory minimum sentence (Heaney, 1991). Given that drug law enforcement typically focuses on areas of the city where the poor and minorities are concentrated (Mauer, 1991), African Americans are adversely affected by these practices.

A final feature of the new sentencing system that precludes its being an effective deterrent to racial disparity in sentencing is its failure to address racial disparity during the first phase of the sentencing process. Sentencing typically involves two decisions. The first, the in/out decision, involves a decision as to whether the defendant should be incarcerated. If the defendant is to be incarcerated, then another decision must be made regarding the length of the prison term. The guidelines attempt to reduce racial disparity during the second phase of sentencing only. And yet, a review of numerous sentencing studies by Free (1996) found that empirical support for racial bias in sentencing is stronger for the in/out decision than for the decision on sentence length.

In conclusion, neither mandatory minimum sentences nor the guidelines have been effective in eliminating racial disparity in sentencing in federal court. Much of the disparity can be attributed to drug laws (especially those pertaining to crack cocaine). Although changing the law to make penalties for identical amounts of powder and crack cocaine the same would reduce the disparity, it would not eradicate it because of the greater likelihood of drug enforcement to concentrate on inner-city neighborhoods. Moreover, selective law enforcement at preprosecutorial stages of the criminal justice system has an adverse effect on African Americans by producing criminal records that culminate in longer sentences under the new standards. Therefore, any meaningful attempt to promote equality between African Americans and Whites must address the dual issues of possible preprosecutorial racial bias as well as possible racial bias during sentencing.

References

Alschuler, A. (1991). "The Failure of Sentencing Guidelines: A Plea for Less Aggregation." *University of Chicago Law Review* 58, 901-95 1.

Berk, R., & Campbell, A. (1993). "Preliminary Data on Race and Crack Charging Practices in Los Angeles." *Federal Sentencing Reporter* 6, 36-38.

"Developments in the Law: Race and the Criminal Process." (1988). *Harvard Law Review* 101, 1472-1641.

Finley, J. (1993). "Crack Charging in Los Angeles: Do Statistics Tell The Whole Truth About 'Selective Prosecution?'" *Federal Sentencing Reporter* 6, 113-115.

Frank, L. (1995, September 24). "Color of Skin Affects Sentences, Study Finds." *Wausau Daily Herald* Pp. 1A, 6A.

Free, M. Jr. (1996). *African Americans and the Criminal Justice System*. New York: Garland.

Heaney, G. (1991). "The Reality of Guidelines Sentencing: No End to Disparity." *American Criminal Law Review* 28, 161-232.

——. (1992). "Revisiting Disparity: Debating Guidelines Sentencing." *American Criminal Law Review* 29, 771-793.

"Justice Agency Urges Congress to Reject Cocaine-Penalty Plan." (1995, April 17). *The Wall Street Journal* P. A7G.

Locy, T. (1995, March 1). "Panel Plans to Amend Sentencing Disparity for Crack Dealers." *The Washington Post* P. D3.

Maguire, K., & Pastore, A. (eds.). (1994). *Sourcebook of Criminal Justice Statistics* 1993 U.S. Department of Justice, Bureau of Justice Statistics. Washington, DC: U.S. Government Printing Office.

Mauer, M. (1991). *Americans Behind Bars: A Comparison of International Rates of Incarceration*. Washington, DC: The Sentencing Project.

McDonald, D., & Carlson, K. (1993). *Sentencing in the Federal Courts: Does Race Matter? The Transition to Sentencing Guidelines, 1986–90 (Summary)*. U.S. Department of Justice, Bureau of Justice Statistics. Washington, DC: U.S. Government Printing Office.

Schulhofer, S. (1992). "Assessing the Federal Sentencing Process: The Problem Is Uniformity, Not Disparity." *American Criminal Law Review* 29, 833-873.

State v. Russell, 477 N. W. 2d 886 (Minn. 1991).

Tonry, M. (1993). "The Failure of the U.S. Sentencing Commission's Guidelines." *Crime & Delinquency* 39, 131-149.

U.S. Bureau of The Census. (1992). *Statistical Abstract of The United States: 1992 (112th ed.)*. Washington, DC: U.S. Government Printing Office.

U.S. General Accounting Office. (1992). *Sentencing Guidelines: Central Questions Remain Unanswered*. Washington, DC: Author.

U.S. Sentencing Commission. (1991a). *The Federal Sentencing Guidelines: A Report on the Operation of the Guidelines System and Short-Term Impacts on Disparity in Sentencing, Use of Incarceration, and Prosecutorial Discretion and Plea Bargaining (Vol. 2)*. Washington, DC: Author.

———. (1991b). *Mandatory Minimum Penalties in the Federal Criminal Justice System*. Washington DC: Author.

United States v. Mistretta, 488 U.S. 361 (1989).

United States v. Rosen, 929 F.2d 839 (1 St Cir. 1991).

United States v. Williams, 746 R Supp. 1076 (D. Utah 1990).

Vincent, B., & Hofer, P. (1994). *The Consequences of Mandatory Minimum Prison Terms: A Summary of Recent Findings*. Washington, DC: Federal Judicial Center.

Wilkins, W. Jr. (1992). "Response to Judge Heaney." *American Criminal Law Review* 29, 795-821.

Wilkins, W. Jr., Newton, P., & Steer, J. (1991). "The Sentencing Reform Act of 1984: A Bold Approach to the Unwarranted Sentencing Disparity Problem." *Criminal Law Forum* 2, 355-380.

Critical Evaluation

1. Should society's concern be with the discriminatory laws or the criminal behavior?

2. Are the penalties for crack too severe or are the penalties for powder cocaine too lenient?

3. The author asserts that drug enforcement tends to be concentrated in inner-city neighborhoods. Is that true? If true, is it appropriate?

Marvin D. Free, Jr., "The Impact of Federal Sentencing Reforms on African Americans." In *Journal of Black Studies* 28:2, pp. 268-286. Copyright © 1997 by Sage Publications, Inc. Reprinted by permission. ✦

Project for Personal Application and Class Discussion: Crime and Deliquency

As noted in the introduction to this section, virtually everyone will be a victim of crime at some point in his or her life. Some people will be the victims of many crimes. There are no failproof defenses against crime, but there are steps that you can take to minimize your chances of becoming a victim.

The eight crimes on the FBI's Index are murder and nonnegligent manslaughter, aggravated assault, forcible rape, robbery, burglary, larceny-theft, auto theft, and arson. To which of those crimes do you feel most vulnerable? Make a list of things you can do to minimize being victimized. Then call your local police department and ask for any information they have on how to protect yourself. Add those suggestions to your list. For example, some of the preventative steps that people report taking include the following:

- Keep car doors locked, even while driving.
- Avoid walking alone at night on dark streets.
- Take a self-defense class.
- Don't use ATMs in isolated or dark locations.
- Keep a light on in your apartment or home when you're away at night.
- Never respond quickly to an offer that sounds "too good to be true." ✦

Epilogue:
Can Social Problems Be Solved?

The answer to the question whether social problems can be solved is both yes and no. Yes, because conditions can be improved and the extent of, or effects of, problems can be reduced. No, because social problems cannot be completely eliminated from a society. It is as unrealistic to think that society can be problem free as it is to expect a marriage to be problem free.

It is instructive to look at the various utopian societies that have been established in the United States. Those societies were efforts to deal with problems in the larger society by creating communities that conformed to some ideal (Lauer and Lauer 1983). Many such groups found their ideal in a religious doctrine; some found it in a socialistic, communistic, anarchistic, or other kind of secular ideology. The best known utopian communities in the United States include the Icarians, in the western United States, the Oneida community in New York, the Amana community in Iowa, and the Owenites in Indiana.

If modern communes are included in the utopian quest, then hundreds of thousands of Americans have sought a problem-free social order in thousands of utopian communities. How did they fare? The majority of them failed to survive more than twenty-five years. The Shakers, a celibate religious community, have been the most successful in terms of survival. The community began in England, spread to this country before the Revolutionary War, and still maintains a small membership today in New England.

Most of the utopian groups dissolved because of internal conflict, loss of members, or inability to survive economically. In other words, they may have avoided some of the problems in the larger society, but they found themselves enmeshed in various problems in their own communities, ranging from poverty to conflicts over the division of labor and various other issues. The utopians all failed to achieve a problem-free social order.

Their experiences vividly illustrate that social problems cannot be avoided. They cannot be eradicated. But they can be attacked and, in some cases, mitigated.

Indeed, if one looks at the record, Americans are making advances in dealing with various social problems. As of this writing, the editors see progress in a number of areas when compared to preceding years. Consider the following information from the Statistical Abstract of the United States (U.S. Bureau of the Census 1997). In the area of the economy and work, the unemployment rate stood at 5.4 percent in 1996, the lowest figure since the early 1970s. Female unemployment rates, which were typically higher than male rates in the past, have been at or lower than male rates during the 1990s. In education, the high school dropout rates for African Americans and Hispanics, although considerably higher than that of whites, are lower than they were in 1980 (and, for African Americans, less than half of what they were in 1970). Similarly, although a much higher proportion of whites complete college, the proportion of college graduates among African Americans increased from 4.4 percent in 1970 to 13.6 percent in 1996, and the proportion among Hispanics increased from 4.5 percent to 9.3 percent (24.3 percent of whites were college graduates in 1996). In the family, divorce rates have declined somewhat in recent years. In the area of health, deaths from AIDS fell 26 percent in 1997—the first decline since the onset of the problem. In the environment, progress has been made in controlling both air and water pollution. In the area of poverty, the 13.8 percent rate of 1995 was higher than some previous years but much below the 22.2 percent figure of 1960. And in the area of crime, the rate of violent crime declined significantly from 1991 to 1995.

These are only a sampling of facts and figures that show progress. They can be balanced, of course, by other facts and figures that show continuing severe, or even worsening, problems. The point is not that we are finally on the road to utopia, but that *serious, informed* efforts at dealing with social problems pay off.

"Serious" here means that the effort must be more than just a show of concern or a partial commitment of resources. At election time, politicians typically identify various ways in which they intend to address the nation's problems. What is actually done after the election is another story. The editors worked in a rural area of a state where the governor was running for reelection. As a part of his campaign, he promised to pave the graveled state highway that ran through the community if he was returned to office. He made similar promises to other communities. A few weeks before the election, road-building equipment arrived in the community. The local people were impressed. The governor was reelected. Shortly thereafter, the equipment was taken away and the road was left unimproved for a number of years.

"Informed" here means that any effort to deal with a social problem must be based on as complete an understanding of that problem as possible. For example, it was indicated earlier that, contrary to what some Americans think, the problem of poverty is not simply a matter of being out of work. Those who think that "workfare" will solve the problem of poverty are unaware of the diverse reasons that people are poor.

Finally, it is suggested that a serious, informed effort is one that follows a number of important principles. In particular, the editors have identified five principles that they believe are central to any realistic effort to deal with social problems. Each of them will be discussed here briefly.

1. Important guidelines for addressing social problems emerge from an analysis of their causes and associated conditions.

Although many of the selections in this book offered suggestions about how to deal with the problem addressed, some did not. But almost all of them contained useful information for formulating a course of action.

For example, Uchitelle's article on downsized workers who return as rentals (Chapter 6) suggests that some kind of government action or collective action by workers is needed in order to provide greater job security and protection against exploitation. These actions could be supported by information about the consequences of the practice, including the possibility that in the long run it is counterproductive to the interests of the organization as well as the workers.

As another example, in Chapter 12, Kurz described some of the negative consequences associated with growing up in a single-parent home. Clearly, any action that strengthens families and reduces the divorce rate will also reduce the varied problems exhibited by children who grow up without one of their natural parents.

The editors do not mean to assert that the way to attack social problems is obvious and straightforward once you know the causes and associated conditions are known. Just how, for instance, does society strengthen families? Whose responsibility is it? Still, it is clear that something needs to be done in that direction.

Furthermore, there are usually unanticipated consequences to social action, even when such action seems dictated by the logic of the situation. For example, the use of antibiotics in the past 50 years to combat infectious diseases appeared so successful that even some physicians believed that these diseases were a thing of the past. The use and overuse of antibiotics, however, has had the unanticipated consequence of creating a new generation of drug-resistant microbes that threaten humankind with a wave of epidemics.

Similarly, advocates of computerization of the workplace envisioned both higher productivity and virtually paper-free offices. But there is no evidence that the computer has increased productivity, and paperwork has proliferated rather than decreased.

The adoption of legalized gambling by a number of cities and states is also an instructive example of unanticipated consequences. The expectation is that legalized gambling will bring in the revenue needed to deal with the needs and problems of the area. But if money from gambling enables local governments to deal more effectively with their problems, it creates a new set of problems with which they must cope, including reduced job productivity, gambling addiction, crime, and insurance fraud (*The Futurist* 1997).

The point is, understanding the causes and associated conditions of problems enables society to identify logical ways to attack them. But the attack always involves a certain amount of trial and error. Having guidelines is not the same as having sure-fire cures.

2. Social problems do not have simple solutions.

The above discussion has already suggested that simple solutions are likely to be inadequate and, therefore, ineffective. For example, "just say no" is a simplistic solution to the drug problem. Showing the help-wanted ads in the newspaper (as a high government official once did) is a simplistic solution to the problem of poverty. "Get an education and work hard" is a simplistic solution to the problems faced by women and racial or ethnic minorities. "Get tough" is a simplistic solution to the problem of crime.

This book has frequently pointed out the diverse factors that enter into a particular problem. Problems that are caused and maintained by numerous factors—both structural and social psychological—are not going to be effectively addressed by a single line of attack.

For instance, Susan Headden (Chapter 24) discussed the problem of Hispanic dropouts. A simplistic solution would be to confront the dropouts with the relationship between education and income, and if that did not work to shrug it off as their choice and, therefore, their fault. Yet this "solution" would ignore the fact that most of the dropouts would have remained in school if they had not been caught up in a web of other problems—poverty that leaves them malnourished and ill-prepared to focus on schoolwork, friends and parents who devalue education, teachers who do not inspire them or believe in them, a curriculum that ignores their culture, and home and neighborhood experiences that dissipate any hope for a better future.

There are no simple problems. There are, therefore, no simple solutions.

3. A variety of resources are needed and must be mobilized.

The fact that there are no simple solutions means that many different resources must be applied to the problem.

Among those resources are government, business, voluntary associations, the schools, churches, the media, and individual volunteers.

Consider how this combination could impact the problem of drugs. Government action is needed to stem the supplies and to prosecute dealers and abusers. Corporate and other business action is needed to provide programs that help employees who abuse drugs and to identify employees whose drug use and abuse endangers others. Voluntary associations (such as Mothers Against Drunk Driving [MADD]) perform the useful function of educating the public and encouraging action by government and business. The schools and churches can reinforce the norm of moderation in the use of legal drugs and abstinence from illegal drugs. The media can portray those who abuse drugs as dangerous rather than comic figures (as movies and TV programs sometimes portray drunks), and can educate people about the hazards of drug use.

Individual volunteers are needed to work in and with the various organizations just discussed. Such volunteers are responsible for starting and helping maintain such organizations as Alcoholics Anonymous, MADD, and self-help groups for those who abuse other kinds of drugs. Finally, individual volunteers include those who offer help to a relative or neighbor or friend with a drug problem.

All of the above, of course, only address the problem directly. That is, what has just been described does not deal with various conditions associated with drug use such as poverty, stress, and peer-group pressure. When all the factors involved in a particular problem are drawn togther, it is clear that a great many resources must be mobilized in order to deal with it.

Unfortunately, a tendency was revived in the 1990s that places greater responsibility for dealing with social problems on state and local resources, including private charities and volunteers. As already indicated, the editors believe that such resources are important. But they are not a substitute for a full mobilization that includes the federal government.

In the mid-1990s, about 93 million Americans reported doing some kind of volunteer work (Gerson 1997). But volunteers alone cannot deal with problems that are rooted deeply in the structure of American society. Nor can volunteers combined with private charities, many of which are largely funded by the government, handle these problems (Lemann 1997). What, for example, can volunteers and private charities do to stem corporate abuse of the environment, corporate exploitation of workers, the flow of illegal drugs from other countries or the indignities suffered by women and racial or ethnic minorities in the workplace, and so on?

It is true that the federal government cannot solve all society's problems. It is also true that society can not solve its problems without the resources of the federal government. Mobilization of the full range of resources is necessary in order to deal with problems effectively.

4. Prevention programs are an important component of the effort.

The old saying that prevention is the best cure applies to social problems. Prevention programs may be costly, but they do not entail the staggering economic and human costs of the problems themselves. If a prevention program in a school persuades one young person to refuse to experiment with drugs, it may have avoided the costs of maintaining a drug habit, physical and emotional damage to the young person, family trauma, law enforcement action, and the loss of positive contributions that the drug-free young person would have made.

In Chapter 34, Hawkins discussed the model for establishing prevention programs. "Risk-focused" prevention involves the same initial step as the editors' first principle—identify the causes and associated conditions of a problem. A number of factors will then emerge that put individuals at risk for that problem. To minimize the number of such individuals requires action that will minimize their exposure to the various risks. Or, as Hawkins put it, action is required to establish those "protective factors" that shield people from the risks.

Thus, to prevent young people from becoming involved in juvenile crime, Hawkins argued that action is needed at the community level. In particular, community leaders need to come together, analyze the risk factors present in their community, and initiate an action plan that is "nothing less than reinventing the community as a protective environment" (Hawkins 1995, 17). This means that every child in the community will be exposed to healthy beliefs and clear standards of behavior. It means that every child will bond with someone (parent or other relative, friend, neighbor, etc.) who cares about him or her and who holds healthy beliefs and adheres to the standards of behavior.

Prevention programs, like other measures, will not of themselves eliminate a problem. They are, however, an integral part of the attack. Educational and lobbying efforts of groups like MADD and the American Cancer Society have reduced the number of drunk drivers and the number of smokers. Efforts by the Environmental Protection Agency and groups such as the Sierra Club have reduced the number of businesses that freely dump pollutants into the air, ground, and waters. Government regulations and pressures have reduced the number of organizations that discriminate against women and minorities.

Prevention alone is not the answer. Yet every prevention effort that works means fewer Americans caught up in the economic, physical and emotional trauma associated with social problems.

5. Eternal vigilance is the price of progress.

Our ancestors knew that liberty, once won, could be lost again. They counseled eternal vigilance. Similarly, progress made in dealing with a social problem cannot be either sustained or retained without continued vigilance and action.

A clear example of the need for continued watchfulness is the problem of inequality faced by minorities. As of this writing, many Americans believe that minorities no longer need such things as affirmative action programs because minorities now have the same opportunities as white males. But government data on income show some disturbing facts.

If one looks at the median income of families, black income was 54 percent that of white income in 1950 (U.S. Bureau of the Census 1975, 297). The civil rights movement enabled African Americans to make some gains over the next two decades. The figure edged up to 55 percent by 1960, and by 1970, median black family income was 61.3 percent of that of white family income (U.S. Bureau of the Census 1997:469). It appeared that although the pace was agonizingly slow, African Americans were making progress in their struggle toward equality.

By 1980, however, the median black family income had fallen to 57.9 percent that of whites, and by 1995 the figure was 60.9 percent (U.S. Bureau of the Census 1997, 469). In other words, the median family income of African Americans has not continued to progress toward equality with whites but has fluctuated and was lower in the mid-1990s than it was in the early 1970s. In addition, 41.5 percent of black children lived in poverty in 1970 (U.S. Bureau of the Census 1997,

475). The proportion has varied since then, reaching a high of 47.3 percent in 1982. By 1995, the figure was 41.5 percent—the same as it was in 1970.

The point here is not to identify the reasons for these figures but simply to assert that the struggle for racial equality is far from won. In fact, in some ways racial minorities were no better off in the mid-1990s than they were in 1970.

The attitude of many white Americans that conditions exist to eliminate racial inequality, is not justified by the evidence. Progress once made does not necessarily continue unabated. In the area of social problems, the price of progress is eternal vigilance.

References

The Futurist. "Gambling on Gambling." 1997. *The Futurist* Jan.-Feb., p. 38.

Gerson, Michael J. 1997. "Do Do-Gooders Do Much Good; Most Volunteers Aren't Solving Core Problems." *U.S. News and World Report* 28 April.

Hawkins, J. David. 1995. "Controlling Crime Before It happens: Risk-Focused Prevention." *National Institute of Justice Journal* August, pp. 10-18.

Lauer, Robert H., and Jeanette C. Lauer. 1983. *The Spirit and the Flesh: Sex in Utopian Communities*. Metuchen, New Jersey: Scarecrow Press.

Lemann, Nicholas. 1997. "The Limits of Charity." *U.S. News and World Report* April 28.

U.S. Bureau of the Census. 1975. *Historical Statistics of the United States, Colonial Times to 1970*. Washington, DC: U.S. Government Printing Office.

U.S. Bureau of the Census. 1997. *Statistical Abstract of the United States*. Washington, DC: U.S. Government Printing Office. ✦